GREAT
OPERAS

GREAT OPERAS

A GUIDE TO 25 OF THE WORLD'S FINEST MUSICAL EXPERIENCES

MICHAEL STEEN

ICON

First published in the UK in 2012 by Icon Books Ltd

This edition published in the UK in 2013 by
Icon Books Ltd, Omnibus Business Centre,
39–41 North Road, London N7 9DP
email: info@iconbooks.net
www.iconbooks.net

Sold in the UK, Europe and Asia
by Faber & Faber Ltd, Bloomsbury House,
74–77 Great Russell Street, London WC1B 3DA or their agents

Distributed in the UK, Europe and Asia
by TBS Ltd, TBS Distribution Centre, Colchester Road
Frating Green, Colchester CO7 7DW

Distributed in Australia and New Zealand
by Allen & Unwin Pty Ltd,
PO Box 8500, 83 Alexander Street,
Crows Nest, NSW 2065

Distributed in South Africa
by Book Promotions, Office B4, The District,
41 Sir Lowry Road, Woodstock 7925

ISBN: 978-184831-611-9

Some of the material in this book has previously been published in a series of individual ebooks, each titled *A Short Guide to a Great Opera*.

Typesetting by Marie Doherty

Printed and bound in the UK by
CLAYS LTD, ST IVES PLC

Contents

Contents

PREFACE

'We're off to the opera in a couple of days,' Rosemary reminded me. 'I'm rather busy. Tell me what I need to know.' She added, 'We'll want a drink when we get there. So I won't have time to read much of the programme.' 'By the way,' she continued, 'Kate and John know all about opera and I want to hold my own with them during the interval.'

'I'll write you a short guide, something informative, but light and amusing, which will help you; you can read the key information in the car,' I promised.

It worked so well that every time we went to an opera I gave her – and her knowledge of the technicalities is that of a typical BBC Radio 4 or Classic FM listener who learnt piano at school – a similar guide. I structured each so that she could get up front the key information on the opera's background and what it is about. She could then 'drill down' if she wanted more information.

Having been to so many operas, and consequently having so many such guides at my fingertips, it has been a challenge choosing which to include in this compendium. I have concentrated on well-known favourites. This means that the operas of Mozart are bound to be well represented. And the contents are necessarily dominated by 19th-century Italian opera, in style, if not always by date.

The popularity of many of the Italian and French operas arises to a considerable extent from the impressive vocal pyrotechnics and gymnastics which enable celebrities, or would-be celebrities, to show off. Verdi, but more notably the Germans to the north, developed a more serious purpose to which the composer Hector Berlioz (who regarded himself as three-quarters German) applied the phrase *un peu élevée*, that is, 'lofty' or 'noble'. They aimed to use music, both vocal and orchestral, to express the drama more effectively than the spoken word on its own could do. So, to reflect this, and to provide breadth, I have supplemented the popular operas with an early and a mature opera by Wagner. As a Dubliner, I would have liked to be able to include something with an Irish flavour. But accepting that Benedict's *The Lily of Killarney* and Stanford's *Shamus O'Brien* fell out of the repertory long ago, I settled for starting and ending with guides to well-known operas by Handel and Britten, both essentially English composers.

The guides vary in length. There is much more to say about *Tristan und Isolde* than there is about *L'Elisir d'Amore*. Besides, the length of the opera itself varies: the Italians, so commercially astute, knew exactly what their impatient audiences would tolerate. Verdi reckoned that 40 minutes was the maximum attention span for an act.

I have been keen to ensure that, for practical use, the reader has all the information he or she needs together in one place, in a stand-alone piece without too much cross-referencing. So it is inevitable that at times there will be some duplication between guides – it should come as no surprise that certain useful knowledge relating to one Puccini opera will be similarly valuable with regard to another. Conversely, biographical box features, which appear in the first guide for each composer, are not repeated in subsequent guides. And the same applies, occasionally, for librettists and other important figures.

In the original language, the first lines of certain arias and choruses can be important and useful milestones. But the translation of the first line of a verse is often not very meaningful, taken on its own. So I have often relied on the surrounding description to convey the overall meaning. I have also assumed that even though most readers do not have a glossary of musical expressions at their fingertips, they have encountered enough Italian waiters to know or guess what many phrases are likely to mean. Most operas are about love.

Some old hands may be disappointed not to see discographies. They can be obtained today at the touch of a button. The efficient and up-to-date way to see what is available is to refer to the internet.

I have drawn the information from my own considerable experience and from various authoritative sources listed in the acknowledgments. Without all these, without the team at Icon, Duncan Heath, Robert Sharman and Andrew Furlow, this book – and the accompanying ebook series of 'Short Guides to a Great Opera' – would not exist. More crucially perhaps, without the great composer, we would not have the opera. To my sources (and Rosemary and the others who have helped me, including Richard Todd and Katharine Hogg on photography, and Dr Guy Deutscher, Dr Janie Steen and David Vaughan on a host of other matters), I am very grateful. I am also indebted to the staff of various libraries, especially the British Library, the City of London Libraries and the City of Westminster Music Library. Their courtesy, helpfulness and responsiveness never cease to astonish me.

* * *

Andrew Porter, the leading 20th-century critic, tactfully drew attention to contradictory trends today: on the one hand, ever greater fidelity to the sounds of a composer's score, and, on the other, 'ever less respect for scenic indications' that might be considered part of the composer's overall creation, his complete, integrated work of art.

These guides help you to appreciate the opera the composer wrote. They cannot anticipate a particular production which is not in line with the composer's original intentions. (Sometimes these are so ignored that I wonder whether the advertising, which holds the work out as being that of the composer, complies with local regulations on trade description.) Maybe the opera-house programme will indicate the thinking behind a particular production.

Rosemary and many friends have found these guides very helpful. I hope you do as well, and have a very enjoyable musical experience.

Michael Steen
Mattingley

HANDEL: *GIULIO CESARE*

THE OPERA AND ITS COMPOSER

Today, Handel's opera about Cleopatra, 'the immortal harlot', is the most popular of the 40 or so Italian operas that were his focus during the first part of his career, before he took up composing oratorios. 'No Handel opera has been staged in so many countries or enjoyed greater success.'

We may be surprised that *Giulio Cesare in Egitto* was composed in Italian by a German resident in England. Handel's contemporaries were amused by this fashion for Italian opera, which could be heard twice a week, starting 'exactly at Six'. Such was the enthusiasm that *The Spectator*, a newly launched journal, feared that future historians might infer that the English spoke Italian. An extraordinary notion! Otherwise, how would the journalist's great grandchildren possibly explain why 'their Forefathers used to sit like an audience of Foreigners in their own Country' in order to hear 'whole Plays acted before them in a Tongue which they did not understand'?

The explanation is found in the enormous sums which Italian celebrities could earn in the booming English economy. Their success was facilitated and exploited by the Herculean efforts of Handel, a leading composer and producer. And *The Spectator* made the odd penny from advertising the opera and the celebrities.[1]

The audience must have found it very novel, not least the bizarre experience of seeing a eunuch purporting to be a Roman general, barking commands and bedding the sexy Queen of Egypt. Indeed, the 'foreign Strumpets and Eunuchs', despite at first being pelted with oranges, enthralled London's aristocratic audiences. Their popularity lasted until, in 1728, John Gay's *Beggar's Opera* undermined Italian opera. The 'squeaking Italians' were lampooned off the stage;

---

[1] Although *The Spectator* drew attention to celebrity grandees who would be present, there was no mention of the composer.

besides, their tantrums had become wearisome. Handel, by then a true Englishman, had to turn his hand to oratorio, such as *Messiah*, to make his living.

Handel's libretto for *Giulio Cesare* was based on an earlier one by Giacomo Francesco Bussani, a prolific librettist. This had been set particularly successfully in the 1670s by a leading composer of operas for Venice, Antonio Sartorio. It was adapted, and compressed to make it suitable for an English audience, by Handel's 'staff' librettist in London, Nicola Haym. It has been suggested that in its final form the libretto of *Giulio Cesare* 'is one of the best Handel ever received', and that it 'presents a historical love story with a subtlety of characterisation worthy of Shakespeare.'

Nicola Haym (1678–1729) was a cellist, composer, book collector and antiquarian. He was born in Rome, where he was a member of the Papal Chancellor's orchestra. He came to London in 1701 to work for the Duke of Bedford and, later, the Duke of Chandos. He took a leading part in the establishment of Italian opera in London. He became secretary and librettist to Handel's 'Royal Academy of Music'. His opinion of the purpose of music is not wholly consistent with modern attitudes: 'Music,' he wrote, 'must always have some Passion or Sentiment to express, or else Violins, Voices or any other Organs of Sound, afford an Entertainment very little above the Rattles of Children.'

Giulio Cesare was composed during the summer of 1723 and premièred at the King's Theatre on 20 February 1724. In that year, London audiences also saw two other operas for which Handel used libretti supplied by Haym, *Tamerlano* and *Rodelinda*.

The production was well-received and ran for thirteen nights. That summer, it was performed in Paris and, in the following year, in Germany. Handel prepared a revised version in 1725, and brought the opera back in the early 1730s.

Giulio Cesare is long: the first act lasts almost an hour and a half, the second and third acts each over an hour. The action unfolds in 'recitatives'. The narrative, this 'speaking in music', has to be quite lengthy to recount the intricate story. Perhaps more significantly, convention required that the story was interjected with arias, in which the characters express their emotional response (rage, love etc.) to the circumstances. These are composed in the standard three-part structure: after the second part, the soloist returns to the start and essentially repeats the first part in a more embellished form in which technical brilliance may be displayed. Cesare has eight of these, as has Cleopatra. They also have two duets together and two substantial orchestrally accompanied recitatives, 'a full half of the set pieces in the opera.'

However, the opera is action-packed right up to the finale. And Handel's art ensures that the listener's interest is constantly drawn forward by presenting the act 'as a complete unit', rather than focusing on each aria separately. Thus cuts made by modern producers, however desirable, can upset the balance of the act, and give the impression of increasing the opera's length.

Handel

In addition, to maintain box-office returns, producers are often tempted to introduce gimmickry and, not least, to commit the cardinal 'sin of mounting irrelevant distractions during the arias' – for example portraying Cleopatra as a gold-digging tart, or Cesare as a buffoon or even as a 'silly-ass President of the United States.' In the effort to popularise it, *Giulio Cesare* has been particularly prone to this tendency, which one commentator has described as 'a desolating vulgarity and contempt for the opera as a work of art.' However, this gimmickry can undeniably add to the entertainment value of the opera.

Several of the arias are memorably beautiful, for example, Cesare's *Va tacito e nascosto*, which is unique in Handel's operas for its solo horn accompaniment; and Cleopatra's Act 2 love song *V'adoro, pupille*, which has been described as 'one of the most haunting tunes ever written.' One can add to the list the *Venere bella*, her lament *Piangerò la sorte mia*, and much more. The listener can settle in and enjoy some truly wonderful music.

The events portrayed in the opera took place about four years before Julius Caesar's assassination, and eighteen years before Cleopatra's death as portrayed almost 2,000 years later in the well-known 1963 film *Antony and Cleopatra*. This starred Richard Burton and Elizabeth Taylor, with Rex Harrison as Julius Caesar.

George Frederick Handel (1685–1759) was to have an exceptional influence on music in England. He was born on 23 February 1685 in Halle, near Leipzig. Rather than becoming a lawyer, as his father, a barber-surgeon, had wished, he turned to music, and worked in Lutheran Hamburg. His talent was spotted by a Medici prince who invited him to Italy, where he continued to study and compose.

Italy provided no future for Handel, a Lutheran. Also, while 'in Italy and France, there was something to be heard and learned', in England, there was 'something to be earned.' So he moved to Hanover and then in 1710 to London. In 1711, his opera *Rinaldo* was a huge success. He also fitted well with the new Hanoverian monarch George I, who acceded to the throne in 1714. During a lull in the fortunes of Italian opera, Handel worked in the household of the Duke of Chandos. After this, about 60 noblemen and gentlemen formed an opera company, the 'Royal Academy of Music'. They employed Handel, Bononcini (Handel's greatest rival in London) and Ariosti. This flourished from 1720 to 1728, and Handel produced fourteen operas for it.

As well as composing operas, and much other secular and church music, and running 'the business', Handel had to deal with the squabbles between actors whose egos were inflated by spectacular fees. The public eventually tired of Italian opera, preferring the ballad style of John Gay's *Beggar's Opera*.

After the Academy folded in 1729, Handel took over in conjunction with a Swiss impresario, but this venture failed three years later. A new 'Royal Academy' was then formed, but this faced such intense competition from the rival 'Opera of the Nobility' (backed by the Prince of Wales), that both companies were almost bankrupted. London could not support one, let alone two, opera companies. All these pressures led to a breakdown in Handel's health.

The last of Handel's London operas was premiered in 1741. By then, he was composing the oratorios for which he became idolised in England. *Messiah* was staged, with an enormous choir, annually in Westminster Abbey in aid of the Foundling Hospital. (Today, Handel memorabilia can be seen at the Foundling Museum near Russell Square, London, and in Handel's own house at 25 Lower Brook Street, off Bond Street.) The operas were shelved in the 1750s and only reappeared 160 years later, at first in Germany where, with modern staging, and somewhat cut and messed about, they were popular as an antidote to Wagner productions.

Handel was central to the entertainment industry in London. He composed a wide variety of music, including works for the pleasure gardens at Vauxhall and Ranelagh. The strains began to show and contributed to his poor health. In 1752, he lost his sight. He died on 14 April 1759.

WHO'S WHO AND WHAT'S WHAT

The story below is based on the libretto. Certain directors may amend
opera stories to suit their production.

It is 48BC. The Egyptians greet **Giulio Cesare**, the Roman general, and his lieutenant, the tribune **Curio**.[2] They have pursued Cesare's rival, Pompey, who has fled to Egypt to seek military support from the effete pharaoh **Tolomeo** (Ptolemy).

Pompey's wife, the beautiful **Cornelia**, and his son **Sesto** want peace, but their initiative grinds to a halt when **Achilla**, Tolomeo's general, formally presents Cesare with a gruesome welcome gift, **Pompey's severed head**. Cesare is furious and orders proper obsequies. Cornelia's distress is not lessened by the hasty amorous advances of Curio, whom she resists; Sesto knows he must seek to avenge his father.

Cleopatra, Tolomeo's sister and Queen, is in her apartment. She is told what has happened by her confidant and pimp, the eunuch **Nireno**. She thinks of visiting Cesare in his camp. Cleopatra and Tolomeo squabble about the exercise of power. Achilla reports Cesare's angry reaction to the gift. He offers to kill Cesare; that is, if he can have Cornelia. Tolomeo is non-committal.

(The action generally alternates between two separate strands until Act 3, when they come together in the battle: on the one hand, there is Cleopatra's intense seduction of Cesare (impelled initially by her desire to outflank her brother); by contrast, there are the antics, comical at times, of Curio, Achilla and Tolomeo, each of whom makes one or more passes at, and is rebuffed by, the wretched Cornelia.)

Cesare is in his camp brooding over Pompey's demise: ***Alma del gran Pompeo***. Cleopatra turns up disguised as a lady-in-waiting, 'Lydia'. He is bowled over by her, as is Curio.

Still disguised as 'Lydia', Cleopatra agrees to help Sesto and Cornelia, and deputes Nireno to take them to confront Tolomeo.

---

[2] Handel sometimes omitted Curio in later productions.

First, however, Cesare has a difficult meeting with Tolomeo. He knows he must proceed with great caution: *Va tacito e nascosto*

Cornelia and Sesto now face Tolomeo. When Cornelia rebuffs his advances, he has her sent to work as a gardener in his harem. Sesto is sent to be locked up. Tolomeo confirms to Achilla that he can have Cornelia. But when Achilla offers to have her freed in return for marrying him, he too is rebuffed.

* * *

Cleopatra (still disguised as 'Lydia'), has got Nireno to create an erotic **pleasure garden**, into which she will lure Cesare: *V'adoro, pupille, saette d'amore*. She will be there at sunset.

Cornelia, in the harem, when escaping the advances of Achilla, falls into the arms of Tolomeo. She rebuffs him as well. Nireno advises her to join the concubines in Tolomeo's folly, his trysting place, where he is unguarded. This will give her (and Sesto) the opportunity to strike at him.

Cleopatra, in her pleasure garden, invokes Venus to help her seduce Cesare: *Venere bella*. Their dalliance is interrupted by Curio who warns that assassins are coming to murder Cesare. 'Lydia', despite being Cleopatra, has insufficient authority to stop them. Cesare, who refuses to flee, has to go and handle the situation.

Cornelia is with the other concubines. Tolomeo gives her the white linen towel, a sign that she is the chosen one for the night. Sesto is about to strike but he is interrupted by Achilla who reports that Cesare has escaped, jumped into the sea, and been drowned. However Cleopatra has declared war. Achilla's renewed but ineffective attempts to have Cornelia anger Tolomeo.

* * *

Cleopatra's forces make war on Tolomeo. Achilla, having been traduced by Tolomeo, is furious. He changes sides. In the battle, the Queen's forces are defeated and she is put in chains. She laments her fate: *Piangerò la sorte mia*.

But Cesare did not drown. He overhears Sesto and Nireno as they discover the dying, and now penitent, Achilla, who advises them how to get into the palace and save Cornelia from Tolomeo. Cesare resolves to lead them to save both Cleopatra and Cornelia.

Cleopatra, desolate at her situation, is with her weeping maidens in her apartment. Cesare comes to the rescue. Sesto kills Tolomeo as he tries to rape his mother

In the grand finale, Sesto claims vengeance for his father. Cesare crowns Cleopatra. She, in turn, agrees to act as a vassal to Rome. Cesare and Cleopatra proclaim their love and fidelity. The Egyptians rejoice at their liberty.

THE INTERVAL: TALKING POINTS

Stage performance in Handel's time

For 17th century audiences, the aim of the entire production was 'not to create realistic illusion, but to excite wonder and delight.' Visual spectacle and scenic effects, with scenery and scene changes which 'transported the audience from scene to scene, almost in the manner of a modern film', were executed in full view of the audience. The theatre in the Haymarket had a 'live' fountain on stage. Lighting effects were considerable. There were gantries packed with lights, and coloured transparencies were used. When a sudden burst of light was needed, sulphur was thrown on the candles.

The recitatives and da capo arias

Handel's operas, typically of Italian *opera seria* (serious opera) of the period, are characterised by soloists singing arias linked together by recitative.[3] Grand choruses are rare. They were usually sung by ensembles of soloists.

Following the action as described or enacted in the recitative, the soloist would step forward onto the apron of the stage, to a position

---

[3] Recitative is usually *secco*, denoting that it is accompanied by a solo instrument, often the harpsichord. For scenes of particular poignancy or rapidly shifting moods, Handel used the *recitativo accompagnato*, in which the recitative is accompanied by the orchestra.

predetermined by the character's rank,[4] and address the audience, providing it with an emotional response appropriate to whatever is taking place at the time. Convention required that the aria express just one single specific mood or feeling.[5]

Usually Handel's arias involve three lines of music: the soloist, an accompanying instrument above, and a base line (the *continuo*), played by the harpsichord or a solo instrument below. He adopted the standardised structure known as *da capo*. This literally means 'from the head' and denotes the repeat of the first part after a contrasting second section. The music returns to the beginning or a point indicated near the beginning and more or less completely repeats the first part, the soloist usually slightly embellishing it with improvised ornamentation.

The section sandwiched in the middle of the aria provided a different and contrasting shade of this basic mood;[6] the repeat allowed the soloist to burst forth again, reinforcing the mood with renewed energy. As the first section usually involved a repetition of the same words, some contrast was essential: no strong passion can be sustained for long.

The soloist, who had unashamedly exploited the opportunity to show off, then made a dramatic exit as the audience thundered its applause. Hence, many of these arias were also known as 'exit arias'.

Later in the century, Gluck, the composer of the 'best tune' *Che farò senza Euridice*, was very critical of the disruptive and unrealistic effect of the da capo aria. In modern times, the series of isolated arias linked by recitative has been called 'not so much a drama in music as a concert in costume.' One critic has called these operas 'pure concert

---

[4] One of Handel's leading ladies had to be reminded that the location depended on the role she was playing, not on her own sense of self-importance.

[5] The technical term for this mood is 'affect' or 'affection'.

[6] Cleopatra's *Piangerò* in Act 3 provides an example. In its first section, she laments her cruel fate. In the second, she threatens that, when she is dead, the tyrant will be haunted by her ghost. While the sections contrast and reinforce each other, both represent her single emotional response to her situation, that is, self-pity and its obverse, rage. The coloratura second section also makes more poignant the return to the beginning; and the word *agiterò* ('trouble', 'haunt', 'shake') is coloured by speedy runs which were absent in the first section.

in fancy dress with plots as thick as porridge in which nothing is said twice if it can be said four times.'

However, Handel could incarnate in music 'the essence of a mood with overwhelming poetic depth and suggestiveness.' To see how effectively he could combine arias and recitative, we only have to look at the scene in Act 1 when Cesare's philosophical broodings on the death of Pompey, *Alma del gran Pompeo*, are interrupted by the arrival of Cleopatra dressed as 'Lydia'. The 18th century writer Dr Burney called this 'the finest piece of accompanied recitative, without intervening symphonies, with which I am acquainted.' The seductive opening scenes of Act 2 provide another example.

Handel's art and characterisation

It has been said that Handel's Cleopatra is the equal of Shakespeare's and 'one of the most subtly drawn characters in opera.' Every one of her eight arias contributes to her portrait; three at least 'are among the supreme creations of their epoch.'

Handel builds up the character 'facet by facet in the course of the arias until he or she stands complete.' Cleopatra's sexuality begins in a very light-hearted way as she teases Tolomeo about his effete behaviour in *Non disperar*. It becomes passionate in the great love scene. She regains some of her kittenish self-confidence in the *Venere bella*. Her mood changes when things look as if they are going wrong. She expresses her anxiety in *Che sento* and her desolation in the *Piangerò*.

To build up her character, Handel selected some arias from his 'stock'. Seven of her arias are based on earlier versions.

The castrati

The parts of Cesare and Tolomeo were sung by male altos. Modern counterparts could not possibly sound the same; so, however much the performance may aspire to be authentic, it cannot be.

Small boys had not sufficiently powerful voices to deliver the ornamented church music that was expected of them. Because St Paul, in his First Epistle to the Corinthians (ch. 14, v. 34), had forbidden women to perform in churches, it became necessary to employ eunuchs to get the appropriate sound. So castration was permitted, provided it was declared to be necessary for medical reasons or was undertaken with consent of the boy. For 300 years until 1898, there were castrati in St Peter's in Rome. The soprano-male concept endured in roles such as Cherubino in *The Marriage of Figaro*, Prince Orlovsky in *Die Fledermaus* and Octavian in *Der Rosenkavalier*.

Usually the castrato grew exceptionally tall and large, and reputedly could provide immense power, while sounding like a choirboy. This sounded very different from the youthful softness of the female voice such as one would hear from the part of Sesto, sung by a female soprano, a 'trousers role'.

Like celebrity footballers today, the few successful castrati were very highly paid. Senesino, the first Giulio Cesare, was majestic in public but, in private, he was touchy, insolent and vain. His contract for 1720 was worth £3,150 at a time when a shopkeeper might earn a pound a week. The less successful castrati led a life of drudgery.

The procedure usually involved the boy being anaesthetised with opium and being put in a hot bath, or being knocked out by compressing the carotid arteries.

Some actually married – apparently, they could ejaculate but were infertile – and the fact that they were 'risk-free' made them attractive to women concerned about unwanted pregnancies. Caffarelli (1710–1783), who purchased a dukedom, was surprised, *in flagrante delicto*, by a husband returning home unexpectedly. The castrato had to take refuge in a disused water tank, thereby causing considerable damage to his health.

A little Roman history

Although the characters, apart from Nireno, are historical, the libretto is only historical in broad outline. All of them, except Cornelia, came to a violent end.

Julius Caesar (c. 100–44BC), who Shakespeare called 'the foremost man of all this world', was born into a family that had held high office in the Roman state. At the age of 40, he took his first important military command in Gaul and Portugal. He pacified Gaul and entered

Britain. On his second visit to Britain, in 54BC, he crossed the Thames, showing that an invasion would be feasible, but he did not conquer it. Those whose Latin education involved reading his *Commentaries* will probably recall the drudgery, and may have forgotten that they were regarded as a masterpiece of literature, faultless in style.

Caesar ruled Rome in a triumvirate with Crassus and Pompey.[7] Crassus had defeated the Spartacus slave revolt and crucified 6,000 slaves. Notorious for his greed, he had become fabulously rich largely from trafficking in slaves and the property of those who had been proscribed by the state; he was killed in Syria in 53BC. This left Caesar, whose power base was in Gaul and the West, and Pompey, who was associated with Roman rule in the East.

Pompey the Great (106–48BC) was the husband of Caesar's daughter Julia. He was 'a cautious general with a cherubic face.' He had been a soldier from an early age. He made his name in Spain, and by destroying the pirates in the Mediterranean who were disrupting Rome's corn supplies. His ruthlessness brought him the title 'the young butcher'. It also amassed him an immense fortune. He became the 'first man in the Roman world': he annexed Syria and stormed the Temple in Jerusalem and its Holy of Holies, killing 12,000 in the process. He returned to Rome for the 'most magnificent triumph which Rome had ever witnessed.'

Caesar and Pompey ruled jointly. After Julia died in 54BC, their relations became strained. It was inevitable that the two protagonists would slug it out. In January 49BC, Caesar crossed over the River Rubicon into Italy, and became its master. In the following year, Pompey experienced his first ever defeat in the battle of Pharsalus in Greece. He fled to Egypt, a vassal state, the bread-basket of Rome, to secure the support of the boy-king Ptolemy XIII, but was murdered by one of his centurions as he stepped ashore. His face must have looked less cherubic when pickled.

---

[7] Caesar duly bedded his rivals' wives. Albeit in his early fifties and 'self-conscious about his balding pate', he was well able to cope with Cleopatra when she arrived in a laundry bag. They had a child, Caesarion, who later ruled jointly with Cleopatra.

Caesar followed close behind, and arrived two days after Pompey had been murdered. This was in October 48BC, at a time when Ptolemy and his 'sister-wife', the 21-year-old Cleopatra VII were also fighting each other.

This is the point at which *Giulio Cesare* takes place.

Caesar's demand that Ptolemy and his sister disband was resented as 'unwarrantable interference'. He was blockaded in Alexandria where the historic library was destroyed in the fighting.[8] He was seduced by Cleopatra. Ptolemy was drowned in the Nile. Cleopatra was placed, as a Roman stooge, on the throne jointly with a younger brother.

Only in June 47BC did Caesar leave for Syria and return to Rome, where he was later created perpetual dictator, and set up with Cleopatra in a scandalous relationship. She was obviously very talented – she could converse in seven languages – but she was also a nasty piece of work: she poisoned her younger brother, and, later, her sister. Curiously, her long, aquiline nose and pointed chin argue against her beauty. Caesar possessed 'almost superhuman energy'. He seems to have governed well: he introduced several administrative reforms, not least the reform of the calendar.

In 44BC, Caesar was assassinated at the foot of Pompey's statue.[9]

The Roman sequel: Richard Burton and Elizabeth Taylor

After Caesar's assassination, Cleopatra fled back to Egypt. Caesar's former lieutenant Mark Antony, and Octavius (Caesar's adopted son, later Augustus) defeated the assassins in 42BC at Philippi, in Macedonia, North-East Greece.

---

[8] Caesar was supported by 3,000 Jewish troops. The Ptolemaic dynasty in Egypt had begun when Alexander the Great's empire was divided following his death in 323BC. Ptolemy I had been one of Alexander's generals. The dynasty ended with the death of Cleopatra in 30BC. After her father died, she ruled jointly with her brother Ptolemy XIII who was seven years younger, but they soon were at war with each other. The Romans at first supported Ptolemy, but when Caesar arrived, his sister seized her chance.

[9] At the bottom of Dante's pit of hell, Lucifer holds in his three mouths the three greatest malefactors the world had ever seen by the 13th century: Brutus and Cassius, who betrayed their sovereign and their country, and Judas Iscariot.

Along with the other assassins, Pompey's younger son Sextus[10] could not return to Italy. He set himself up in Sicily, where he disrupted Rome's corn supplies. He was eventually murdered by one of Mark Antony's officers. According to a 19th-century expert, 'He had his father's bravery as a soldier, but seems to have been a rough uncultivated man.'

Mark Antony followed Cleopatra to Egypt where he offered her his support in return for her favours. She was fourteen years younger than him. They had three children. As enthusiasts of the film will recall, Antony and Cleopatra lived together 'in the most profuse and wanton luxury.' It is therefore perhaps appropriate that it is said to be the most expensive film ever made, when adjustment is made for inflation.

There were various comings and goings in the intervening years. But Antony and Cleopatra were, in their turn, defeated in 31BC by Octavius in the naval battle at Actium in Western Greece, and they fled back to Egypt. There, she had her ships hauled from the Nile to the Red Sea so as to flee in the direction of India, but they were burnt by local Arabs. She was trapped. Antony fell on his sword, but must have made a bad job of it because he was just able to join her in a mausoleum where they died together. She killed herself either by applying an asp to her bosom, or by using a poisoned comb; nobody knows which.

The original cast

Giulio Cesare was composed with a specific cast in mind. It took great determination to control this unruly lot. Early in 1724, Senesino, the Cesare, insulted Anastasia Robinson, the Cornelia. The Earl of Peterborough, who she had already secretly married, 'publicly and violently caned him behind the scenes.' Another problem for Handel was the Cleopatra, the soprano Francesca Cuzzoni (1698–1770). During rehearsals, he lost his temper with her, grabbed her by the waist and threatened to throw her out of the window. Subsequently, there were fisticuffs on stage between her and her rival, the more aristocratic Faustina Bordoni.

---

[10] Sextus (75BC–35BC) was actually Cornelia's stepson rather than son. Although the opera portrays him as a youth, he was already in his mid-twenties when Pompey was murdered.

Senesino

The arrogant, vain and insolent Senesino – real name Francesco Bernardi (*d.* 1759) – dominated London opera in the 1720s until superseded by Farinelli. He had a sweet alto contralto voice and was particularly skilled in recitatives. His performance in *Giulio Cesare* was described as being 'beyond all criticism'. Horace Walpole, who came across him in Siena in 1740, thought he looked like a fat old woman, but spoke 'in a shrill little pipe.'

Surprisingly, the stage performance of Cuzzoni was said to be cold, and her figure was not too favourable. She came from Bologna and made a sensational debut in London in January 1723. In contrast to her subsequent rival, Faustina Bordoni, who excelled in the fiery music, Cuzzoni's strength was the expressive and pathetic cantabile (her *Piangerò* must have been sensational). Later, she joined the opera company that competed with Handel's.[11]

---

[11] Notorious for her extravagance, Cuzzoni was imprisoned for debt and spent her last years making buttons in Bologna, where she died in obscurity and extreme poverty.

Anastasia Robinson

Anastasia Robinson (1692–1755), the daughter of a portrait painter, was described by a contemporary as being 'of moderate beauty but of the highest spirit'. She retired shortly after *Giulio Cesare* was produced. The elderly Earl of Peterborough only acknowledged her as his wife around ten years later.

The Sesto was Margherita Durastanti, who had been Cuzzoni's predecessor as the Academy's leading soprano. Although coarse and masculine, and even described as an elephant, she was musically very versatile, and had a longer personal association with Handel than any other singer. He had first encountered her in Rome when she sang at the regular Sunday afternoon salons. Handel wrote the part of the Magdalen for her in one of his first oratorios. By 1724, she was already old with a worn-out voice.

The Tolomeo was another alto castrato, Gaetano Berenstadt; the Achilla was Giuseppe Boschi, said to be best in the role of a tyrant or villain.

In the revised version, Handel omitted the part of Curio. Nireno, originally designed for the alto castrato Bigonzi, who was unequal to singing anything other than recitative, was reduced to a mute.

ACT BY ACT

Act 1

In 48BC, Cesare lands in Egypt where he is hailed as the equivalent of Hercules (Alcides), the greatest of the Greek heroes. He accepts the praise: *Presti omai*. His legate Curio describes how he came, saw and conquered.[12] Pompey, his rival, has appealed to Tolomeo the King of Egypt for military support.

Pompey's wife Cornelia and his son Sesto appear, seeking peace. But just as Cesare is giving a suitably magnanimous response, Tolomeo's general, Achilla arrives. He invites him to stay in the palace and bears diplomatic gifts. One of these is the severed head of Pompey. Not surprisingly, Cornelia swoons. Cesare expresses rage at Tolomeo's behaviour: *Empio, dirò, tu sei* ('A king should be merciful, not pitiless').

When Cornelia revives, she tries to kill herself, the first of several such attempts. It quickly becomes clear that she is 'sufficiently attractive to provoke violent and instantaneous desire in every man she meets' except, for some unexplained reason, Cesare. Although Achilla has already eyed her, Curio is the first to make a pass and get the brush-off. She is bereft at the loss of her husband: *Priva son d'ogni conforto*. By contrast, her enraged son is duty-bound to avenge his father's death: *Svegliatevi nel core*. Indeed, his father's shade expects this of him.

* * *

The scene changes to Cleopatra's chamber. Her eunuch and royal pimp Nireno interrupts her musings about her ambitions. He brings news of Pompey's death. She resolves to go to Cesare's camp. Tolomeo interrupts her, and brother and sister argue about the exercise of power. He says that the woman's role is with needle and thread, not the sceptre. She flippantly teases him about his effete behaviour: will

---

[12] Julius Caesar actually pronounced *Veni, vidi, vici* later, following the battle of Zela in northern Turkey, after he had punished one of Pompey's allies, Pharnaces. This was in 47BC, after Ptolemy had been defeated by him and Cleopatra.

he will be more fortunate as an effeminate philanderer than as a monarch: *Non disperar, chi sà?* – who knows?

Achilla returns to warn Tolomeo that Cesare was none too pleased with the gifts. He suggests that, in return for having Cornelia, he would arrange for Cesare to get the same treatment as Pompey. Tolomeo rages about Cesare coming to disturb his peace: *L'empio, sleale, indegno vorria rapirmi il regno.*

Meanwhile, in his camp, Cesare broods over the death of his great rival. The once-great Pompey is nought but dust: *Alma del gran Pompeo.*

Cesare's reflections are interrupted by the arrival of Cleopatra, disguised as a lady-in-waiting, 'Lydia'. Cesare is bowled over, and admires her hair. Curio is obsessed with her breasts, and reckons that if he cannot have Cornelia he will have a go at Cleopatra instead. Cesare expresses his admiration of her face, which is as beautiful as a flower in a meadow: *Non è sì vago e bello.* Once he has gone, Nireno and Cleopatra congratulate themselves on her success. There is nothing a pretty woman cannot do: *Tutto può donna vezzosa.*

* * *

Cornelia, still grieving over the death of her husband, intends to destroy Tolomeo, but is stopped by Sesto, who claims that revenge is his prerogative. Cleopatra, disguised as 'Lydia', overhears this. She almost reveals who she is by offering to introduce them into Tolomeo's presence to enable Sesto to take his revenge. Nireno will guide them. Sesto is now optimistic that he will succeed: *Cara speme, questo core.*

* * *

Tolomeo, accompanied by Achilla, frostily receives Cesare in his palace. Cesare suspects a plot and determines to proceed, like an expert huntsman, with great caution: *Va tacito e nascosto.*[13]

---

[13] Handel originally composed this superb aria for another of his operas, *Berenice*, about Cleopatra's cousin. In that, she is urged to be careful in her approach to Caesar. So, not surprisingly, the aria can be criticised for contributing nothing to the characterisation of Cesare. However, it wholly satisfies an important requirement of Handel's market, which he outlined

When Cornelia arrives in the palace, it is Tolomeo's turn to be utterly captivated by her. But he is annoyed by her insults. He orders her to be taken to the harem, and Sesto to be locked up. Out of respect to Achilla's request to enjoy her, he pretends that she is condemned only to dig the flowerbeds rather than perform the more usual duties of the place. Achilla makes a pass at her (in a style consistent with his position as a senior officer): *Tu sei il cor di questo core*. But he is rebuffed.

As they are taken away, Cornelia and Sesto sing a sad duet lamenting their fate: *Son nata a lagrimar, Son nato a sospirar*.

Act 2

With the help of Nireno, Cleopatra (still 'Lydia') has created the ideal setting in which to seduce Cesare: a cedar grove with a backdrop of Mount Parnassus, the home of the Muses. This scene has been called 'an epitome of seductiveness seldom equalled in any opera of any period … seldom has the process of seduction been so vividly expressed by musical means.' The love music is 'a glorification of sexual passion uninhibited by the shadow of matrimony.'

Cesare, guided by Nireno, gasps as he espies Virtue[14] surrounded by the Muses, with a stage orchestra playing a delightful sinfonia, as if it were accompanying the Muses. Virtue proceeds to sing the exquisite *V'adoro, pupille, saette d'amore* ('I adore you, dear eyes, arrows of love').[15] Cesare is captivated and interrupts her: such a beautiful sound is not heard in heaven. He demands to be taken to her, and to the accompaniment of a solo violin compares her to a songbird in a beautiful meadow: *Se in fiorito ameno prato*.

* * *

to the composer Gluck: 'The English like something they can beat time to, something that hits them straight on the ear drum.'

[14] The notion of Cleopatra clothed as Virtue may be politely described as 'delicate irony'.

[15] The stage orchestra provides the main accompaniment. The pit orchestra interjects with echoes when the voice pauses for breath. The plaintive second section, with the pit orchestra again silent, hints at the same material in the minor mode. Before the return to repeat the first part, Cesare interrupts, musically gobsmacked.

Meanwhile the unfortunate Cornelia is hard at work hoeing the garden of the harem. When Achilla comes to seduce her, she runs away, only to find herself falling into Tolomeo's arms. Achilla renews his supposed deal with Tolomeo, but the pharaoh actually wants her for himself. The brusque soldier tells her that, if she yields to him, he will be faithful; if not, she can expect rough treatment: *Se a me non sei crudele*. Tolomeo then tries his luck, again without success, so his love turns to hatred: *Sì, spietata, il tuo rigore sveglia*.

Cornelia is about to kill herself by throwing herself from the battlements, but is prevented from this by Sesto. Things get worse for her when Nireno arrives to say that Tolomeo has ordered her to join his concubines. But he explains that he is on her side, and that Tolomeo's trysting place is where he is undefended and Sesto can easily take revenge. Cornelia sees an end to her troubles and her sighing: *Cessa omai di sospirare*! And Sesto, likening himself to an angry snake, contemplates his revenge: *L'angue offeso mai riposa*.

* * *

We return to Cleopatra's pleasure garden, where, in a confident mood, she awaits her lover. She implores Venus to enhance her attraction: *Venere bella*. She pretends to be asleep when Cesare arrives. Again, he is overwhelmed by her beauty and, out loud, contemplates 'Lydia' as his *sposa e consorte* – his wife and consort. He is disconcerted by Cleopatra's positive response to this ill-considered proposal – after all, 'Lydia' is just a servant. When Cesare is initially taken aback by her presumption, she threatens to go back to sleep.

But Curio rushes in to warn that Tolomeo's assassins are on their way.[16] Cesare is surprised when 'Lydia' says that Cleopatra will come to his aid, and that her authority will halt them. At this, her cover is blown, and she rushes out to head off the assassins.

---

[16] On hearing that a squad has been sent to assassinate him, Cesare boasts: *Cesare non seppe mai che sia timore* ('Caesar has never known what it is to be afraid'). In the 1732 revival, at this juncture, a piece of machinery fell down on him. 'The poor Hero was so frightened, that he trembled and lost his Voice and fell a-crying.' Cleopatra's immediate response, *O Dio*, must have seemed particularly appropriate.

But she is unsuccessful and returns to advise Cesare to flee: *Fuggi, Cesare, fuggi!* However a warrior of Cesare's stature is not fazed by this: *Al lampo dell'armi*. He rushes out to deal with it. Cleopatra is left behind to utter the anguished *Che sento?* followed by the aria *Se pietà di me non senti*: Heaven, if it were merciful, would let her die and release her from her torment. This sequence reveals unsuspected depths of suffering and has been described as being among the finest creations of any age, 'Bach-like in its harmonic probing of emotion and scored in rich dark colours.'[17]

Back in the harem, Tolomeo hands Cornelia the linen towel, the sign that she is selected for the night. Sesto emerges from his hiding place and is about to strike, but is interrupted by Achillla, who reports that Cesare has escaped, jumped into the sea, and been drowned: Cleopatra's troops are coming to avenge his death. Achilla again demands Cornelia in return for his support. This infuriates Tolomeo, who reneges on the deal, and enrages Achilla. Sesto is about to fall on his sword. But his mother stops him, thus reinvigorating him: *L'aure che spira*.

Act 3

In a wood near Alexandria, the betrayed Achilla resolves to change sides and support Cleopatra with his sword: *Dal fulgor di questa spada*. Unfortunately, in the surprisingly short and brisk battle which follows, represented by a sinfonia, Cleopatra's forces are defeated. She is put in chains. Tolomeo resolves to tame her pride: *Domerò la tua fierezza*.

In the truly exquisite aria *Piangerò la sorte mia*,[18] Cleopatra laments her cruel fate; when she is dead, her ghost will haunt the tyrant.

Fortunately for her, Cesare has actually survived his swim in the sea. His first thought is of course for his lover: *Aure, deh, per pietà*, although all he sees around him are the corpses of Cleopatra's forces.

[17] The conspirators shout 'Death to Caesar' in B flat. Cleopatra's horror and concern are expressed immediately with dissonance on F sharp, as far removed as is possible.

[18] The *Piangero* is on a bass descending by steps over a fourth. Bars 26–29 comprise an eloquent sequence from an earlier cantata, associated with cruel fate and separation.

He meets Sesto and Nireno who, still in search for revenge, come across the mortally wounded Achilla. He expresses a dying wish that Cornelia should be told that it was he who contrived both the death of Pompey and the attempted assassination of Cesare. This does not go down too well with Pompey's son and Cesare. But fortunately Achilla, before expiring, tells them that in a nearby cave they will find a relief force with which they can enter the palace via an underground passage, save Cornelia, and kill Tolomeo.

Cesare takes control and determines to rescue the ladies and destroy, like a torrent rushing down the mountain, everything that gets in his way: *Quel torrente, che cade dal monte*. Achilla's death renews Sesto's confidence that he will avenge his father: *La giustizia ha già sull'arco*.

In her apartment, Cleopatra is still bemoaning her fate, when Cesare arrives. She is so surprised that, at first, she thinks he is a ghost. He dismisses the guards so that they can be alone together. They have a brief kiss, but he says that there is no time to hang about, and he rushes off with his soldiers. Cleopatra is overjoyed, and expresses in a bravura aria how she feels like a battered ship finally reaching a safe haven: *Da tempeste il legno infranto*.

Back in the palace, Tolomeo is still at it, trying to rape Cornelia, who resists him: after all, she is a Roman: *Scostati, indegno, e pensa che Cornelia è Romana*. She draws a dagger and is about to kill him when Sesto arrives and claims this honour for himself. Tolomeo falls. Cornelia now feels that she has nothing more to fear: *Non ha più che temere*.

The grand finale takes place at the port of Alexandria. It begins with a sinfonia with four horns providing a suitable sense of occasion. A somewhat self-satisfied Sesto recounts how he has avenged his father, and he swears loyalty to Cesare, who takes the crown and hands it to Cleopatra. She, in turn, agrees to act as a vassal of Rome. Cesare and Cleopatra sing a duet about their love and fidelity, *Caro! Bella! Più amabile beltà*. As the opera seria draws to its customary happy close, the Egyptians rejoice at their liberty.

MOZART:
THE MARRIAGE OF FIGARO

THE OPERA AND ITS COMPOSER

'Sheer perfection' was how Brahms described Mozart's groundbreaking opera. 'Never,' he said, 'has anything like this been created, not even by Beethoven.'

The première of *The Marriage of Figaro* took place on 1 May 1786 in the Imperial Court Theatre (the Burgtheater) in Vienna. Mozart was almost halfway through a ten-year period he spent freelancing in Vienna. This followed his dismissal – 'with a kick on the arse', as Mozart himself put it – by the chamberlain of the Archbishop of Salzburg, his former employer, who found the young musician totally impossible to manage.

Mozart composed *Figaro* five and a half years before his death, aged only 35, in late 1791. He was at the height of his career, working so hard that his family back in Salzburg hardly ever heard from him.

At this time, Mozart was enjoying considerable success, particularly from subscription concerts, and living a handsome lifestyle. But, as the chamberlain had warned him, celebrity status was brittle. Mozart's father was very worried about the powerful cabals ranged against his son. Competition from other composers was intense. Mozart's popularity would decline. As it waned, fees from operas and foreign touring became an increasingly important source of income. His fee for *Figaro*, however, amounted to less than one year's rent of his expensive accommodation.

Figaro was based on a successful but thoroughly disrespectful play, *La Folle Journée ou Le Mariage de Figaro*, written by Beaumarchais, which had finally been allowed its first public performance in Paris two years earlier.

Mozart. This has been called the most lifelike of all the portraits of him.

This play about love in all its guises, good and bad, features an insubordinate valet, a duplicitous noble and a flighty wife. It followed the French playwright's earlier but less contentious comedy featuring the same characters, *Le Barbier de Séville*. This had recently been staged extremely successfully as an opera by the celebrated and wealthy Neapolitan composer Giovanni Paisiello (1740–1816).[1] It would be a further 30 years until Rossini's version of *The Barber*, with which we are today far more familiar.

Mozart had studied more than a hundred libretti before he chose the Beaumarchais play. He then found a librettist in whom he could have confidence. This was Lorenzo da Ponte, who he had met a few years earlier. Da Ponte cut the play considerably but, despite this, the opera was 'the longest and most complicated one ever staged in the Burgtheater', and is almost always itself subject to cuts today.

The Viennese première starred, in the title role, the celebrity bass-baritone *buffo* Francesco Benucci, 'the greatest of his generation'. In the role of Susanna was his putative lover, the ideal soubrette, the

[1] Paisiello, Martín y Soler (the composer of *Una cosa rara*) and Antonio Salieri were major competitiors. Mozart was on good terms with Paisiello. Salieri, however, gets a bad press as a result of the drama *Amadeus*. He was in fact a 'witty, explosive little man who had a passion for sweetmeats and could never pass a cake-shop without going into it.'

The Mozart family was employed in the service of the highly influential Archbishop of Salzburg, the local potentate where **Wolfgang Amadeus Mozart** was born on 27 January 1756.

From the age of six, he spent much time away on tour. His father Leopold needed to extract, while it lasted, the most value out of his son and daughter Wolfgang and Nannerl, who were both infant prodigies. When Mozart was seven, the family went on a three-and-a-half year European tour to London. Between the ages of thirteen and seventeen, Wolfgang went on three tours to Italy.

As an adult, his father wanted him to get a permanent and secure position, which he never did. He went to Paris in fruitless search of a job, accompanied by his mother, who died there. Later, aged 25, he left Salzburg and fell out with the Archbishop. This did not provide a good basis for his ambition to work as a freelance in the capital of the Habsburg Empire, Vienna. There, the challenge was to distinguish oneself from the many other competing composers. At first, Mozart was successful in this precarious existence.

He married Constanze Weber, whose sister had earlier rejected him. With Constanze, he had two sons. It seems she was a liability: she was often away at a health spa, and Mozart was very worried by her tendency to flirt. He got into debt, fell ill, died and was buried in a common re-usable grave. The cause of his death, on 5 December 1791, is not known, and has been famously attributed to Salieri, not least in a play by Pushkin, an opera by Rimsky-Korsakov and in Peter Shaffer's drama *Amadeus* (1984). Mozart had worked himself to death: he spent almost a third of his 36-year life – 3,720 days – away from home. Yet the piled-up volumes of the 'Mozart Edition' on display in Salzburg measure over six feet high.

Lorenzo da Ponte (1749–1838) wrote libretti for many composers, but is remembered particularly for Mozart's *The Marriage of Figaro*, *Don Giovanni* and *Così fan tutte*. He was born near Venice.

As custom dictated, he took the name of the local bishop when his father, who was Jewish, converted to Christianity. Da Ponte was ordained priest, but because of his views and his serial adultery – he consorted with Casanova and ran a brothel – he was banned from Venice.

After enduring a year of great poverty, he managed to get Emperor Joseph II to appoint him librettist to the Italian theatre company in Vienna. He made his name as the librettist for 'one of the most outstanding operatic successes that Vienna ever witnessed,' *Una cosa rara* by the Spaniard Martín y Soler (1754–1806). This eclipsed *Figaro*. At this time, it was recalled that 'in sooth, the abbé stood mightily well with himself and had the character of a consummate coxcomb; he had also, a strong lisp and broad Venetian dialect.'

Once the Emperor died, Da Ponte fell out with the authorities, partly because of his radical views, and was dismissed. He went to London with his wife, and was librettist at the King's Theatre; he also ran a bookshop at 55 Pall Mall and a printing business. He backed somebody's bill of exchange (cheque), and was arrested for debt no less than 30 times in three months – so he fled to New York and Elizabeth Township, New Jersey, where his financial problems continued on and off during his varied career as a poet, a grocer, and even as a haulier – in 'L. de Ponty's Wagon'. He was also a collector of Italian editions and an enthusiast of Italian operas when they came to New York.

He later became a distinguished teacher of Italian at Columbia College. His advertisements for pupils stated, 'Every attention will be paid to the morals of those entrusted to his care.'

His astonishingly turbulent, long and varied life evinced some characteristics of Liszt (whose appearance, with long mane and hooked nose, was also somewhat similar). He died in the USA in 1838.

London-born soprano Nancy Storace.[2] The Irish baritone Michael Kelly sang both Don Basilio and Don Curzio.

It seems that the opera was at first only moderately successful. Yet by the third performance, there were so many encores that it took almost twice the normal time, and the Emperor Joseph II, the eccentric Habsburg monarch and patron of the arts who had commissioned the opera, had to forbid the encoring, except for solo numbers. But it had a short run, and this may be attributable to the 'perceived difficulty of Mozart's music.' In Prague, however, *Figaro* fared particularly well and Mozart and his wife were given a wild reception. Mozart wrote to one of his pupils, 'Here they talk about nothing but Figaro. Nothing is played sung or whistled but Figaro. Certainly a great honour for me!'

Emperor Joseph II supported Mozart's venture. He was a monarch enlightened before his time, who was 'bitten by the ambition to become his own theatre director.' Although himself a very competent musician, Joseph thought *Figaro* rather heavy. (Famously, he had similarly complained that there were too many notes in Mozart's *Die Entführung*.) For us, *Figaro* is far from heavy, although the details of the plot can be difficult to disentangle. Perhaps it seemed less complex to an audience who would have been familiar with the original plays.

As was normal in opera, the action is moved along by the frequent use of 'recitatives', 'speaking in music'. Even as far back as the 1620s, one composer stressed the importance of arias in breaking up 'the tediousness of the recitative.' In Mozart's hands this is actually an art form, but much of this and its Italian subtlety may be lost on the majority of audiences, so chunks of it are usually cut. *Figaro*'s arias and ensembles however provide an almost relentless succession of wonderful tunes – 'each item a miracle,' as Brahms said – most of which are amongst the most popular classical music today.

---

[2] Her manner was coarse, in the opinion of Emperor Joseph.

WHO'S WHO AND WHAT'S WHAT

The story below is based on the libretto. Certain directors may amend opera stories to suit their production.

Three years ago, the **Count of Almaviva**, a Spanish grandee, wooed the lovely Rosina, who is now his **Countess**.[3] **Figaro**, the Barber of Seville, helped them defy the wishes of her elderly guardian, **Doctor Bartolo**, who wanted her for himself. (Those who know the story of Rossini's *The Barber of Seville* will be familiar with this.)

Figaro, who became the Count's valet, is now about to wed **Susanna**, the Countess's lady's maid, a pert soubrette. The Count wants to resurrect his ancient feudal right to deflower the bride (***droit de seigneur***), even though he himself recently took credit for abolishing it. There is also an impediment: Figaro is already pledged to **Marcellina**, Doctor Bartolo's former housekeeper, who lent him money.

The story revolves around Figaro's complex scheme to thwart his master's objective.

Figaro plans to utilise the Countess's pubescent page and godson **Cherubino**, who will chase anyone in a skirt, and who is infatuated with the Countess even to the extent of compromising her dignity and reputation. The Count has already ordered him away after catching him trying to seduce **Barbarina**, the daughter of Susanna's uncle Antonio, the gardener.

* * *

The opera takes place on the wedding day at the Count of Almaviva's castle about nine miles from Seville. Figaro and Susanna are moving into their married quarters, which are dangerously near the Count's bedroom. Susanna is visited by Cherubino, who has to hide when the Count comes to visit her. The Count himself also tries to hide

---

[3] It is inappropriate to speak of either the Countess or Susanna as the prima donna. The parts are treated equally. Elisabeth Schwarzkopf progressed from Susanna to the Countess, having earlier been Barbarina. Kiri Te Kanawa made her name with the role of the Countess. Audrey Mildmay, the wife of Glyndebourne's founder John Christie, was a leading exponent of the role of Susanna.

when **Don Basilio**, the music teacher and thus an inveterate intriguer, comes to persuade Susanna to give in to the Count's advances.

Figaro's scheme involves firstly accelerating events so that he can consummate his marriage before the Count has the chance to deflower Susanna; and secondly, he will take revenge by publicly exposing the Count's hypocrisy. He has sent the Count an anonymous letter insinuating that his wife is having an affair.[4] This will divert the Count's attention. And, to expose the Count's hypocrisy, an assignation will be fixed for that night in the park where everyone will congregate. The Countess will catch her husband up to his old tricks. Specifically, he will be caught trying to seduce Cherubino dressed up as a girl.

The Countess is depressed that the Count no longer loves her, but she joins in the scheme. They start to dress up Cherubino as a girl just at the moment that the Count, having received the anonymous letter, comes to confront his wife. He finds her seemingly compromised with Cherubino in a state of undress. Fortunately, Cherubino escapes out of the window and Susanna takes his place. Unfortunately, the escape was seen by **Antonio** the gardener, who informs the Count. So the Count remains deeply suspicious.

However, his spirits rise when Susanna appears to accept an assignation with him in return for her dowry: the money will be used to pay off Marcellina. Meanwhile, Marcellina's claim against Figaro must be adjudicated. When it transpires that Figaro is her long-lost son by Doctor Bartolo, the court lawyer **Don Curzio** points out that marriage between her and Figaro is now forbidden. Although Susanna is at first upset and confused by this, a double wedding is arranged, for Figaro and Susanna on the one hand, and the Doctor and Marcellina on the other.

Meanwhile Cherubino is still hanging around, now dressed as a village girl, despite being sent away to join the army.

The Countess regrets that she has to stoop so low to confront her husband. But she and Susanna compose **another letter** to the Count,

[4] This first letter might seem a red herring, but Figaro's convoluted plan prompts the cross-dressing that soon takes place in the Countess's boudoir and brings the Count prematurely back from the hunt to catch them all red-handed.

confirming the assignation that night in the pine grove. They seal it with a **pin**. The Count pricks himself with the pin when he opens it during the preliminary wedding celebrations. Despite this, he responds graciously to the villagers and invites them to continue the celebrations in the grounds that night.

In the pine grove, in the dark, events evolve slightly differently to Figaro's original plan as outlined to the Countess earlier. In that, there was no question of the Count actually seducing Susanna. But Figaro finds Barbarina searching for the pin, which the Count asked her to take, as a love token, back to Susanna. To his horror, he interprets this to mean that his fiancée has indeed agreed to give herself to the Count. Cherubino, who has come to find Barbarina, of course gets in the way.

The Count starts to make love to the person he thinks is Susanna (but is actually the Countess dressed as Susanna). It is only when Figaro recognises Susanna's voice, coming from the person he took to be the Countess, that he realises at last that the two women have exchanged clothes.

Figaro now knows that he too has been tricked, and, in revenge, feigns making love to 'the Countess' (who is actually Susanna dressed in the Countess's clothes). The real Susanna at first is furious; and the Count denounces 'the Countess' when he discovers Figaro trying to seduce her.

The real Countess then discloses herself, and graciously forgives the Count for his misbehaviour. Everybody lives happily, with love providing the solution to all confusion, ever after.

THE INTERVAL: TALKING POINTS

Characterisation

Some might be tempted to regard *The Marriage of Figaro* as a light-hearted romp of chocolate-boxy puppets or caricatures, displaying the 'harmless merriment' found in the general run of comic operas. That is a mistake. Each character is a carefully 'sculptured individual', whose 'flesh and blood vitality' is illuminated by Mozart's music.

In the past, music had often been descriptive; but for the first time, a way had been found, by Mozart, for it to encapsulate the feelings, passions, thoughts and responses of real human beings and their inter-relationships. They all inhabit 'an actual world, enchanted yet recognisable, companionable but full of danger.'

Their feelings emerge realistically from the bottom of their hearts: as a distinguished American musicologist has said, 'their anger is just as real as their merriness.' The Count's wish to have Susanna develops into a real passion, and the Countess's fun and games with Cherubino run the risk of escalating into the very affair envisaged by Beaumarchais for a later, third play.[5] This is not cardboard cut-and-paste; it is for real.

Should we attribute the characterisation to Mozart's music, or to the superb libretto of Lorenzo da Ponte, or to the 'brilliant political satire' of Beaumarchais on which the opera is based? And what does it mean to say that the characters are illuminated by the music? There are limitations to what music alone can describe.

Mozart's music is perfectly blended with the characters and their attitudes. For example, the upper-class dignity of the Countess, and her purity, despite her fooling around, is perfectly conveyed in her two cavatinas, *Porgi amor* and *Dove sono*, in which Mozart uses a melodic structure that he had already used (and would again) in religious music. It is hard to imagine these being sung by the soubrette serving girl Susanna.

But a musician does not have to be a great artist to improvise music appropriate to the circumstances: quiet music to accompany sadness, loud music for rage, light music for a flighty person, or martial music for a soldier. So composing dignified music for a Countess is not in itself an exceptional achievement, even if the sheer beauty of the music is unsurpassable.

---

[5] Beaumarchais planned that the Countess would have a baby by Cherubino in a third play, *La mère coupable*.

Mozart's monumental achievement is well illustrated in the second half, in the Act 3 sextet of which he himself was particularly proud. This follows the surprise revelation that Marcellina is Figaro's mother. Thus, the impediment to him marrying Susanna, disappears. Susanna, however, still does not know this, and thinks that she has been jilted. The Count's schemes are frustrated. Each of the six characters is bound to have a different response to this turn of events. Their entirely different reactions are realistically and perfectly portrayed in the music, blended together by Mozart into a single ensemble. The result is so realistic, natural and effortless that it can pass one by.

On the straight theatre stage, it would sound chaotic if the actors in this sextet were to give their response to the circumstances all at once. If they were to do so consecutively, the result would be unrealistically stilted: people do not trot out their feelings one after another. But music as an art form provides the facility whereby the whole picture can be presented, at once, very effectively.

We see this again in *Don Giovanni*, when the wild, dangerously rapacious character of Don Giovanni is so famously depicted in the so-called 'Champagne aria' (*Fin ch'han dal vino*). A writer would need reams of paper to make the same point: Mozart does it conclusively in less than 90 seconds. Such is the power of music in his hands.

The relationship between music and words, and which should take primary place, was a topical subject at the time. Three months before *The Marriage of Figaro* premièred, there was a state banquet at the imperial summer palace at Schönbrunn. At one end of the orangery, Salieri's *Prima la Musica, poì le Parole* (which included a caricature of Lorenzo da Ponte) was performed;[6] at the other end, Mozart's *Der Schauspieldirektor*. Both of these one-act operas included a serious consideration of the relationship between music and words.

---

[6] In the twentieth century, Stefan Zweig, the prominent novelist and biographer, unearthed the libretto to inspire Richard Strauss to create *Capriccio*.

Cherubino

Opera generally is full of ludicrous characters. If it were not for the momentum of Mozart's music, Cherubino would seem to be one of them. Even then, is this fizzy, frothy page, about to be officer cadet, sung by a mezzo-soprano, convincing?

For a countess to be chased by a pageboy was relatively safe in terms of political correctness. Also, audiences in Mozart's time were far more used to breeches roles than we are – they were a hangover from the days when the male opera stars were *castrati*. Today, the tenor dominates opera. Then, the tenor role was not well developed and there was a shortage of them. Besides, one half of the audience took some pleasure from the male costume disclosing the shape and curves which female dress customarily hid from view.

It has been suggested that Cherubino, for all his oddities and eccentricities, has a real soul. Maybe in the Countess's mind, he is a surrogate for an earlier version of the Count? Maybe his successful adolescent exploits even indicate an incipient Don Giovanni?

Political aspects

Beaumarchais's *Figaro* was staged shortly before the French Revolution. It is not surprising that it had taken a long time to get it past Louis XVI and the French censors. The play contains a relentless current of insubordination from servants, indeed, 'there is a positively dangerous spirit of revolution.' In the last act of the play, Marcellina becomes the focal point for a feminist outburst against the 'state of servitude' to which women are condemned.

In Vienna, the political problems facing Louis's brother-in-law Emperor Joseph II were different. He was strait-laced and would not tolerate the immorality and obscenity which had shocked Paris audiences. But he tolerated critical political comment. This was because, unlike in France, which was bankrupt, the opposition to him came from aristocrats who he upset with the considerable reforms he tried to implement. They wanted to turn the clock back, not forwards. He wanted to shake them up.

Pierre Augustin Caron, 'de Beaumarchais' (1732–1799)

This improbable Frenchman took the name 'de Beaumarchais' from the lands belonging to an elderly court official whose wife he seduced, whose appointment as Contrôleur de la Bouche du Roi he purloined, and whose assets he inherited when he married the widow. She herself soon died; some suspect she was poisoned. As well as being a dramatist, Beaumarchais was a chancer, royal fixer, high-class pimp and dealmaker, who got into many scrapes and duels. He was an expert at working the system.

He was the son of a watchmaker of Calvinist origins. Aged 21, he invented a new mechanism, which was pirated. He successfully challenged this before the authorities, whereupon he styled himself Watchmaker to the King. Working for the royal family of Louis XV, he taught the princesses the harp and arranged favours, which included his own appointment as a regulator of the game laws. He worked for a time in Spain, probably in the slave and tobacco trades.

He became entangled in a court case with the legatees of a banker who had been his patron and business associate on his way up. Beaumarchais was invited to bribe the judge's wife, but nevertheless lost the case. He was accused of corruption but, knowing he had not a chance in court, defended himself by publishing witty pleadings, his *Mémoires*. This gained him great notoriety.

Beaumarchais was employed by the royal court to destroy scurrilous pamphlets, one about Louis XV's mistress Madame du Barry, another about the young Louis XVI's reproductive problems. He also became an armaments supplier, at his own expense, to the American rebels. He supplied the Revolutionaries in France with muskets from Holland, but came under attack for his great wealth and splendid mansion. He was lucky to be released from prison just a few days before the inmates were massacred.

He worked hard to protect authors' rights and developed a drinking water system for Paris.

Emperor Joseph seems to have undertaken an enlightened piece of risk analysis and put aside any fear that *Figaro* would foment social discontent. Peasants rebelling in far-off Transylvania, currently giving him a headache, would not see it. Provided Mozart's opera was performed in Italian and not in German, the only people who would understand it were the upper classes.

So it was no bad thing to pillory the aristocrats, exemplified particularly by the Count, dissolute from boredom, jealous from vanity. The Emperor did not mind the valet describing his boss with the diminutive *'Signor Contino'*, with its second-beat sideswipe, in the familiar *Se vuol ballare, signor Contino*. Nor did he mind the Countess being put to the indignity of wearing servant's clothes, and even being dragged into the bushes. However, Joseph would not tolerate anything that might portray the servants as low, ugly or ill-behaved by comparison with aristocrats. And he insisted on cleaning up the sexual freedom displayed by everyone in the play, including the Countess; thus a lot of Beaumarchais's feminist material was cut.

As Sir Geraint Evans has pointed out, the part of Figaro, played properly, needs to be played with sufficient 'revolutionary intent': 'Figaro is a fighter.' He needs to be rebellious and resolute. His truculence is consistent with Mozart's attitude to his Archbishop (not a character trait which endeared him to potential sponsors in Vienna).

Length

The opera closely follows the structure and content of Beaumarchais's play, albeit with considerable pruning of individual lines, and much toning-down, for example the role of Marcellina.

The play lasted four-and-a-half hours, so it is with some relief that one finds that Da Ponte reduced the opera to three. Even then, the stretches of recitative which Mozart needs to keep the complicated story moving can be hard on the audience, especially one not familiar with Italian. In the last act, all the main characters have to be accorded their separate showpiece arias or cavatinas, and this contributes to the length.

The story runs the risk of being engulfed by its own complexity, something most librettists would take enormous care to avoid. Some of the detail, such as Cherubino's love song (albeit *Voi, che sapete* is one of the most popular items in the opera), the anonymous letter, the seal on the commission and the pin, could all have been pruned or dealt with differently.

It is also arguable that some of the roles could have been cut, for example Doctor Bartolo and Barbarina. But the Doctor's *La vendetta* in which he patters that he can find some legal quibble to stop Figaro's wedding going ahead, is a 'consummate portrait of pomposity mingled with stupidity.' And Barbarina's cavatina lamenting that she has lost the pin, *L'ho perduta, me meschina*, sung in the garden at night, is glorious.

Success?

It is not really clear whether the opera was the immense success that Michael Kelly, the performer in the première, claimed subsequently that it had been. In 1787, it did not even feature in a list of top popular operas performed in the Burgtheater. And it was quickly eclipsed by Martín y Soler's *Una Cosa Rara*.

Mozart's music was found difficult – 'complex, innovative and ambiguous' – and, at its first hearing, it often puzzled listeners, including the Emperor. In Mozart's operas, the singers found that the accompaniment drowned them. In his chamber music, Paisiello found that he and his fellow string quartet members could at first only play the slow movements of Mozart's quartets.

Some actual tomfoolery

Not surprisingly, various humorous and unfortunate incidents have occurred during performances of this opera. Here are some:

In Act 1, when Figaro first greeted Susanna with a light kiss, she was leaning back against her basket and unfortunately lost her balance and fell backwards. Sir Geraint Evans fell forward and found himself kissing Elisabeth Schwarzkopf's bosom.

Another notorious incident involving Evans took place in rehearsal. Very early in her career, he was rehearsing Figaro with the inexperienced and self-conscious Joan Sutherland as the Countess. They were sitting around in a break, and Sutherland leant forward leaving a gap between her jumper and skirt, just as Evans, in a paternal and reassuring way, put his arm round her and asked, 'And how are we today?' Feeling the bare flesh, he added, 'And very nice too.' The mighty Sutherland stood up and felled him.

A lot of practice is needed for the fooling around in Act 1 when Cherubino and the Count both try to hide. Once, when the singer taking the part of the Count was indisposed, there was no time for a rehearsal with the understudy. There were so many chairs, with so many covers, that the stand-in did not know which one to lift in order to reveal Cherubino. He took so long going from chair to chair, lifting covers, that in the end Cherubino had to jump out.

Opera singers are not trained carpenters. In the boudoir scene, when the Count begins to knock the closet door down, he has been known to hit his thumb with the hammer rather than the door.

Papers handed over on the stage from one actor to another, perhaps a song or a letter, provide an opportunity for performers to write messages, rude or suggestive or silly, to each other. *Figaro* provides ample opportunity for this.

ACT BY ACT

The overture begins with what is almost a chuckle.[7] Mozart 'abandons himself without reserve to the whirl of life' in what has been described as 'the most endearing and happy opening scene in all opera.'

---

[7] The overture of *Figaro* reflects the general mood of optimism prevalent at the time. But, like Mozart's own fortunes, a reversal was imminent. Emperor Joseph was about to introduce some commendable, far-reaching but badly implemented governmental reforms. His changes 'shot too far ahead of the prevailing sentiment of his people.' One trivial but notorious reform was to economise by requiring corpses to be buried in reusable graves, an eighteenth-century instance of the nanny state. As a consequence, Mozart's grave is lost.

Act 1

A servants' room, partly furnished, in the castle of the Count of Almaviva

It is the wedding day of Figaro and Susanna. They prepare their new quarters, which have conveniently been allocated so that Susanna will be easily available when 'needed' by the Countess, as will Figaro by the Count: *Cinque, dieci, venti*. Susanna explains that Basilio, the court music teacher, has warned her that she may be expected to perform duties for the Count as well as his wife.

Although the Count has given up his *droit de seigneur*, he has arranged things so that, once he has got Figaro out of the way, he can seduce Susanna. He has been appointed ambassador to London, and proposes to take Figaro as a travelling courier and Susanna as his own personal secretary (*secreta ambasciatrice*). Deeply troubled, Figaro sings the obviously insubordinate *Se vuol ballare, signor Contino* ('Hey Countikins! If it's dancing you want, you can skip to *my* tune').

* * *

From a conversation between Doctor Bartolo and his former house-keeper Marcellina, we learn that Figaro borrowed from her against the security of a promise to marry her. She now intends to enforce her contract and scupper the marriage. (There is no love lost between her and Susanna.) The Doctor, who once hoped to marry his erstwhile ward Rosina – now the Countess – but was cheated out of doing so by the intervention of Figaro, relishes revenge: *La vendetta*. He is confident that he can find some legal quibble to stop the wedding.

* * *

Marcellina and Susanna exchange insults before Marcellina goes. Cherubino, the page, comes to see Susanna to tell her the disaster that has befallen him. He has been banished for trying to make love to Barbarina, the gardener's daughter. However, as well as chasing most people in skirts, he personally has a serious crush on the Countess. Susanna, as her lady's maid, undresses her – Cherubino wishes he could do the same! He has written a song which he exchanges for one of the Countess's ribbons, and he sings about his infatuation with women: *Non sò più cosa son, cosa faccio.*

When the Count comes to pay court to Susanna, Cherubino knows he had better get out of the way and hide. The Count says he will pay Susanna for a few moments in the garden at dusk. Because it would not be in order for him to be found alone with Susanna, he too has to hide when they are interrupted by Don Basilio, who has come looking for him. This reptilian music teacher expresses surprise that Susanna does not prefer the Count to the pageboy, who he insinuates is enamoured of the Countess.

This disclosure causes the Count to erupt in a rage from his hiding place: the page is impossible – only yesterday the Count went to visit the gardener's daughter Barbarina and found her looking distinctly flustered. He looked around and gradually lifted the tablecloth only to find Cherubino hiding underneath. He illustrates this by lifting the chair cover under which Cherubino has been hiding. The Count explodes when he realises that the page has just overheard his own attempt at seduction. He rounds on Susanna and demands that Figaro is fetched to witness the visitors she has been receiving in her room. Basilio rubs his hands as he cackles, '*Così fan tutte le belle*' ('All pretty women are like that') – words which would be immortalised in a later opera by Mozart and Da Ponte.

* * *

Figaro is keen to accelerate the wedding ceremony and thus frustrate the Count's *droit de seigneur* objective. He brings the villagers to praise the Count's magnanimity and ask him to start the proceedings. Cherubino is silent because he has been dismissed. The villagers ask for clemency, whereupon the Count says he will forgive him, but sends him away to join a regiment.

The Count realises he can use Marcellina's claim to play for time. The act ends with Figaro singing the ever-popular *Non più andrai, farfallone amoroso* ('Oversexed butterfly, you won't have the opportunity to chase women any more, because you will be standing to attention, or marching in the mud, or fighting for glory among the blazing guns').

Act 2

The Countess's boudoir

Countess Rosina, whom we now meet for the first time after over three-quarters of an hour, provides a dignified contrast to all these other characters and their goings-on – a brilliant *coup de théâtre*. In a famous cavatina[8], she despairs about the withering of her husband's passion for her: *Porgi amor qualche ristoro*. She talks to Susanna about the previous events, and the unfaithfulness of men.

Figaro, is heard coming along. He is furious about the Count's behaviour and explains his preposterous scheme to trap him. He has sent the Count an anonymous letter, suggesting that his Countess has arranged an assignation for that night.[9] This will divert the Count's attention, and Figaro's wedding can go ahead in the meantime. When the Count investigates the nocturnal goings-on, the Countess will actually catch him seducing Cherubino, who he thinks is Susanna (because the page will be dressed in Susanna's clothes). The Count will be caught in the act, but everyone else's reputation will be intact. The Countess is nervously shocked that events have come to this. Figaro suggests that they start dressing up Cherubino to play his role in the scheme.

Cherubino actually comes to say goodbye. He is off to his regiment, although the Count has overlooked the need to seal his commission. He sings the song which he composed, *Voi, che sapete che cosa è amor* ..., imploring the ladies, who know all about love, to tell him whether his conflicting emotions – pleasure, torment, heat and cold – indeed constitute love. Susanna suggests that Cherubino should change into her clothes: they are about the same height. There is much tomfoolery while Cherubino, who will do anything to oblige the

---

[8] A 'cavatina' is a short solo song that does not repeat the beginning again, which an aria may be expected to do. *Porgi, amor* has been regarded as one of 'the most difficult singing challenges in opera.' The Countess comes on to the stage and sings it straight away without any warm-up. Sir Colin Davis advised Kiri Te Kanawa, at her 'début', to sing it four or five times in her dressing room before going on.

[9] Not surprisingly the Countess is none too happy with this outrageous proposition, not least coming from a servant. It is of course necessary to give rise to Cherubino's clothes-changing, and the disguises later in the opera.

Countess, changes: *Venite, inginocchiatevi*. They discover that he has bandaged a cut with the piece of ribbon belonging to the Countess. They notice that his commission has no seal. Susanna goes to fetch some clothes.

Suddenly, there is a knock at the door: the Count has returned early from the hunt in order to confront his wife about her supposed infidelity, disclosed in the anonymous letter. Cherubino, her putative lover, has to hide quickly, so they lock him in the closet.

The Count's suspicions are aroused because the Countess has locked her room door. When she lets him in, and he hears a noise, he is sure that he has caught her 'in the act', and her lover has taken refuge, locked in the closet. Although the Countess explains that the noise he heard was Susanna trying on her wedding dress, her husband works himself up into a rage. Having secured the door of the room so that nobody can get in or out, he forces the Countess to accompany him as he fetches some tools with which to break into the closet. While they are away doing this, Cherubino changes places with Susanna, who has quietly returned to the room. He escapes by jumping out of the window.

The Count returns with his wife. Before he breaks down the door, she, the epitome of honesty, nervously confesses that he will find Cherubino in the closet. But when he does break in, both are equally astonished to find not Cherubino, but Susanna, in there. The Countess splutters that she was only testing the Count when she conceded that Cherubino was hiding there.[10] The Count craves forgiveness.

Figaro comes to invite everybody to the wedding celebrations, which are beginning. He is accused of writing the letter in which it was suggested that the Countess was compromised. The Count's lingering suspicions are magnified when the gardener Antonio arrives to say that he has seen someone escaping from the window. As the fugitive jumped, he broke a flowerpot and dropped a piece of paper: it is Cherubino's commission, so it was quite clearly him. The others

[10] Lorenzo da Ponte prudently excised a line in the play in which Susanna says she can see how moving in high society provides a good education in how to tell lies without showing it.

accuse the gardener of being drunk. Fortunately though, he did not actually see who it was that jumped, so Figaro can say that it was him: he jumped from the balcony and twisted his ankle. He has some difficulty explaining why he needed to jump, but concocts an explanation that he was on his way to get the Count to seal the commission, which he must have dropped.

The act ends with the Count being presented with Marcellina's claim that Figaro is contractually bound to marry her. The Count delays; he insists that everything must be done properly, in accordance with good governance.

Act 3
A large room, decorated for the wedding

The Count ruminates suspiciously, but knows that, at heart, the Countess is unlikely to be 'guilty'. Susanna, urged on by the Countess, visits him on the pretext of fetching smelling salts for her mistress. He is overjoyed when she seemingly flirts and accepts his invitation to an assignation in the garden, but he chides her for her cruelty in being so slow to agree: *Crudel! Perchè finora.*

The Count has promised to give Susanna a substantial wedding present, with which she knows Figaro can pay off his debt. But when the Count hears Susanna telling Figaro that she is confident that they will win the case with Marcellina, his suspicions revive: he is acutely jealous of Figaro, who is but a base serf: *Vedrò mentr'io sospiro.*

* * *

The lawyer Don Curzio tells Figaro that he must repay Marcellina or marry her. Figaro answers that he cannot marry without the consent of his parents, who were gentlefolk. To prove his origins, he refers to a birthmark ('*una spatula impressa*') on his arm. When Marcellina asks if it is in the shape of a spatula, and he does not deny it, she realises that Figaro is actually the love child of herself and Doctor Bartolo.

Everyone rejoices at the outcome. That is, apart from the considerably discomfited Count. As Don Curzio points out, any marriage between Figaro and Marcellina is now forbidden.

When Susanna arrives with the money to pay off the debt, she is appalled to find everyone embracing. She assumes that she has been betrayed. The different reactions of the characters to the turn of events is portrayed in the marvellous sextet, led by Marcellina, *Riconosci in questo amplesso una madre, amato* ('My dear, your mother enfolds you in her embrace').

Once everything has been clarified, and Marcellina has waived her son's debt, a double wedding is arranged for Figaro and Susanna on the one hand, and the Doctor and Marcellina on the other.

Barbarina, the gardener's daughter, has arranged for Cherubino to be dressed as a village girl so that he can partake in Figaro's wedding ceremonies and be in the chorus which is going to present flowers to the Countess. The Count is tipped off by Antonio, the gardener, that Cherubino is still in the castle, dressed as a woman – Antonio has found the page's hat.

* * *

Meanwhile, the Countess again laments her circumstances, not least the indignity of being asked to dress up as a servant girl: *Dove sono i bei momenti* ('Where are those happy moments of the past?').[11] If only she could turn the clock back to the time when she and the Count were in love. But this aria ends on an optimistic note: maybe she will be able to reform him. (One wonders if this music is so especially effective because it somehow reflected Mozart's own personal relationship with his wife.)

Susanna and the Countess prepare a letter (which has little to do with the earlier letter) to the Count, confirming his assignation among the pines in the grove. They sing the duet *Che soave zeffiretto* ('How soft the breeze will be in the pine woods this evening'). The envelope is sealed with a pin, which is to be returned as evidence of receipt (perhaps an early example of 'Request Read Receipt').

* * *

---

[11] Mozart's melodic sketches show that he took 'infinite pains' with this item.

The Countess is about to be further compromised with Cherubino. When the village girls arrive to present their flowers to her, the Count catches his wife and Cherubino seemingly flirting. Just as she is picking out Cherubino from among them, Antonio comes up behind and places the boy's hat on his head. In a bid to save Cherubino, Barbarina cheekily reminds the Count that, when 'making love to her', he would offer her anything she asked for: she now says she wants Cherubino for a husband. The Count's suspicions are further aroused when he notices that Figaro no longer limps from the injury he supposedly suffered when he twisted his ankle jumping out of the window. Antonio, still obsessed with the person who jumped and destroyed his flowers, accuses Figaro of being a liar. But they are all interrupted when the villagers come to start the celebrations for the double wedding.

During the villagers' song and dance in which the Count is praised for giving up *droit de seigneur*, Susanna surreptitiously passes him the letter. He pricks himself on the pin when he opens the envelope. Despite this, he responds graciously to the villagers and invites them to the wedding celebrations.

Act 4
Night-time, by a pavilion in the garden

Barbarina, in a flap, searches for the pin which she has been told by the Count to return to Susanna, and which she has lost: *L'ho perduta, me meschina*. When Figaro hears that it is destined for Susanna, he fears that his fiancée is really going to accept the advances of the Count. He despairs of his fate to his mother. She uses this to launch an attack on the perfidy of *men*, and their treatment of women.

Everybody is fooling around in the dark. Barbarina searches for Cherubino. Basilio explains to the confused Doctor Bartolo what he thinks is happening. Figaro overhears Susanna deliberately musing aloud about her forthcoming assignation: *Deh, vieni, non tardar* ('Come, don't delay, my love'). He angrily condemns the perfidy of *women*.

Cherubino gets in the way, as he always seems to. While searching for Barbarina, he finds 'Susanna' (that is, the Countess disguised as Susanna). He seizes the opportunity of having a peck at her. The Countess is not too happy with the prospect of being caught being kissed by Cherubino. 'Why can't I do what the Count's about to do?' he asks, and plants a kiss – which actually lands on the Count. The Count wallops Cherubino but the blow lands on Figaro. Who else but Cherubino would compound the confusion and create slapstick at this chaotic moment?

Once Cherubino is out of the way, the imminent arrival of torches gives the Count the pretext to pull his prey (his wife dressed as Susanna) into the bushes. First, he presents her with a diamond ring. When she protests about going into the dark, the Count explains that this does not matter because they are hardly going into the bushes to read a book. This delights the Count.

During a lull, Figaro laments to the 'Countess' (Susanna in disguise) that all is quiet while Mars seduces Venus: *Tutto è tranquillo e placido*. When Susanna, dressed as the Countess, tells him to shut up, he recognises her voice, and the penny drops. To obtain his revenge for their attempt to trick him, he starts to seduce her (giving the appearance of seducing the Countess). For this, he enjoys a cuff over the head from his fiancée. He manages to calm her down: he knew it was her; he recognised her voice: *Pace, pace, mio dolce tesoro*.

The Count returns. Having lost 'Susanna' in the bushes, he finds Figaro ostensibly seducing his wife. Outraged, he clamours for revenge. He calls to his retainers to come and help him. The 'Countess' (i.e. Susanna) pleads for forgiveness, but the Count refuses. The real Countess then reveals herself, and the Count realises his mistake and himself pleads for forgiveness, which the Countess grants. Everybody lives happily ever after, with love providing the solution to all confusion.

MOZART: *DON GIOVANNI*

THE OPERA AND ITS COMPOSER

Don Giovanni, which Charles Gounod, the French composer, called 'that unequalled and immortal masterpiece', was first produced in Prague on 29 October 1787, to tremendous acclaim. This was around four years before Mozart died, aged only 35.

Mozart had already been freelancing in Vienna for six years after being unceremoniously expelled from the household of his former employer the Archbishop of Salzburg. His celebrity concert performances were no longer as popular, and he was increasingly dependent on opera and foreign touring for his income. He was living expensively: the fees for *Don Giovanni* covered less than his rent for a year and a half. And he was already borrowing money from friends. He had other preoccupations at this time, as well: his father Leopold had died unexpectedly in the previous May and there was a lot of correspondence necessary to wind up the estate: the auction of the assets took place the following September. However, Mozart seems to have taken this 'in his stride', and some believe that his father's death may have generated a creative urge.

The residents of Prague were enthusiastic about Mozart. As the conductor Bruno Walter has said, 'the enthusiasm of the Prague audiences "shed a ray of sunshine"' upon Mozart's sorrowful life. Eighteen months before *Don Giovanni*, Prague had given *The Marriage of Figaro* such a welcome that, 'for the first time since his childhood, Mozart knew what real success and acclaim meant.' There, he was far better appreciated than in Vienna, where the reception accorded to *Figaro* had been lukewarm: audiences in Vienna regarded it as heavy and difficult, and it was quickly superseded by other operas such as Martín y Soler's *Una cosa rara*, rarely heard today, but quoted in the supper scene in *Don Giovanni*.

As *Figaro* was such a success in Prague, in the early months of

1787 the theatre director there gave Mozart a commission for another opera. The director's wife would subsequently sing the part of Zerlina, the peasant girl chased by Giovanni.

Lorenzo da Ponte

The librettist of *Figaro* had been Lorenzo da Ponte, who was up to his eyes in work.[1] He was working for twelve hours at a stretch, fortified by a bottle of tokay, a box of tobacco and frequent revival by his housekeeper's sixteen-year-old daughter, who brought him coffee and much else. He also claimed that it was he who suggested to Mozart using the familiar old tale about Don Juan and 'hellfire and seduction'. Over the years, it had featured in a wide variety of theatre. The French and Venetian dramatists Molière and Goldoni had written plays using the story and Gluck had composed a very successful ballet-pantomine. Less reputably, it featured in *Commedia dell'arte* – pantomime-and-puppet shows at fairgrounds. The story had also been treated 'ad nauseam' in other operas, and in the same year as Mozart's, there were two other 'Don Giovanni' operas.[2]

[1] Da Ponte was working on libretti for Martín and Antonio Salieri at the same time as Mozart. It is possible that Da Ponte was given some assistance by Casanova, the notorious womaniser, as well.
[2] Molière had written a 'Don Juan' as far back as 1665, 35 years after Tirso de Molina's *Stone Guest* was published. Goldoni wrote one in 1736. *L'empio punito*, composed by Alessandro

Da Ponte based his libretto on one already written by Giovanni Bertati, (1735–1815) a poet whom he described uncomplimentarily as a 'frog blown up with wind'.

The high-minded Emperor Joseph, the autocratic and eccentric ruler of the vast Habsburg Empire, and a music enthusiast, would never have suggested such an old-fashioned and vulgar subject for his court theatre: it was a subject for popular theatres. Nor would his censors have tolerated sentiments like *Viva la libertà*, expressed by everyone at the climax of Act 1. But for Prague, which was relatively provincial and dowdy, it was safe: Dr Johnson's friend Hester Thrale thought that everything in Prague seemed to be at least five centuries behind. And Da Ponte seems to have successfully duped the censors, by omitting contentious material from the copy 'filed' with them.

At the beginning of October, Mozart, with his wife Constanze, took the three-day journey from Vienna to Prague. He was joined there by his librettist a few days later. The overture and the finale were still incomplete. The première had to be delayed and then a singer was ill. So *The Marriage of Figaro* was put on again instead. Because the show was to have been graced by the Emperor's sister, the Archduchess Maria Theresa, who was passing through on her honeymoon, the irreverent *Figaro* might have been thought unsuitable. However, she commanded it to be performed. According to one story, Mozart, fortified with punch, then completed the overture of *Don Giovanni* during the night before the première. It was ready by 7am. The ink was still wet on the copies from which the orchestra had to play, so the story goes.

Afterwards, the Prague management tried to persuade Mozart to stay and write another opera, but he was too busy and had to rush back to Vienna.

Six months later, Vienna gave Mozart's opera a disappointing reception, as it had *The Marriage of Figaro*. Perhaps the subject was too threadbare (for a long time, the Italians also found *Don Giovanni* too difficult and refused to stage it). For that Vienna performance,

Melani (1639–1703) was performed at the Teatro Colonna in Rome in 1669. Purcell had written music for Shadwell's *The Libertine* in 1676.

Mozart's first love, his wife's sister Aloysia, was the Donna Anna. Caterina Cavalieri, who was later the mistress of Mozart's competitor Antonio Salieri, was the Donna Elvira.

Giovanni is a fascinating figure. He would be 'inexcusable in real life', but he is also a fantasy figure who many men would like to emulate and many women would like their man to be, as we sense in the famous and delightful duet with Zerlina, *Là ci darem la mano*.

The opera was staged by the great Manuel Garcia in New York in the 1825/26 season, and was attended there by Lorenzo da Ponte himself. Garcia's daughter, the great diva Pauline Viardot subsequently bought the autograph score for around £200. When she showed it to Rossini, he lowered his bulky frame to the floor and prostrated himself in deepest reverence before it.[3] No wonder.

Don Giovanni was part of the staple repertoire of the Royal Italian Opera in London right through the middle of the nineteenth century. Even the flames which in mid-century reduced the Covent Garden theatre 'to a shapeless mass of ruins',[4] did not prevent the Don popping back up in the following year in the Lyceum down the road. He was on stage in three London houses two years later.

(More on the lives of Mozart and Da Ponte can be found on pages 25–26.)

WHO'S WHO AND WHAT'S WHAT

The story below is based on the libretto. Certain directors may amend opera stories to suit their production.

The setting is a city somewhere in Spain. The attempted rape of **Donna Anna** by the nobleman **Don Giovanni** is interrupted by her

---

[3] She later presented the priceless manuscript to the Paris Conservatoire and stipulated that the manuscript should never leave its library.

[4] The fire, in March 1856, started in the carpenters' shop above the gas-lit candelabra. A masked ball was just coming to an end at the time; amazingly, the only two people who had been missing turned up later.

father, the Commander (**Commendatore**).[5] Don Giovanni kills him. Her rather 'wet' fiancé **Don Ottavio** swears revenge, and Anna's thirst for revenge becomes one of the driving forces of the opera.

Also demanding satisfaction for Don Giovanni's earlier seduction of her (or renewal of it) is the dignified **Donna Elvira**, who is still a young woman.

The murder and Elvira's outrage are all familiar stuff to **Leporello**, Don Giovanni's servant, who describes his master's successes in the **'catalogue aria'**: in Spain alone, there are already 1,003 – *mille e tre* – in all classes, shapes and sizes.

The wedding celebrations of two bumpkins, **Masetto** and **Zerlina**, provide the Don with an opportunity to add to his tally by seducing the bride, who is impressed by his wealth and class. With the beautiful duet, *Là ci darem*, he persuades her to go along with him, but she is rescued by Elvira, who Don Giovanni explains away as mad.

Anna and Ottavio identify Don Giovanni's voice as that of her father's murderer. Ottavio's hopes of marriage rest on her achieving peace of mind, as he expresses in another 'best tune': *Dalla sua pace*.

In the **'Champagne aria'**, Don Giovanni orders Leoporello to 'keep the party going'; by morning, he will have another ten to add to the list.

Zerlina protests her fidelity to Masetto, but he catches Don Giovanni making another pass at her. Don Giovanni invites them to the ball in his palace. In the **ballroom scene**, he greets them with *Viva la libertà* ('Hurray for freedom!'). While the dancing takes place, he makes off with Zerlina. When she shrieks for help,[6] Don Giovanni, having fixed the blame on Leporello, manages to escape.

* * *

---

[5] Today, his rank has no obvious analogy. We may perhaps assume that he would have the status of a Commander of the Order of the British Empire, a 'CBE'.

[6] In the final rehearsal before the Prague première, Mozart apparently was not content with Caterina Bondini's scream, so he leapt on to the stage and pinched her. When she let out a sufficient yell, Mozart told her 'That's the way to do it tonight.'

Out in the street, the thoroughly disgruntled Leporello is persuaded to stay in Don Giovanni's employment, by the award of a bonus. The Don exchanges clothes with Leporello so that he can make his next conquest – Elvira's maid. Thus, Elvira mistakes Leporello for the Don and goes off with him. The Don's **serenade** of the maid at the window is interrupted by Masetto and some mates intent on revenge. But Don Giovanni (dressed as Leporello) separates Masetto from his friends and thrashes him. Zerlina consoles her bruised fiancé.

Leporello (disguised as his master) is in a tight corner, surrounded by the others. In the **sextet**, Elvira wants him, but the rest have come for revenge. To escape, he has to disclose who he really is. Eventually, he manages to make a dash for it.

Ottavio proclaims that these goings-on provide proof that Don Giovanni was the murderer of Anna's father. Ottavio will be able to tell his 'treasure' that she is avenged: *Il mio tesoro*. And, alone, Elvira confesses that, despite the scoundrel's evil behaviour, at heart she really loves him: *Mi tradì quell'alma ingrata*.

In the **graveyard scene**, at almost 2am, Don Giovanni catches up with Leporello. He describes his exploits, even insinuating, with a laugh, that he has enjoyed Leporello's own woman. At this lewd and tasteless remark, the Commendatore's funerary monument, his **statue**, declares that Don Giovanni will have his last laugh before dawn. The Don forces the reluctant Leporello to invite the statue to dine with him.

Back in Anna's house, Ottavio is confident that Anna will be avenged, and proposes marriage, but she says he must wait.

During the **supper scene**, the Don dines in his palace. Elvira comes to plead with him to mend his ways, but he dismisses her. As she leaves, the statue comes to dine. It grasps Don Giovanni's hand. When he refuses to repent, he is pulled down and engulfed in flames.[7] The others are too late to take revenge.

---

[7] Although a scenery collapse early in the opera has been known to precipitate Don Giovanni down to hell prematurely, it is in the final moments that there is ample opportunity for something to go wrong. In one production, the stage lift which was supposed to drop the Don down got stuck halfway, so he had to pop up again. After several attempts by the lift operator to get it to work, it failed again. Someone in the gods called out, 'Jasus, that's great, sher Hell must be full.'

Ottavio proposes to Anna again, but she requires him to wait one more year. Elvira heads for a convent; Zerlina and Masetto go off with each other; Leporello goes to the pub to find a new master. They all agree with the moral of the tale: scoundrels get what they deserve, the sentiment expressed in the original title of the opera, *Il dissoluto punito*.

THE INTERVAL: TALKING POINTS

Why *Don Giovanni* is so great

Don Giovanni is regarded as 'one of the greatest masterpieces of all time.' Gounod called it a 'revelation of perfection.' It has been claimed that 'The very first ensemble … with the dying Commendatore writhing in pain, the imperturbable Don laughing at the misery unfolding before him, and his servant trying to find a way of escaping from this dangerous situation, is a scene of such dramatic intensity, with murder, death, fear, lust, defiance, and cunning all condensed in a few measures, as can hardly be matched in the whole history of theatre.'

Musicologists have analysed remarkable key structures, demonstrated symmetries, detected erotic chromatic upward surges, and drawn attention to recurring themes such as those in the supper scene and the overture. But the audience is mainly enjoying a succession of 'best tunes', and is unlikely to notice or to be especially interested in these details, however important they may be, just as very few are interested in the type of paint used for a picture by a painter. The music just moves on too quickly.

Crucially, Mozart presents us with realistic characters, and brings them together in an ensemble which no straight performance on stage could do. The greatness of *Don Giovanni* lies in this totally credible presentation of what the characters are doing, and what is going through their minds as they do it. That is what makes it so accessible to the audience.

The Irish playwright and music critic Bernard Shaw made the simple observation that, while the Don, Leporello and Masetto all have a baritone part in much the same range, 'the dramatic distinction between these parts is so strong that only an artist of remarkable versatility could play one as well as the other.'

Two examples of Mozart's art will specifically illustrate his achievement. First, the musical contrast between the characters of Don Giovanni, as depicted in the explicitly erotic Champagne aria, *Fin ch'han dal vino*; and Don Ottavio in his melodious *Dalla sua pace*. Secondly, there is the musical composition of the ballroom scene.

In the Champagne aria, the priapic Giovanni orders Leporello to invite everyone to a party: tomorrow morning he will have another ten names to add to his catalogue of conquests. 'This explosion of licentious energy in which the whole essence of the Don is summed up,' as Berlioz described it, lasts less than two minutes. The relentless thumping chords in the orchestra confirm that he has something more physical in mind than the flirting he mentions.[8] One leading expert has commented, 'If the censors had only known how suggestive of the erotic Mozart's music could be, they would surely have banned it.' 'Care is thrown to the winds. Its animation,' said Gounod, 'is that of one possessed and its drive never halts for a moment.'

This is presented shortly after we have heard Don Ottavio sing unctuously that 'if she sighs, I too must sigh.' Although his music is beautiful, Don Ottavio is essentially tedious: Mozart designed him deliberately to contrast with and highlight Don Giovanni. According to E.T.A. Hoffmann (1776–1822), whose 'Tales' became the basis of a famous opera by Offenbach, Ottavio could have prevented the attempted rape of Donna Anna, but he 'had to dress first and did not like much going out at night.' Placido Domingo described him as 'a lily-livered fop'. Half a century earlier, he would have been sung by a castrato (in his case, appropriately).

Not only did Mozart understand the psychology, he could use music to convey it, almost instantaneously.

The astonishing ballroom scene provides a second example of Mozart's greatness. In around five minutes, Mozart succeeds in

---

[8] The bassoons rise chromatically as he rises to the thought of adding ten more names by morning.

projecting 'the whole world onto the stage' and the different amorous inclinations of the characters. The suave Don Giovanni, the vengeful three masked guests, the buffoon Leporello, the soubrette Zerlina, the oaf Masetto, all blended together.

This scene is a triumph of composition, a tour de force, probably unsurpassed. There are three orchestras – two of which are on the stage – each playing a different dance, relating to the social status of the characters.[9] As is appropriate in the Don's palace, it begins with the most courtly and graceful dance, the minuet. Then, a rustic quadrille, the country dance or contredanse, in double time, is played at the same time as a minuet and a waltz, both in triple time.[10] The orchestras even tune up in fifths some eight bars before each begins to play its dance!

Mozart must have enjoyed composing the ballroom scene immensely. He loved dancing, as did his family.

The libretto

Mozart's art is, if anything, enhanced by his choice of the wretched old legend of Don Juan, with its mixture of love, debauchery, murder, blasphemy, the supernatural and a moral ending in rather bad taste. The Victorian art critic and author John Ruskin (1819–1900) regarded the tale as the 'foolishest and most monstrous of conceivable human words and subjects of thought … No such spectacle of unconscious (and in that unconsciousness all the more fearful) moral degradation of the highest faculty to the lowest purpose can be found in history.'

The libretto has come in for considerable criticism: it has been called 'a loose string of episodes without organic development.' The story is criticised for losing momentum by the end of the first act:

---

[9] It was quite normal to have different dance music going on at either end of dance halls, and chaos was not unusual.

[10] The minuet is for the ladies and gentlemen; the quadrille is for the peasants and the Don before he goes off with Zerlina; Leporello distracts Masetto into dancing the Deutscher/Teitsch, a predecessor of the waltz, then recently introduced to Vienna. The Deutscher required a close grip, so Leporello whisks Masetto around with a tight grip so that he is distracted and stuck as Zerlina is taken off by Giovanni.

until the dramatic end, to keep the libretto going, Lorenzo da Ponte had to resort to disguise, which was a threadbare stock-in-trade item used in comedy. The music critic Ernest Newman (1868–1959) even went so far as to say that the libretto was 'one of the sorriest pieces of stage joinery ever nailed together by a hack in a hurry.' Despite the opera being driven forward by Donna Anna's thirst for revenge, and Don Giovanni's quest for pleasure, it has been suggested that all producers face the problem of how to maintain the momentum in the latter stages of Act 2, without sacrificing great dramatic music.

For the Vienna première, Mozart inserted various arias which tend to disrupt the flow, for example Don Ottavio's *Dalla sua pace*, a great favourite for modern audiences (Ottavio's difficult *Il mia tesoro* in Act 2 was replaced by this, which did not appear in the Prague original). At Caterina Cavalieri's request, Donna Elvira was given the additional and splendid *Mi tradì quell'alma ingrata*. Zerlina and Leporello were given a duet, followed by a recitative by Leporello as he tries to escape.

One should not be too hard on the librettist. He deserves great credit for a very clever and effective work: we can point to the juxtaposition of the comedy (Leporello and the peasants) with the tragedy of the attempted rape, the actual murder and the death of the Don. And the characters of the women are so different, yet so realistic. Donna Anna momentarily wanted the Don and feels guilty about deceiving her dreary Don Ottavio, so she thirsts for revenge. Elvira, who has fallen, is desperate to possess him for herself and longs for his redemption. Zerlina, who for a brief moment senses the opportunity to do far better for herself than tie herself to her oafish fiancé, demonstrates shrewdness as well as peasant coquetry.

Domingo reminds us that Don Giovanni's character is far more complex than either an aggressive macho or a cold, calculating seducer. He must have the distinction and charm of the Spanish gentleman. He must be capable of considerable tenderness without which he would not succeed. Occasionally, in order to succeed, he may have to become theatrical, but those moments are 'temporary departures from his normal behaviour.' This is no puppet show.

Far from there being too much music, however, it is the sheer quality of Mozart's music – virtually each item being a popular favourite – which keeps up the interest of a modern audience and drives the opera forward.

But perhaps there is too much libretto, however clever it may be, for an audience unfamiliar with Italian. However, we may not wish to go so far as Bernard Shaw who – appalled by some very second-rate performances in London – recommended that the director take 'a pot of paste, a pair of scissors and some tissue paper ... and reduce all the rest to such sentences as are barely necessary to preserve the continuity of the action.'

Giovanni's success rate

We know from Leporello's 'catalogue aria' that Don Giovanni has had 1,003 Spanish, 640 Italian, 231 German, 100 French and 91 Turkish women (a ratio which is in itself quite illuminating, even if partly determined by poetic scansion and rhyme).

And we know from the Champagne aria that he would expect to have another ten Spanish women by the morning. One might well wonder about such matters as terminology and psychology – fantasy or real, and extent – and biology (including speed).

But it can perhaps be more entertaining to speculate about how many women the Don seduces in the course of the opera. Some say none; others have counted six.[11] Three of these could be: Donna Anna in her bedroom; Zerlina in the bushes during the wedding festivities; and Leporello's wife just before the graveyard scene – otherwise Don Giovanni would not roar with laughter at the suggestion and declare it 'better still' if the girl he had seduced in the street had been Leporello's woman. He must have had at least a couple of peasants in the interval, otherwise why would he be in such good form at the beginning of Act 2, having had to escape ignominiously at the end of Act 1. And he must surely have had Elvira's servant girl after he serenaded her,

[11] The question that exercises the voyeur is whether Donna Anna was in fact seduced. Possibly Donna Anna was expecting a nocturnal visit from her fiancé, who was resident in the house, and found that in the dark she had yielded to Giovanni instead.

since, in the opinion of one writer, 'no woman could possibly resist being sung to like that.'

Donna Elvira

Much has been written about the dignified Elvira who has been called 'the central female figure of the opera' and 'far the most interesting character in the opera after Don Giovanni himself.' She weaves her way in and out of every situation.

The role used to be secondary, less important than Donna Anna, or Zerlina, whose relatively undignified part was given, in the first performance, to the theatre director's wife.

Donna Elvira is a very remarkable character, and the choice of it by Elisabeth Schwarzkopf as one of the five roles on which she would concentrate[12] emphasises the importance of the character and the challenges it presents.

It is probably best to assume that Donna Elvira's earlier seduction by Don Giovanni was a turning point in her life; she wants to win him back, and to save him from annihilation.

ACT BY ACT
Overture and Act 1

At night, in the garden beneath Donna Anna's bedroom; later, in the street and afterwards in another garden; finally the 'ballroom scene'[13]

In the overture, the ominous opening chord of D minor conjures up from the outset the drama of the dénouement. For Gounod, the first chords established 'at once the majestic and formidable authority of Divine Justice, the Avenger of Crime.' This may be a *dramma giocoso in due atti* – a comic opera in two acts[14] – but for Mozart it was ser-

---

[12] Schwarzkopf's other four were the Countess in *The Marriage of Figaro*, Fiordiligi in *Così fan tutte*, the Marschallin in Richard Strauss's *Der Rosenkavalier* and Countess Madeleine in his *Capriccio*.

[13] Effecting the large number of scene changes quickly enough to avoid disrupting the flow in the music has provided a challenge to producers of this opera.

[14] Donna Anna, Don Ottavio and Donna Elvira are stock characters out of the main opera genre of the eighteenth century, '*opera seria*', which was often based on mythological subjects.

ious. There is some evidence that Da Ponte was concerned that he was being too serious. But Mozart put his firm imprint on it in the overture, and in the characterisation of Don Ottavio and the Donnas.

It is night-time in a Spanish city. Leporello, the servant of the extremely dissolute nobleman Don Giovanni, keeps watch, somewhat jealously, in the garden of a prominent citizen, the Commander (Commendatore). Inside the house, Don Giovanni is attempting to rape the daughter, Donna Anna.

Donna Anna escapes, raises the alarm and tries to detain Don Giovanni, who is masked. Her father challenges him, they fight and the Commendatore is killed. Donna Anna, who has gone to fetch help, returns with her fiancé Don Ottavio, who has to cope with the murdered father and the swooning daughter.[15] In a duet, Anna, who just wants to be left alone to die, and Ottavio pledge revenge: *Fuggi, crudele, fuggi*.

* * *

Leporello chides his master for his behaviour. They take cover when Donna Elvira, a lady from provincial Burgos arrives, ostensibly thirsting for revenge: she has been seduced by Don Giovanni. However, she really loves him and wants him back: *Ah, chi mi dice mai*. The Don thinks he had better disappear. In the humorous 'catalogue aria',[16] Leporello explains to Elvira that she must accept that she is just one of many, of all types, classes, sizes and nationalities, who Don Giovanni has seduced – the younger the better. He has a list of them: *Madamina, il catalogo*. In Spain, there are already 1,003, *mille e tre*. Donna Elvira vents her frustration.

'*Dramma giocoso*', 'a comedy with seria parts woven into it' was a concept developed by Goldoni, one of Italy's most distinguished playwrights.

[15] Sometimes at such moments of great drama, opera singers play tricks on each other. Birgit Nilsson tells of one Commendatore who used to 'tickle her knee' after she had collapsed over his body in Act 1. She got her revenge by opening his shirt to examine the wound and pulling the hairs on his chest. Once, she pulled too hard and a false 'toupee' came away. Convulsed with mirth, she had to pretend that she was overcome by tears.

[16] The 'catalogue' was standard at fairground performances. Don Juan's servant would produce a list of female names and hint that the spectators' wives were on it.

* * *

As if to underline Leporello's point, the scene changes to the countryside where some peasants are preparing for the wedding of two bumpkins, Masetto and Zerlina: *Giovinette che fate all'amore*. Don Giovanni appears and sets to work. He sends them all off to his villa for a party, promising them *cioccolata, caffè, vini, prosciutti*. But, to Masetto's considerable concern, his fiancée is detained by Giovanni, who tells her that Masetto is not good enough for her, and that she has a glorious future with him, the Don. He proposes marriage. In the beautiful duet *Là ci darem la mano*, she almost yields. But Donna Elvira overhears them and whisks her away, just in time.

It is not one of Don Giovanni's good days. It gets worse when Donna Anna and Don Ottavio, little suspecting that he is the masked man who killed her father, come and seek his help. But Donna Elvira creates a scene by denouncing him: *Fermati, scellerato ... Ah! fuggi il traditor*. Although Don Giovanni says she is mad, the going gets too hot and he escapes, but only just before Donna Anna recognises that his voice is that of her father's murderer. She tells Don Ottavio the story of the attempted rape: *Or sai chi l'onore*. Unfortunately, she mistook the intruder for Don Ottavio, she tells him. He expresses relief that she got away. Now she wants vengeance. In an aria specifically inserted for the first Vienna production, Don Ottavio expresses surprise that a nobleman can be so base. On her peace of mind his hopes rest: *Dalla sua pace*.

Leporello returns with Don Giovanni and tells him that he got the peasants drunk. Who should arrive but Zerlina with a ranting Donna Elvira! Leporello manages to get rid of her and lock her out. In the so-called Champagne aria, Don Giovanni orders Leporello to keep the party going; by morning, he will have another ten conquests to add to the list: *Fin ch'han dal vino*.

* * *

Outside Don Giovanni's house, Zerlina has to deal with Masetto, who is furious that she abandoned him. She assures him that Don

Giovanni has not molested her. She will love Masetto however much he punishes her: *Batti, batti, o bel Masetto*. But Don Giovanni is heard coming. In a piece of pure farce, the suspicious and oafish Masetto decides to hide in the bushes and spy on his fiancée. Zerlina also tries to hide from Don Giovanni. Having ordered everybody to go inside to the party, the Don tries to join her, and the three of them bump into each other. Don Giovanni, never short of the quick response, pretends that he is bringing Zerlina into the bushes because Masetto cannot do without her. The three then follow the others inside to the ball.

* * *

Ottavio, Anna and Elvira are on their way to Don Giovanni's palace, intent on revenge. But they are masked, and, on Don Giovanni's instructions, Leporello invites them to the party. The ballroom scene follows. There, Don Giovanni is chasing the girls, including Zerlina: *Riposate, vezzose ragazze*. This causes Masetto to work himself up into a considerable sweat. The masked trio is welcomed by Don Giovanni with *Viva la libertà* ('Hurray for freedom!').[17] The various characters dance, and Leporello forces Masetto to dance so as to distract him while Don Giovanni makes off with Zerlina. She shrieks for help, and Don Giovanni pretends that it is Leporello who has had designs on her. The masked trio unmask themselves and, amid considerable confusion, and thunder and lightning, Don Giovanni, having fixed the blame on Leporello, manages to make a timely escape.

Act 2
In the street; later moving to the graveyard, then a dark room and finally Don Giovanni's dining room

The disgruntled Leporello wants to hand in his notice, but he agrees to stay on once he is offered a bonus. Don Giovanni, who reckons being faithful to one woman is being cruel to others, now has designs

---

[17] Mozart and Da Ponte were 'lucky to be writing in the 1780s, the decade when the enlightened rule of Joseph II eased formalities, relaxed censorship and encouraged pleasure-loving audiences.' Earlier, the subversive subject matter of the three Da Ponte operas would have fallen foul of the authorities.

on Elvira's maid. In a standard *Commedia dell'arte* gig, he exchanges clothes with Leporello to pursue her. Donna Elvira appears, still hankering after Don Giovanni, who feigns repentance and thus ruthlessly engineers things so that she goes off with Leporello (dressed as him).

In another *Commedia dell'arte* routine, Don Giovanni proceeds to call the maid to the window where he serenades her on his mandolin: *Deh vieni alla finestra*. Masetto, with some mates, has come to beat up Don Giovanni. The Don, in the guise of Leporello, offers to help. He instructs Masetto's friends to go off in various directions to search for – him. Once they have gone off ahead, Don Giovanni disarms Masetto, then thrashes him. After this, Zerlina consoles her fiancé. She will provide his cure: *Vedrai, carino, se sei buonino*.

* * *

The scene changes to a dark courtyard in Donna Anna's house. Before Leporello, still disguised as his master, can extricate himself from Donna Elvira, who thinks he is Don Giovanni, the man she craves, he is confronted by the others, bent on revenge.

In the sextet, Mozart draws together the opera's main dramatic ideas in a single concentrated ensemble. Leporello tries to escape from Elvira; Donna Anna is still expressing her grief to Don Ottavio, who reckons she has been at it long enough; and Zerlina and Masetto come in search of Don Giovanni and think they have found him when they see someone (Leporello) disguised as him. Elvira defends 'her husband' while the others go for him. Leporello patters away nervously.

To save himself, Leporello has to disclose who he really is. The sextet reaches a climax as everyone admits to being completely confused: *Mille torbidi pensieri* ('A thousand thoughts whirr round my head'). They are furious at being tricked. Leporello pleads for mercy: *Ah, pietà, Signori miei*.

Leporello makes a dash for it. Don Ottavio proclaims that these goings-on provide proof that the murderer of Donna Anna's father was Don Giovanni. Don Ottavio will be able to tell his 'treasure' that she is avenged: *Il mio tesoro*. And Donna Elvira sings about how, despite Don Giovanni's evil misbehaviour, at heart, she really loves him: *Mi tradì quell'alma ingrata.*

* * *

It is almost 2am. The scene moves to the graveyard where the tomb and monument of the Commendatore are located. Beneath his statue[18], a plaque reads, 'I shall be avenged on the evil one who killed me.' Don Giovanni reports that he managed to pick up a girl on the street – a nice little piece, who at first thought he was Leporello. When she began to scream, he had to escape into the graveyard. Leporello accuses him of being callous. What if the girl had been his, Leporello's, wife? Don Giovanni says 'better still' and roars with laughter. At this moment, the statue declares that before dawn Don Giovanni will have his last laugh. Don Giovanni forces the reluctant Leporello to invite the statue to dine with him.

* * *

Back in Donna Anna's house, in a badly lit room, Don Ottavio tells her that she will be avenged, and proposes marriage, but she says he must wait. At this, he suggests that she is being hard-hearted. Not so, she tells her beloved: *Non mi dir, bell'idol mio.*

* * *

Don Giovanni is dining in his palace.[19] While Don Giovanni (and Leporello) stuff themselves with the excellent meal which the cook has produced, the band plays popular songs, from Martín y Soler's smash hit *Una cosa rara*, from an opera by Paisiello, and from Mozart's

---

[18] The statue, sometimes called the Stone Guest (Pushkin wrote a poem called 'The Stone Guest' in the 1830s) is a difficult part for the designer. In a Glyndebourne production, the singer was surprised to find the make-up assistant flicking yellow paint at him after he had put on his grey outfit. When asked what on earth was happening, the make-up assistant explained, 'Pigeons'.

[19] Don Giovanni declares, *A che piatto saporito!* ('What a savoury dish!'), a pun on the name of the first Donna Anna, Teresa Saporiti. Mozart repeats this several times so that the point is not missed. He makes a similar pun – what might be considered a sales pitch – saying the cook ('cuoco') is excellent. 'Cook' was the name of the musician who did the piano reductions for both *The Marriage of Figaro* and *Don Giovanni*.

own *The Marriage of Figaro*. Donna Elvira arrives to plead with Don Giovanni to mend his ways, but he dismisses her.

The statue arrives just as she goes. When Don Giovanni asks for a place to be laid for the stone guest, the statue declares that it has no need of food but has come for more serious matters. It invites the Don to come and dine with it. The Don is not a man to be afraid, and he accepts. The statue offers him its hand on it, which Don Giovanni shakes. But the statue grips the Don's hand and demands that he repent. He refuses, and is engulfed in flames.

The others, Anna and Ottavio, Zerlina and Masetto, and the lonely Elvira, arrive to take revenge on the villain. Leporello explains that they are too late.

Ottavio proposes to Donna Anna again, but she requires him to wait one more year. Elvira heads for a convent; Zerlina and Masetto go off with each other; Leporello goes to the pub to find a new master. They all agree with the moral of the tale: scoundrels get their just deserts.

MOZART: *COSÌ FAN TUTTE*

THE OPERA AND ITS COMPOSER

Così fan tutte – they're all like that! Such generalisations about female behaviour may hardly seem a safe subject for the 21st century. Yet, ironically, *Così fan tutte* is among the most popular and widely performed operas in the repertoire today, and considered 'the best of all Lorenzo da Ponte's librettos and the most exquisite work of art among Mozart's operas.'

Yet, almost within two years of its première in 1790, the German press attacked *Così fan tutte*, as absurd, frivolous and immoral. People were disgusted that Mozart could possibly have wasted 'heavenly melodies on such a worthless libretto.' And for a long time the standard view was that the libretto was 'of rather doubtful character'. On the occasions when it was staged, it was often 'improved', even by its music being fitted to different words and action.

Da Ponte, then the Poet to the Imperial Theatres, himself rarely mentioned it later in his life, when he was so proud of his earlier association with Mozart which led to *The Marriage of Figaro* and *Don Giovanni*. Emperor Joseph II, the eccentric ruler of the Habsburg Empire, who micro-managed (as he did most things)[1] the music performed at his court, has been blamed for the misogyny and the immorality in the plot. He found women difficult to handle: he is said to have looked at them in the way that people normally look at statues. He has long been held responsible for encouraging Da Ponte to write the libretto called *La scuola degli amanti*, 'The School of Lovers', which evolved into Mozart's opera.

The eccentric Emperor may have suggested the story himself. Alternatively, it may have been based on an actual incident that had

---

[1] Royal encouragement was tantamount to an order. As well as everything else, the monarch was up to his eyes with political and social reform, and waging an expensive war in the Balkans at the time.

taken place recently. Whatever, Da Ponte seems to have drawn on the work of two distinguished playwrights, the Venetian Carlo Goldoni (1707–1793), and the Frenchman Pierre de Marivaux (1688–1763), the latter described as a specialist in 'the coming to awareness of the state of being in love, particularly in young ladies.'

Da Ponte blended two themes which have a long history in literature: one in which the man wagers his lady's fidelity of which he is (foolishly) convinced; and the other whereby a suspicious husband disguises himself as a stranger and tests his lady's fidelity by attempting to woo her.

Da Ponte's plot was unusual in that it was not based specifically on an existing play or story, nor some ancient or classical subject, and it did not involve royal or aristocratic characters in some way. Although obviously absurdly fictional, it was fundamentally about down-to-earth characters (people such as the composer, even), in ordinary surroundings and, importantly, wholly contemporary. The cast would be small: necessarily so, in view of a cost-cutting program that the Emperor was implementing.

Antonio Salieri, the more senior composer in the very hierarchical Viennese structure, and known to many as the villain of the film *Amadeus*, was offered the first crack at composing the opera, but gave up. Indeed Mozart's widow later suggested that Salieri's legendary hatred of her husband arose because Mozart took on this libretto, which Salieri 'could make nothing of' and had rejected as being unworthy of musical invention.[2]

At the time Mozart took on the commission in 1789, he seems to have been in surprisingly bad form. His creativity and rate of composition were dropping off. The public lost interest in his keyboard virtuosity, and his downward trajectory began. His cash flow had deteriorated and he was borrowing from a fellow freemason, most

[2] Constanze Mozart said this at the age of 66, when she was 'still of sound mind and body', despite all her health problems during her husband's last years. She was notoriously unreliable in her recollections, and her attribution of Salieri's jealousy is improbable. He started to respond negatively to Mozart some six years before Mozart's death. Constanze's explanation also does not accord with Salieri's normal behaviour: he did not normally turn down libretti on the grounds that they were weak, and he usually completed works once begun. It seems possible that, in this case, Salieri was de-energised following the recent failure of his opera *Il pastor fido*.

recently against the 'security' of his prospective fee. It is perhaps no coincidence that in the second half of the year, his louche wife, whom he adored, was enjoying the high life in Baden, the health resort some twenty miles to the south of Vienna. (Her behaviour, justifying his conclusion '*così fan tutte*', caused him sufficient concern that he wrote to remonstrate with her about it.)

Mozart's wife Constanze

Mozart himself coined the title. He derived it from a snippet of melody and text from Act 1 of *The Marriage of Figaro*, the moment when Don Basilio, the reptilian music teacher, discovers the bedroom shenanigans involving the Count, Susanna and Cherubino.

Così fan tutte was premièred in the Vienna court theatre, the Burgtheater, on 26 January 1790. There was a star cast: Guglielmo was played by the 'best comic singer in Europe' Francesco Benucci, the original Figaro.

Unfortunately, less than a month later, after there had only been four performances, Mozart's primary sponsor, Emperor Joseph, died. He went to his grave almost certainly without hearing *Così fan tutte*. The theatres were closed for court mourning until April. By the end of August, *Così fan tutte* had been performed ten times. But although it toured – for example in the British Isles – 'it fell out of the repertoire'. Fifty years later, a distinguished critic in London dismissed it: 'there is no hope for *Così fan tutte* on the stage as the work stands.' It was occasionally staged, however, and some of its numbers featured in collections of Mozart's popular tunes.

As is normal, the action is moved along by the use of 'recitatives', that is, 'speaking in music'. Recitatives are in themselves an art form. Although they are very clever and witty, they result in the opera being long. A normal performance of *Così fan tutte* might run for two-and-three-quarter hours, even after the recitatives have been substantially cut (some would say 'butchered'). The cuts mean that the audience misses music in which (many people feel) Mozart demonstrates his supreme art. They tend to be made especially in Act 2, by which time the story is obvious, and the words are less necessary. That is so, provided the singers' diction is clear, because, as one great baritone has observed, in this opera 'it is essential for the words to be clear, whatever the language used.'

To be successful, and to compliment Mozart, *Così fan tutte* also needs great elegance of style.

(More on the lives of Mozart and Da Ponte can be found on pages 25–26.)

Who's who and what's what

The story below is based on the libretto. Certain directors may amend opera stories to suit their production.

We are in the sensual South. **Ferrando** and **Guglielmo**, smooth army officers based in the metropolis of Naples, are betrothed to two sisters from the 'provincial' town of Ferrara in northern Italy.

Ferrando is betrothed to the flighty, superficial **Dorabella**; Guglielmo is betrothed to the high-minded, conscientious, earnest **Fiordiligi**.[3]

---

[3] Cognoscenti of names like Grace, Patience, Prudence, etc., will recognise that Dorabella and Fiordiligi could mean 'blond beauty' and 'budding constancy'. They are sometimes compared with the Dashwood sisters in Jane Austen's *Sense and Sensibility*. To get the relationships straight,

To the men's annoyance, **Don Alfonso**, a crusty old misogynist and a philosopher of reason, has the temerity to question their ladies' avowed fidelity and constancy. He wagers that, provided the men strictly cooperate with his arrangements, he will demonstrate the superficiality and fragility of these qualities.

Alfonso arranges that the officers will pretend to have been called up to go to war. The disguised Ferrando is then to return and seduce Guglielmo's Fiordiligi; and the disguised Guglielmo will seduce Ferrando's Dorabella. **Despina**, the pert, sexually experienced, insolent ladies' maid, and the butt of the girls' fury, encourages their infidelity.

The men reappear disguised as two Albanian nobles who threaten to poison themselves if their ardent love is not reciprocated. To their great relief, this scheme at first does not succeed. They think that Don Alfonso should concede and call off the wager.

Alfonso presses on. He achieves the girls' fall by suborning Despina, who first disguises herself as the doctor who supplies an 'antidote' for the 'poison'.

Dorabella soon weakens: Guglielmo succeeds in replacing her miniature of Ferrando, which hangs around her neck, with a heart, a symbol of Guglielmo's supposed love for her. (He takes some pleasure in his relative prowess and Ferrando's discomfiture.)

Fiordiligi is a harder nut to crack. She tries hard to resist, even threatening to join up and leave for the front herself. But she eventually yields to pressure from Ferrando. Both men are now horrified with the outcome, and have lost their wager. When the seduction has succeeded, Don Alfonso claims that he has demonstrated that women are all the same: *Così fan tutte* – they're all like that.

Alfonso arranges a (mock) wedding between the girls and their newfound lovers. This is presided over by Despina, posing this time as a notary. In the middle of the ceremony, martial music indicates that the original lovers are returning. The girls, caught seemingly

the listener may find it helpful to remember that neither of the F's (Ferrando, Fiordiligi) is affianced to the other, so neither F should be chasing the other.

having signed a marriage contract, are greatly embarrassed, until all is revealed. They round on Don Alfonso, who proclaims the importance of being guided by reason.

THE INTERVAL: TALKING POINTS

'La Ferrarese', the prima donna

Mozart designed the music to suit his original cast, as was normal. The roles of his first Fiordiligi and Dorabella were to be performed by Adriana Gabrieli del Bene and Louise Villeneuve. Some believe that these two were sisters; others do not.

Adriana, known as 'La Ferrarese' because she herself came from Ferrara, was Da Ponte's mistress – a status in which her husband acquiesced. Da Ponte was besotted by her 'heavenly voice, wonderful eyes and lovely mouth', and promoted her relentlessly and obsessively. She had successfully appeared as Susanna in *Figaro*. But she was disliked by the theatre world in general, and Mozart thought she was a useless actress. Her unpopularity contributed to Da Ponte's downfall in Vienna. When he ceased to be of use to her, she dropped him like a stone, a step which he was later in a position to reciprocate when the tables were turned.

She had an unusually wide vocal range, which Dr Burney, the English musical historian, had noticed when he heard her in her youth in Venice. In Fiordiligi's arias, we hear gigantic vocal leaps, which Mozart used to depict the character's divided emotions. Within five bars in the short introduction to *Come scoglio*, the range exceeds two octaves and she sustains a top B flat.

Some have suggested that the angular music was designed to mock her, because she tended to bob up and down depending on whether she was singing a high or low note. More probably Mozart designed it to portray a determined character, impervious to the addresses of men – an irony which an audience familiar with La Ferrarese's reputation for sleeping around would have hugely enjoyed.

A great baritone advised that the best way for an aspiring prima donna to succeed is for her to concentrate on five roles. Elisabeth Schwarzkopf made Fiordiligi one of her five.[4] It was also one of Kiri Te Kanawa's 'most successful and best-loved' parts.

A musical farce?

Wagner thought that Mozart's music for *Così fan tutte* matched its feeble and trivial libretto. An eminent German musicologist rashly concluded that 'Mozart's greatness would not suffer if *Così fan tutte* had remained unwritten.' He added, 'one could take it for a work from the times of Mozart's first operatic essays.'

This judgement has been described as an 'appalling misconception'. Sir Peter Hall, the theatre director, has pointed out that *Così fan tutte* is 'unblinking in its realism and uncomfortable in its pain.' He has observed that 'we avoid its disturbing perception if we can. And we do so by turning this most serious of comedies into a farce.' Elisabeth Schwarzkopf made the same point by walking out of a production where the characters were cast as puppets.[5]

Comedy *Così fan tutte* certainly is. Apart from its obvious absurdities, it is full of histrionics. In Act 1, after Dorabella's *Smanie implacabili*, about the implacable pangs which only death will assuage, both girls fling themselves, absurdly, on the sofa. A few minutes later, Fiordiligi's *Come scoglio* (in which she claims her steadfastness is as solid as a rock), with its wide melodic leaps and even shrieks, is mockingly serious. According to convention at the time, this big item should have been an 'exit' aria, followed by the dramatic exit of the singer in order to generate thunderous applause. However, Fiordiligi is left standing and looking fatuous; when she starts to make her dramatic exit with her sister, they are pulled back by Ferrando with 'Here, you two, come back!' thus allowing Don Alfonso to sarcastically observe how simply too frightful it all is.[6]

---

[4] Schwarzkopf's other four were Donna Elvira in *Don Giovanni*, the Countess in *The Marriage of Figaro*, the Marschallin in *Der Rosenkavalier* and Countess Madeleine in *Capriccio*.

[5] Her biographer has written, '*Così* is always tempting fare for a producer with a theory.'

[6] There are also clever little nuances, such as when, in a piece of recitative, Fiordiligi tells her sister's fortune: she reads it as an M and P, which she interprets as '*matrimonio presto*' (foretelling imminent marriage), but which could also signify Mozart and Da Ponte.

But, there is also much more to this opera than the 'harmless merriment' found in the general run of comic operas. In *Così fan tutte*, composer and librettist expose many pessimistic and disillusioned truths about human nature and behaviour. In particular, they show that the enlightened and educated upbringing, from which these affluent young girls have been privileged to benefit, fails under pressure to provide a defence against basic raw human emotions. And the cocky playboys get their comeuppance: they too learn what reality is all about.

Mozart and Da Ponte collaborated on the opera, and it represents 'a summation of their combined gifts.' It is difficult to apportion the credit for its comedy, irony, textual characterisation and subtleties. Given that Salieri had a first crack at it – he composed versions of the Act 1 trios, *La mia Dorabella* and *È la fede delle femmine come l'araba fenice* before giving up – it is possible that the die was cast by the time Mozart got to it.

One can get the impression that some commentators make rather heavy weather of Mozart's contribution, analysing melody and key relationships which the audience – which in any case was probably chattering and not attending too carefully – cannot be expected to have noticed in a fast-moving stage performance. Mozart, who is unlikely to have had his eye on university music faculties of the future, must presumably have designed these features for his own edification.

Using music to illuminate character

Much of Mozart's greatness arises from his art of using music to illuminate, differentiate and sculpture his operatic characters so that they come across with 'flesh and blood vitality'. His music portrays their sentiments as real, coming from the bottom of their hearts. And it portrays the heartbreak which 'lurks beneath the surface of the comedy.'

As might be expected, Mozart often gives the pert soubrette Despina patter music suitable for her status as a servant; and normally we hear Don Alfonso display an expansive style suited to a philosopher, except when he degenerates to the level of his accomplice, and sings patter. Violin scales depict Dorabella's surging emotions in the recitative before her *Smanie implacabili*. Mozart also paints the background scenery most effectively, as when the violins imitate the lapping waves by the seashore in *Soave sia il vento*.

To the ordinary listener, the delineation may be less obvious in the many ensembles, but should be discernible in the solos and duets. At its simplest, we can hear it in the two girls, who at first seem comically inseparable, singing identical lines, often in parallel thirds, with identical coloratura; their characters then diverge, the hysterical Dorabella singing her *Smanie implacabili* and Fiordiligi, infuriated by the unwelcome visitors, exploding with her angular *Come scoglio*.

In the duet early in Act 2, the two sisters are both heading in the same direction, Dorabella planning to have 'the dark one' who is more fun ('*Prenderò quel brunettino*'), while Fiordiligi is aiming to have a laugh with the fair one. However, the capricious Dorabella's rhythms are more flamboyant and irregular ('dotted') than those of the more sentimental Fiordiligi, whose rhythms are softer.

The use of music to illuminate a character is best found in the music of Fiordiligi, the prima donna. The *Come scoglio* makes us chuckle at her self-importance, while her *Per pietà* ('In pity's name, my love, forgive the weakness of a loving soul') 'brings us close to tears.' In the *Per pietà*, stresses emerge which weaken her defences and which permit her final seduction. Her vacillation is even accompanied by a wobbling horn, itself the instrument of the cuckold.

After a bit, she steels herself and dresses up to join her fiancé at the front, much to the delight of the down-to-earth Guglielmo (her fiancé) who marvels at her constancy: *Si può dar un amor simile a questo* ('Can there be such love as this?'), he expostulates. Six minutes later, it ends with her complete capitulation to her sexy sister's extremely seductive fiancé Ferrando: *Fa di me quel che ti par*, that is, 'you can have me'. Fiordiligi is unified with him, either exactly so, singing in parallel sixths, or in imitation, one after the other. The music makes it totally convincing.

And, with great irony, Mozart illuminates the '*fa di me*' of her capitulation with a series of notes similar to that used by the two girls to protest their perpetual love for their fiancés at the outset when they were about to go away: *No, crudel, non te ne andrai* ('Cruel one, do not leave me'). The audience is most unlikely to notice this, but the irony here is considerable, and it perhaps reflects Mozart's own personal concerns about what his wife might be up to at Baden.

Political correctness

It is not hard to see why audiences in the nineteenth and early twentieth centuries took exception to *Così fan tutte*, and why Mozart had to be excused with the explanation that it was not in his power to turn down the Emperor's commission. His early biographer wondered 'how that great mind could lower itself to waste its heavenly melodies on so feeble a concoction.' A prominent actor called *Così fan tutte* a 'miserable thing which lowers all women; it cannot possibly please female spectators and will therefore not make its future.'

The title itself is indeed a slanderous generalisation.[7] Beethoven was shocked by the sentiments expressed. Everything about the story is wrong and even flippant: the women are seducible; the men set about seducing them and succeed; instead of being sacked, the saucy, insubordinate and immoral servant is praised. The philosopher unscrupulously practises a deception, and even organises a wager. The only acceptable material is the routine lampooning of the professionals, the doctor and the lawyer.

Although plays featuring 'wife' swapping were not unknown at the time, they were rendered acceptable by the underlying cause being supernatural or magical (and thus, officially, unrealistic) as, for example, in *A Midsummer Night's Dream*. Wife swapping among contemporary, real human beings was a wholly different matter, and condoning it struck at the very foundations of society. It has been suggested that, within the conventions of his time, Mozart was trying to express the idea that it's possible to be genuinely in love with more than one person. If so, this view would have been revolutionary.

---

[7] Lorenzo da Ponte, on the few occasions he referred to the opera, called it by its original title at the time when Salieri took it on, *La scuola degli amanti* ('The school of lovers'). The title *Così fan tutte* was Mozart's.

What is more surprising, perhaps, is that *Così fan tutte* has been such a popular opera from the middle of the twentieth century, during a time when feminism has progressed. There is considerable irony in modern audiences applauding all this without even a token objection. It must be fiction. Maybe there is indeed a moral in the tale: its happy ending may signify that, in a genuine relationship, the first love will still be the strongest and will remain so, and thus will be worth returning to.

ACT BY ACT

Before the overture moves into a lively Mozartian 'presto', we hear the strings play the five-note theme that will reappear towards the end of the opera when Don Alfonso pronounces *'così fan tutte'*. This is repeated again, quietly, just before the end of the overture. Early in the presto, we also hear the snippet of melody heard in Act 1 of *The Marriage of Figaro* when Don Basilio sings *'così fan tutte le belle'* ('All the beauties are like that').

Act 1

We enter what Sir Thomas Beecham, the conductor, once called 'a long summer day spent in a cloudless land by a Southern Sea.' The scene is actually a coffee house, in Naples, Italy. We know we are in the classical period contemporary to Mozart, from the style of the opening trio of 'exquisite gracefulness', *La mia Dorabella*.

Army officers Ferrando and Guglielmo assure the doubting Don Alfonso, a philosopher, that their fiancées are paragons of fidelity and virtue. When he observes the men's naivety, they cite as evidence the girls' assurances, their tears, sighs and so forth. Don Alfonso maintains that woman's constancy is like the phoenix:[8] everybody swears that it exists, but 'try and find some examples of it': *È la fede delle femmine come l'araba fenice*. The men are irritated by his attitude

---

[8] The text of *È la fede delle femmine* would have been recognisable as a send-up of the style of poetry written by the court poet Metastasio, who was responsible for a large number of opera libretti.

and they suggest the matter be settled by duel; but Don Alfonso wagers one hundred sequins (Venetian gold coins) that he will show them he is right. However, he insists that they must cooperate with whatever he stipulates. The men confidently discuss what they will do with their winnings. The romantic Ferrando (Dorabella's fiancé) will arrange a serenade – *Una bella serenata* – and the more down-to-earth Guglielmo will have a banquet.

By the seashore, the serene and serious Fiordiligi and the more jaunty Dorabella natter while awaiting their lovers, whose looks they praise and whose miniatures hang round their necks: *Ah, guarda sorella*. Fiordiligi reads Dorabella's fortune and foretells marriage. But instead of their lovers arriving, Don Alfonso comes in and slowly reveals to them dreadful news. Their men have been called up and are off to war. They are coming to take their leave: *Vorrei dir, e cor non ho*. The men approach hesitantly and nervously: *Sento, o Dio*. But Don Alfonso says that heroes have to be brave. When the girls ask them to plunge their swords into their hearts, the men don't, but feel reassured.

A drum roll is sounded and soldiers are heard singing *Bella vita militar*; it is time for the men to leave. While they have been tarrying, their ship has sailed and they must go out to it in a tender. They swear fidelity and to write to each other. With the strings imitating the lapping of water on the seashore, the girls and Alfonso wish them Godspeed in the most exquisite little trio, *Soave sia il vento*, ('Gentle be the breeze, and calm the waves'). Don Alfonso leaves to join the men and repeats his misogynist sentiments.

Despina, the girls' maid, brings in their breakfast. She rebels at her status, expressing insubordinate sentiments that the audience might not have been surprised by, but would not have tolerated. Why should she make the chocolate and not taste it, she asks. And taste it she does. When she gives it to the girls, they fling it to the ground, and, to her amazement, express their sorrow and distress: Dorabella hates everything, including herself, those who take pleasure in her bad news[9]

---

[9] Mozart uses a few notes of melody similar to those which Fiordiligi will use later when expressing her unshakeable fidelity, and when she is beginning to waver.

and those who comfort her. Her surging emotions are preceded by rushing violins, as she sings of her pain – *Smanie implacabili* – after which both girls fling themselves on the sofa. Despina expresses some surprise at the histrionics. For her, the fiancés' departure would provide an opportunity: if they're killed, there would indeed be two fewer men, but think of all the others. Meanwhile, have fun, she suggests, and make love as vigorously as the men will be doing while they are away. She is a strong feminist: for her, men are no better than quivering leaves – despite all their endearments, they just use women for their pleasure: *In uomini, in soldati*.

Don Alfonso is worried that Despina may recognise the men, so he decides to take her into his confidence by bribing her. He tells her he has need of her, to which she saucily retorts that she has no need of him. But he persuades her to join his scheme, which carries a bonus if it succeeds. He then brings in the lovers, disguised: *Alla bella Despinetta*. She reckons these foreigners, whether Wallachians or Turks,[10] are sufficiently ugly to make anybody renounce love.

The ladies are furious to find strangers in their house and they jointly tell Despina to send them away. The men fall at their feet and express their undying love. The girls' outrage delights them. Don Alfonso pretends to recognise them as old friends, 'the dearest friends he has in this world.' The men continue to protest their love. Fiordiligi tells them in no uncertain terms to get lost and gives them a sound ticking off. (Despina runs out, terrified.) Fiordiligi will remain a bastion, true to her oath of faithfulness.[11] Her heart is like a rock impervious to storm and tempest: *Come scoglio immota resta*. Don

[10] Wallachia was part of modern Romania. At the time *Così fan tutte* was written, it was ruled by the Turks against whom the Emperor Joseph was fighting in the Balkans.

[11] To underline this pledge and its importance, in a beautiful piece of recitative, Mozart uses the same snippet of melody Dorabella used when wringing her hands at the news that their lovers had gone away, and which will recur later when Fiordiligi begins to waver. At this stage, Fiordiligi is utterly determined, as the two trumpets with which Mozart reinforces her *Come scoglio* make abundantly clear. The use of trumpets was conventionally reserved for martial music (and choruses). This also points forward to her later plan to don soldier's clothes and go to the front – shortly before her abject collapse.

Alfonso protests that the ladies should at least treat his friends with due courtesy.

The lovers continue their attempt at seduction. Guglielmo asserts that their mustaches are the very plumages of love: *Non siate ritrosi*. When the girls storm out, the men fall about laughing at the collapse of Don Alfonso's wager: *E voi ridete?* They offer to settle for half of it; but Don Alfonso advises them not to count their chickens before they are hatched. The men reckon they will enjoy their celebratory dinner after all this. The romantic Ferrando declares, in a beautifully lyrical aria, that a mere breath of love will be sustenance enough for him: *Un'aura amorosa*.

Don Alfonso, despite appearances, actually feels a bit unnerved. He consults his accomplice. She regards the women as absurd: 'If one lover leaves, take two others; it's just common sense,' she suggests. Don Alfonso should leave it to her to run the show. She has led a thousand men by the nose, and should be able to manage these two.

The girls pine about how their lot has suddenly changed, *Ah che tutta in un momento*.[12] Then the foreigners arrive threatening to take arsenic in order to set themselves free from such hard-hearted ladies. They drink the potion. When they collapse, Don Alfonso suggests that the girls should at the very least show some compassion. At this, the girls call for Despina to help. She tells them to comfort the men while she and Don Alfonso find a doctor who has an antidote.

When the girls set about comforting the expiring men, they notice that they are actually rather attractive. They find that their bodies are ice cold; they feel their pulses, which are almost non-existent. Despina, however, returns, disguised as a doctor. At first, she utters obscure Latin phrases, and, to the impatient girls and Don Alfonso, she enquires formally about various irrelevancies. In a topical reference, she then she takes out an iron magnet, such as Doctor Franz

---

[12] With its delicate woodwind and horn accompaniment, this finale has been praised for its 'gentle note of sighing sensuality.' Mozart displays an unusually wide range of orchestral colour in this opera.

Mesmer[13] would have obtained in Germany and used in France. She waves it over the men, who immediately convulse, recover, and attempt to embrace and kiss the girls. Despina and Don Alfonso explain to the reluctant girls that this behaviour is merely a further consequence of the poison. The men are delighted that the girls are suitably outraged when asked for a kiss: *Damme un bacio, o mio tesoro.* The act ends in a lively sextet with the men becoming increasingly nervous, while Despina and Don Alfonso are confident that the girls will eventually capitulate.

Act 2

Despina tells the girls that they should pull themselves together, treat love lightly and seize 'the opportunity' – like soldiers, they should go recruiting. They regard her as immoral. To their objection that to entertain the foreigners would lead the neighbours to gossip, the servant retorts that they can just say that the men have come to see her. She attributes the men's ardent behaviour to the effect of the poison. The girls should get on with it: at fifteen, she says, a woman should know the ways of the world and should market herself properly: *Una donna a quindici anni.*

Although Fiordiligi is worried about scandal, Dorabella begins to weaken – they do need some relief from boredom – especially if it can be pretended that the men actually came to see Despina. Dorabella says she will have the dark one who is more lively: *Prenderò quel brunettino.*

While they are anticipating the fun they will have, Don Alfonso calls them into the seaside garden, where they can see the men reclining in a barge decorated with flowers. Accompanied by singers and musicians

---

[13] Franz Mesmer (1734–1815), was a friend of the Mozart family. Mozart's early opera *Bastien et Bastienne* was played in his garden in Vienna in 1768. Mesmer's interest in astrology led him to imagine that the stars exerted an influence on humans. It followed that magnetism would also do so, and that stroking with magnets could therefore have medical, curative effects. Later, Mesmer discarded magnets, and supposed that some occult force within himself could effect cures. In Paris, where some thought he was a charlatan, his patients would hold hands in his dimly lit consulting room, which was furnished with mirrors. Music was played and the air was perfumed; Mesmer glided around. This technique gave rise to our word 'mesmerise', and later influenced the development of hypnosis.

playing woodwind and horn, the men implore the friendly breezes to aid their romance: *Secondate, aurette amiche*. The girls are still reticent and the men know they must be cautious, so Don Alfonso, with Despina's help, intervenes to bring them together. He takes Dorabella's hand – *La mano a me date* – and leads her to her lover.

When Don Alfonso and Despina leave them to it, the conversation becomes rather stilted, and the couples talk about the weather. Fiordiligi then suggests to Ferrando that they go for a stroll. Dorabella thinks that Guglielmo, who is a bit disconcerted that the other two have gone off together, is still suffering the after-effects of the poison, but he says he is inflamed by the fire of love. She asks him to cool it a bit. But Guglielmo asks for some token of her pity for him, to which Dorabella responds positively. Despite her initial protestations (and to his concern), he succeeds in putting a heart in the place where she wears the miniature of Ferrando.[14] 'Poor Ferrando,' he exclaims to himself, and keeps up his pretence in *Il core vi dono*.

Meanwhile, Ferrando is experiencing more resistance from Fiordiligi. But, under her breath, she tells herself that her emotions are already confused.[15] 'You're robbing me of my peace,' she exclaims; and he responds, 'Just to make you happy.' Ferrando is also unsettled when Fiordiligi looks at him and sighs. When she has sent him away, she expresses her remorse as well as her overwhelming temptation to succumb – 'In pity's name, my love, forgive the weakness of a loving soul' – and wishes she had the strength to banish the dishonourable desire which fills her with shame and horror: *Per pietà, ben mio*.[16]

[14] It may seem simple for Guglielmo to replace a locket from around Dorabella's neck with one from around his, but Sir Geraint Evans has observed that to do it elegantly, while not interrupting the vocal line, needs great stagecraft and a considerable amount of practice. Guglielmo has to avoid catching her wig, or her costume, or his own. And it would be quite easy to give her back the wrong chain, her original one.

[15] As she wavers, Mozart reminds us ironically, by using the same snippet of melody that Fiordiligi used when she resolved to be faithful, and that Dorabella used when expressing histrionics at the departure of their fiancés.

[16] It is worth going to *Così* just for this item, which Mozart wrote specifically for the wide vocal range of the first Fiordiligi, 'La Ferrarese'. Note the woodwind accompaniment, and in particular the unusual figures on the horn, for which Mozart uses notes whose intonation tends to sound uncertain when played on horns of the period.

Meanwhile, the men meet to assess progress. Ferrando jocularly reports his failure to seduce Fiordiligi, who, all right, had teased him a bit by seeming to melt, but then fobbed him off. When he asks about Dorabella, the cocksure Guglielmo nervously breaks the bad news that she has capitulated: he shows Ferrando the miniature of him that he, Guglielmo, took away and replaced with the heart locket. Ferrando is outraged and swears revenge.

Guglielmo sententiously shrugs it all off: in his considerable experience, women, the lot of them, are all like that; even to the extent that it actually becomes rather a bore, and justifies men in objecting to their behaviour: *Donne mie, la fate a tanti a tanti*. Ferrando is not quite so relaxed, because, betrayed and scorned by a faithless heart, he still loves Dorabella: *Tradito, schernito*. He rounds on Don Alfonso, who advises him to calm down. Guglielmo, however, continues to preen himself on his success, and suggests that Don Alfonso immediately settles up his share of the wager, fifty sequins. 'Not so fast,' says the philosopher.

Despina compliments Dorabella on her common sense in accepting her new lover. Fiordiligi arrives, cursing everybody because she is in the course of falling head over heels for her Albanian. Dorabella advises her conscience-stricken sister to stop worrying. After all, their fiancés may be killed in the war; so they should 'move on'. If their lovers do return, well, when they do, they will be married and far, far away. In a jaunty aria, she advises Fiordiligi to give in, because love is like a little thief: *È amore un ladroncello*. Fiordiligi is not so sure. Guglielmo is delighted to overhear her resistance.

Fiordiligi, starting the most memorable sequence in the opera, orders Despina to get one of the uniforms which the soldiers have left behind: the girls will dress as soldiers and go and join their lovers in the war. She starts to put on the uniform:[17] Soon she will be away and in the arms of her beloved: *Fra gli amplessi in pochi istanti*.

---

[17] Her suggestion that Ferrando's uniform will fit her, and that Dorabella can have Guglielmo's, is perhaps an admission that she knows her situation is hopeless, as was suggested by her earlier sigh. She adds, looking in the mirror, 'I can hardly recognise myself.'

But Ferrando persists with his seductive and tender charms, and pleads with her. She has wavered enough and can no longer resist. She falls from her great height: *Giusto ciel, Fa di me quel che ti par* ('Merciful heaven, do with me as you will').[18] They sing a love duet, in which synchronised thirds denote that they are indeed one: *Abbracciamci, o caro bene* ('Embrace me, my love').

It is now Guglielmo's turn to rage at his betrothed, who appears like the chaste Diana but is actually a strumpet and a bitch. When he suggests that they deserve punishment, Don Alfonso suggests that an appropriate punishment could be for the men to marry them. He reassures them that the women are actually not that bad. It may be a sin, it may be a habit, but it is a necessity of the heart. Women are all the same; all women act alike: *Così fan tutte*.

Despina announces that the ladies are ready to marry the Albanian noblemen. The servants and musicians prepare for the wedding and the ceremony begins. The girls and the men toast each other: any reluctance on the girls' part is now long past.

Despina returns disguised as a notary. In nasal tones, she holds forth pompously and legalistically. The marriage contract has just been signed when distant martial music, the same as accompanied the men's departure, is heard. Don Alfonso goes to look: horror, panic, the soldiers are returning. The Albanians take refuge by disappearing into the closet.

Having shed their disguise, the lovers return to claim their sweethearts, and are disappointed at the lack of enthusiasm with which they are received. When the servant puts their trunk in the closet, the notary is found in there: Despina reveals that it is her, and pretends that she has returned from a fancy-dress ball. Then the men see the contract, and act outraged.

The girls are overwhelmed with remorse, and hasten to blame Despina and Don Alfonso. To their horror, Don Alfonso encourages

[18] For this, Fiordiligi uses a series of notes similar to that to which her words 'Cruel one, do not leave me' were set in Act 1, at the time when Guglielmo went off to war.

the men to look in the closet. They go in, and emerge again disguised as the Albanians. Guglielmo returns the miniature.

The truth dawns on the girls. Don Alfonso says that everyone will be wiser for the experience, and everybody has a good laugh. Indeed, happy is he who looks on the bright side, and makes reason his guide.[19]

[19] From Mozart's 'almost manic setting of these words' – in the score he indicates that it should be taken at high speed, '*Allegro molto*' – we may suppose that he had little confidence in this conclusion, which was unlikely to provide a practical solution to the problems he faced in his own life.

MOZART:
THE MAGIC FLUTE

Mozart took his seven-year-old son, Karl, and his granny to *The Magic Flute*. Karl was allowed out from a school which his parents thought was pretty useless. He 'was absolutely delighted at being taken to the opera', according to his father. Children have always been enchanted by *Die Zauberflöte*. Why? It has a strong resemblance to pantomime.

But it is no pantomime. There have been many different interpretations of what it is about, some elaborate and psychological. It has roots deep in Freemasonry, but also in the *Commedia dell'arte* played by the traditional strolling masked players, and various other sources.

It is an allegory. Two 'lofty', 'noble' lovers must pass through various trials of constancy, endurance and discretion, before they can come together and attain ultimate bliss. The story contains messages, conveyed using the symbolism of Freemasonry, about love for humanity, and its role in the quest for self-betterment. Progress, presided over by a priesthood, is made through the reconciliation of opposites: light and darkness, good and evil, enlightenment (i.e. the use of reason) and superstition.

The opera ends with a hymn to beauty and wisdom; and, at 'half-time', the chorus proclaims that when virtue and justice prevail, Earth becomes Heaven, and mortals become gods. Later, the High Priest declares in his second exquisitely beautiful aria that happiness comes from fraternal love, not from revenge.

The target audience for Mozart and his librettist was not the usual sophisticated high society. It was suburban, and middle or lower class. In a development well ahead of its time, they were using opera to disseminate ethical messages. To appeal to this new audience, the high-faluting material needed softening, lightening. Thus, it was interspersed with farcical incidents involving a comic, primitive man who has no hope at all of achieving 'lofty' objectives. These are the pantomime aspects which delight children. They also provide dramatic contrast.

The 'lofty' and the comical merge, almost embrace, in the beautiful duet *Mann und Weib*, which audiences since the first night have greatly applauded. A 'lofty' woman and the primitive man declare that husband and wife, whether high- or low-born, together strive towards the divine. Not surprisingly, the modern conception and the music have impressed people of great stature, such as Goethe.

Mozart began to compose *The Magic Flute* in March 1791. The libretto was provided[1] by Emanuel Schikaneder, a fellow Freemason, whom Mozart had known for over ten years.

Emanuel Schikaneder

Mozart was working frantically hard. He finished *La Clemenza di Tito* in a coach as he headed to Prague for Leopold II's Coronation

[1] They were helped by Ignaz von Born, a metallurgist and anti-clerical writer who was the Masonic Grand Master, and by J.G. Metzler, who became a famous microbiologist.

festivities. This was just in time for its production in the first week of September. *The Magic Flute* was produced in Vienna at the end of that month, on 30 September 1791, in the Theater auf der Wieden, a somewhat rudimentary building in the Vienna suburbs. Mozart conducted from the clavier. Schikaneder, the star attraction, played the comical Papageno. It was a tightly knit production: Mozart's sister-in-law Josefa sang the sensationally difficult part of the Queen of the Night.[2]

Less than ten weeks later, on 5 December, Mozart was dead. Two days before the première, Mozart had completed the 'March of the Priests' and his greatest instrumental prologue, the overture. These constitute his farewell to the musical stage. The *Requiem* was unfinished at his death.

Emanuel Schikaneder (1751–1812) has sometimes been described as a rogue, sometimes as 'one of the most talented and influential theatre men of his age.' He was certainly remarkable. He was a travelling actor, a famous Hamlet, a Lear and a Macbeth. He met Mozart in Salzburg when his troupe was performing there. He was at first a chorister in Regensburg, a Free City which was a considerable centre of Freemasonry. At the end of the century, he directed the company at Vienna's Theater auf der Wieden. In 1801, he created the larger Theater an der Wien, which became an epicentre of Viennese theatrical and musical life and, although bombed in the Second World War, is still in existence today. Schikaneder overreached himself financially and had to move to Brno in the modern Czech Republic. Still beset by financial difficulties, he went mad and died in penury back in Vienna.

---

[2] Josefa Hofer particularly suited the role because Mozart thought she was 'as cunning as a fox'. Pamina was played by a seventeen-year-old who, five years earlier, had been the first Barbarina in *The Marriage of Figaro*: Anna Gottlieb survived into her eighties, in poverty. She described herself as the 'the first Pamina and the last living friend of Mozart.'

It has been suggested that Schikaneder knew of Mozart's difficult personal circumstances and need for cash, and proposed the creation of an opera in a brotherly, 'masonic' way. Others have suggested that Schikaneder himself was in financial trouble, and he approached Mozart for a show that could put him back on the rails. Maybe Mozart and his friend just had a vision that art would be an excellent medium through which to broadcast important messages about the Age of Reason. There are differing views about almost everything to do with *The Magic Flute*.

The Magic Flute, a success when first performed, has not always been as well received since. In 1816, a performance at La Scala was such a flop that it almost bankrupted the theatre. Many of the fashionable and distinguished, in their time, have taken a negative view, and have suggested that *The Magic Flute* is 'incoherent', 'a jumble of nonsense'. Ruskin, the English essayist, thought it was 'a silly extravaganza'. The Parisians decided it should be rehashed in what Berlioz called 'a lamentable concoction', *The Mysteries of Isis*, which included items from other operas, (including Don Giovanni's 'Champagne aria' rearranged for two sopranos and a bass). A mid-nineteenth century critic referred to 'the extreme wearisomeness of this elaborate puzzle'. For him, the music was admirable, and suitable as 'concert and home music, but not as part of a drama, which has no clear meaning on the stage' – even when performed by top-flight singers.

The negative views do not prevail today. Goethe thought them shallow and uneducated. He said that 'more knowledge is required to understand the value of this libretto than to mock it.'

A role reversal in the middle of the opera confuses the story. In the first half, evil appears to be personified in the High Priest Sarastro, from whom the Queen of the Night – the mother of the heroine – wishes to rescue her daughter. In the second half, Sarastro becomes the High Priest of Enlightenment, and of all that is good, whereas the Queen of the Night becomes tainted by the forces of darkness.

Many commentators have tried to rationalise this. It has been suggested that, halfway through the composition, Mozart and Schikaneder feared that they might be accused of plagiarising a similar story which was already on stage,[3] so they undertook a 'drastic revision in mid-course'. Apparently the story of *The Magic Flute* is fully comprehensible to people initiated into the ritual of Freemasonry.

Mozart's opera was written as a Singspiel, a form of opera in which music was interspersed with spoken German dialogue, instead of musical recitative. Mozart's earlier *Die Entführung* (*Il Seraglio*) took this form. The Emperor had encouraged this form of opera: it was less exclusive and more suitable for the people. But, as a result, the libretto is long, so today it is usually truncated, with some of the heavier material about virtues, trust and so forth being omitted. The cuts did not save Sir Geraint Evans, a famous Papageno, from being ticked off because he spoke his lines with a Welsh accent.

On the day Mozart took Karl and his granny, he also drove his rival Antonio Salieri and his mistress, a top diva, out to see *The Magic Flute*. They were extremely enthusiastic about it and thanked him profusely. This incident is reported in Mozart's last letter, and would seem to indicate that Mozart had a cordial relationship with Salieri, the villain of the film *Amadeus*.

How the ordinary folk comprising the audience must have been awestruck by the music! The Queen of the Night has two arias which rank among the most sensational ever composed by Mozart. Bernard Shaw, the writer and critic, thought that Sarastro's music was fit to emerge from the mouth of a god. Pamina's *Ach ich fühl's* has been called 'forty-one bars of musical perfection.' The music of the others, including that of Papageno, is also very beautiful, popular and entertaining. All this in the dingy Vienna suburbs, with an audience heaving their sides at the antics of the clown. This was the propagation of the Enlightenment. Is it surprising that Mahler chose *The Magic Flute* as the Mozart opera with which to make his début as conductor at the Vienna Hofoper a century later?

(More on the life of Mozart can be found on page 25.)

---

[3] The other show was called *Kaspar der Fagottist oder Die Zauberzither*. Schikaneder seems originally to have envisaged a puppet show in which a wicked sorcerer has stolen the Queen's daughter, who is restored by a Prince, by means of magic. The puppet show was to be called 'Lulu', based on a story by Liebeskind.

WHO'S WHO AND WHAT'S WHAT

The story below is based on the libretto. Certain directors may amend
opera stories to suit their production.

Because of the complexity of the opera and its themes and messages (as referred to earlier), a much-simplified outline of the story is first provided.

Prince Tamino falls in love with Pamina, the daughter of the Queen of the Night. She has been abducted by the Queen's enemy Sarastro, the High Priest, and is guarded by Monostatos, the head slave. The Queen promises Tamino that he can wed Pamina if he rescues her. He is given a magic flute to protect him from misfortune. He is accompanied by Papageno, the Queen's comical bird catcher, who also needs a wife. He is given a glockenspiel: a set of bells.

Three young boys lead them to the Temple of Wisdom, which surprisingly is presided over by Sarastro. They have to undergo various trials before being admitted. These involve staying silent under pressure, and braving the elements. Tamino endures the trials and wins Pamina, but the ignoble Papageno is less successful. However, he is also found a wife, Papagena, who is first presented to him in the guise of an old woman. The Queen of the Night and her accomplices are despatched in thunder and lightning.

Tamino, an Egyptian Prince, is saved from a serpent by **three ladies** in veils, who fancy him, and rush off to tell the **Queen of the Night**, their mistress. **Papageno**, the Queen's simple but popular and cheerful bird catcher, is punished for claiming that it was he who saved the Prince: his mouth is clamped with a golden padlock.

Pamina, the Queen's daughter, has been abducted by **Sarastro**, the High Priest whom the Queen loathes. Tamino falls in love with Pamina's portrait. The Queen confirms that he can marry her if he saves her. To protect him from misfortune, Tamino is given a **magic flute**. Papageno, told to accompany Tamino as his servant, is given a **glockenspiel**: a set of bells. **Three young boys** will lead them to Sarastro.

In Sarastro's fortress, **Monostatos**, the lecherous head slave, guards Pamina. Papageno comes to announce the arrival of the Prince who will rescue her. She wonders if Papageno has another half who also awaits him. He replies that he longs for one. They declare that there is nothing nobler than man and wife together reaching towards the Deity.

Tamino arrives in a glade with three temples. In order to save Pamina, he needs to demonstrate, by **trials** of constancy, endurance and discretion, that he can adopt the **virtues of manhood**. A **Speaker** tells him that he has been misled about Sarastro's character.

He is warded off from the Temples of Reason and Nature. He is surprised to hear that the Temple of Wisdom, in the middle, is Sarastro's and represents love and virtue. To gain access, he needs to extend the hand of friendship. When he plays his flute, wild animals come and go as he starts and stops.

Pamina escapes with Papageno. His bells even charm Monostatos and his slaves when they are chasing after her.

When Sarastro arrives, Pamina insists that she and Papageno must tell the truth. She confesses that she escaped for fear of Monostatos. Sarastro will not return her to her mother, because she needs to be guided by man. Mozart's music makes it clear that he is not the 'baddie' that the Queen has depicted him as. But he is not going to let her go back to the Queen.

Tamino has been caught by Monostatos and is brought into Sarastro's presence. For Tamino and Pamina, it is love at first sight. After a bit of pantomime from Monostatos, the lovers are led away for their trials. The chorus proclaims with a fanfare that when virtue and justice prevail, Earth becomes Heaven, and mortals become gods.

* * *

Three priests lead Tamino and Papageno into the temple precincts. Sarastro prays to Isis and Osiris for the couple to be granted wisdom and endurance.

Tamino affirms that they have come in love and friendship, for which they will fight. Papageno is not quite so sure. All he wants is food and sex, but he is tempted with the possibility of a wife, **Papagena**.

The first trial is the **trial of silence**. They are warned that women may try to make them talk. The three ladies try to break their silence. The men stand their ground. Tamino has passed the first test. Papageno is taken away.

Monostatos again ogles Pamina but is forestalled by the arrival of the Queen of the Night. She is furious to hear that Tamino has transferred his loyalty to Sarastro. She commands her daughter to take revenge and stab him.

When Pamina asks Sarastro not to take revenge on her mother, he says that, where he presides, there is no revenge just fraternal love.

In the next trial, Tamino and Papageno are again commanded to be silent. Papageno cannot keep quiet, especially when an old woman offers to quench his thirst.

The three boys return the magic flute and bells, which had been taken away from them, and give them some refreshment. When Pamina returns, Tamino waves her away. She is distraught.

Sarastro and the priests are optimistic that Tamino will be successful. He is presented with Pamina, who is told that Tamino is about to leave her forever. He remains silent, and, with gestures, rejects her: they part.

Papageno is told that he can never join the priesthood. He does not seem to mind; he just wants a wife. A woman appears, but she is an old hag. When told that the alternative is imprisonment, he decides he will take her. She turns into a young girl, **Papagena**, but a priest prevents him from going with her.

The three boys say that superstition will be banished and mortals will be like gods. Pamina, following the rejection by her lover, is about to stab herself. The boys stop her and say they will take her to Tamino.

Two armoured men take Tamino to the final ordeal, **The Fear of Death**. Pamina joins him, and they resolve to face it together, protected by the magic flute.[4] They walk through the gates of death, through fire, wind and flood. The priests hail their achievement.

---

[4] We hear that the flute was carved by Pamina's father out of the heart of a thousand-year-old oak.

Meanwhile Papageno, having lost Papagena, resolves to hang himself. But the three boys stop him and tell him to play his bells and Papagena will reappear. She does, and they embrace.

The Queen and the three ladies come on a rescue mission led by Monostatos, to whom she has now promised Pamina. But they cannot resist the force of the elements and are driven away.

Sarastro proclaims that light has driven out darkness. The opera concludes with a chorus praising Isis and Osiris: beauty and wisdom have been given an eternal crown.

THE INTERVAL – TALKING POINTS

The exceptional quality of the music

The Magic Flute has been described by the late Sir Charles Mackerras, the conductor, as 'a musical mosaic of such richness that it is unusual even for Mozart.' He added that 'with all its apparent simplicity, it is one of its creator's most sophisticated works.' For the French novelist Stendhal, it was a 'masterpiece'. For him, it illustrated how music can 'transform even the cheap fancies of the vulgarest imagination into conceptions of noble grace and individual genius.'

Stylistically, *The Magic Flute* is 'probably the most many-sided opera ever written.' Papageno and Papagena sing in the popular style of the Viennese suburbs. The three ladies and the three boys are also like something out of a musical comedy. The arias of the Queen of the Night are in the tradition of great Italian opera. Tamino and Pamina combine German melodic line and Italian aria; the priests and Sarastro follow Gluck. Mozart melds the various styles together. Listened to on a CD, uncluttered by the confusing fable, one is given a succession of some of the most beautiful music ever written.

To a great extent the difference in styles is a direct consequence of the characters, the 'nobility' of Sarastro and Pamina, the 'resentful lustfulness' of Monostatos, the vengeful Queen of the Night, who the writer Ernest Newman described as 'a vulture with the throat of a nightingale.' But the characters are not depicted in the orchestra with the subtlety demonstrated in the operas where Lorenzo da Ponte was librettist, *The Marriage of Figaro, Don Giovanni* or *Così fan tutte*.

Mozart broke new ground with this opera. The 'March of the Priests', and Sarastro's *O Isis und Osiris* at the start of Act 2, with the basset horns and trombones, exhibit a new sound. And this is the first time the glockenspiel was used in opera. Wagner built upon the speech–song dialogue between Tamino and the Speaker who emerges from the Temple of Reason, a combination of recitative and arioso, as a model for his own style. The opera has been called 'the ancestor, not only of the Ninth Symphony, but of the Wagnerian allegorical music-drama.'

Political correctness

The libretto gives directors various challenges with equality, ethnic equality, and feminism.

The opera portrays a clear class distinction between the 'nobility' and the lower classes: Tamino and Pamina, as against Papageno and Papagena. The lower classes are given a simple folk-song style of music, whereas princes and noble ladies are given elegant arias.

Monostatos, the slave, is specified as black. Papageno is comically alarmed at first sight of him, but he supposes that there are bound to be black men because there are black birds. In Act 2, Monostatos asks, 'Am I to forswear love because a black man is ugly? Do I then not have a heart?'

In Act 1, when asked for proof of his accusation that Sarastro is a tyrant, Tamino points to the unhappy lot of Pamina. The Speaker responds, 'So you've been beguiled by a woman; but women do little and chatter a lot.' Much the same sentiment is expressed when the three ladies tell Tamino that he is heading for Hell: he dismisses this as female gossip.

There is a less flippant and more deeply misogynist sentiment as well. On the one hand, male and female (for example, Papageno and Papagena), need each other, and Pamina and Tamino are given equal status as they go through the trials in search of the truth. On the other, the female has to be kept in check by an enlightened male, because, if not, the result will be someone as disastrous as the Queen of the Night (who so misled everybody in the first half of the opera). In the trials in Act 2, two priests sing an aria which begins 'The brotherhood's duty is to beware of woman's wiles' – *Bewahret euch vor Weibertücken.*

Sources of the opera

The Magic Flute has been scrutinised for sources. For information on Egypt, Mozart and Schikaneder will have used Abbé Terrasson's *Sethos*, published in 1731, a forgery and novel, purporting to be a historic treatise about ancient Egypt and Isis and Osiris.[5] Mozart knew something about Egypt already. He had written music for a play entitled *Thamos, King of Egypt*, back in the late 1770s.

Shakespeare is another source cited. Sarastro has been compared with Prospero, the magician in *The Tempest*, 'so reputed in dignity, and for the liberal Arts without a parallel'; 'all dedicated to closeness, and the bettering of my mind.' And Papageno has been compared with Caliban, the 'mis-shapen knave', 'disproportioned in his manners as in his shape.'

The fantastic plot in an oriental setting, accented with spectacular stage effects, has its roots in the works of the Venetian Carlo, Count Gozzi (1722–1806), a playwright, wit and satirist. Gozzi was fiercely opposed to the new realistic style of writing introduced by 'the most illustrious of the Italian comedy-writers' in the mid-eighteenth century, Carlo Goldoni.

Gozzi promoted the old style of theatre, in particular the *Commedia dell'arte*, the traditional strolling masked players, the Harlequins and Columbines, who improvised their ribald humour, often featuring sex, disease, cuckolds and geriatrics. He saw that this type of dramatic material could be used to convey messages to a large audience,

---

[5] The reference to the gods Isis and Osiris conjures thoughts of temples built by stonemasons in Egypt, just as Sarastro's name gives the flavour of Zoroaster, the Persian philosopher. In the complex and shifting pantheon of sun worship in ancient Egypt, Osiris, the funerary god, was a 'good' god, associated with sunrise, resurrection and light, the beneficent power of nature. Isis was his consort, or even his female form.

including (in his case) one about the treatment, in Eastern countries, of women as inferior.

Gozzi is largely forgotten today, except for his profound effect on opera: Puccini drew on his fable *Re Turandote*;[6] Wagner's early opera *Die Feen* was based on his fable *La donna serpente*; Prokofiev's *The Love for Three Oranges* was based on his *Fiaba dell'amore delle tre melarance*; and, more recently, Hans Werner Henze's *König Hirsch* was based on a Gozzi fable.

Papageno is comparable to Gozzi's comic Truffaldino, the average man.[7] Prince Tamino in *The Magic Flute* strives for noble action, like Gozzi's Prince Tartaglia; and in a sexist, misogynist way, Tamino and Sarastro are the saviours of mankind who overcome The Queen of the Night, who is comparable to Gozzi's sorceress Fata Morgana. The comical slave Monostatos is also comparable to characters in Gozzi's works.

Freemasonry in the plot

The plot is apparently not so absurd to persons initiated into the secrets of Freemasonry. To them, we are told, serpents, veils, golden padlocks etc., and the story generally all make considerable sense.

The 18th century was the Age of the Enlightenment, which emphasised the use of reason to advance society. Freemasonry, with its hierarchical structure (apprentices, brothers, masters), its ritual and its aspirations, took root in this environment. The intellectual classes were attracted to Freemasonry; many Freemasons saw themselves as explicitly advancing Enlightenment principles: consistent with the 18th century Age of the Enlightenment were their aims for the improvement of man through the respect and observance of ideals of a rigorous morality. Man should strive to achieve a society founded on

---

[6] Carl Maria von Weber wrote an overture and incidental music to *Re Turandote*. Goethe particularly liked the play. Schiller, the great German dramatist, translated and adapted it into German.

[7] Truffaldino, an incarnation of the standard Harlequin character in *Commedia dell'arte*, is a birdcatcher in Gozzi's *The King Stag*.

truth, justice and equality, and thus raise himself to a higher level of happiness than that of primitive man (e.g. Papageno).

Freemasonry was brought to Austria by Emperor Francis, Maria Theresa's husband. But, after his death, she banned it, because it was associated with the ideals of revolutionary France: liberty, equality and fraternity. Her son, Joseph II, removed the ban, and, during its 1780–1785 heyday in Vienna, the membership of Freemasons tripled.

Joining a typical Masonic lodge was perhaps similar to joining a gentlemen's club in Britain. Mozart and Haydn became masons, shortly before Emperor Joseph re-imposed restrictions on the Order. Mozart was exceptionally zealous. He hoped to change men's hearts through music, which has the power to create harmony among different people. It has been suggested that Masonic spirituality occupies a place in Mozart's works that is equivalent to that of Lutheran Christianity in the works of J.S. Bach.

Joseph, who was in favour of the Enlightenment, but regarded Freemasons as 'slightly silly but pretty harmless', was prepared to allow their activity and meetings within limits. He sensibly wanted to ensure that Freemasonry remained under control, that its leadership was dominated by 'his men', and that it was not a threat to public order.

At the end of 1785, very suddenly, the Emperor's attitude hardened. He tightened his squeeze in an edict in which he described Freemasonry as 'charlatanry', and which restricted it and brought it under police control. This was four weeks after Mozart had provided music for a grand memorial event for a leading Freemason, the Hungarian chancellor, who was opposed to Joseph's policies. There was bitter infighting among the lodges, and by 1790, the year of Joseph's death and the year before *The Magic Flute*, there were only 200 Freemasons in Vienna. Joseph's successors took a harder line towards Freemasonry, which was closed down for good in the mid-1790s.

Within a few years of its première, it was suggested that the opera was based on Masonic principles or ritual. Some of the suggestions are more obviously credible than others: the opera is clearly based on a progress towards enlightenment; Sarastro's second aria *In diesen heil'gen Hallen* asserts that happiness comes from fraternal love, not from revenge; the candidate for initiation knocks thrice on the door; the three boys may represent the three officers who must be present when a request for admission to the Order is made.

Mozart may have been presenting Freemasonry in a favourable light at a time when it was under attack; and possibly asserting the rights of women to be admitted on the same terms as men, if they were found worthy.

Perhaps less credible are suggestions that the Queen of the Night represents Joseph's mother Empress Maria Theresa and Tamino represents Joseph. And that Schikaneder saw the stage as an alternative way of presenting the rites which had been banned.

It is sometimes suggested that Mozart was murdered because he divulged Masonic secrets. However, it seems that information on Masonic ritual was readily available in bookshops. And indeed, in the mid-1780s, a play was staged about a woman who tries to penetrate a Masonic lodge.

Freemasonry in the music

Connections with Freemasonry are cited when the number three arises. This number has significant symbolism for Freemasonry.[8] In *The Magic Flute*, triple time – three beats in a bar – applies in various items and, in places, the melody moves in intervals of thirds and sixths. The predominant tonality of the opera is E flat, with three flats, a key convenient for wind instruments used in the Masonic ritual. And the overture sets the scene by opening and concluding with three chords based on E flat; and, unusually, it is interrupted almost exactly halfway through with a similar three-fold repetition.

However, it is hard to write classical music without employing triple time, or the key of E flat. And there are borderline matters:

[8] There were three witches in *Macbeth*, which long preceded Freemasonry.

the opening section of the Act 2 finale is scored for clarinets, bassoons and horns, the instruments apparently most frequently used in the ritual. But only two clarinets, two bassoons and two horns are specified.

Comedy or farce?

The Magic Flute has provided its share of farcical incidents with which the cast and conductor have had to cope. For example, the serpent has got entangled in the scenery and refused to fall and die, and an inexperienced Sarastro has stepped imperiously out of his chariot, got caught in his cloak, and found himself splayed out on the stage.

The boys' chariot, passing high over the stage, has got stuck, resulting in some difficulty in returning the bells to Papageno. On one occasion, he temporised, remarking, 'No wonder it's late, the chariot is run by British Rail.'

The considerable number of scenery changes specified in Act 2 can be challenging. One designer provided several freestanding triangular pillars. The scenes painted on each of the three faces, when rotated by a stagehand concealed inside, resulted in a temple quickly becoming a forest and so on. Unfortunately, two stagehands fell over. Papageno rescued them by lifting up the pillars, while improvising some dialogue based on the strapline of a contemporary advertisement: 'Guinness for strength'.

The Queen of the Night has great potential. Once, dressed as a Chicago tart clad in a feather boa, she entered in a white Rolls-Royce, protected by her 'hoods'.

Intended to be less humorous, at least by its performers, was the trio sung by Queen Victoria in a private concert at Buckingham Palace. Tamino was sung by the leading high tenor of the day Rubini; and Sarastro by the Queen's singing teacher Luigi Lablache, an enormous bass, the first Don Pasquale. A courtier made the comment about Pamina's performance, which sustains a top A and even reaches a brief B flat, 'How well Her Majesty sings, and *correctly* too.' Her comment was sufficiently cryptic to allow for several interpretations – some complimentary, some not.

ACT BY ACT

The overture starts with three big chords, suggestive of the three-fold knock at the door of a Masonic Lodge given by an aspiring Freemason. As well as recurring later in the overture, this is repeated in the temple when Tamino is about to demonstrate his fitness, his courage and his constancy.

Act 1

Tamino, an Egyptian Prince, is saved from a serpent by three veiled ladies who work for the Queen of the Night. He collapses, exhausted. The ladies each fancy him, so they dispute which of them will stay behind and which will go to tell their sovereign what has happened. They cannot agree, so they all go.

Tamino recovers to find Papageno, a popular, cheerful, but dense, bird catcher, singing how he wishes he were as good at catching girls as he is at catching birds: *Der Vogelfänger bin ich ja*. He is amazed that Tamino does not know who he is. He tells him that he is well known for making his living by selling birds to the Queen. She has never been seen by a mortal, but her ladies collect them from him. When Papageno tries to take credit for killing the serpent, the ladies return and punish him for lying by giving him water and a stone to eat, and clamping his mouth with a golden padlock.

The ladies show Tamino a portrait of the Queen's daughter, Pamina. He immediately falls in love with the girl in the picture: *Dies Bildnis ist bezaubernd schön.*[9] The ladies tell him that the Queen has selected him to save her daughter, who has been kidnapped by the wicked Sarastro, who lives in a fortress nearby.

When Tamino asks to be shown the way, the Queen appears and describes the kidnapping of Pamina. If Tamino can save her, she will be his: *O zittre nicht, mein lieber Sohn.*

Tamino wonders whether this is real. The lock prevents Papageno explaining: all he can do is to mumble *Hum Hum Hum*. The ladies

---

[9] In Gozzi's play on which Puccini based Turandot, the hero also falls in love with a miniature portrait taken from an executed rival when on the scaffold.

return. They remove the lock, and tell him not to lie in future. Love and brotherhood would triumph over hatred and malice, if all liars were punished in this way. One of them gives Tamino a magic flute, which will protect him from misfortune in his endeavours. Papageno is reluctant to accompany Tamino, because he has heard that Sarastro is as merciless as a tiger and will roast him and feed him to the dogs. To ward off evil, the three ladies give him a glockenspiel: a set of bells. Three young boys will lead them to Sarastro's fortress.

The scene changes to a magnificent chamber in Sarastro's palace. Pamina, who is worried about her mother, is incarcerated there. Her jailer is Monostatos, the head slave. He is about to try to rape her when he is confronted by Papageno. The two comical characters look at each other in horror, and Monostatos runs away. Papageno explains to Pamina that he has been sent on ahead to announce the arrival of the Prince who will rescue her. He is not worried about being caught by Sarastro, because, if he is, he will not have to make the return journey. Pamina wonders if he has a wife who is awaiting him. Sadly not. Pamina and Papageno sing of love: there is nothing nobler than man and wife reaching towards the Deity: *Mann und Weib, und Weib und Mann.*

* * *

The setting changes completely. We are in a glade in which there are three temples, of 'Nature', 'Wisdom' and 'Reason'. The three boys escort Tamino and advise him that, in order to save Pamina, he needs to demonstrate by his constancy, endurance and discretion that he possesses the virtues of manhood.

Tamino wonders if he is in the abode of the gods: in these temples, discernment, industry and the arts are to be found. Priests turn him back from the Temples of Reason on the right and Nature on the left. But a Speaker emerges from the central temple, the Temple of Wisdom, where Sarastro presides. When Tamino explains that he is in search of love and virtue, the Speaker observes that this is hardly consistent with his anger and thirst for revenge.

Tamino is about to leave when he hears that Sarastro is there. He hates Sarastro but he cannot give any compelling reasons why. He has been deceived about Sarastro being a tyrant! And deceived by a woman. Only when he comes with friendship will all be revealed, he is told.

Tamino is overjoyed when he hears that Pamina is still alive. He plays his flute and its sound calls up wild animals, which disappear when he stops: *Wie stark ist nicht dein Zauberton*. When he calls to Pamina, his flute is heard by Papageno, who answers on his bells. He rushes off to find him.

Pamina and Papageno are trying to escape. But Monostatos and the slaves restrain them, until, at the sound of the bells, they are charmed: they dance, sing and go away. Pamina and Papageno observe that if only harmony prevailed, then the world would be free and peaceful: there would be universal friendship.

When the arrival of Sarastro is announced, they despair. What should they do? Pamina answers: tell the truth, regardless.

Sarastro arrives in a coach drawn by six lions. Pamina, with compelling beauty and nobility, pleads forgiveness for her escape by saying that she was terrified by the wicked Monostatos. Sarastro's 'tone'[10] makes clear that he cannot be the pantomime 'baddie' we had been led to believe. He explains that he knows that Pamina is in love, but he will not release her into the hands of her mother. A man must guide her.

At this moment, Monostatos brings in Tamino. Tamino and Pamina fall in love at first sight, and they embrace. Although Monostatos claims credit for preventing Pamina's escape, Sarastro orders him to be punished with 77 strokes on his soles.

The heads of Tamino and Pamina are covered and they are led into the temples for their purification and trial. The chorus proclaims with a fanfare that when virtue and justice prevail, Earth becomes Heaven, and mortals become gods.

---

[10] Sarastro goes down to bottom F.

Act 2

The precise location now changes constantly, although the action is all set in the area of the temples and Sarastro's fortress. It starts in a palm grove, with the 'March of the Priests'.

Sarastro welcomes Tamino with the hand of friendship: he possesses discretion, virtue, charity. Sarastro explains that Pamina has been destined for Tamino. This was why he rescued her from her deceitful and superstitious mother. The threefold sound is heard, as at the beginning of the overture. But Tamino must first undergo various trials before he can be admitted. The Speaker wonders if Tamino can survive these, because he is merely a Prince. Sarastro answers that he is a human being. Sarastro prays that Isis and Osiris will grant the couple wisdom and endurance: *O Isis und Osiris*.

There is a thunderclap. In the forecourt of the temple, Tamino declares, when challenged, that they have come in love and friendship. When Papageno is asked if he too will fight to the death for wisdom, he replies that all he actually wants is food and a woman. The priests indicate that he might have one if he is sufficiently strong-willed not to say a word to her. They are both required to be silent. The priests counsel them both to be aware of the machinations of women.

The three ladies appear and say they are both lost. Tamino tells Papageno, who chatters, to be quiet. The ladies try to tempt them. But the priests expel the ladies. Tamino is told that he has passed the first trial.

Pamina sleeps. Monostatos desires her: *Alles fühlt der Liebe Freuden*. He is about to molest her when the Queen of the Night arrives and is told by Pamina that Tamino has gone off with the priests.

In an aria 'of the utmost difficulty', reaching top F,[11] the Queen swears vengeance and threatens to disown Pamina if she does not kill Sarastro with the dagger that she has brought for the purpose: *Der Hölle Rache kocht in meinem Herzen* ('Hellish rage seethes in my heart').

[11] This trumps even the notoriously difficult Mad Scene in Donizetti's *Lucia di Lammermoor*, in which the top E flats have presented a considerable challenge to the greatest sopranos, such as Maria Callas and Joan Sutherland.

Monostatos takes the dagger from Pamina and tries again to rape her. But in the nick of time, Sarastro arrives. When Pamina asks him not to take revenge on her mother, he says revenge is unknown in this place, only fraternal love: *In diesen heil'gen Hallen kennt man die Rache nicht.*

Mozart then provides a light contrast. Two priests command Tamino and Papageno to be silent. Papageno cannot keep quiet. He is thirsty and an old hag appears with a jug. Papageno converses with her. She says that he is her sweetheart. They are interrupted by a loud clap of thunder.

The three boys arrive in a chariot suspended high above the stage, guaranteed to raise a laugh and applause. They return the magic flute and bells, which had been taken away from Tamino and Papageno, and also give them some refreshment.

Pamina hears Tamino playing the flute. But Tamino, in the trial of silence, waves her away, as does Papageno, whose mouth is full of food. She laments in a 'simple expression of utter desolation … in forty-one bars of musical perfection' that Tamino's love has vanished: *Ach ich fühl's, es ist verschwunden.* A slight discordance on the woodwind accentuates the anguish, also expressed in her coloratura.

Sarastro and the priests are optimistic about Tamino's performance so far: *O Isis und Osiris, welche Wonne!* Pamina is brought in and she is told that Tamino is about to leave forever. The determined Tamino, together with Sarastro, leaves her: *Soll ich dich, Teurer, nich mehr sehn!*

When Papageno tries to follow, a voice orders him to go back. The priests say that he will not be punished but can never have the joy of joining the priesthood. Papageno says that the only joy he really wants is a glass of good wine, which appears. They ask if he wants anything else and the answer is a little wife: *Ein Mädchen oder Weibchen wünscht Papageno sich.* An old woman appears, and Papageno is less certain he wants an engagement to her. When told that the alternative is imprisonment, he decides he will take her. She turns into a young girl, Papagena, but a priest prevents Papageno from going with her.

The three boys reappear and say that superstition will be banished and mortals will be like gods. Pamina, feeling betrayed by her lover, appears with the dagger, about to stab herself. The boys are sympathetic; they stop her from suicide and tell her they will take her to Tamino.

The scene moves to a site beneath two mountains, one spewing fire, the other cascading a waterfall. Two armoured men take Tamino to the final trial, 'The Fear of Death'. This is sung to an old German chorale. Pamina is allowed to join him, and they resolve to go together, protected by the magic flute. They walk through the gates of death, through fire and flood. The chorus of priests proclaims that they have overcome the danger and invite them into the temple.

Meanwhile, in a garden, Papageno has lost Papagena, and resolves to hang himself. He counts to three, but she does not come.[12] The three boys stop him and tell him to play his bells and Papagena will reappear. She does, and they sing of the little children they will have.

Monostatos reappears with the Queen and the three ladies. The Queen has promised Pamina to Monostatos. But they cannot resist the force of the elements, and are driven away.

Sarastro proclaims that light, the sun's rays, have driven out the night. The opera concludes with the chorus praising Isis and Osiris for rewarding beauty and wisdom.

---

[12] The whistle call he gives has been compared to a whistle call that Wolfgang and his sister Nannerl used to give to each other.

ROSSINI:
THE BARBER OF SEVILLE

THE OPERA AND ITS COMPOSER

Rossini's *Il barbiere di Siviglia* has been called 'perhaps the greatest of all comic operas.' When he selected the story of 'The Barber of Seville' for the 1816 carnival season in Rome, he was being particularly brave. This was a well-known story with a great track record. Forty years earlier it had been sketched by the distinguished French playwright Beaumarchais (about whom more can be read on page 34) as an informal opera to entertain house-guests in a château. He later developed it into a straight play – so successfully that he was subsequently persuaded to write a sequel about Figaro in love, *La folle journée, ou Le mariage de Figaro* (1784).

By the time Mozart used this for his opera, an opera about 'The Barber' had been composed by the famous Neapolitan composer Paisiello. This had been very popular indeed: it ran every season in Vienna in the mid-1780s.

Paisiello was in his mid-seventies by the time Rossini composed his opera. He was a distinguished, if contentious, figure: when the Bourbon monarchy was restored in Naples in 1815, he was sacked from all his posts; he had backed the wrong side. He had no interest in Rossini having a success.

It was to no avail that, to avoid upsetting him, Rossini changed the title to *Almaviva, ossia l'Inutile Precauzione* (*Almaviva, or the Useless Precaution*). The disruption by Paisiello's supporters of the première in Rome on 20 February 1816 has been called one of the three major operatic fiascos, the others being the 1861 Paris production of Wagner's *Tannhäuser* and the first night of *Carmen* in 1875.

At the première, the part of the Count was taken by the famous tenor Manuel Garcia. Early in Act 1, when Garcia, disguised as

'Lindoro', began to serenade Rosina, a string on his guitar broke, so he had to stop and mend it. The derision of the partisan audience increased when Figaro was seen entering with a replacement guitar. Soon after the Count resumed his serenade,[1] Rosina urged him on with *Segui, o caro* ('Continue, my love, continue'). This caused a further hullabaloo. It was disastrous. At the end of Act 1, Rossini shrugged his shoulders and clapped, an attitude which so annoyed the audience that Act 2 could not be heard for the disruption.

There were other problems that night: apparently the music teacher, Don Basilio, tripped over a trapdoor and had a persistent nosebleed; and a cat – not part of the cast – walked onto the stage and caused havoc.

Rossini's libretto was reluctantly provided by Cesare Sterbini, a civil servant and dilettante who had supplied him with the libretto for an unsuccessful opera *Torvaldo e Dorliska*, which Rossini had already composed for that same 1816 carnival season. Sterbini was competent in French, and kept very close to Beaumarchais's text. He also had the Paisiello opera to use as a model. He delivered his libretto of *The Barber* in twelve days.[2]

Rossini was said to have composed his score in a fortnight, although in fact it was more like six weeks. He borrowed (as was the custom) considerably from other works of his. The overture had already been heard in his *Elisabetta, Regina d'Inghilterra* and that in turn had been borrowed from his *Aureliano*. The music for Don Basilio's well-known aria *La calunnia* came from Rossini's *Sigismondo*. The music for the cavatina *Ecco ridente* had also done service in *Aureliano*.

Although the first night was a fiasco, the mood quickly changed. On the second night, Rossini thought it prudent to stay at home

[1] Manuel Garcia was the father of the famous singers Maria Malibran and Pauline Garcia. His granddaughter claimed that, because of the rush, Rossini got him to write his own first-act serenade. This was not exceptional. Performers often substituted a different aria at any stage during an opera, however irrelevant it might be, if it suited their purposes, particularly by showing off their voice to better effect. These were known as *arias di baule* – 'luggage arias'. Jenny Lind, when singing Rosina, used to import an *aria di baule* into the singing lesson. In this case, it is more likely that Garcia was merely left to improvise the accompaniment, the tenor part being written by Rossini himself.

[2] In the middle of the rehearsals, the owner-impresario of the Teatro Argentina, who had signed Rossini's contract, dropped dead. But the show had to go on.

and went to bed. He was woken by the sound of applause outside his lodgings, people shouting 'bravissimo Figaro'. The opera has been a resounding success ever since. According to a mid-19th century English critic, Rossini, with his vivacity, 'the freshness of his melodies, the richness of his combinations' succeeded in 'intoxicating the general public as no other composer earlier or later has done.' The critic admired 'his wondrous grace, his fertility of invention, his admirable treatment of the voice, and his simple and effective taste in arrangement of the orchestra.'

And his music invited comparison with that of Mozart. But few today would accept the view of the distinguished French novelist Stendhal, who in 1823 reckoned 'the slow sad strains of Mozart' were 'dull and heavy' compared to the music of Rossini; and that if Mozart were to appear anew, in Italy, 'at the première, he [too] would be hissed off the stage.' Stendhal however emphasised the Italianness of Rossini, and pointed out that 'Love is not the same in Bologna as it is in Königsberg.'

Doubtless, Rossini succeeded in providing a 'kind of freshness, which evokes a smile of pleasure at every bar.' *The Barber* is full of great tunes, the best known being Figaro's famous *Largo al factotum*. The roles are very balanced and all the principals have great music. Some of the memorable items are the Count's serenade *Se il mio nome*, Rosina's cavatina *Una voce poco fa*, the Doctor's patter song *A un dottor della mia sorte*, and the quintet when Don Basilio is sent off home to bed, *Buona sera, mio Signore*.

However, Rossini went out of fashion in the 1830s. His music was regarded as 'overcharged and out of taste.' As the century wore on, and 'commentators wrangled about outer forms and inner meanings', he seemed simply superficial, 'the spoiled idol of fashion, a mere tune-spinner whose seductions must prove transient, palling, unreal.' Amazingly, we hear that 'there were some good and cultivated Englishmen, who, on principle, when Signor Rossini entered one music shop, repaired to another.'

It has been suggested that Rossini brought comic opera, the *opera buffa*, to its peak. Although composers such as Donizetti (in *Don*

Pasquale and *L'Elisir d'Amore*) wrote some good comedies, there was nothing quite like *The Barber* until Verdi's *Falstaff* in 1893.

When Rossini visited Beethoven towards the end of his life, the great composer complimented him on *The Barber* and suggested that he restrict his output to comic opera. As this was regarded as a relatively inferior form of opera, the compliment may have been suitably backhanded. Looked at in retrospect however, it seems certain that 'Signor Rossini will endure so long as the art of Music lasts.'

Gioachino (Joachim) Rossini was born in a leap year, on 29 February 1792, in Pesaro, on the Adriatic coast near Ravenna. As a boy he was a gifted singer. He studied at the academy in Bologna. His first opera, a one-act farce, was staged in Venice when he was only eighteen. By the time of *Tancredi* (which includes the well-known tune *Di tanti palpiti*), a further seven of his operas had been staged, and he was still only twenty. *Tancredi* assured his fame. Although both *The Barber* and *La Cenerentola* were written for theatres in Rome, Rossini moved to Naples where he was able to build his fortune, not least from his partnership in the gambling business run in the theatre foyer.

In 1822, Rossini married Isabella Colbran, a Spanish soprano and mistress of Domenico Barbaja, the colourful theatre director in Naples. He had composed many operas for her, including *La donna del lago* and *Semiramide*, but not the opera buffa for which he is best known today.

In 1823 he moved to London, and then to Paris, where he directed the Théâtre-Italien, and later the Opéra. By the age of 31, he had already written 34 operas. His pace slowed and he adapted earlier operas – for example, much of *Le Comte Ory* was taken from *Il viaggio a Reims*.

After *Guillaume Tell* in August 1829, he composed no further operas, even though he lived for a further 40 years. There are various explanations: pressure from his father; urethral disorders and depression; the fact that he was now economically secure. Also, he may have been concerned that he was out of date, and being overtaken by the grand operas of Meyerbeer.

Rossini began an affair with a prominent courtesan, Olympe Pelissier. He moved to Bologna with her, and he married her in 1846 after Isabella died. Having returned to Paris in 1855 for medical help, he took on a new lease of life. He regained his former exuberance and appetite for good food, and composed again.

At that time, Paris was well known for its salons, presided over by aristocratic and plutocratic ladies. In great houses, artists, writers, musicians, scholars and politicians congregated regularly. The Rossinis' salon included most of the leading artists and public figures. Rossini died in his villa in Passy, then just outside Paris, on 13 November 1868.

WHO'S WHO AND WHAT'S WHAT

The story below is based on the libretto. Certain directors may amend opera stories to suit their production.

Count Almaviva, an important grandee, has arrived, using the incognito '**Lindoro**', at the house of **Doctor Bartolo** on a piazza in Seville. He has come to woo the lovely **Rosina**, whose guardian is the elderly and miserly Doctor, who has his eye on her fortune and wants to marry her himself.

The Doctor's house is also the base for the barber, **Figaro**, a former employee of the Count. Figaro is now, as a by-product of his business, Seville's indispensable 'fixer'. As he puts it, the cheese has fallen on the macaroni: that is, the Count has come to the right place. And Figaro knows that he can get a good tip if he helps the Count achieve his objectives. (The role of the 'purse', the 'harmonising influence of gold' in oiling the wheels is a recurrent feature of this opera.)

The opera begins at dawn, when the Count's servant **Fiorello** creeps in with various musicians to perform the serenade. At first,

Rosina does not appear. When at last she does, she drops a message in which she asks her serenader to identify himself.

Rosina wants Figaro to help, and he reveals that the serenader is 'Lindoro'.

The Doctor, ever suspicious, interrogates the servants, the manservant **Ambrogio** and the governess and housekeeper **Berta**. Rosina's music teacher **Don Basilio**, an idle but grasping scoundrel, warns the Doctor that Count Almaviva has arrived in town; however, appropriately remunerated, he can spread scandalous rumours about him so that he will be driven out.

Rosina is caught by the Doctor having written a billet-doux to her lover. None of her explanations or excuses cuts any ice with him: *A un dottor della mia sorte*. He resolves to keep her under lock and key.

To obtain access, with the assistance of Figaro, the Count disguises himself first as a drunken soldier. There is such a commotion that the Watch arrives and the **officer** attempts to arrest the Count, but he pulls rank and avoids it.

After the interval, the Count arrives, disguised now as 'Alonso', a music teacher substituting for Don Basilio, who is ill. He ingratiates himself by giving Bartolo the letter which Rosina wrote to 'Lindoro'. This could be helpful to the Doctor's cause. During the **Singing Lesson**,[3] Rosina and Lindoro/Alonso, arrange to elope, and Figaro, who has come to shave the Doctor, gets the keys to the window to facilitate her escape. But they are interrupted by Don Basilio, who they manage to persuade that he looks as if he has scarlet fever and should go home to bed: *Buona sera, mio Signore*.[4]

Bartolo calls Rosina aside. He claims to have got from the jealous mistress of Count Almaviva the love letter which Rosina sent to him. Clearly Lindoro/Alonso is merely a decoy working for the rakish

[3] The Singing Lesson provided a particular opportunity for a 'luggage' *aria di baule*, of the variety referred to earlier. A popular one has been *Di tanti palpiti* from Rossini's *Tancredi*. Stendhal said this drew the sobriquet *aria dei risi*, a 'rice aria', because Rossini, a gourmet, composed it in the time it would take to cook a bowl of rice, four minutes.

[4] Berta, the elderly governess, is given her own aria: she expresses herself disgusted with all the goings-on, and with love. However, even at her age, she reckons that she is not beyond a bit of a romp: *Il vecchiotto cerca moglie*.

Count who wants to abduct and seduce her. She is shocked and out-raged that she is not loved by the impecunious Lindoro, the man she actually wants. She betrays the plan to elope.

It is night. There is a **storm**. Figaro and the Count arrive for the elopement. Rosina, in her fury, at first repels 'Lindoro', claiming that he pretended to love her in order to sacrifice her to the lust of the wicked Count. Whereupon 'Lindoro' reveals that he is not 'Lindoro', but is actually Count Almaviva himself.

The Doctor meanwhile has gone to fetch the police to prevent the elopement. He first takes the precaution of moving the ladder by which they planned to escape. The couple has no choice other than to get married immediately. Fortunately a **lawyer**, who the Doctor had brought to marry him to Rosina, is at hand to sign the register before the Doctor returns.

The police arrive to arrest 'Lindoro', but he discloses that he is in fact Count Almaviva. He waves the marriage contract, which shows that he and Rosina are already united. The Doctor realises that the game is up and that he should have allowed them to elope: the removal of the ladder was indeed a futile precaution.[5] All wish the happy couple well.

THE INTERVAL: TALKING POINTS

Features of Rossini's style: coloratura, crescendo, and patter

Rossini was faced with a narrative comprising long stretches of rela-tively boring recitative necessary to take complicated, even if comic, action forward. This was interspersed with arias where internal intro-spective feelings are expressed. He recognised the severe risk of the action freezing and the audience becoming bored. He avoided this by his use of glittering coloratura, his 'trademark' crescendo, and his use of patter. There is no possibility of feeling that the action has become

---

[5] In the play, Figaro concludes that when youth and love are at one, anything that age tries to do to stop them is 'a futile precaution'.

static: the listener is just gobsmacked by the fantastic tour de force of the singers, and the composer himself.

Coloratura is the elaborate ornamentation of melody with dazzling runs and arpeggios, either notated in the score itself or extemporised by the singer.[6] Sometimes these appear in solos; often, they are sung in duets, for example, by the Count and Rosina in a moment of passion, when they are about to elope. The technical demands, achieving clarity and uniformity, are enormous.

Rossini's crescendos are extraordinarily effective, but generally surprisingly simple in structure. High-speed percussive rhythmic figures, built around the simplest of sequential chord progressions, are repeated relentlessly, mainly on the strings, with the singer(s) almost on a monotone.

The crescendo provides the perfect medium to convey Don Basilio's explanation about how well-placed slander can spread like wildfire, *La calunnia è un venticello*: the raw material appears first in the strings during the recitative, then there is a gradual increase in orchestral power, and an enormous crescendo with the big drum giving a thunder crash.

Figaro's *Largo al factotum,* when the barber first swaggers onto the stage, is 'one of the most rapid patter songs ever written'. The libretto is simply Figaro describing his role in life. Even with a good tune, this description could be tedious and grind to a halt. Not so; it is driven forward by the comic and almost breathlessly high speed of delivery, and an added crescendo, so that the listener has no option other than to applaud.

A similar effect is created in *A un dottor della mia sorte* to depict Doctor Bartolo at first being reasonable, then working up his sense of outrage that the girl will not confess. There is a dramatic key

---

[6] Much of Rosina's *Una voce* is written out in the score. A diva will usually add her own decoration, like the conventional decoration of her penultimate bar on the high B, or previously on the G for 'I can be obedient, ruled, guided ...' Schumann complained that Pauline Viardot, as Rosina, 'transformed the whole opera into a great variation. She scarcely left one melody untouched.' Another soprano sang *Una Voce* to Rossini and interpolated masses of coloratura. When she stopped, Rossini, ever the humorist, asked, 'But what were you singing?'

modulation to underline the climax when he tells her that if she won't pull herself together, he will have her locked up in her room.[7]

Characterisation: Rosina

There is no great subtlety, no careful musical characterisation such as we would find in Mozart. Once Rosina has had a chance to appear more than fleetingly, after around three-quarters of an hour of the performance, she tells us in *Una voce poco fa* that 'if crossed in love, I shall be a viper.' But there is nothing in the music to underwrite this characteristic, just glittering coloratura. The role is very difficult to put across.

Stendhal, the French novelist, criticises a non-musical flaw in her character. He accuses Rossini of falling into the 'vulgar error, common to sensual and unrefined persons in every land, of thinking all women alike.' By this, Stendhal alluded to the brazen women Rossini had doubtlessly been consorting with that evening.

Thus Rosina does not come across as a modest virgin of eighteen, as she should, but rather as 'some good-looking woman, perhaps twenty-six years of age, ardent in temperament and more than a little inclined to flirtation, debating with a confidant upon the ways and means to grant an assignation to a man who has caught her fancy.' She has no reservations about falling for 'Lindoro' without knowing anything whatsoever about him.

And the part itself is not one in which a prima donna can really 'star'. It has been said that 'no single artist can shift the emphasis from Figaro and all the colourful characters so beautifully balanced by Rossini.' The bravura performances demanded from Figaro, the Count, Doctor Bartolo, Don Basilio – all of them – inevitably compete with Rosina and prevent her from shining out in the way in which the prima donna does in, say, Donizetti's *Lucia di Lammermoor*.

Yet the part demands a prima donna with top-quality performing ability. Apart from the demands of the coloratura, her range is very wide and demanding indeed. In *Una voce*, she hits top G several

---

[7] Patter was used extensively later in the century by Gilbert and Sullivan.

Nellie Melba was a renowned Rosina

times and concludes on top B. The top C she reaches almost at the end of Act 1 is at the top of the normal soprano range. By contrast, the bottom A flat when she declares herself dumbstruck like a statue (*Freddo ed immobile come una statua*) is almost at the bottom of the contralto range; as is the A flat she descends to when she senses that the elopement is becoming a real possibility. The role requires an unusual singer, such as Pauline Viardot was in the 19th century, one who can reach the high notes as well as luscious deep mezzo and contralto notes.

Paisiello, the first composer of 'The Barber'

Giovanni Paisiello (1740–1816), a contemporary of Mozart, was born in Taranto in the heel of Italy. He died just over three months after

Rossini's première, having composed more than 80 operas, and having been very successful and influential. His 'Barber' was performed in September 1782, when he was based at the court of Catherine the Great in St Petersburg. Later, back in Naples and working for the Bourbon Monarchy, he became 'the most favoured musician in the city.'

But he had to play his cards carefully, what with the gyrating politics during the Napoleonic period. When he was first introduced to Napoleon, who at the time was only a general, Paisiello, who knew how to creep, addressed him as 'Sire'. Napoleon told him not to, whereupon he called him 'Your Majesty', adding that he was used to addressing sovereigns who were pygmies by comparison with him.

The Bonapartes became considerable patrons: Paisiello was successively chapel composer to Napoleon, his brother Joseph, King of Naples, and Napoleon's brother-in-law Marshal Murat, also King of Naples. But when the Bourbons were restored in 1815, he was disgraced for having supported the wrong side. Murat was shot.

ACT BY ACT

The overture calls the audience to attention. There is then a jaunty rhythm, followed by a good tune and then repeated crescendos, Rossini's trademark. While the audience may have thought that the overture portrayed the spirit of the opera, including 'the threats and bluster of Dr Bartolo the elderly, jealous and enamoured guardian, and all the plaintive sighs of his pretty ward', this cannot be so: it had already been used in two of Rossini's operas.

Act 1

It is dawn, beneath the balcony of Doctor Bartolo's house on a piazza in Seville, the time when Rosina habitually comes out on the balcony, and the Count comes beneath, intending to serenade her. His servant Fiorello creeps in with several musicians. With guitar accompaniment, the Count starts his serenade, *Ecco ridente in cielo* ('Behold, in the smiling sky the lovely dawn is breaking'). But she does not appear.

So the musicians are dismissed brusquely. Somehow the city remains asleep despite the Count shouting *Basta, basta* and the orchestral crescendo that accompanies him. The Count observes the depths to which love leads a man of his status when he has to go about serenading his beloved at dawn![8]

Figaro is heard going to work, singing the famous *Largo al factotum*: make way for Seville's indispensable fixer! He enjoys his job, not least for the mixture of add-on services and errands he carries out for a great variety of customers, male and female: he knows everything, does everything.

During a long recitative, Figaro bumps into the Count, his former master. Their conversation tells us the necessary background. The Count has seen Rosina and has fallen in love with her, but wants to remain incognito and be loved for himself rather than his status. It turns out that Figaro in effect runs the Doctor's household. The Doctor wants to marry Rosina, who is not his daughter but his ward.

Rosina appears on the balcony with a piece of paper, which she tells the Doctor is an aria from the new opera, 'The Futile Precaution'. She drops it over the ledge, giving the Count the chance to take it while the Doctor descends to retrieve it (unsuccessfully). The Doctor, most put out by this, and highly suspicious, tells her to get back into the house: he is determined to marry her himself that very day, and sets off to hasten the wedding.[9]

The letter is a message, in which Rosina asks the serenader to identify himself. When the Count espies Rosina behind the shutters, he serenades her again, this time with *Se il mio nome*: 'If you want to know my name, call me Lindoro' – he does not want to disclose his identity or wealth; indeed he pretends he has nothing but his heart to offer her.

---

[8] There is less political innuendo in *The Barber* than in *Figaro*. This is one example.

[9] Sir Geraint Evans, as Bartolo, wanted to indicate a more substantial reason for leaving the house. He borrowed the white miniature poodle of the Count (Peter Glossop) and took it for a walk. With Glossop in the wings on the other side of the stage, the dog strained at the leash and seemed suitably keen to go. They also gave the dog a bow matching the one Bartolo was wearing on his wig.

The Count and Figaro sing the almost breathless duet *All'idea di quell metallo*. Tempted by the prospect of gold,[10] Figaro agrees to help the Count get into the house before nightfall, and suggests that he disguise himself as a soldier who has been billeted on the house. He should also pretend to be drunk so that the Doctor will be less suspicious. He tells the Count how to find his shop: number 15. Rapturously, the Count anticipates his rendezvous. Equally rapturously, Figaro contemplates his fee.[11]

The scene shifts to the inside of the Doctor's house where Rosina sings of her love for Lindoro: *Una voce poco fa*. The voice she has just heard has thrilled her heart. Come what may, she will get her way and Lindoro will be hers. Maybe Figaro can help her?

She tells Figaro that living in the house is like living in a tomb, and wants him to take a letter. When Doctor Bartolo returns, he suspects that she has been speaking to Figaro, who he curses for his barber-surgeon's stock-in-trade, including the sneezing powder which makes everyone in the house sneeze. The Doctor asks the servants, Ambrogio the manservant and Berta the governess and housekeeper,[12] whether Rosina has been talking with Figaro, but their sneezing precludes a reply.

Don Basilio, who has recently become Rosina's music teacher, arrives. He is an idle fellow, but a busybody. He warns the Doctor that Count Almaviva, who is suspected of being Rosina's amour, has arrived in town. However he, Basilio, appropriately remunerated, can fix it – he will spread scandalous rumours about the Count so he will be driven out: *La calunnia è un venticello* ('Calumny starts as a gentle

---

[10] The ebullient Figaro is perhaps surprisingly obsessed with money. By the time of Mozart's *The Marriage of Figaro*, the Count has taken both Figaro and Don Basilio into his service, so they were well rewarded for their part in helping him win the Countess.

[11] Rossini combines his coloratura, his crescendo and his high-speed patter in the duet, which enables much detail to be covered, and the action to be moved forward. In other circumstances, this might have necessitated the use of yet another piece of recitative. This is a tour de force, despite the fact that Figaro and the Count participating in the same music belies any possible suggestion that music is being used to delineate different characters.

[12] Berta in Mozart's *The Marriage of Figaro* becomes Marcellina. In *The Barber*, Marcellina is a name given to Figaro's daughter, although she does not appear.

breeze but develops into a resounding thunderstorm [note the big drum], and finishes a man off'). A perfect aria for a Rossini crescendo.

Bartolo and Basilio go off together to draft the marriage contract. But Figaro overheard their conversation and warns Rosina that the Doctor is planning her marriage that very day. Figaro invents a story that his cousin has arrived and is in love with her, and wants some sign, a couple of lines in a letter will do, that she is in love with him. She already has the note tucked away in her bosom.

When the Doctor comes back, the ink on her fingers, the usage of notepaper and the quill show that she has been writing a note to somebody. He dismisses her excuses that she has used one sheet to wrap sweets to send to Figaro's daughter Marcellina and the pen to design a flower to embroider. In another patter song, he tells her that none of this cuts any ice with him: *A un dottor della mia sorte* ('To a doctor of my standing, you should try some better excuses'). When she does not respond, he threatens to have her locked in her room whenever he leaves the house.

Berta lets the Count in. He is disguised as a soldier, and seems drunk: he cannot get Doctor Bartolo's name right. Anyway, the Doctor claims that he is exempt from having soldiers billeted on him. When the Count refuses to leave, there is a brawl. Meanwhile Rosina has tried to pass the Count the note. By the time the Doctor gets hold of it, he finds it is just the laundry list. The ensuing commotion draws crowds of people.

The Watch arrives and an officer arrests the Count. But, once he shows the officer his papers, they salute him and withdraw. Everyone is astonished. The act ends with the six protagonists joining imitatively in a chorus: *Freddo ed immobile come una statua* ('I'm dumbstruck like a statue. My head thumps like hammers on an anvil'). This gives Rossini ample opportunity for rhythmic thumping, crescendo and patter. At the end, Rosina hits top C.

Act 2

The act opens in Bartolo's music room. He suspects that the soldier had something to do with Almaviva. The Count arrives, disguised now as the absurd and ingratiating 'Alonso', a music teacher substituting for Basilio, who is ill: *Pace e gioia sia con voi.*

The Doctor is suspicious. To reassure him and to get access to Rosina, 'Alonso' explains that he has come from the inn where Count Almaviva is staying. There, he has got from the Count's jealous mistress the love letter which Rosina sent to Lindoro. Rosina will be outraged if she hears that he let Count Almaviva have it.

The Doctor fetches Rosina for a music lesson. She recognises that 'Alonso' is 'Lindoro'. The Singing Lesson begins and Rosina sings a love song to him, ostensibly an aria from the new opera 'The Futile Precaution': *Contro un cor che accende amore* ('Love will always triumph').

While Bartolo dozes off, Rosina pleads with 'Lindoro' to rescue her. Bartolo wakes up and also sings a love song, in which he has changed the words so that they are addressed to Rosina; he also does a little dance.

Figaro arrives to shave the Doctor. While 'Lindoro' and Rosina snatch another moment together, Figaro fetches the shaving equipment from the locked closet. This enables him to obtain the house keys, including the key of the window; and his clumsiness also causes a considerable diversion.

When the shaving of the Doctor begins, Don Basilio turns up, much to the surprise/consternation of everybody. But amidst the confusion, and with the help of a purse of money, they persuade Don Basilio that he looks as if he has scarlet fever (then a very dangerous disease, and the cause of many complications) and they send him off home to bed: *Buona sera, mio Signore.*

While the Doctor is distracted by the shaving, the Count arranges to elope with Rosina at midnight. The Doctor, ever suspicious, overhears the lovers whispering sweet nothings (and mentioning the word 'disguise'). He chases the Count and Figaro out of the house. Rosina retreats to her room.

Berta, the elderly governess, expresses herself disgusted with all the goings-on, and with love, except that, even at her age, she is not beyond a bit of a frolic: *Il vecchiotto cerca moglie.*

The Doctor returns with Basilio, who tells him that he has never come across an 'Alonso'. Indeed, for all he knows, the man could be the Count, especially in view of the size of the purse he received from him. The Doctor is confused by this; he panics and realises that it is essential that he marry Rosina immediately. He sends Basilio to fetch the lawyer, there and then.

The Doctor then taunts Rosina, by waving at her the letter she sent to Lindoro, insinuating that it was obtained from Count Almaviva's mistress. The Count had been showing it off as evidence of his prowess; indeed he has been using Lindoro to procure Rosina for himself. Rosina falls for this deception, this calumny. She is furious because she loves Lindoro and not Count Almaviva. In her rage, she betrays the plan to elope. Bartolo goes to fetch the police.

There is a storm. It is night. Figaro and 'Lindoro' arrive for the elopement. Rosina however repels 'Lindoro', who only pretended to love her in order to procure her for the wicked Count. She loves Lindoro. At this, 'Lindoro' explains that he and Count Almaviva are one and the same – *Almaviva son io; non son Lindoro* – whereupon Rosina is overjoyed, and the Count proposes. Figaro gets worried that they should be getting along instead of falling into each other's arms: *Zitti, zitti, piano, piano*.

They see two people and a lantern. When they try to go, they find that the ladder by which they planned to escape has been removed by the Doctor, when he left to fetch the police. When the lawyer and Basilio arrive, the Count bribes Basilio to push off, and tells him that if he does not he will shoot him. He gets the lawyer to marry him to Rosina there and then.

The police arrive with the Doctor. When they try to arrest 'Lindoro', he discloses that he is in fact the Count Almaviva. He waves the signed contract, which shows that he and Rosina are married. For Bartolo, the game is up. *Cessa di più resistere*, sings the Count. Bartolo laments that he took the futile precaution of removing the ladder from the balcony in order to prevent the elopement. The Count says he does not need Rosina's dowry, which he presents to the Doctor. Figaro's work is done. All wish the happy couple well: *Amore e fede eterna*.

ROSSINI:
LA CENERENTOLA

THE OPERA AND ITS COMPOSER

Within just a year of the première of his *The Barber of Seville*, which has been described as 'perhaps the greatest of all comic operas', Rossini staged *La Cenerentola* for the carnival season[1] in Rome. It was first performed at the Teatro della Valle on 25 January 1817.

Rossini had not yet reached his 25th birthday but *La Cenerentola* (Cinderella) was already his twentieth opera. He had staged the première of *Otello* in Naples less than eight weeks earlier, such was the frantic pace at which he worked.

As librettist, Rossini used Jacopo Ferretti.[2] Ferretti wrote over 50 opera libretti, of which *La Cenerentola* is the most enduring. Around Christmas in 1816, the censors in Rome, then ruled by the Roman Catholic Church, were being difficult about another subject which had been proposed by theatre management. So, having discussed between 20–30 alternatives, some of which were deemed too serious or complex, some too costly, some unsuitable for the singers available, we are told that Rossini and Ferretti lit upon the story of Cinderella. Ferretti had originally thought of calling Rossini's opera 'Angioline', but then the censors had difficulty with this title because there was a celebrity beauty called Angiolina who was turning the hearts of all the men in Rome at the time.

La Cenerentola (*Cinderella or Goodness Triumphant*) was written, composed and staged within 24 days. During this time it had to be

---

[1] Carnival was a relic of pagan times and ran for about eight weeks between Epiphany (early January) and Shrove Tuesday, the day before Lent.
[2] As well as administering the tobacco monopoly in the Papal States, Jacopo Ferretti (1784–1852) was associated with the Teatro della Valle where he later wrote libretti for three of Donizetti's more obscure operas.

cleared with the censor, the libretto had to be typeset, the musical parts copied, the scenery and dresses designed, and the singers, orchestra and chorus rehearsed. It is not surprising, therefore, that Ferretti cribbed from earlier Cinderellas; nor that Rossini borrowed the overture from another opera of four months earlier and outsourced the routine recitative work and some of the numbers to a minor composer. Rossini also used a part of an aria from *The Barber* for the grand finale; and he was accused of basing one aria on a popular opera by Cimarosa, who had died nearly two decades earlier.

In view of the rush, we can appreciate why *La Cenerentola* was not an immediate success. In his old age, Rossini joked that the sound of a train whistling would remind him of the reception of some of his operas, including *La Cenerentola*. The venue did not help. The orchestra was virtually amateur; the standard of performance was poor. Because the Papal authorities disapproved of theatrical activity, performances took place in temporary wooden buildings, which were dark, dirty and pungently short of facilities.

Within a few years, however, the popularity of *La Cenerentola* had increased enormously. For example, in Trieste in the early 1820s, a scheduled run of 30 performances was extended to 100. It became the first opera to be staged in Australia. It then went out of fashion, as did most of Rossini's works other than *The Barber*. *La Cenerentola* was revived between the First and Second World Wars. Today, it features among the most popular operas.

(More on the life of Rossini can be found on pages 110–111.)

WHO'S WHO AND WHAT'S WHAT

The story below is based on the libretto. Certain directors may amend opera stories to suit their production.

Don Magnifico, a down-at-heel and comical baron, has two unpleasant daughters **Clorinda** and **Tisbe**. He also has a pretty and charitable stepdaughter, **Angiolina (Cinderella)**, who is oppressed and abused by the family.

Cinderella

The Cinderella fairytale had been used in operas already. An extremely successful version of *Cendrillon* composed by Nicolas Isouard (1775–1818), the Maltese composer and music publisher, had been staged in Paris in 1810, and led to 'a vogue for fairy tale operas.' Another opera based on the story was produced in St Petersburg in 1810 by the Prussian composer Daniel Steibelt (1765–1823).

The rags-to-riches tale had already featured in many cultures and over many centuries. In 1696–1697, a collection of fairy stories was published, having been assembled by Charles Perrault (1628–1703), a Parisian lawyer who worked in the office of the finance minister of Louis XIV. This included stories such as Sleeping Beauty, Little Red Riding Hood, Blue Beard and Puss in Boots.

Perrault's collection was the source of the Cinderella story most familiar to modern pantomime audiences. This features a fairy godmother who turns a pumpkin into the coach in which Cinderella, magnificently dressed, goes to a ball, from which she must return before midnight. In the rush to get away in time, Cinderella leaves behind one of her glass slippers, which the Prince uses to track her down.

However, Cinderella's glass slipper could not feature in Rome in Rossini's time. Ankles then had connotations which subsequent centuries have associated with attributes of the female form higher up the body (the Greek epic poet Homer celebrated women for their ankles and cheeks rather than for their legs and breasts). The rulers of the Papal States would not tolerate the display of an ankle, in public at least.

Don Ramiro, Prince of Salerno, has returned to his country estate nearby. He is about to throw a party at which he will choose his bride. To identify the true personality of his potential spouse, he swaps clothes with his valet, **Dandini**.

The prince's tutor, the philosopher **Alidoro**, disguises himself as a beggar to test the charity of the candidates (he substitutes for the traditional fairy godmother in the fairy story). He conveys Angiolina to the ball. The prince, disguised as Dandini, proposes to her, but she hurriedly leaves, having given him one of her matching bracelets, and tells him that he must seek her out. Alidoro arranges to have the prince's coach break down outside the baron's house. This happens in a **storm**. Thus Ramiro arrives at Don Magnifico's castle and finds his bride.

THE INTERVAL: TALKING POINTS
The moral of the tale

Rossini labelled *La Cenerentola* a *dramma giocoso* rather than an *opera buffa*, or comic opera. While the subject matter and its treatment, with its many comic elements, is necessarily lighthearted, the moral of *La Cenerentola* is essentially serious: it portrays the triumph of virtue over snobbery. But perhaps it is an exaggeration to claim, as one distinguished critic has, that it 'is neither a million miles from Jane Austen, nor two million miles from any British panto tradition.'

Angiolina (Cinderella) is presented as an essentially sentimental character rather than as the superficial soubrette we might expect to find in a farce or pantomime. This 'seriousness' is underlined by her part being composed for a contralto rather than a soprano. Her music, which drops to bottom A, contrasts effectively with the light-headed high-pitched sopranos of her sisters.

Lead parts in Rossini's time were often written for a contralto. Later in the century, the contralto and mezzo-soprano had been superseded by the high soprano, and *prima donna* roles for the former two were consequently fewer. Verdi was the primary cause of this; he had demanded and promoted much higher voices, a development which listeners sometimes have reason to regret.[3]

Differing views on the quality of the music

Commentators sometimes compare the depth of Mozart's operas with the apparent shallowness of Rossini's. Berlioz was 'disgusted' by Rossini's familiar trademark, the 'brutal crescendo[4] and big drum', and we can be irritated by another of his mannerisms, the frequent but sudden hiccup on the second beat of a bar.

Rossini has had many detractors and many apologists. In the 1820s, Stendhal, the novelist of *La Chartreuse de Parme*, deplored the triviality, distasteful vulgarity and superficiality of *La Cenerentola*, and went so far as to say that some of it afflicted him with 'a faint feeling of nausea.' Later in the century, in 1892, at the time of the centenary of Rossini's birth, Bernard Shaw, the Irish music critic and playwright, disliked Rossini's sensationalism. For him, Rossini was 'one of the greatest masters of claptrap that ever lived.'

However, many commentators praise Rossini's music for its warmth, its ebullience, its wit, its 'ethereal feather-lightness'. Wagner conceded that he was as important to his age as were Palestrina, Bach and Mozart to theirs. And it has been suggested that Rossini brought the 'opera buffa' to its peak. Although Donizetti wrote some good comedies, for example *L'Elisir d'Amore*, *La Fille du Régiment* and *Don Pasquale*, there was nothing quite up to Rossini's *The Barber of Seville* until Verdi's *Falstaff* in 1893.

We know that Rossini borrowed, subcontracted and plagiarised, liberally. This is bound to be disconcerting, because music is expected to support specific feelings and emotions, and these are not easily transferable from the topic of one opera to another. How can it be

---

[3] Verdi was invited to write the Violetta part of *La Traviata* for a contralto, but he refused. He emphasised that he wrote operas so that they could be re-performed (thereby making him money), and any work written for the contralto would not be hired out more than two or three times a year.

[4] Rossini created his distinctive crescendo by using high-speed percussive rhythmic figures, built around the simplest of sequential chord progressions. These are repeated relentlessly, mainly on the strings, with the singer(s) often on, or virtually on, a monotone.

suitable for the overture to an opera about Cinderella to be the same as that composed for an opera which starts with a crowd of travellers disagreeing about who should look first at the newspaper? How can the same overture plausibly be used for *Elisabetta, regina d'Inghilterra* and *The Barber*? How can Queen Elizabeth plausibly sing very similar music to that of Rosina from *The Barber*?

Rossini was in the entertainment business, where he made a colossal fortune. To succeed, he worked in a rush, at great speed. We should not be surprised that he cut corners. As well as musical weakness, there are moments when the drama also comes unstuck. There is no obvious reason why Cinderella should give the Prince one of her matching bracelets and tell him that he must seek her out. This might perplex the audience, but the entertainment proceeds at such a frantic pace, and the story is so much part of our heritage, that the audience hopefully will not have time to wonder.

The music: power and colour

Rossini's music moves with tremendous energy, momentum, verve and power. It is also notable for its coloratura, the elaborate ornamentation of the vocal melody, either extemporised by the singer or notated in the score itself. There can be no gainsaying the infectiousness of this 'brisk and impetuous style.' Rossini himself said that 'in rhythm lies all the power of music.'

The coloratura is dazzling; for example when Cinderella announces that she is not a fortune-seeker but wants her husband to display kindness, love and respect, she whizzes up two octaves from bottom B flat to top B flat.

Patter

Rossini's use of patter is not just another of his affectations. It can be very clever, such as when Don Magnifico daydreams of being a member of the Prince's family, and works himself up into a state of great excitement about the potential for fees, perquisites and bribes. Rossini also uses patter, combined with a big crescendo, to describe the astonishment on the faces when the official register provides the evidence that Don Magnifico has a third daughter, Cinderella: *Nel volto estatico*.

It requires great coordination and skill to bring off these high-speed numbers. But done well, they are extremely effective.

Rossini's wit

Rossini was well known as a considerable wit and bon viveur, who enjoyed his food and drink.[5] He himself cut a comical figure. He was completely bald, but he had a selection of wigs. He had one for each day of the week and two for Sunday. When he went to Mass, he put one wig on top of the other and if it was cold he put on a third one, curlier than the others so as to provide more warmth.

Rossini

This sense of humour infects his music. For example, when the Prince arrives with the bracelet, we hear of the confusion, the tangled web, the tangled knot – *Questo è un nodo* – which is enough to make your head spin. The music for this, perhaps the musical climax of the opera, is hilariously funny.

---

[5] For Rossini, the four acts of the comic opera we call 'Life' were Eating, Loving, Singing and Digesting, which he described as evaporating like the bubbles of a bottle of Champagne. 'Appetite is for the stomach what Love is for the heart,' he said.

The opera is of course dependent on the cast, including a very effective and comical Don Magnifico. But surely even Rossini himself would not claim, as one distinguished critic has done, that Don Magnifico is 'one of the most complex and rewarding characters in all opera.' There is nothing obvious in the music to support this claim, indeed it is not clear that Rossini reveals anything exceptional through his music.

'I cannot say "Rest his soul", for he had none,' Bernard Shaw observed in Rossini's centenary year. Shaw's 'fervent aspiration that we may never look upon his like again' is surely going too far. Maybe Carl Maria von Weber, the composer of *Der Freischütz* and *The Invitation to the Dance*, who disliked Rossini and his music, got it right when he suddenly left a rendering of *La Cenerentola* muttering, 'I'd better go; I'm beginning to like the stuff.' We enjoy Rossini's comedy: it is an excellent vehicle for a good production and a great evening.

ACT BY ACT

The jaunty 'sinfonia' which opens the opera awakens the audience with a knock at the door and a couple of big Rossini crescendos, which are based on a theme we will hear again in the big ensemble with which the first act climaxes.

Act 1

At first, in the decaying castle of Don Magnifico, Baron of Monte Fiascone

Clorinda and Tisbe, the daughters of Don Magnifico, preen themselves while Angiolina (Cinderella), his stepdaughter, blows the cinders in order to heat the coffee. She sings somewhat hopelessly about a time when there was a king who was looking for a wife; he chose an unfortunate girl who was sweet and kind instead of choosing one of the vain ladies who hovered around him: *Una volta c'era un re.* Her sisters are irritated by this song, but Cinderella asks them to let her be.

At this moment, a beggar knocks at the door. The sisters try to shut him out, but Cinderella takes pity on him and gives him some coffee. Her sisters give her a cuff over the ears for her pains. But the beggar tells her that she may reap her reward before the day is out.

Courtiers from the prince's entourage announce that Don Ramiro, Prince of Salerno, who has recently arrived at his country estate nearby, is about to take the sisters, 'the lovely daughters of Don Magnifico', to his mansion, for a party at which he will choose his bride: *O figlie amabili di Don Magnifico*. This sends the sisters into a tizz as they prepare for the arrival of the prince. To the amusement of the beggar, they get very excited, building up to a big crescendo. But poor Cinderella realises that she will be excluded from all the fun.

Clorinda gives the prince's servants a tip, and is angry to see that the beggar has not yet gone. Cinderella tells the beggar that she is sorry she could not have given him the coin. Then the sisters bicker as they compete to wake their father with the news. He enters, pompously addressing his female offspring: *Miei rampolli femminini*. He is furious because they interrupted him during an odd dream about a donkey who grew wings and flew off and landed on a church steeple: *Mi sognai fra il fosco e il chiaro*. He interprets this as meaning that their fortunes will rise, and his daughters will be royal ladies with lots of babies; however, he is somewhat disconcerted that, on this interpretation of the dream, he is the ass.

When the sisters tell their father about the invitation which is about to arrive, he is overwhelmed with excitement. He was expecting the bailiffs, yet now the principality seems to be within his grasp. They all rush off to get ready.

Don Ramiro arrives, dressed as a servant, and finds the place deserted: *Tutto è deserto*. He had hoped to find the good and pretty girl described to him by his tutor Alidoro – for the beggar was the philosopher in disguise. He is appalled by the thought of marrying without it being for love. At this moment Cinderella walks in with the coffee and is so surprised that she drops it. In the duet *Un soave non so che*, the prince and Cinderella express their instant attraction to each other. He tells her he is looking for the baron's daughters and asks who she is. She is the baron's stepdaughter, she says, her mother having remarried after being widowed.

The sisters are heard calling Cinderella. She tells the prince that her sisters do not allow her a moment's peace. He is entranced by her simplicity and her pretty face.

We hear that the prince has swapped clothes with his valet Dandini because, so disguised, he will discover the true hearts of women. On meeting Don Magnifico, he is less sure.

Dandini arrives dressed as the prince. His retinue urges him to find a bride and keep the succession going. Dandini jokes about being like a bee buzzing from flower to flower on an April day: *Come un'ape*. The sisters obsequiously introduce themselves to him, and each assumes she has caught him, but Ramiro already longs for Cinderella. Dandini pretends that he has returned from abroad; his father on his deathbed, he claims, advised him to get married. He whisks the sisters off to his palace, in the expectation that later in the day there will be bad news for these awful women.

While Magnifico prepares to follow them, Cinderella begs her father to be allowed to go too. Magnifico asks Ramiro to excuse her behaviour; she is a mere servant, he says, who has got too big for her boots. When he sends her to her room, Ramiro is infuriated. Cinderella despairs that she is condemned forever to a life with the cinders.

Alidoro appears with a register which shows that there should be three daughters in the house. While Magnifico tries to restrain her, Cinderella protests that she is the third. Magnifico says the third is dead. Their expressions show their confusion: *Nel volto estatico*.

Alidoro returns, disguised again as the beggar. He explains that pride will bite the dust; Cinderella will be collected and taken to the party. She thinks he is mocking her. But he tells her to come with him, despite her clothes. And he (being a philosopher) can reassure her that the good God in heaven will indeed look after her: *Là del ciel nell'arcano profondo*.

* * *

In Don Ramiro's mansion, Dandini, still disguised as the prince, has to cope with the two sisters and Don Magnifico. Don Magnifico has lectured him about wine, so Dandini sends him to the cellars, promising to promote him to Master Sommelier of the Prince's Wines if he demonstrates his tasting ability and remains sober.

Ramiro tells Dandini to find out more about the girls. The brainless sisters bicker, Clorinda claiming that, being the elder, she has prior rights and is more experienced; Tisbe arguing that, being younger, she will not grow old so quickly.

Don Magnifico, despite the tasting, is still sober, and thus is hailed grandiosely as Master Sommelier: *Conciossiacosacché*. His first official act is to issue a decree to be posted up throughout the town (printed appropriately with capitals, suitable references to his many titles, and countless etceteras) prohibiting watering the wine. He also offers a prize to whoever drinks the most fortified wine.

Dandini and Ramiro catch up quietly: *Zitto, zitto, piano, piano*. They cannot understand Alidoro's recommendation that the prince should marry one of Don Magnifico's daughters, because the two sisters are so frightful. But they had better keep up the pretence. The sisters rush in. They are horrified to hear that the runner-up will be married to the valet, even though the valet says that he will be fond and obedient.

Then a commotion is heard. An unknown and veiled lady has arrived with Alidoro. Ramiro recognizes the voice and blissfully anticipates who it might be. Dandini feels like a honeycomb, with a swarm of bees buzzing around. Cinderella announces that she is not seeking fortune: whoever she weds must offer kindness, love and respect.

When the veil is lifted, the courtiers are amazed and the sisters are gobsmacked: *Parlar, pensar, vorrei*.[6] Don Magnifico and his daughters are horrified that she looks so like Cinderella.

At Dandini's invitation, they all go in to dinner. There is a colossal finale for the ensemble: *Mi par d'essere sognando*. We again hear

---

[6] The singers follow each other in imitation, rather like Beethoven's *Mir ist so wunderbar* in *Fidelio*.

the crescendos from the opening sinfonia, as everybody worries that, beneath them, that, despite all the fun, a volcano is about to erupt and dash all their hopes. A fit moment for an interval!

Act 2

After dinner, Don Magnifico confers with his daughters. The unknown lady looks so like Angiolina (Cinderella)! Tisbe observes that, whether or not she is their stepsister, the outlook is bad for them. Don Magnifico worries that it will be discovered that he has misappropriated and squandered the fortune that should have gone to Cinderella from her mother's bequest. Then he feels reassured that one of his daughters is bound to win the prince and ascend the throne. Whichever daughter does so, his celebrity status is certain: *Sia qualunque delle figlie.* He daydreams about queues of supplicants and petitioners using him to oil the wheels, and he speculates on the considerable potential for fees, perquisites and bribes.[7]

Ramiro ponders about how much the unknown beauty resembles Cinderella: *Ah! Questa bella incognita.*[8] He is delighted to hear her resisting Dandini's advances, and saying that she prefers the valet over the attractions of wealth. This also pleases Alidoro. But, when Ramiro proposes, she tells him not to be so fast: he must seek her out. She gives him one of her matching bracelets, and she departs.

The prince orders his coach. In a 'brilliant show-piece for a competent tenor', he swears (to himself) that he will find her: *Sì, ritrovarla io giuro.* He treasures her bracelet and he declares that they will keep searching until they do find her.

Alidoro plans to have the prince's coach break down outside the baron's house. While Dandini regrets that he has reverted to being a

---

[7] A contemporary of Rossini wrote: 'Such indeed is the accepted standard of behaviour in the wretched city of Rome, and such, in consequence, are the tasteless satires which may be perpetrated without provoking an outcry; such, finally, is the normal way in which affairs are managed within the boundaries of the Papal State! In Paris, we draw a more becoming veil of discretion over such transactions.'

[8] Rossini outsourced this to a minor composer.

servant again,[9] Don Magnifico, unaware of this, presses him to make his choice. In a 'brilliantly witty' sequence, he is let into the important secret: *Un segreto d'importanza*. Dandini tells him that the decision has been taken and the result will make him reel. 'Don't worry, I will be as still as a statue,' Don Magnifico replies.

To the baron's delight, Dandini consults him on the type of household he would expect his daughter to have. Dandini then observes that the reality will be far from the baron's expectations, and, to his fury, he reveals that he is only a servant, the valet. It has all been fiction, like a novelette: *È un romanzetto*. Alidoro is glad that his scheme seems to be working.

* * *

Back in the baron's castle, Angiolina (Cinderella) sings again her lament about the king choosing the simple, sweet bride. She longs for the prince's valet to come with the other matching bracelet. She reflects that she much prefers the servant to the prince. When the sisters and their father return home, they are again disconcerted by the likeness between Cinderella and the unknown lady.

There is a great and dramatic storm and the sound of a coach crashing. Dandini arrives to say that the prince's coach has overturned outside. Don Magnifico orders Cinderella to bring the best chair for the prince to sit in. As the lovers recognise each other, and the Prince sees the bracelet, he asks, is it you? *Siete voi?* It is, everyone says, all very complicated, a tangled knot, enough to make your head spin: *Questo è un nodo.*

The baron and his daughters are enraged and hurl insults at Cinderella. They order her to return to the kitchen where she belongs. Ramiro is infuriated by this. But Cinderella asks him to forgive them: *Ah, signor.*

Ramiro's fury increases, and he sarcastically imitates some of Don Magnifico's earlier insults to him when he believed him to be a

---

[9] His recognition in *Ma dunque io son un ex* that he is now an 'ex' must surely be one of the earliest uses of a word which is so frequently used in the tabloids today.

servant. When Cinderella tries to kiss her sisters, their fury increases. Tempers rise. We'll all end up in a loony bin, they rage.

At last, it dawns on the sisters that they have been made fools of. Clorinda despairs at her misfortune: *Sventurata*.[10] She, who was born to command, will now have to obey. Alidoro explains his part, and predicts that the castle will have to be sold to liquidate the baron's liability for squandering Cinderella's fortune. The sisters must either choose misery or throw themselves on Cinderella's mercy – a bitter pill to swallow, perhaps, but a necessary one. Tisbe reckons it will not be that bad.

* * *

In his throne room, Ramiro presents his bride, and she pleads for him to forgive her sisters; it will be her vengeance to grant them pardon. Cinderella is grateful for her change in fortune, which is fickle: *Della Fortuna instabile*. She was born to sorrow and tears, and until now her life has been sad and unfortunate: *Nacqui all'affanno e al pianto*. She tells her family to dry their tears and embrace her as daughter, sister, and friend. At such a display of magnanimity, all applaud the fact that such a good and worthy girl has become princess. No longer will Angiolina (Cinderella) sit by the cinders sighing.[11] Time has moved on.

---

[10] Rossini outsourced this to a minor composer.
[11] *Non più mesta accanto al fuoco* is borrowed from Almaviva's well-known aria at the end of *The Barber of Seville*. If you have composed a very good tune, why not use it again?

DONIZETTI:
L'ELISIR D'AMORE

THE OPERA AND ITS COMPOSER

Opera in the 19th century was usually a wholly commercial activity: there were no subsidies, and the audience was merciless. In the early 1830s, a theatre manager in Milan needed an opera quickly because he had been let down by another composer. He asked Donizetti to rework one of his, make it appear new, and have it available in a couple of weeks.

Donizetti did not take kindly to the suggestion that he adapt one of his existing works, but nevertheless undertook to provide an opera in time. He needed a librettist; these were two a penny at the time, but often expert in the needs of the musical stage. He turned to Felice Romani,[1] who had recently provided the libretto for his very successful *Anna Bolena*, and gave him a week to prepare the text. The result was *L'Elisir d'Amore*, which Donizetti composed in his meticulous and careful script. He met the deadline and it was premièred at the Teatro della Canobbiana (known more recently as the Teatro Lirico) in Milan on 12 May 1832.

L'Elisir d'Amore was cribbed from a text produced by Eugène Scribe, the prolific French librettist, who in turn derived the story from a play by an Italian, Silvio Malaperta. Eleven months earlier, Paris audiences had heard Scribe's libretto used in *Le Philtre*, an opera by Auber, a prominent French composer, known for his *La Muette de Portici*, which, because of its nationalistic sentiments, had caused a riot in Brussels a few years earlier.

---

[1] Felice Romani (1788–1865) came from Genoa and was well used to working in a hurry. In one year, he produced eight libretti. He often based his texts on French plays. Romani provided texts for more than 100 composers, most importantly Bellini, all of whose libretti from *Il Pirata* to *Norma* were written by him.

Donizetti

Donizetti's opera ran for 32 performances and became an 'instant and enduring delight.' Its success was not unalloyed however. The first performance in Rome seems to have been a disaster, with great hissing, directed especially at the producer: indeed the government had to close the theatre for four days.

A few days after the Milan première, young Hector Berlioz went to see it. However, he could not hear much other than the bass drum, despite the singers apparently 'yelling their lungs out.' The audience were making a great noise, chatting away with their backs to the stage, even gambling. He walked out.

Five years later, a leading English critic much preferred Auber's version, which became extremely popular in the middle of the century, and which was soon being blended with Donizetti's in a pastiche. The stage versions of Donizetti's had not been a 'profitable' success in England, although, in concert-rooms 'the music has been hackneyed to a death after which it is hard to fancy any possible resurrection.' How wrong the critic was! Today, this hilarious comedy is included in Opera America's twenty most performed operas. Its success has been assured by very popular tunes, including Nemorino's[2] *Quanto è bella*

---

[2] The role of Nemorino was a favourite of Pavarotti, who could identify himself with this 'simple country boy' who possessed a lot of naïve intelligence. The analogy is surprising: Dulcamara says that in all his travels, he has never come across a 'gonzo', an idiot, quite like this one.

and *Una furtiva lagrima*, Dulcamara's *Udite, udite, o rustici*, and the duet with Adina *Io son ricco, e tu sei bella*. One Italian critic after the première observed that 'to say which of the arias, duets, trios etc. is better than another is not any easy task.' Soon they had been translated into many languages, including even the Piedmontese version of Italian.

Gaetano Donizetti (1797–1848) was born into a poor family in Bergamo in the north of Italy in 1797. After an uncertain début, he settled in Naples. He composed at a frantic pace, 50 operas in 20 years, sometimes at the rate of five a year, and around 70 in all. He had composed 30 by the time *Anna Bolena* made his name internationally in 1830. This was followed by *Lucia di Lammermoor*, *La Favorite*, his successful comedies *L'Elisir d'Amore*, *La Fille du Régiment* and *Don Pasquale,* and many other operas no longer remembered.

He never really recovered from the death in July 1837 of his wife Virginia and their young children. He moved to Paris and later took a post in Vienna. He began to show symptoms of syphilis and acute sexual depravity. He was incarcerated in an asylum near Paris before being allowed to return, in an appalling state, to Bergamo for the nine months before his death there in April 1848.

L'Elisir d'Amore illustrates 'Donizetti's special gift for light farce, for the sweeter forms of satire.' Few operas are easier on the ear and the brain. This irritated the high-minded Berlioz, who believed that the Italians were impervious to the 'evocative and poetic side' of music, 'as well as to any conception which is remotely lofty, *un peu élevée*, or out of the ordinary, *excentrique*.' They had hardly any more respect for the noble expression of the mind than they had for the art of cooking (in his view). 'They want an opera that, like a plate of macaroni, can be consumed straight away without their having to make a mental effort to appreciate it,' he wrote. Whether or not one agrees with Berlioz's taste in cuisine does not matter: *L'Elisir d'Amore* provides a very entertaining experience. And we must always remember that this lively, brilliant opera was knocked together in a couple of weeks.

WHO'S WHO AND WHAT'S WHAT

The story below is based on the libretto. Certain directors may amend opera stories to suit their production.

Peasants take their midday break, with **Giannetta** observing that, though shade can reduce the heat of the sun, the flame of love is unquenchable.

One of them, **Nemorino**, is besotted with the capricious and far more affluent **Adina**, who is uninterested, largely out of pique that he is not more forceful. She has been reading the story of Tristan falling for Isolde after drinking a magic love potion, an elixir.

Belcore, the over-inflated sergeant from the garrison, considers that he is irresistible. He proposes to Adina. She accepts and turns Nemorino away.

Doctor Dulcamara, a grandiose itinerant charlatan, purports to have a universal cure for sale. Nemorino purchases what he thinks is a love potion with his remaining coins. He is warned that the elixir (actually a bottle of cheap wine) takes about a day to be effective (by which time Dulcamara will have pushed off). That's fine for Nemorino: it will activate before the wedding. But when the news comes through that the garrison must move on, the marriage must take place immediately. Nemorino is horrified because his potion won't have had time to become effective. Adina and Belcore's wedding preparations go ahead.

* * *

Dulcamara is the centre of attention at the wedding party. The **notary** arrives and Adina flutters with concern that Nemorino is nowhere to be seen.

Although Nemorino notices that the elixir is beginning to have some effect, Dulcamara tells him that to speed it up he must double the dosage. To acquire another bottle, Nemorino uses the bounty he receives for joining Belcore's regiment.

* * *

The rumour reaches the village that Nemorino's uncle has died and has left him heir to a fortune.

Adina realises that she has been in love with Nemorino all along. The teardrop in her eye is an indication that she has fallen for him: *Una furtiva lagrima*. But he must not appear too keen. Then she confesses she loves him, and Belcore concedes defeat. Adina secures Nemorino's release from his contract with the regiment. Dulcamara claims that his elixir not only brings love, but also riches.

THE INTERVAL: TALKING POINTS

The music

Donizetti's successful comedies followed on from comedies by Rossini, such as *The Barber of Seville*, *La Cenerentola* and *Le Comte Ory*.

As noted in the guide to his *Lucia di Lammermoor* (see pages 147–163), Donizetti has been criticised for being insufficiently passionate about his music: his high-speed rate of production, possibly driven by his recognition that his life would be short, was inconsistent with any depth of feeling. Bellini, the composer of *Norma* and *La Sonnambula*, who was Donizetti's contemporary, simply regarded him as a musical hack who deliberately sacrificed quality for money.

He has been criticised for his limited range of harmonies, and for his use of the orchestra as a mere accompaniment to the voice. He was not an innovator, and did not use music, as Mozart did, to illuminate the character of his cast. While serious opera was breaking new ground with composers such as Bellini and Verdi, comic opera ('opera buffa') as exemplified by Donizetti was in a stagnant period. Verdi's comic masterpiece *Falstaff*, in which 'the orchestra supplies a commentary of incomparable flexibility and wit', would only appear well over half a century later.

More positively, however, we can observe in *L'Elisir d'Amore* Donizetti's 'perfection of sentimental comedy in a pastoral setting' and the 'blend of humour and tenderness' which is the hallmark of his style.

Pavarotti and *L'Elisir d'Amore*

Pavarotti regarded *L'Elisir d'Amore* as 'an operatic masterpiece'. His manager suggested tactfully that 'Pavarotti was no intellectual', and reminded his readers that his client did not go to the University of Modena (the city near which he was born). He had great difficulty learning his lines. His popularity and his immense success are attributable to his exceptional voice, but his absence of intellectualism may have been another factor.

Pavarotti used *Una furtiva lagrima* as a means of checking the state of his voice. If it went well, he knew his voice was OK. The piece is unusual because it does not have a sensational climax. 'The music is very restrained which, for me, makes it more difficult to sing correctly,' he said.

During one performance of *L'Elisir d'Amore*, Pavarotti had to rush to the side, and the curtain was hurriedly let down. He needed water: he had gone on a diet and had taken 'what to most mortals would be a near-fatal overdose of diuretics.'

Other suppliers of elixirs

Doubtless W.S. Gilbert (and Sullivan) had Dulcamara in mind when he invented, in *The Sorcerer*, Mr John Wellington Wells, the purveyor of a patent 'Oxy-Hydrogen Love-at-First-Sight Philtre'.

At a garden fête, this gentleman announces, 'I'm a dealer in magic and spells, In blessings and curses, And ever-filled purses, In prophesies, witches and knells.' His potion is on sale, with a 25 per cent discount offered to 'members of the Army and Navy Stores.' It has the effect of sending people to sleep and falling in love with whomever they first see on waking, however young or old, rosy or pale, more or less buxom in build, and indeed however unsuited in age or temperament. This naturally leads to some unfortunate, but entertaining, combinations.

It is only by Mr Wellington Wells going up in smoke that the effects of his sorcery are undone and couples are restored to normality. Meanwhile, some long-yearned-for attachments are sealed. After this diversion, everybody can return to their mustard and cress sandwiches and strawberry jam.

Some eleven years before *The Sorcerer*, at the outset of his career, Gilbert wrote a burlesque, or extravaganza, entitled 'Dulcamara'. Clearly he thought it a good subject for light musical entertainment; and a bit of satire.

ACT BY ACT

Act 1

Adina's farm, then the village square

The jolly peasants on a farm take a midday break. Led by Giannetta, a village girl, they observe that, though the heat of the sun can be reduced by shade, the flame of love is unquenchable. Nemorino, a bumpkin, is in love with Adina, who comes from one of the more prosperous families in the area. As he watches her reading, he wonders how he can possibly succeed with her, because she is clever while he is a dunce: *Quanto è bella, quanto è cara!*

Adina is amused by the story of how Tristan won the cruel Isolde after they drank a magic potion, an elixir.[3] She wishes she could try such a potion. The peasants ask her to tell the tale, which she does,

---

[3] The reference to the ancient myth about Tristan and Isolde predates Wagner's opera of that name, which was first produced in 1865. The circumstances were rather different to those encountered by Nemorino. In that opera, Isolde, out of revenge because Tristan slew her fiancé, gives him a cup of poison. Isolde's lady-in-waiting substitutes a love potion for the poison, resulting in their having a passionate and forbidden affair. They are caught *in flagrante delicto*. Tristan, badly wounded when they are discovered, escapes back home to Britanny. Isolde arrives too late to save him. (For more on Wagner's *Tristan und Isolde*, see pages 183–206.)

giving herself the opportunity to sing some tremendous coloratura flourishes above the chorus: *Della crudele Isotta*.

Martial music heralds the arrival of Belcore, the pompous sergeant. Just as mythical Paris presented an apple to Aphrodite, thereby selecting her as the most beautiful goddess,[4] so he presents Adina with a bunch of flowers: *Come Paride vezzoso*. She is bound to fall for him: nobody can resist a soldier in uniform. So, to Nemorino's horror, he proposes to her and is increasingly importunate. She is irritated by Belcore's self-confidence and vanity.

Nemorino and Adina are left alone. In a tender duet, she tells him in no uncertain terms to 'get lost', to go and look after his uncle in the city. Besides, she is too flighty and wayward for him. He swears undying love, to no avail.

There is a commotion in the village square. A cornet announces that something important is about to happen. A grandee seems to have arrived.[5] Maybe he is a duke, a marquis or a baron? No, he is Doctor Dulcamara, who is in fact a charlatan. As a 'famous scientist and physician', he has a cure for everything; this has been certified in writing. He can supply rejuvenating potions, medicines for every ailment. Because he likes the village, and he comes from the area, and of course particularly because of his philanthropy, he is offering his products at bargain prices and substantial discounts: *Udite, udite, o rustici*.

Nemorino sees his opportunity, and asks the doctor if he has Queen Isolde's potion. At first, this odd request puzzles the doctor, but he quickly understands what is wanted. Of course he has it, and indeed it is in great demand. Marvelling at the simpleton, Dulcamara

---

[4] A deliberately idiotic reference. In the Judgement of Paris, which has been a subject for many artists such as Raphael and Rubens, Paris was asked by Zeus to present the Golden Apple – actually the Apple of Discord – to the most beautiful of his daughters. Aphrodite/Venus offered him Miss World, Helen, as a bribe, and accordingly won the prize. The vengeance of the goddesses who lost in the contest led to the Trojan War.

[5] Sometimes Dulcamara arrives by coach, sometimes by balloon or some other contraption. A Glyndebourne producer specified the use of a donkey. This caused some difficulty when on tour. A donkey had to be found at each location visited. The 'auditions' for this role caught the press headlines. In one newspaper, the critique of the performance was devoted almost exclusively to Ringo the donkey, his owners and his diet. There was however a reassuring postscript to the press reports: 'The opera itself is superbly presented.'

sells Nemorino a bottle of Bordeaux, in return for all the money he has, a small coin. He gives him the instructions, and warns him that it usually takes about a day to be effective (by which time Dulcamara plans to be long gone). Cautiously, he tells Nemorino to keep it all very secret.

Nemorino quaffs the liquor, which immediately invigorates him. He deliberately ignores Adina because he needs to wait until the next day when the potion will be effective. Meanwhile, he must appear to show some lack of interest. This annoys and piques her. He is totally unfazed when she agrees to marry Belcore in a week. This infuriates her even more.

But a message arrives that the soldiers have been ordered to move on. Belcore tells Adina that, as a result, they must be married forthwith. Nemorino is horrified and says that she must wait until tomorrow: *Adina, credimi*. He looks frantically for the doctor. Belcore is furious at the delay and Adina tries to calm him. They prepare for the celebrations.

Act 2

Inside Adina's farmhouse, then outside in a 'rustic courtyard'

The wedding party is taking place at Adina's home. The guests call for a song and Dulcamara, ever ready to oblige in any way, supplies one and sings a duet with Adina: *Io son ricco, e tu sei bella* ('I am wealthy; you are beautiful').

The notary appears. As the wedding group leaves to sign the wedding contract, Adina expresses concern that Nemorino seems to have stayed away.

Dulcamara stays behind, taking advantage of the food. Nemorino comes to tell him that he is desperate because the medicine will not take effect until the next day. The doctor advises him to double the dosage. But, too bad, he has no money to pay for another bottle.

Belcore provides the solution: the 'King's shilling'. He enlists Nemorino into his regiment, which Nemorino does reluctantly, considering he will have to leave home. But he acquiesces. With the money, the bounty on his enlistment, he can buy his treasure.

Meanwhile, outside in a rustic courtyard, Giannetta and the village girls chatter about secret information which has been leaked. Nemorino's uncle has died and has left him heir to a fortune. He is now quite a catch and the girls start to flirt with him. This reinforces his confidence that the elixir is working; it annoys Adina, and amazes Dulcamara. While Adina upbraids him for joining up, he is delighted that she is jealous of all the attention he is getting.

Dulcamara tells the sceptical Adina that he deserves the credit for Nemorino suddenly being so much in demand: he has supplied him with the elixir. Never one to miss a chance, he tries to sell her some of it. But she realises that she is in love with Nemorino. She also knows, as does Dulcamara, that Nemorino will fall for her charms, not for some potion.

Nemorino sings *Una furtiva lagrima*. He has seen a teardrop in Adina's eye, a sure sign she has fallen for him; all he now wants is to feel the palpitations of her heart and to exchange sighs. For these he could die. But he knows that he must still appear stand-offish. He tells her that he has not yet decided who to marry. She tells him that here is the place to be; she has bought out his agreement to join up. She confesses she loves him.

Belcore concedes defeat: he knows that there are many more women around. Dulcamara, as he departs, claims that his elixir not only brings love but also riches. Everyone praises him, apart from Belcore.

DONIZETTI:
LUCIA DI LAMMERMOOR

THE OPERA AND ITS COMPOSER

Donizetti composed his operas at a frantic pace, at the rate of five a year, and around 70 in all. His *L'Elisir d'Amore* had been composed in a couple of weeks. He is said to have composed *Don Pasquale* in eight days, or at any rate in less than a month. It took rather longer to bring *Lucia di Lammermoor* to the stage – about four months – but that was mainly because the theatre in Naples, the San Carlo, was virtually bankrupt. The Lucia, the 'incomparable' Fanny Persiani, one of the greatest sopranos, refused to rehearse until paid; and Donizetti himself almost went on strike.

The première of *Lucia di Lammermoor* was on 26 September 1835. Donizetti had composed the music as fast as his librettist, Salvatore Cammarano,[1] the official 'poet' at the San Carlo, could write the words. Donizetti had begun work during the previous June. The score was finished on 6 July, but it was not until 20 August that it was finally accepted by the management.

Lucia di Lammermoor is the 'archetype of Italian Romantic opera', and it might almost be regarded as an absurd parody, if it were not for the extraordinarily effective and dramatic 'Mad Scene', in particular.

The Bride of Lammermoor by Sir Walter Scott, who had very recently died and whose novels were still the rage at the time, was used as a basis, although not in much more than outline. This was not the first time Scott's story had been used: around six years earlier Paris had first seen a version of the story in an opera by a composer in the second division,

---

[1] *Lucia* was the first of several librettos Salvatore Cammarano (1801–1852) wrote for Donizetti. A well-known drawing of Donizetti has been attributed to him. He wrote for several other Italian composers: his libretti include Verdi's *La Battaglia di Legnano* and *Luisa Miller*. The libretto for *Il Trovatore* was incomplete at Cammarano's death.

147

Michele Carafa. Even before that, there had been a version in Denmark, in which the fairytale writer Hans Christian Andersen was involved.

As in the story of Romeo and Juliet, the lovers come from different sides of warring factions. Scott based his tale on an incident in the life of a top lawyer in Scotland, Lord Stair, from the Dalrymple family. His daughter had pledged herself to marry someone other than the person her family forced her to marry. She stabbed her bridegroom and was discovered, as Scott wrote, 'dabbled in gore'.

Lucia was a great success. In Paris, one commentator reported that 'it is a miracle; Donizetti has succeeded in electrifying the dead.' It became one of the most universally popular operas of the nineteenth century. Great novelists have used it to colour dramatic moments in their works. It arises in Flaubert's *Madame Bovary* when she is at the opera with her dull husband, and her former lover returns into her life. It features in Tolstoy's *Anna Karenina* when the heroine, a fallen woman, caused a sensation and was snubbed in the opera house.

In England it was also a sensation and, although expensive to stage, it became a great standby. It was beloved of audiences but less acclaimed by critics. Indeed, it became sufficiently hackneyed that the playwright and critic Bernard Shaw became utterly fed up with it. He suggested that it needed some element of comic relief, such as a 'highlander with a fling and a burlesque chorus to liven the precepts of Raimondo.' Earlier a leading critic in London had taken a dim view: 'Never was a story so full of suggestion for music tamed into such insipid nothingness, even by an Italian librettist, as this.'

The title role has attracted an unending succession of high sopranos. In the twentieth century, Joan Sutherland was perhaps the most famous exponent: her ability to sing her Mad Scene while running among the wedding guests greatly enhanced the effectiveness.

And he who sings Edgardo knows that he has the final scene, 'the darling of tenor singers', almost entirely to himself. Pavarotti, aged twelve, was inspired by Gigli singing Edgardo.[2] And later, with

---

[2] After the performance, the star-struck Pavarotti asked Gigli how long he had studied. 'I stopped three minutes ago; I never stop studying,' was Gigli's reply.

Sutherland's help, he himself made his American début in 1965 in the role, filling in for another tenor who had cancelled at the last minute. Three years earlier, Domingo had made his US début in the role of the unfortunate Arturo, and later went on to sing Edgardo opposite Lily Pons (who had sung opposite Gigli thirty years before that) and, of course, opposite Sutherland.

Whatever view one takes about the quality of the music, there is no doubting that *Lucia* can be great entertainment, a truly great show. It requires a star 'coloratura' performance from the soprano, and an excellent production. Lucia's nuptial nightie needs to be suitably 'dabbled in gore', and the baronial hall, the fountain and the Wolf's Crag suitably 'gothick'. Oh, and the kilts need to be of suitable tartan.

(More on the life of Donizetti can be found on page 139.)

WHO'S WHO AND WHAT'S WHAT
The story below is based on the libretto. Certain directors may amend opera stories to suit their production.

It is around 1700, a time when the Scottish Puritan Presbyterians have successfully opposed the Jacobite supporters of the exiled Roman Catholic King James.

Edgardo Ravenswood, a Jacobite, has been dispossessed by the Puritan family of **Lucia Ashton**, the girl he loves. Her family is headed by her brother **Enrico**. Because the wheel of fortune has moved, the family reputation and standing can only be salvaged if Lucia marries **Arturo, Lord Bucklaw**, a local grandee.

In Ravenswood park, **Normanno**, the evil captain of the guard, searches for an intruder who often has an assignation with Lucia. Enrico, who is accompanied by the chaplain **Raimondo**, is appalled to hear that this intruder might be Edgardo, his deadly and sworn enemy.

Lucia and **Alisa**, her lady-in-waiting, walk near a fountain haunted by the ghost of a woman who was murdered by her lover, a jealous Ravenswood. In the past, the ghost has appeared to Lucia and beckoned her towards the fountain, which was covered in blood.

Lucia has come to warn Edgardo that her brother has returned to Ravenswood.

Edgardo tells Lucia he is leaving for France. She is concerned by his wish to make peace with Enrico, their bond sealed with her hand in marriage: she believes that this is fanciful and unsustainable. They pledge themselves to each other eternally, with rings.

In the castle, Normanno is confident that the wedding between Lucia and Arturo will go ahead. He has interfered with Lucia's post and has interposed a forged letter indicating that Edgardo has fallen for another woman. This letter is produced to persuade the reluctant Lucia to marry Arturo. Raimondo, who has been on her side, also concedes that she must marry him. They tell the bridegroom that the bride may seem unenthusiastic because she is mourning her mother's death.

At the moment the marriage contract is signed, Edgardo reappears. The emotions of the lead characters are depicted in the well-known **sextet**. Raimondo then intervenes to stop a fight developing. When Edgardo is shown the contract, he curses Lucia for breaking her pledge, and flings the ring at her. He demands his own one back, and grinds it in the dust.

In **The Wolf's Crag**, the ruined tower where he lives, Edgardo broods to the background of thunder. Enrico gallops to challenge him. They arrange to meet at dawn in the Ravenswood family grave-yard. Neither can wait.

The wedding celebrations continue. Raimondo announces that he has been to investigate a shriek he heard from the nuptial chamber: there he found Arturo dead and Lucia insane, holding a dagger.

Lucia enters for the **Mad Scene**, which the audience has been waiting for, one of the best-known scenes in all opera. She recalls her love for Edgardo; she imagines the ghost stepping between them; she thinks it is the day of their wedding; she recalls the contract and Edgardo stamping on the ring. She tells him they will be joined in heaven. She sings *Spargi d'amaro pianto* ('Sprinkle my corpse with bitter tears'). It ends in a galaxy of coloratura.

Unusually, the dénouement is left to the tenor. At the Ravenswood family graveyard, Edgardo prepares for death. He trusts that Lucia and her husband in future will not pass by without shedding a tear. Some people report that she will soon be dead. When he hears that she has indeed died, he stabs himself.

THE INTERVAL: TALKING POINTS

Coloratura and bel canto

Donizetti composed during the era of the coloratura soprano who, 'with great ability and a high range, is able to warble rapidly and neatly in the most acrobatic fashion.' The melody is elaborately decorated, with runs, trills and arpeggios, much of it at the top range ('tessitura') of the voice.

Another expression that is sometimes applied to Donizetti's music, and even more so to that of Bellini, is *bel canto*, meaning 'beautiful voice' or 'beautiful singing', connoting long, lyrical lines of melody. As with coloratura, pigeon-hole terms such as this can be confusing, because bel canto is a phrase which we may also find applied to lyrical and florid music of the much earlier baroque period.

In the Italian opera of the early nineteenth century, the orchestra has a merely supportive role and the human voice reigns supreme. Bellini, the composer of *La Sonnambula* and *Norma* (both produced around four years before *Lucia*), was perhaps the greatest exponent of bel canto, and for a long time it was claimed that he had inspired Donizetti in his composition of *Lucia*. It has been said that 'emotions are created by variations in the melodic line itself – its rhythms, its intervals, its speed, its phrasing, and particularly by the shadings and dynamics of the human voice.' However, despite this, the objective much of the time seems to be a glittering vocal display by a celebrity coloratura.

An earlier, well-known example of coloratura is provided by the Queen of the Night in Mozart's *The Magic Flute*, who, after a few top Cs and Ds, should reach top F, although is sometimes not altogether successful. The spectacular cadenza in Lucia's Mad Scene ends on high E flat.[3]

---

[3] The E flats, the top of Fanny Persiani's range, have been the bane of several celebrities. During a performance in Dallas, at a time when her private life was in shreds, Callas missed the final E flat.

Donizetti is sometimes reported as having said that he wrote *Lucia* as a monument to Bellini. The claim is improbable because the première of *Lucia* was three days after Bellini's untimely death in curious circumstances outside Paris. The two composers were actually fiercely competitive: Bellini regarded Donizetti as a musical hack who deliberately sacrificed quality for money whereas Donizetti accused Bellini of being a musical sponger upon elderly wealthy ladies.

Sir Walter Scott (1771–1832) died almost exactly three years before the première of *Lucia*. He had quite recently visited Naples, and been fêted there.

Scott virtually invented the historical novel, and has been described as perhaps being 'the first lifelong and repeated best-seller in history.' He came from a warring Border family not unlike the Ravenswoods or the Ashtons, and he knew people who had been around at the time of the Jacobites. He grew up in Edinburgh when Romanticism was succeeding classicism: the new movement was brilliantly intellectual. Scott, however, disliked many of the components of Romanticism, such as the emphasis on feeling and sentiment, the cult of nature and Byronic exhibitionism.

Scott was apprenticed to his father's law firm and became Clerk of Session, a position he held for most of his working life. He worked half a day, six months of the year. His emoluments and the income he gained from his early poetry, such as *Marmion*, financed his taste for being a hospitable laird at Abbotsford, his estate by the river Tweed, in the Borders about 40 miles south of Edinburgh. He only began writing novels when he was in his forties. An early publication was *The Lady of the Lake*, which made

As she made her way back to the dressing room, she gave five E flats, and kept asking herself, 'I had the note but what happened?' As all performers know, there is no going back once the note is sung or played. Sutherland in her later performances had the aria transposed down a tone. For a time it suited Lily Pons, the French-born American coloratura, to sing the Mad Scene a whole tone higher than written.

Perthshire fashionable for tourists and formed the basis of Rossini's *La donna del lago*.

Despite being lame from polio, Scott had phenomenal energy. He has been called 'an immensely careless and rapid writer.' However, Anthony Trollope claims to have exceeded Scott's rate of two to three novels a year. The first group of Waverley novels began in 1814 with *Waverley* – about the Forty-Five Rebellion – and ended with *The Legend of Montrose* in 1819. Work and worries took a toll on Scott's health. Parts of *The Bride of Lammermoor* were dictated because his gallstones were giving him so much trouble.[4]

By this time, Scott's finances were precarious, although he was a phenomenally successful author. He had provided finance for the printing and publishing business of an old school friend, John Ballatyne, which had links with publishers we still recognise: Murray and Constable. Unfortunately, Scott became an inactive, sleeping, partner. His liability, though, was still unlimited, and when the business went bankrupt in 1825, Scott was called on for £130,000. The rest of his life was spent in a heroic effort to pay off his creditors. Although £40,000 was paid off in the first two years, his health deteriorated. He had a stroke in 1830, but kept going. The British government provided a ship to give him a holiday in the Mediterranean. He had his own mad scenes in which he thought he had satisfied his creditors, when in fact he had not. He was brought back across Europe to die, on 21 September 1832, at Abbotsford.

The Bride of Lammermoor by Sir Walter Scott

In January 1835, the audience at the Paris Theâtre-Italien saw the première of *I Puritani di Scozia*, Bellini's opera based on Scott's *Old Mortality*. Eight months later, the audience in Naples was entertained by *Lucia*, based on Scott's *The Bride of Lammermoor*.

---

[4] Scott avoided trying out a cure that was recommended to him – sleeping on twelve stones taken from south-flowing streams, the stones wrapped in the petticoat of a widow who had never wanted to be remarried.

Scotland and its literature, such as the works of Ossian[5], already provided a major influence on the Romantic movement. Balladry, stories about Border warfare, Gothic medievalism, the Jacobites and the Forty-Five Rebellion were all part of this. So we will find settings of poems by Scott among Schubert's songs; Berlioz composed his *Waverley* and *Rob Roy*[6] overtures; and, six years before *Lucia*, Donizetti had composed the now-redundant *Elisabetto al castello di Kenilworth*, based on another Scott novel.

The Bride of Lammermoor was published in 1819. A dramatised version was staged in London less than two weeks after the appearance of the novel. By the time Donizetti came to it, 'it was one of the best-known works of fiction in all Western Europe.' A modern marketing professional could probably not have suggested a more eye-catching title for a West End show.

Sir Walter Scott

[5] *Fingal* was published in 1762. The Ossian poems were alleged to be early translations of Celtic poems but were actually a forgery by James Macpherson (1738–1796) who then had to write the originals.

[6] The eventual popularity of 'Auld Lang Syne' owed much to its being sung in *Rob Roy*, composed by John Davy, a Devonshire-born composer and alcoholic who also wrote an opera entitled *What a Blunder*.

The libretto is a travesty of Scott's novel, which brims with imagination and humour, especially when characterising the parvenu Ashtons and the aristocratically threadbare Ravenswoods. Scott's dénouement, from the start of the wedding, takes around a twentieth of his novel, whereas it absorbs around a third of the opera. Indeed, the climax and focus of the opera, Lucia's madness, is disposed of in about fifteen lines. Cammarano, the librettist, finds room to include a hunt and a thunderstorm (both conventional in musical settings), but he bypasses witches, a grave-digger, the appearance of the ghost – all of which were possibly considered too colourful for an art-form where the technicolour is supposed to be provided by the music.

The librettist's task is far more difficult that it may seem. For Scott, Lucy's formidable and detestable mother, and her wily father, a lawyer, are the cause of the disastrous turn of events at Lammermoor. Again, they are perhaps too starkly drawn to fit easily into an opera. The character of Lucy, pale and palely drawn, is more convenient: she is a 'winsome, sweet creature, soft and flexible, exquisitely beautiful' who has a predictable tendency to tremble or faint.

One can perhaps sympathise with Cammarano having his *primo uomo* stab himself. Even though the novel foretold that he would ride into the quicksands on the Kelpie's Flow, such an end would have been considerably more difficult to stage.

The Mad Scene

Mad scenes were fashionable in Donizetti's time and their like are found in his *Anna Bolena*, *Lucrezia Borgia* and *Maria Stuarda*, and also in Bellini's *Il Pirata*, *La Sonnambula* and *I Puritani*.

It was quite normal for a soprano to insert an elaborate coloratura cadenza at the end of any great aria. So one should not be surprised that Donizetti did not compose the formidably demanding cadenza,[7]

---

[7] In 1959, on the first night of her sensational Covent Garden début as Lucia in the Zeffirelli production, Joan Sutherland had throat problems. She was advised by the throat specialist to drink hot Ribena between the Acts. The performance was a triumph.

in which Lucia echoes the flute. Some say that it was created by Teresa Brambilla (1813–1895), the first Gilda in Verdi's *Rigoletto*. Another view is that it was composed by Mathilde Marchesi for Nellie Melba's 1889 performance at the Opera Garnier in Paris. In the last hundred years, it has been the highlight of the opera.

The vocal line in the Mad Scene runs the risk of sounding merely like an acrobatic display of technical brilliance. As Sutherland's biographer described it, 'There is the crooning softness of the feeble-minded; the shrinking fear of the hallucinated; the joyous rapture of the deluded – but no strident madness.' In the Zeffirelli production with Sutherland in February 1959, instead of the music just being a soprano echoing the flute in the pit, the music was presented as 'distracting sounds that Lucia imagined she heard and, having imagined, repeated … notes that existed only in a destroyed mind.'

Lucia's Mad Scene does not conclude the opera.[8] This either annoys the soprano (as it did Fanny Persiani), because the Edgardo in the final scene gets the final applause, or it provides an anticlimax to the opera, because the tenor is no match for her.

The music

Lucia has been described as 'Donizetti's finest work', 'its composer's masterpiece.'

Many would disagree with this view on the quality of the music, including his contemporary Bellini, as we have seen. However, Berlioz, who took a dim view of Italian opera generally, with its gay and brilliant music that was often wholly inappropriate to the circumstances, makes an exception for *Lucia*, in which he admired the pathos in the Act 2 sextet *Chi me frena*, and the final scene of the opera.

A leading English critic of the nineteenth century regarded Donizetti as 'essentially a second rate composer.' He received a chilly blast from the German attack on Italian opera, typified by Wagner,

---

[8] At Sutherland's first performance of Lucia at the Met, despite dipping the lights several times, the audience would not quieten down after the Mad Scene, making it difficult to begin the final Edgardo scene.

The first Lucia

The first Lucia, Fanny Persiani (1812–1867), was no beauty, and her only asset was her profuse hair. She was taught by her father, a distinguished Italian Othello, who was himself so ugly that he would ask composers to write parts for him that he could start in the wings; thus, the sound of his voice would precede his appearance. Fanny was pale, plain and anxious. It sounds as if she suited *Il pallor funesto, orrendo*, with which she begins Act 2.

Mendelssohn said that there was a bitter tone to her 'acute soprano' voice, which others described as 'acrid and piercing'. The sound may have seemed so in the years after 1830, before the high soprano took over from the previously dominant mezzo. So it may have sounded 'worse' to contemporaries than to us today. But, despite having a voice and appearance far from as good as her outstanding competitors, Fanny was a consummate professional. The leading London critic said 'she was such a mistress of the art of singing as few women in her time, or ever had been … Her voice was developed to its utmost capacities. Every fibre of her frame seemed to have a part in her singing.' Her ascent to the highest notes of the scale was 'unrivalled' and 'every conceivable passage was finished to perfection.'

In contrast to the demands of the tragic Lucia, according to the Russian novelist Turgenev, she fitted perfectly into the role of the naughty woman in comic opera. A gesture that she made as Adina in *L'Elisir d'Amore* reminded him exactly of one of his mother's chambermaids.

who had far greater ambitions for the art form. Donizetti's high-speed mass-production has been derided, and he has been considered insufficiently passionate about his own work. He is also criticised for not being an innovator in the development of music and for not using music, as Mozart did, to illuminate the character of his cast.

Let us take as an example the cabaletta[9] *Spargi d'amaro pianto* at the end of the Mad Scene. This jaunty little tune actually accompanies a verse in which the mood is anything but jaunty: she asks him to sprinkle tears on her corpse; only when united with him in heaven, will it be heavenly. Not surprisingly, one commentator says that this 'shows a curious indifference to the mood of Cammarano's text' and that 'some of the Mad Scene remains on a purely decorative level.'

There are many other instances, although the librettist Cammarano also takes a considerable responsibility. Fortunately, the audience is still settling down, so it does not have to think too hard about the relevance of the huntsman's chorus, which has been described as 'not too well motivated.' Also, the male protagonists seem to be hurling too much furious abuse. When one would expect the music to be furious, it is not: for example, Enrico's *Cruda, funesta smania* at the opening of the opera, when his bitter hatred is aroused by Normanno's mention of the name Edgardo. The rollicking music when Enrico tells Lucia that unless she marries Arturo, he faces the axe, hardly presages the scaffold. Similarly, the orchestral accompaniment is hardly appropriate (however lovely it may be) to Edgardo's final, famous aria before he stabs himself. The roles of the supporting cast, Alisa and Raimondo, are wishy-washy. Alisa is not even given her own solo to sing at any stage in the opera. In the 1839 Paris production she was omitted.

As against these and similar criticisms, experts praise the popular sextet *Chi me frena*, usually just before the interval. This portrays the different reaction of all the participants to the sudden and dramatic reappearance of Edgardo during the wedding. Enthusiasts[10] have claimed, perhaps with some exaggeration, that this 'ranks as one of the finest pieces of dramatic music in all opera … the greatest ensemble number in Italian opera' and is rivalled only by the quartet in *Rigoletto*.

---

[9] A cabaletta is usually the final section of a multi-part aria, as it is here. Sometimes it is also a short aria, with repeats. In the latter case, Rossini said that the first statement should be sung as written, but thereafter the singer was totally free to embellish with ornamentation.

[10] At the Met, following Enrico Caruso's début in the sextet, there was such applause that a policeman rushed into the auditorium brandishing a truncheon. He thought the audience was creating a riot, whereas in fact they wanted an encore.

ACT BY ACT
Act 1
In the garden of Ravenswood castle, around 1700

Instead of an overture, there is a very short orchestral introduction that gives us a premonition of mystery and tragedy. Normanno, the captain of the guard, searches for an intruder. He is accompanied by the chorus, which the orchestral horns denote are huntsmen. We hear of honour, duels and vengeance.

Enrico Ashton comes on the scene, accompanied by Raimondo the chaplain. Enrico explains that his political circumstances have deteriorated; the wheel of fortune seems to be turning again, this time to the Ashtons' disadvantage.[11] His problems are compounded by Lucia's refusal to marry Arturo Bucklaw, the one person who could save the family reputation.

Raimondo tries to calm Enrico down, and points out that Lucia is still in mourning for her mother. However, Normanno says she is in love with someone else. Every day at sunrise, she has an assignation with a man who saved her when she was in danger: he shot a bull that was charging towards her. When it is suggested that the man is Edgardo Ravenswood, a Jacobite, and a sworn enemy of the Ashtons, Enrico is enraged and determined to be avenged: *Cruda, funesta smania* ('Bitter raging furies'). The huntsmen return and confirm Normanno's suspicions.

* * *

An opening harp solo, giving a feeling of flowing water, prepares us for a scene in the park of the castle, near a fountain. Lucia and Alisa, her not-too-happy lady-in-waiting, walk there. She has come to warn Edgardo that his opponent, her brother Enrico, has returned to the castle. Lucia explains that the place is haunted by the ghost of a woman who was murdered there by her lover, a jealous Ravenswood.

---

[11] The anti-Jacobite King William of Orange is rumoured to be dead, so the throne will revert to Queen Mary, his wife and the daughter of King James. In fact, King William died nearly eight years after Mary! Neither Sir Walter, nor the librettist, is a wholly reliable historian.

The victim fell into the fountain. In *Regnava nel silenzio*, in which the clarinet plays a prominent part, Lucia describes how on a still, silent night she saw the ghost of the woman, who beckoned her towards the fountain, which was covered in blood. Lucia feels she must expunge Edgardo from her heart. But, with the harp returning to the fore, she tells Alisa that she cannot: she has a sense of ecstasy when he says that he loves her: *Quando rapito in estasi*. Alisa predicts tears, and leaves when Edgardo arrives.

* * *

Edgardo has come to tell Lucia that he must set off to France on state business. Before leaving, he is going to see Enrico Ashton to make peace, with her hand as a pledge. Edgardo is not too happy when she explains that this is fanciful, indeed impossible. In the lyrical *Sulla tomba*, he warns her that over his dead father's tomb he swore vengeance on her family. So his hatred could easily reignite. She must swear to love him eternally as his wife. So, with a ring, they pledge themselves to each other eternally. As they part, they sing[12] of their sorrow at being parted, and of their love, borne by wind and wave across the sea, *Verranno a te sull'aure*. Again, the harp, supported by a clarinet, lends colour to this beautiful number, in which Lucia concludes their farewell high on top B flat.

Act 2

The Ashtons' castle

The wedding between Lucia and Lord Arturo Bucklaw – who will rescue the Ashtons from their impending disgrace – is about to take place. Normanno, the captain of the guard, tells Lucia's brother Enrico that it is unlikely that she will refuse Arturo. He has been intercepting and monitoring Lucia's post. He also has a forged letter insinuating that Edgardo has fallen for another woman.

A very unhappy Lucia accuses her brother of cruelty. Enrico

[12] *Verranno a te sull'aure* is reputed to have come from the melodies of a street bagpiper who Donizetti had heard.

blames her for loving Edgardo and produces the letter showing that he has fallen for another. Lucia laments, *Soffriva nel pianto* ('In weeping I suffered'). When horns indicate that the bridegroom is arriving, Enrico emphasises that only by Lucia marrying Arturo can the family fortunes be saved: otherwise he faces the axe – and she will be for ever haunted by it: *Se tradirmi tu potrai*. Lucia just wants to die.

Raimondo explains that he had circumvented Normanno and got a letter to Edgardo in France, but had received no response. He persuades the reluctant Lucia to marry. He commends her for sacrificing herself for her family.

* * *

In the great hall of the castle, the guests congregate joyfully: *Per te d'immenso giubilo*. Enrico lightheartedly warns Arturo that Lucia may appear downcast, because she is still mourning her mother's death. Still protesting, but forced by her brother, she signs the marriage contract.

At that moment, to everyone's horror, Edgardo reappears. The lead characters then sing the sextet *Chi me frena in tal momento*. In this, Edgardo talks of his fury which is restrained by love for Lucia; Enrico remorsefully realises he has made a bit of a mistake; Lucia wishes that death would have prevented this hopeless situation; Raimondo just fears the worst; Alisa and Arturo pray that there will be no bloodshed.

Edgardo draws his sword: he will die, but others will as well. Raimondo, the chaplain, demands, with the authority of the church, that they put up their swords, and shows Edgardo that Lucia is contracted to Arturo. Enrico tries to pass it all off casually. Edgardo turns on Lucia and curses the eternal pledge which he and she swore. He produces the ring and throws it at Lucia. He demands his own one back and grinds it in the dust. His corpse, he declares, will make a good wedding present for Lucia.

Act 3

At first, the ruined tower, Wolf's Crag; then back in the Ashtons' castle

Edgardo sits brooding in a room in his ruined tower, Wolf's Crag. He compares his destiny to the storm raging outside: *Orrida è questa*

Artist's impression of Fast Castle in Berwickshire, which possibly gave Scott
the inspiration for Wolf's Crag

notte. And from the pit, we hear a thunderstorm, and then a horse
galloping. Enrico has come to challenge him. Enrico is given a very
frosty reception: the spirit of Edgardo's unavenged father resides there:
Qui del padre ancor respira.

Edgardo is particularly enraged and jealous when Enrico informs
him that Lucia is now ensconced in her nuptial bed. They swear to kill
each other: they arrange to meet at the Ravenswood family graveyard,
at the first rays of dawn. They 'can't wait' for sunrise: they sing a loud
and lively duet, *O sole più ratto*.[13]

* * *

Meanwhile, the wedding reception has been continuing, with dancing and
rejoicing, although (as we know) by now the bride and groom have already
gone to bed: *D'immenso giubilo*. The chaplain Raimondo suddenly orders
the guests to shut up. He announces that scarcely had the couple gone
to the nuptial chamber when he heard a scream: *Dalle stanze ove Lucia*.

---

[13] Marked in the score '*marziale*', this has, perhaps improbably, been described as 'an excellent
example of passion expressed by broken rhythm.'

He went to investigate and found Arturo dead and Lucia holding a dagger. She is insane.[14] This information subdues the chorus of guests.

* * *

To an introduction from the flute,[15] Lucia enters for the Mad Scene. She imagines she has escaped back to Edgardo and heard his gentle voice: *Il dolce suono*. She recalls the happiness of her earlier days at the fountain with Edgardo and recollects the music of *Verranno a te sull'aure* when they pledged, one to the other, eternally. She imagines, with horror, the ghost stepping between them; and they hide. The shrine is strewn with roses; she hears celestial music: *Sparsa è di rose! Un'armonia celeste*. Then in a beautifully pathetic section, she thinks that it is the day of her wedding to Edgardo, the censers are burning, the tapers are flaring: *Ardon gl'incensi*. There is even a priest there, Raimondo, to join them together. With a gymnastic cadenza, at last she is, in her deranged mind, Edgardo's.

After this lovely music, Donizetti gives the Lucia a much-needed break by having her briefly interrupted, insensitively, by a furious Enrico. Then she proceeds to recall signing the contract and Edgardo stamping on the ring. He must not be furious with her: *Non mi guardar sì fiero*. She has always loved Edgardo: they will be joined in heaven. She gets confused with Arturo and pleads forgiveness. To a lilting tune, far from obviously suitable to the circumstances, she sings the famous *Spargi d'amaro pianto* ('Sprinkle my corpse with bitter tears'). After the assembled company has had difficulty restraining their tears, she recapitulates this in even more ornamented form. The Mad Scene ends in a galaxy of coloratura.

* * *

[14] To the audience, her insanity, her delirious imaginings of a union with Edgardo, are important for dispelling the unwomanly effect of her violent and criminal assault on Arturo.

[15] In a recent edition of the opera, the glass harmonica was used rather than the 'traditional' flute. It would appear that the confused circumstances at the San Carlo at the time of the première resulted in Donizetti replacing the glass harmonica with the flute in the score. As, surprisingly, 'shakes', or trills, were not Fanny Persiani's (the first Lucia's) strong point, it would be interesting to know how she fared in *Spargi d'amaro* where they are such a feature.

The scene changes to the Ravenswood family graveyard where Edgardo, the last of his ill-fated line, hopes to die at the hands of his enemy: he sings of the tombs of his forefathers: *Tombe degl'avi miei*. He can see the castle lit up where he jealously imagines Lucia with Arturo, and he calls on Lucia and her husband not to pass by without shedding a tear: *Fra poco a me ricovero*.

He is horrified to hear from some passersby that Lucia will be dead by nightfall. She is calling for him. The death knell is heard, and Edgardo tries to dash to her.

Raimondo comes to tell him of her death. As her soul rises to heaven, Edgardo calls on God to unite their spirits: *Tu che a Dio spiegasti l'ali*.[16] And, to the horror of the rest of the cast, he stabs himself and dies, envisaging himself with her in Paradise.

---

[16] Donizetti provides for the tenor (if he so wishes) to reach high C sharp as he sings of ascending to heaven. The notorious high C's in *La Fille du Régiment*, which Pavarotti made famous, are 'mere' C naturals. Extraordinarily, Donizetti is reputed to have suffered from a searing headache when he composed *Tu che a Dio spiegasti l'ali*.

WAGNER: *TANNHÄUSER*

THE OPERA AND ITS COMPOSER

Tannhäuser is a favourite not least because it comes from the early part of Wagner's career, the era also of *The Flying Dutchman* and *Lohengrin*. In his works of this period, Wagner took German Romantic opera to its ultimate conclusion. Today, these operas are 'the most loved and often performed works of that kind that there are.' This was before, for many, his works became relatively inaccessible. Wagner realised that he had 'exhausted the possibilities of the genre', and he developed the new style to which his towering greatness in the development of opera is attributable.

Starting with the overture, which is occasionally heard at the beginning of orchestral concerts, *Tannhäuser und der Sängerkrieg auf Wartburg*, to give the opera its full name, is full of good tunes. We can enjoy the Pilgrims' Chorus, the Knight's Chorus, Elisabeth's Prayer, Wolfram's 'Song to the Evening Star' ... and the opera only lasts around three hours!

Tannhäuser and others of the cast, notably Wolfram von Eschinbach and Walther von der Vogelweide,[1] were real-life poet-musicians known as *minnesinger*. *Minne* signifies chivalrous love. The minnesinger, many of them aristocratic musicians, flourished from the end of the 11th century to the end of the 13th, the Age of Chivalry. They had evolved from the Provençal and French troubadours and trouvères, whose poetry was often expressed in the language of courtly love. Its essence was the knight's courteous striving for the grace and favour of a respected but unreachable lady, sometimes associated with the Virgin Mary (Mariolatry). But their subject matter was various, and included a lament on the death of Richard the Lionheart, who

---

[1] Walther von der Vogelweide was, fictionally, in Act 1 of Wagner's *Die Meistersinger*, claimed as 'teacher' of the knight who wins Eva with his Prize Song.

himself was one of their number. One of their favourite themes was the story of Tristan and Isolde.

Wagner drew his story from two principal sources. A 13th-century collection, the *Sängerkrieg*, refers to the unorthodox minstrel Heinrich von Ofterdingen, who was defeated in a song contest, ostracised and threatened with death. (Thus Tannhäuser's colleagues in the opera keep calling him Heinrich.) The second source was a ballad, believed to date from 1400, which appears in the well-known early 19th-century compilation *Des Knaben Wunderhorn*. In this, the hero extricates himself from the delights of 'Venus', like Odysseus from the temptations of Calypso and Circe, and goes on a pilgrimage to Rome.[2] Wagner wove the two stories together.

In April 1842, Wagner left Paris, itself a veritable Venusberg, a city of commonplace pleasures. He went to Germany, the land of the great, the sublime, the noble. With his first wife Minna, he travelled over the Rhine on the road to Dresden for the première of his *Rienzi*, which he had failed to get staged in Paris. On the way, the sun broke through the clouds and shone on the fortress of the Wartburg, some 1300ft (400m) high above. Seemingly he was inspired to write his opera about Tannhäuser, the story of which he had already been introduced to in Paris.

A few months later, he told a friend about the pleasure he had obtained from a picture of the Madonna attributed to Carlo Dolci, a 17th-century Florentine painter. He observed that, if Tannhäuser had seen it, he would have fully understood how he turned from Venus to Mary, 'without being gripped by any great piety.'

In 1843, Wagner was appointed one of the conductors at the Royal Dresden Opera, and he also completed the *Tannhäuser* libretto, which he then called 'Der Venusberg'. In that summer, he composed the Venusberg music.[3] He completed Act 1 in the following January,

---

[2] Other sources were Romantic poets, especially Heine, and E.T.A. Hoffmann and Tieck, and the writings of Feuerbach. 'Des Knaben Wunderhorn' was drawn on by many composers, including Mahler.

[3] His technique was to sketch the voice part on the top of two staves, and the orchestral bass, harmony, and important motifs on the bottom. Then he produced a complete draft for each act on two staves.

Wagner in 1842

but owing to delays, the entire opera was only finished in April of the following year.

The first performance, held in Dresden on 19 October 1845, did not go well. Extravagantly expensive scenery for Act 2, especially ordered from Paris, failed to turn up in time and they had to make do with scenery from Weber's *Oberon*. Venus was too large;[4] the Tannhäuser became hoarse. The cast were confused by the style and some of the unusual harmonies; the audience were confused by the story, because, at the conclusion, Wagner left too much to the imagination, even though he had depicted it in the music.

After the first night, there was no further performance for a week, so as to enable the tenor to recover. This delay allowed rumours to circulate that the opera was Roman Catholic propaganda – surprisingly because, if anything, its description of a Pope who refuses absolution was hardly flattering. The house was nearly empty for the second performance, which went better. And for the third and fourth

---

[4] It was written for Wilhelmina Schröder-Devrient, a singer who Wagner admired greatly. Wagner's brother's adopted daughter Johanna, aged nineteen, sang the role of Elisabeth.

performances, it was full. Thereafter, *Tannhäuser* proved a steady draw. By the early 1850s, it was being performed widely in Germany, although its composer's reputation as an outlawed revolutionary was unhelpful. In the second half of the 1850s, it reached the larger court theatres, Munich, Vienna and Berlin.[5]

Liszt regarded it as 'the most remarkable opera, the most harmonic, the most complete, the most original and independent as regards both substance and form, that Germany had produced since Weber.' It also received support from Hanslick, a severe critic who later turned against Wagner.

Wagner in 1861

But Wagner was disappointed that his novel dramatic ideas had not been appreciated 'in all their subtlety of poetic detail.' Even when the opera became a success, he persuaded himself that it was not the kind of success he wanted, because the public failed to appreciate his ideas. No opera of his was so much revised.

[5] The Berlin opera house turned it down at first, and Wagner was told that if he wanted to dedicate it to the King, the King would have to hear it first. The best way of securing this was to have various sections arranged for a military band so that it could be heard at the changing of the guard.

In the first revision, for the Dresden production in August 1847, Wagner clarified the end of the story, and made other changes. The opera was 'an immense success with the public.' The greatest changes were made for the sensational Paris production in 1861. This had to be withdrawn after three nights, because of the riot which took place. This has been called 'the greatest theatrical scandal of the age.'

Richard Wagner was born in Leipzig on 22 May 1813. His father was either an official in the police, or his mother's lover.

Wagner was a small man with almost superhuman ability, and an outsize ego – justifiably perhaps. Verdi, his opponent, said that he could never quite believe that *Tristan* had been created by a mere human being. However, Wagner's reputation has been tarnished by his anti-Semitism.

His early years – 'professional purgatory as a conductor in small-time provincial opera-houses', including two years in Riga and around two-and-a-half years in Paris – were a time of considerable struggle and poverty. *Rienzi*, with which he had hoped to succeed in Paris, and *Der fliegende Holländer* were staged successfully in Dresden. Wagner's appointment as conductor at the Dresden Royal Opera House followed in 1843. During his work there, he composed *Tannhäuser* and *Lohengrin* and did some very preliminary work on *Die Meistersinger*.

Wagner's journalistic output was colossal; he wrote hundreds of articles and pamphlets. His 'fame as a writer ran ahead of his fame as a composer.' He became involved in the politics that led to the 1848 Revolution in Europe. During the 1849 rebellion in Dresden, Wagner was a lookout on the steeple of a city church. He was fortunate to escape, with Liszt's help.

Wagner immersed himself in the philosophy of Schopenhauer; later, Nietzsche was for a time a personal friend. During his exile, Wagner was provided with a house and finance by Otto Wesendonck, a Zurich businessman. His relationship with Wesendonck's wife Mathilde inspired *Tristan und Isolde*, which he began in late 1856. When Wagner's first wife kicked up a fuss about the friendship, Wagner had to move on. (A few years later, during the Paris rehearsals of *Tannhäuser*, Otto apparently observed to him, 'What totally voluptuous sounds these are!' Wagner imagined that Wesendonck was afraid 'he had been dancing something like that in front of his wife.')

Wagner resumed the project for *Die Meistersinger* when, despite being in a period of desperate insecurity, he was living expensively in Vienna. He was short of money, and thought that this project might provide a quick financial return before he returned to his *The Ring* project (which had reached Act 2 of *Siegfried*).

Eventually, on 3 May 1864, he received a call from King Ludwig of Bavaria, as a consequence of which his financial position immediately improved. After joining the King in Munich, and then being expelled for interference in politics, he settled at Triebschen near Lucerne. Meanwhile, Liszt's daughter Cosima von Bülow had arrived with her daughters, and had proceeded to consummate her liaison with a somewhat surprised and hesitant Wagner. Nine months after this, Isolde was born. In 1870, Cosima became Wagner's second wife.

During 1868–1870, the premières of *Die Meistersinger*, *Das Rheingold* and *Die Walküre* took place. Wagner built his own opera house on a hill above Bayreuth, in scenic Franconia (northern Bavaria). He moved there in 1872. This was a suitable venue for the première of a complete cycle of *Der Ring des Nibelungen* (1876), including *Siegfried* and *Götterdämmerung*. *The Ring* had taken 26 years to complete. Wagner died in Venice on 13 February 1883, just over six months after the première of *Parsifal*.

The music of *Tannhäuser* is glorious. The themes of the story are considerable. Wagner depicts 'a new sensuality in art and life, and a longing for 'unrestrained sexuality' which brings the lovers, and the artist, into conflict with the surrounding social order, in particular with an ossified form of Christian morality. We see flesh versus spirit, Hell and Heaven, Satan and God.

We also get glimpses of ideas which Wagner subsequently developed, such as the *Liebestod* (Love-Death) which, in later operas such as *Tristan und Isolde*, Wagner worked up into a complex philosophy: the woman Tannhäuser loves dies for him 'and thus makes possible his own ultimate release in death.' The opera anticipates 'the antagonism between Old Art and New Art portrayed in *Die Meistersinger*.' And it is almost 'a preliminary study for *Parsifal*.'

The result is however a bit of a mishmash of themes and ideas. To the end of his life, Wagner himself was uncomfortable with it and, had he lived longer, might have reworked it: indeed, three weeks before his death, he told his wife that he still owed the world *Tannhäuser*.

For modern producers, *Tannhäuser* provides a considerable challenge, one which is indeed 'well-nigh unsolvable in the 21st century.' The presentation of medieval times in a 'realistic' way – however enjoyable a spectacle it may be for an audience – is unfashionable and liable to be savaged by critics (a problem also faced by producers of *Die Meistersinger*). But, following a 'modern' production, many in an audience may well feel that the producer's attempt to stamp his or her mark upon this great work does more to spoil it than to resolve its inherent difficulty, which is that, in the final analysis, it is far from clear what *Tannhäuser* is actually about. Does that matter?

Who's who and what's what

The story below is based on the libretto. Certain directors may amend opera stories to suit their production.

Early in the 13th century, in an exotic and magic grotto called the Venusberg, the minnesinger **Tannhäuser** (the name given to Heinrich von Ofterdingen) has been seduced by **Venus**, the pagan goddess of love. He has left the respectable Christian court of Hermann, **Landgraf** (Earl) of Thuringia and deserted **Elisabeth**,[6] the Landgraf's

---

[6] Elisabeth owes no more than her name to the historical St Elisabeth who was married to the real Landgraf Hermann's son, and became St Elisabeth of Hungary. She was the daughter of King

beautiful and virginal niece. The **Venusberg music** depicts the scene in the grotto.

Venus has enjoyed her seamy activity with Tannhäuser, who is exhausted and has had enough: he wants to go home, a wish she is reluctant to grant. However, when he invokes the Virgin Mary, Venus and her grotto instantly disappear.

In a valley near the fortress of the Wartburg, a **young shepherd** sings about love, and the **pilgrims** congregate for the journey to Rome. Tannhäuser is found there by the Landgraf, with his retinue of knights and minnesinger including **Walther von der Vogelweide**, **Wolfram von Eschinbach** and **Biterolf**.[7] They recognise him as Heinrich, and try to persuade him to return to the Wartburg and their company. He is reluctant. But the mention of 'Elisabeth' persuades him. He has forgotten all about Venus.

In the Great Hall of the Wartburg, Tannhäuser and Elisabeth are reunited. The knights and nobles convene for the song contest, over which Elisabeth will preside. The contest, in which the competitors sing about love, is called to order by **four noble pages**. It is soon disrupted by Tannhäuser, who argues that his competitors have no clue about the true nature of love. He lets slip that he has had practical experience, with Venus. Horrified, they threaten to kill him. He is told to join the pilgrims and seek redemption in Rome.

Time passes. Wolfram, who is in love with Elisabeth, realises that his love is not reciprocated. He finds her praying and awaiting the return of the pilgrims. But when they come, Tannhäuser is not among them. She leaves to intercede with the Virgin, and to go to her death.

Tannhäuser appears, looking like a tramp; he is returning to the fleshpots of the Venusberg, his only option: the other pilgrims have all been absolved, but he was damned for eternity. There was as much chance of his being forgiven as the Pope's staff sprouting leaves.

Andrew II of Hungary and a niece of St Hedwig. After her crusader husband's death, she devoted herself to the relief of the poor and was canonised three years after her own death aged 24.

[7] Other minor roles in the retinue are two minnesinger, **Heinrich der Schreiber** and **Reinmar von Zweter**.

Venus returns and claims her prize. But Wolfram tells him that redemption is still possible through the intercession of an angel in Heaven: Elisabeth. Tannhäuser's cry 'Elisabeth' dispels Venus again. Elisabeth's funeral cortège arrives, and Tannhäuser falls, united with her in death. A staff sprouts leaves, implying that he is indeed redeemed.

Legend and reality: the Wartburg and the song contest

High above Eisenach, the birthplace of J.S. Bach, in the centre of Germany, is the Wartburg, a fortress founded in 1067 by a local robber baron known to posterity as Louis the Jumper. There, Martin Luther later took refuge after being declared a heretic at the Diet of Worms. In it, he began to translate the New Testament into German, and, as legend has it, he threw an inkpot at the Devil, who was attempting to weaken his resolve. There in 1817, students from eleven universities took part in the first student protest. Against the background of a celebration of 300 years of the Reformation and the anniversary of the Battle of Leipzig, they were protesting against the repressive policies of the Austrian Chancellor, Prince Metternich.

Holda, the goddess of spring, who had become identified with the goddess of love, dwelt nearby on the Hörselberg, a long limestone feature and the scene of the opening of the opera. She made a practice of seducing the knights from the Wartburg. The Cave of Venus, where Tannhäuser was reputed to have been ensnared, is to be found there.

Tannhäuser and Wolfram von Eschinbach (who wrote the epic *Parzival*) actually participated in a contest, a 'Sängerkrieg', held at the Wartburg in around 1207. Legend has it that the loser, Tannhäuser, or Heinrich von Ofterdingen, faced execution. He was reprieved on the footing that the contest should be held again in a year's time. Heinrich went to Hungary and persuaded Klingsor, the wizard, himself a poet and singer, to act as referee. In the second contest, Klingsor 'achieved a conciliatory decision.'

THE INTERVAL: TALKING POINTS

The Paris fiasco – the causes

In August 1859, Wagner, still a political refugee following his involvement in the revolution in Dresden ten years earlier, moved back to Paris, where he enjoyed the patronage of Princess Pauline Metternich, the wife of the Austrian Ambassador.[8] Many of the literati of Paris were enthusiastic about him: Baudelaire, poet and essayist, wrote an essay entitled 'Richard Wagner and *Tannhäuser* in Paris'. However, others, such as Berlioz, were not.

Napoleon III issued an edict that *Tannhäuser* should be performed in preference to *Tristan*, which Wagner had recently composed and wanted staged. It was just as well: as it was, he faced enough problems getting *Tannhäuser* staged. There were two particular difficulties to be overcome: Paris audiences demanded that the second act of all operas performed at the Opéra include a ballet; and, secondly, Wagner wanted to conduct the performance. However, the resident conductor at the Opéra, the respected local musician and *maître de chapelle* at the Madeleine, Pierre-Louis Dietsch, although exasperated and exhausted, insisted on his traditional right to do so.

The Venusberg scene was ideal for ballet but it was in Act 1, not Act 2. Wagner knew that an Act 2 ballet in *Tannhäuser* would be a dramatic absurdity, 'pure nonsense', but he underestimated the strength of the convention and its origin. The timing of the traditional ballet in Act 2 was determined so as to suit the rakes of the Jockey Club.[9] They would turn up for it, that is, to see the pretty girls. Great pressure was put on Wagner to comply. The ballet master offered the best ballet dancers in Paris for an Act 2 ballet, but for Act 1 it would have to be three Hungarians from the Porte St Martin theatre. The Minister tried to conciliate, but Wagner was adamant.

---

[8] She was both the granddaughter of Prince Metternich, the Chancellor of Austria, and married to his son (her uncle), the Ambassador in Paris. She was a close confidante of Empress Eugénie, the wife of Emperor Napoleon III.

[9] The Jockey Club 'brought together members of the Parisian aristocracy and the grande bourgeoisie.'

Wagner accepted that the Venusberg could be 'hotted up', and composed some more ballet music for that. He also arranged for the performance to start later than usual, at 8pm, so that the Jockey Club members could get there in time.

The Minister refused Wagner's request to allow him to conduct. The 'aurally deficient' conductor of the Opéra pressed ahead from a partially complete score. The Emperor tried to conciliate and said that Wagner could have as many rehearsals as he liked. There were 163 of them. In the final ones, there were two conductors: Dietsch from the rostrum, Wagner from a seat on the stage, conducting forcefully with his foot. The prompter in his box nearby was almost choked by the dust rising from beneath the composer's shoes. It did not help that Wagner refused to bribe the claque.[10]

The Paris fiasco – the riots

On the night, the court, which had promoted the opera, was present in full strength, so it should have been received enthusiastically. The staging was superb. But whistling and shouting began with the cor anglais melody of the shepherd boy in the second half of Act 1. Those who wanted to hear the opera started shouting the objectors down and threatened to throw them out. The performance struggled on.

For the second night, Wagner conceded a few cuts. Napoleon and Eugénie were present again, but this did not stop 'the shock troops of the Jockey Club going into action' with dog whistles and cat-calls. The Tannhäuser, 'a toneless baritone', threw his hat at the audience in the middle of Act 3. Princess Metternich was so furious that she broke her fan to pieces. Somehow the performance continued. By now, hawkers of toys on the boulevards were selling 'Wagner whistles'.

Wagner wanted to withdraw his score, but was persuaded to allow the third performance to go ahead. During this, Act 1 was twice suspended for fifteen minutes. After this performance, the Paris

---

[10] The claque were paid to applaud or hiss. *Rieurs* laughed during comedies; *pleureuses* wept during tragedies; *bisseurs* called for encores. The claque leaders, who received monthly payments from the actors and free tickets from the management, were very influential.

authorities allowed Wagner to cancel further performances. For him it was a financial disaster.

Verdi's Paris publisher told him about the fiasco: 'Words cannot convey what actually happened. The whole audience, apart from some Prussian and Austrian shoemakers, laughed out loud, then hissed, and finally whistled.' He added, 'So we have got rid of a madman who imagined that one could boldly write music without a trace of melody: he made a lot of noise.'[11]

For some of the audience, the riot may have been an opportunity to demonstrate against the court, its favourite Princess Metternich (and by extension Austria) and her German republican protégé. There were also some more fundamental issues. The French liked operas to have wit, charm and 'delicate cleverness'. In *Tannhäuser*, there was 'nothing pretty, nothing light, nothing graceful.' German composers, such as Liszt and Wagner, recognised that progress in the arts implied something more than 'auditory hedonism'; cultivated minds look beyond 'a vague pleasure, a gentle and rhythmic thrill, but prefer to use analogous thoughts and images to interpret the meaning of all music.'

Different editions

Wagner continued to make changes[12] right up to the 1875 Vienna production, his last production of it. He also published, at his own expense, an essay, 'On Performing *Tannhäuser*: A Communication to the Conductors and Performers of this Opera' and further guidance in 'Staging the Opera *Tannhäuser*'.

Today, there are two standard editions, the Second Dresden version of 1852, which takes account of all his revisions while he was there, and the Paris revision of 1861. For the Paris production of 1861, the main change was to enlarge the bacchanal, in response to the

---

[11] Rossini was asked by the composer Auber how he liked the performance of *Tannhäuser*. He answered, 'It is a music that one must hear several times. I am not going again.' Gounod declared, 'If only God would grant it to me to write a flop like that.'

[12] In the first edition, Venus did not reappear in Act 3, and Elisabeth's death was not reported, but merely indicated by tolling bells. For the 1847 performances, the introduction to Act 3 was altered and Venus was brought in again at the end, so as to show Tannhäuser's thoughts returning to her; Elisabeth's death was made clear by staging her funeral procession.

Paris authorities' insistence on a ballet, and to make changes to the song contest. He also incorporated his *Tristan* style in some of the new music.

The place of *Tannhäuser* in Wagner's oeuvre

The style of *Tannhäuser* is very different from later operas. It is still sectional (e.g. Elisabeth's aria stands alone) rather than composed in a continuous flow with the surrounding music.

Tannhäuser also displays a more highly developed use of 'leitmotifs' than is found in previous operas. Although the association of chords or snippets of melody with people, places, things or states of mind, so as to create 'musical reminiscence', can be found in operas by composers long before him, nevertheless, in the words of Liszt, Wagner had made 'a striking operatic innovation' in their use: 'Such recurrence not only gives rise to moving recollections; it reveals the emotions it expresses. Barely glowing when these impressions still stir only vaguely in our heart, the melody vigorously unfolds when they forcefully grip it once again.'

However, we have to turn to Wagner's operas subsequent to *Tannhäuser* to hear Wagner's use of leitmotifs in their more highly developed form, where they both enable the music to enhance the meaning and bind the opera together.

ACT BY ACT

Overture

In the words of a modern expert, this 'looks back to Mendelssohn rather than to a brave new operatic world in the future.' It opens with the melody of the Pilgrims' Chorus and gives us a taste of both the Venusberg music and the music when the minnesingers attack Tannhäuser for his heretical song in the song contest. It concludes with the pilgrims' music which perhaps presages the final forgiveness of Tannhäuser. This overture was the first piece of Wagner that Verdi ever heard; his comment, echoing that of his publisher, was, 'He's mad.'

Act 1

In the Venusberg, an exotic and magic grotto, Tannhäuser has been seduced by its queen, Venus, the pagan goddess of love. There has been a row in which he proudly and haughtily stormed out of the Great Hall at the Wartburg – the court of Landgraf (Earl) Hermann – nobody knows quite why. In so doing he has deserted Elisabeth, the Landgraf's beautiful and virginal niece, who has bestowed her love upon him.

In the opening chorus, *Naht euch dem Strande*, Sirens lure men to the subterranean grotto in the Venusberg which contains dancing fauns, water-nymphs, cupids and satyrs and even the Three Graces, and Leda and the Swan. Presiding over this bacchanalia is Venus herself, with Tannhäuser in her arms. Tannhäuser's harp (which every Minnesinger would have had) is nearby.

Tannhäuser has had enough: *Zuviel! Zuviel!* He wants to go home (and see things like nightingales, green fields and the stars of heaven), a wish Venus is reluctant to grant him. She commands him to pull himself together, take his harp and sing of love. Accompanied by the harp, he does so – *Dir töne Lob* – but ends by declaring that he wants to leave: *O Königin, Göttin, Lass mich ziehn!* ('O queen, O goddess, set me free').

Venus is not too impressed with this, and tries to seduce him again – *Geliebte, komm!* – but to no avail: he wants to go. In a rage, she sends him packing: *Zieh hin, Wahnsinniger!* She curses him and says that he will never find the happiness he seeks, indeed he will eventually return to her. Tannhäuser invokes the Virgin Mary: *Mein heil ruht in Maria!* The mention of Mary makes Venus, and her grotto, disappear.

In a change of scene, Tannhäuser finds himself in a valley near the Wartburg, where the pilgrims are congregating. A young shepherd sings, to cor anglais accompaniment, a song about Holda, the goddess of love: *Frau Holda kam aus dem Berg hervor*. Pilgrims assemble for the journey to Rome and sing the Pilgrims' Chorus seeking forgiveness and redemption: *Zu dir wall ich, mein Jesus Christ*. The young shepherd gives them a wave. Tannhäuser sees them and falls to his knees.

Landgraf Hermann, with his retinue including Walther von der Vogelweide, Wolfram von Eschinbach and Biterolf, come on the scene and find the wandering knight, who they recognise as their former colleague who has left them, Heinrich von Ofterdingen (alias Tannhäuser). Tannhäuser has amnesia about where he has been. He protests that he is just passing through and must move on, but they invite him to stay: *O bleib, O bleib bei uns*. He is persuaded to stay when Wolfram mentions of the name of Elisabeth: *Bleib bei Elisabeth!* She is the 'maid of matchless virtue', a typical object of adoration of the minnesinger. And she has been pining for him ever since he left. Tannhäuser agrees, to their great enthusiasm.

Act 2[13]

Act 2 is set in the Great Hall of the Wartburg, where the song contest is about to take place. Elisabeth awaits Tannhäuser there, the scene of their earlier rupture: *Dich teure Halle, grüß ich wieder*. Now that Tannhäuser has returned, she has recovered. Tannhäuser (Heinrich) enters, still suffering from amnesia about where he has been. They rejoice in each other's company, and sing a love duet, *Den Gott der Liebe*, in which it is clear that she had fallen in love with him, and experienced emotions and longings previously unknown to her. Wolfram, who also pines after Elisabeth, realises that he is no longer in with a chance.

The Landgraf enters and announces a song contest, a festival of which Elisabeth will be the princess. The knights arrive and sing the Knight's Chorus: *Freudig begrüssen wir die edle Halle*. The Landgraf likens the contests that have taken place in the hall to the battles for the supremacy of the German state. However, the theme for the present contest shall be the 'nature of love' and the prize shall be whatever the victor requests of Elisabeth.

---

[13] The Chilean tenor Ramon Vinay had a fit of nerves before Act 2, and fled out through his dressing-room window. The management, not finding him, found Wolfgang Windgassen out taking a stroll; they shoved him into the car and, as soon as he was in costume and make-up, the second act could begin.

The order of singing is chosen by lot, and Wolfram begins. He sings the praises of the lovely ladies he sees around him: *Blick ich umher in diesem edlen Kreise*. He sings of the one single shining star for whom he would devotedly shed his blood. Changing his metaphor, he sings of the fountain of delights, which he would never contaminate with impure thoughts. The knights and ladies express their approval.

Tannhäuser however intervenes and declares that he too worships the star, but for him the true nature of love is the insatiable thirst he has to drink of that fountain.

The contest resumes with Walther von der Vogelweide singing his song. The atmosphere becomes increasingly fraught, with Tannhäuser trading insults with the other participants. Tannhäuser argues that the contestants have no clue about the true nature of love (the enjoyment in which he would participate with Elisabeth). This riles Biterolf, who becomes violent. Eventually, Tannhäuser gets to the point: only someone who has been to the Venusberg can actually appreciate what love is all about.

The lust displayed in the Venusberg is the antithesis of all that the minnesinger, the courtly 'would-be guardians of morality', stand for. At the mention of the Venusberg, the knights realise that Tannhäuser has been there, and in effect treat him as a heretic. They threaten to kill him.[14]

The Landgraf tries to maintain order. Wolfram is indignant. When they draw their spears, Elisabeth intervenes (reaching top B): *Haltet ein*. They should not be his judge, she declares: *Zurück von ihm! Nicht ihr seid seiner Richter!* She demands that Tannhäuser be allowed to seek salvation through atonement.

Tannhäuser, somewhat suddenly upon hearing that his behaviour has broken Elisabeth's heart, repents his lascivious longing for her.[15]

[14] This is bad luck on Tannhäuser, because originally he had not intended to stay in Thuringia, as we know, but had only done so at the knights' behest.

[15] Tannhäuser's cry *Erbarm' dich mein* is a pivotal moment, and without it there is no motivation for the pilgrimage to Rome. This has also been called a 'gaping flaw' in the drama: 'violently but naively, Tannhäuser lurches from one form of enchantment into another.' Wagner spent much time coaching his first Tannhäuser in singing this.

But the Landgraf passes judgement: *Ein furchtbares Verbrechen ward begangen*. He exiles Tannhäuser and tells him to join the pilgrimage to Rome and seek atonement, and not to come back until he has received absolution. The younger pilgrims are heard in the background, and the act ends with all crying, 'To Rome.'

Act 3

There is an introduction, depicting Tannhäuser's pilgrimage. The act opens with Wolfram discovering Elisabeth at prayer at a shrine to the Virgin in a valley near the Wartburg. Wolfram, the only really likable male in the cast (Tannhäuser himself is not a pleasant character) observes her devotedly. She awaits the return of the pilgrims from Rome: *Wohl wuss'ich hier sie im Gebet zu finden.*

We hear the Pilgrims' Chorus, *Beglück darf nun dich, O Heimat*, as they rejoice to be back; but Tannhäuser is not among the older ones. Elisabeth's Prayer, *Allmächt'ge Jungfrau*, in which she intercedes for Tannhäuser, has been immortalised by many great sopranos.[16] But the rest of the pilgrims pass by; and Tannhäuser is not among them, much to Elisabeth's despair. She rejects Wolfram's offer to accompany her, and goes away to intercede for him with the Virgin in Heaven; that is, to die of grief. Wolfram is left to sing his 'Song to the Evening Star', *O du, mein holder Abendstern*,[17] in which he declares his love for her.

Soon, Tannhäuser appears, looking like a tramp. He has heard the sound of the harp: *Ich hörte Harfenschlag*. He horrifies Wolfram by explaining that he is returning to the fleshpots of the Venusberg, his only option. He describes his appalling experience in Rome, where all the pilgrims were absolved apart from him: *Nach Rom gelangt' ich so*. The Pope had refused him absolution[18] and proclaimed that those who had visited the Venusberg were damned for eternity. There was as much chance of Tannhäuser's forgiveness as the Pope's staff sprouting leaves.

---

[16] Birgit Nilsson once sang Elisabeth and Venus in the same performance.
[17] This was turned into a popular drawing-room ballad.
[18] Tannhäuser was guilty of the sin of 'desperatio', doubt in the possibility of divine forgiveness (a sin against the Holy Ghost).

So Tannhäuser is on his way back to the Venusberg, just as Venus in Act 1 had predicted. Venus appears and claims her prize: *Willkommen, ungetreuer Mann!* But Wolfram declares that redemption is still possible through an angel (Elisabeth) in Heaven who is interceding for him:[19] *Ein Engel bat für dich auf Erden.* Just as the name 'Maria' had dispelled Venus in Act 1, so does Wolfram and Tannhäuser's cry 'Elisabeth' dispel Venus again. Elisabeth's funeral cortège arrives, and Tannhäuser falls down dead, united with her in death: *Heilige Elisabeth, bitte für mich.* Young pilgrims come forward with a staff that sprouts leaves, implying that Tannhäuser is indeed absolved and redeemed.

Wagner's first wife, Minna

[19] There is a parallel with Gretchen who atones for Goethe's Faust. By Elisabeth's dying for Tannhäuser, he can die a pure death. Wagner later claimed that Elisabeth's renunciation and mortification of the longing was the same as Schopenhauer's concept of 'denial of the will'. Arguably, the original opera was not about renunciation, but about redemption through love.

WAGNER:
TRISTAN UND ISOLDE

THE OPERA AND ITS COMPOSER

Within less than five weeks of his accession to the throne of Bavaria, King Ludwig, later known as 'the Mad King', came to the rescue of Wagner who was then in dire straits financially. After they met in May 1864, they planned the realisation of their dreams. The first of these was the staging, just over a year later, of *Tristan und Isolde*, the opera which Wagner had completed six years earlier but had not yet succeeded in getting premièred.

It has been said that *Tristan* is 'an opera intoxicated by passion almost to the point of depravity', so much so that Duchess Sophie, the King's cousin and future fiancée, was not allowed to attend. Wagner's first wife Minna complained that the passion in it is almost indecent; she, we shall see, had good reason to complain. Not surprisingly, its theme of sexual love leading to death was adored by the decadent writers, including Frenchmen such as Baudelaire, who might otherwise have been expected to have loathed all things German.

Puccini declared, 'Enough of this music! We're only mandolinists, amateurs: woe to him who gets caught by it! This tremendous music destroys one and renders one incapable of composing any more!' The great conductor Bruno Walter, then a boy, hearing it for the first time, declared, 'Never before had my soul been so deluged with floods of sound and passion, never had my heart been consumed by such yearning and sublime bliss, never had I been transported from reality by such heavenly glory.'[1]

---

[1] Others have been concerned about 'the swollen erotic vapour' in the *Tristan* music, and what Richard Strauss's collaborator Hugo von Hofmannsthal called 'intolerable erotic screamings'. When a distinguished Tristan was criticised for having sung the love duet out of tune, Sir Thomas Beecham, the conductor, averred that it was not the tenor who was out of tune, but Wagner.

This opera, love having nowhere else 'been shown in such grandeur or elaborated to such psychological and metaphysical depths', is one of the pivotal works in the development of music. Its 'incessant modulations, the constant wavering of tonality', had an immense influence. It has been suggested that its 'terrific erotic power poisoned the minds of the composers of the succeeding generations.' Put another way, *Tristan* has been described as 'the moment when modern music began.'

Tristan was based principally on the epic by Gottfried von Strassburg dating from 1210, which itself was based on earlier traditions. Wagner blended this outstanding poem with his somewhat eccentric (at least by modern tenets) philosophical views as articulated by both himself and the philosopher Arthur Schopenhauer (1788–1860).

Wagner was living in Zurich. During the summer of 1857, he was in the middle of composing *Siegfried* when he broke off to work on Act 1 of his *Tristan*. He may have felt it had commercial potential, and he needed the money. Although he told his fellow composer (and future father-in-law) Liszt in 1854, 'I have planned in my head a Tristan and Isolde', the inspiration for it can be traced back to the arrival in Zurich four years earlier of the affluent Wesendoncks,[2] 'Merchant and wife, from New York.' 'With her artistic gifts and enthusiasms,' Mathilde Wesendonck (1828–1902) entered into the intellectual life of Zurich. She was a little more than fifteen years younger than Wagner.

Both husband and wife soon became great friends and supporters of Wagner. Otto Wesendonck provided finance; Mathilde became his confidante and provided him with the inspiration which his then wife, Minna, who was sometimes high on opium, and was 'an illiterate, unimaginative woman, whose mind, such as it was, was all foreground

[2] The Wesendoncks originated from the Rhineland. Otto (1815–1896) was a partner in a firm of New York silk importers. Within just over a year of knowing him, Wagner had touched him for cash. Otto tried to straighten out Wagner's tangled financial affairs and gave him budgeting advice. Wagner's appetite for lavish furnishings – his inspiration was dulled by anything that would remind him of crude reality – led him to run up commitments he could not meet. Otto bailed him out.

Schopenhauer

without perspective', was incapable of providing.³ Wagner's friendship with Mathilde gave rise to gossip; and Minna, understandably (although not to Wagner) became increasingly suspicious and jealous of her.

Wagner required an artistic confidante, rather than sex; and Minna was totally unsuitable. As his leading biographer Ernest Newman put it, 'During the gestation of a big work, the temperature of Wagner's whole being was raised' and led him to 'idealise the woman who, at the moment, seemed to harmonise most perfectly with his inner world.' When that work was finished, 'the scales gradually fell from his eyes, and he came to see the woman not as an ideal but as an ordinary reality.' The woman of the moment, now, was Mathilde.⁴

³ Minna was exceptionally beautiful and was on the stage when Wagner met her. They married when he was 23. She was three and a half years older than him. Her behaviour then belies the bourgeois attitudes which grated with Wagner when their marriage came asunder. Minna's ostensible sister Natalie was in fact her child, born when she was barely 17. In the first year of their marriage, Wagner had had to pursue Minna around Germany after she had absconded with a businessman.
⁴ The love music in *Die Walküre*, composed in 1851–1852, had been annotated with abbreviations which indicate that Wagner saw himself and Mathilde as Siegmund and Sieglinde, two leading characters in that opera. Some years later, Wagner set to music five of Mathilde's poems, subsequently known as the *Wesendonck-Lieder*. In these, there are 'several veiled references to the

Early in 1857, the Wagners were invited to move into a cottage on a piece of land next to the grand residence overlooking Lake Zurich which Otto was having built on land which he had acquired to stop its redevelopment as a mental institution. Around Easter, the Wagners moved into their quarters, known as the 'Asyl' ('Sanctuary'); four months later, the Wesendoncks took up residence.

The first complete musical draft of *Tristan* was composed during that autumn. The score of *Tristan* Act 1 was finished on 3 April 1858. Four days later, Minna intercepted a letter from Wagner which enclosed the sketch of the Prelude, and, as he described it, communicated the feelings he felt at the time. The letter, though it began 'Just out of Bed', was actually largely about Goethe's *Faust*. As Newman observed, 'anything less like a love-letter in the common acceptance of the term could hardly be imagined.' Nevertheless, Minna seems to have been determined to misinterpret it.

She went ballistic. She showed the letter to Mathilde who told Otto. They apparently remained totally calm and went off on holiday. They regarded Minna's mental state as the issue, and would have preferred the Wagners to remain in the cottage. But it became clear to Wagner that Minna's instability was an impediment to his art. By mid-August, the only way forward for Wagner and his art was for him to leave. He made his way to Venice. He spent the next twelve months living in the Palazzo Giustiniani, where he composed Act 2. He was still a political exile as a consequence of his involvement in the revolution in Dresden some ten years earlier, and in March 1859 he was ordered to leave Venice. He finished *Tristan* in the Schweizerhof Hotel in Lucerne, on 6 August. It had taken no more than two years to complete.

The score was rejected by opera houses in Dresden, Paris, Karlsruhe, Vienna, Hanover and Leipzig. Vienna eventually accepted

---

secret sympathy' between them, not least because two of them were 'studies' for *Tristan*. One was played under Mathilde's window as a birthday greeting in December 1857. There is no certainty that Mathilde reciprocated Wagner's passion and its extent, let alone consummated it (it was the 19th century). She lost interest in him. Many years later, she offered his rival Brahms the text of a cantata she had written on the subject of cremation. Nothing came of it.

The Wesendoncks: Otto provided cash, Mathilde inspiration

it in 1862, but, after 77 rehearsals, the production was cancelled. One Berlin newspaper described the work as an art work of the future (the title of one of Wagner's publications), because it was unperformable at present.

The outlook seemed bleak until King Ludwig came to the rescue. In the December after they met, Wagner included the Prelude and Liebestod of *Tristan* in a concert which he put on for the King.

The lead-up to the full performance, scheduled for summer 1865, was punctuated by a series of incidents. On the day of the first rehearsal, Cosima, Liszt's daughter and the wife of the distinguished court conductor Hans von Bülow,[5] gave birth to Wagner's daughter Isolde. Then there was an argument about accommodation for the orchestra: Bülow wanted the removal of 30 seats to make more space. He was overheard asking the southerners angrily, 'What does it matter whether we have 30 *Schweinhunde* more or less?' This infuriated

---

[5] Hans von Bülow (1830–1894), born in Dresden, was a virtuoso pianist and conductor who made the German orchestra the envy of the world. He married Liszt's daughter Cosima in 1857. She left him for Wagner in 1869. Bülow liked to have two pianos on stage at the same time, so that he could present his face or his back to the public.

the Munich press and people. Next, on the day of the première, the bailiffs arrived to enforce an old debt due from Wagner, and he had to be bailed out by the Treasury. Later that day, it was found that the Isolde had lost her voice, so the performance had to be postponed, until 10 June. When it finally took place, Wagner was delighted with it. A further three performances were staged. But nine years passed before a second theatre dared attempt the work, in Weimar.

All the brouhaha around the première was followed by real tragedy. Wagner had found the ideal Tristan and Isolde in the burly 29-year-old Ludwig Schnorr von Carolsfeld, who he had heard as Lohengrin, and his wife Malvina. On 21 July, Schnorr died. Indeed, the opera has been beset by tragedy: two well-known conductors, Felix Mottl (1856–1911) and Josef Keilberth (1908–1968), collapsed when conducting performances, and died.

It may be hard for us today to realise how novel *Tristan* seemed at the time. A final full rehearsal, in effect a private performance, had been held to which 600 guests were invited. The reaction of an intelligent listener to Act 2 probably sums up the audience's reaction. 'The singing consists of nothing but screaming and shrieking; the singers storm, rage and roar while the orchestra accompanies them with the most outrageous discords.'[6]

Even today, *Tristan* can sound untypical in a number of respects. It is not made up of separate arias, traditional choruses and so on – after all, people do not speak in arias – but of a seamless strand of music through each act.

The typical opera goer is conditioned to singers taking the lead, accompanied and underpinned by the orchestra. In *Tristan*, there is no intention to have some 'best tune', and some, although not all, of the music is in the nature of speech-song. For Wagner, the voice has become just another prominent instrument in the overall sound created within a completely integrated *Gesamtkunstwerk* ('art-work'),[7]

---

[6] This kind of response comforts modern composers (and artists) whose work is at first thought to be outrageous.

[7] The idea of an all-embracing work of art was by no means new: it was a central tenet of Romanticism.

in which 'words, stage setting, visible action and music all come together in closest harmony toward the central dramatic purpose.' There are relics of traditional opera, such as the chorus of the sailors; but sailors do tend to talk or shout to each other at the same time, so a chorus of them is realistic.[8]

Tristan has the least action on stage of all Wagner's works. Wagner was greatly influenced by Greek drama, in which most of the action takes place off the stage and is 'reported'. As each act lasts for about an hour and a quarter, there can be what one leading musicologist has called 'undeniable moments of ennui'.

Also, the obscure language of Wagner's poetry and philosophy may seem confusing and even counter-intuitive: the lovers yearn for 'Night', 'Endless night', 'Death' and 'Darkness', and seem to reject the 'Day', and 'Light'. However, this longing is wholly consistent with notions as expressed, for example, by Novalis,[9] 'the prophet of the Romantic school'. He wrote, 'a marriage that gives us a companion for the Night is also a union concluded unto Death. In Death is love most sweet; for the lover, Death is a bridal night, a secret full of sweet mysteries.'

The Night became 'one of the mightiest symbols of the Romantic movement', and *Tristan* was called by its composer a 'Romantic Opera'. However, at the end of Act 2 and during the soliloquies of Act 3, when his poem ventures into the territory of Schopenhauerian philosophy, understanding Wagner's poem becomes more challenging.

It is best to avoid dwelling on the philosophical aspects and to let the intoxicating power of the *Tristan* music surge over you, as would a symphony in a concert hall. Indeed, the Liebestod is really a symphonic piece, 'a drama in the Beethovenian sense' and can be performed without actors or vocal parts. *Tristan* is an orchestral opera.

---

[8] Brahms, who was Wagner's leading antagonist, said that if he looked at the *Tristan* score in the morning, it made him cross for the rest of the day. Rossini, a great wit, was found reading the score of *Tristan* upside down. He said he could not make head or tail of it.

[9] 'Novalis' was the pseudonym of the consumptive poet and philosopher Friedrich von Hardenberg (1772–1801).

In that sense, its words are inessential.[10] Wagner advised Nietzsche, 'Take your glasses off! You must hear nothing but the opera!' And he wrote to Mathilde, 'I have never written anything like it before – you will be amazed when you hear it!' Just so.

(More on the life of Wagner can be found on pages 169–170.)

WHO'S WHO AND WHAT'S WHAT

The story below is based on the libretto. Certain directors may amend opera stories to suit their production.

Some time ago, **Marke**, King of Cornwall and England, had a sister Blancheflor. She died giving birth to **Tristan** who is now heir to the childless King.

When the Irish chieftain Morold came to collect his tribute from Cornwall, Tristan killed him in a fight in which he himself was badly wounded. Tristan sent Morold's head back to Ireland. Morold's fiancée, **Isolde**, the Irish Princess, found a splinter in the skull. She discovered that this matched the nick in Tristan's sword when Tristan, disguised as '**Tantris**', sailed to Ireland to get medical treatment from her (she was renowned for her healing powers).

She knew that she had her betrothed's killer, lying helpless in front of her. She could have taken instant revenge, but, as the poet put it, 'whatever a maid may survey in a man all pleased her very well.' She dropped the sword when *Er sah mir in die Augen* ('he looked me in the eyes').

Tristan, cured by her, returned to Cornwall, to resume his position as King Marke's most honoured and honourable courtier. Peace between Ireland and Cornwall is about to be sealed by the marriage of Princess Isolde to the elderly King Marke, who has sent his favourite, the Lord Tristan, to fetch her home.

* * *

[10] For Romantics, language alone was an inadequate means of communication; it needed to be emancipated into music.

The opera begins with the well-known **Prelude** (which opens with the 'Tristan chord'). This sums up the irrepressible love-hatred which Isolde now holds for Tristan, unknown to him. They are aboard ship on the return journey. Isolde is in a vile mood, infuriated at a **common sailor** insinuating that she is a trophy bride; distressed that her forthcoming marriage constitutes a betrayal of her country and her dead fiancé; and frustrated that the haughty Tristan, who honour obliges to keep distant from her, shows her no gratitude (or love).

Brangäne, her lady-in-waiting, cannot understand her mistress. The proposed marriage seems ideal: she tries unsuccessfully to calm her down. Isolde reveals to her the story of the pathetic **Tantris**. She also asks her to get the phial of poison in the **box of potions** which her mother gave her as a leaving present.

She has Tristan summoned. The atmosphere is further soured by **Kurwenal**, Tristan's hearty, truculent, but supremely loyal knight, who is enraged at the disrespect being shown to his lord. Isolde intends that both she and Tristan should, unknown to him, drink a cup of poison. When she explains her grounds for hating him, he offers her his sword; but she cannot arrive at her wedding having killed the man who was escorting her there.

Brangäne, instead of poison, gives them a **love potion**, which results in them falling wildly in love just as **King Marke** comes aboard to receive his bride. This concludes Act 1.

King Marke is away on a hunt. In the garden of his castle, despite Brangäne's apprehension, Isolde has an assignation with Tristan. She indicates the all-clear by quenching the torch, the light. The **love duet** *O sink hernieder* portrays their passionate affair. Their bliss can however only be fully consummated in **death**, in which they will be united for eternity.

They ignore Brangäne's warnings and are caught *in flagrante delicto*. Tristan's only explanation is that he is about to return to the land of **Darkness**,[11] the wondrous realm of **Night**, from whence his mother brought him at birth. The King, in **King Marke's Lament**, is appalled

---

[11] Despite it seeming to us counter-intuitive, Darkness (Night, eternity) is infinitely preferable to Light (Day). Wagner's complex views in this regard are touched on later in this chapter.

at the betrayal. Tristan's supposed 'best friend' **Melot** mortally wounds him to avenge the cuckolded King.

Tristan is taken by Kurwenal back to his home, **Kareol** in Britanny, where a **shepherd boy**, playing a lament, is posted to act as a lookout for Isolde. Kurwenal has sent for her: she alone has the healing powers to save Tristan. Tristan raves at length about his condition and his (Wagner's) philosophy. The shepherd boy's mournful tune indicates that Isolde has not yet arrived. Eventually, she arrives and he finally dies in her arms, and enters another world.

A second ship lands, bearing King Marke with Brangäne and Melot. Kurwenal assumes that the King has come to attack them. He attempts to fight them off and kills Melot. Kurwenal goes for Marke and is himself killed. Marke, who has heard about the potion, laments that they are all dead. But Isolde is already in another world. The opera concludes with the **Liebestod**, 'the scene all Wagner lovers wait for.' She and Tristan are united in supreme bliss, in death.

THE INTERVAL: TALKING POINTS

The demanding roles

Pavarotti's manager described the role of Isolde as 'hands down the toughest soprano part in the repertory: hardly anybody can sing the thing, let alone sing it well.' It is the longest female role in opera. In Act 1 alone, the role is longer than the entire role of Aïda.

Although Maria Callas sang Isolde, most of the specialists in Italian opera have not tended to sing the part. Isoldes are however sometimes also performers of Turandot; the Swedish singer Birgit Nilsson being a notable example of this.[12]

---

[12] The Mayor of Bayreuth addressed her, after a *Tristan* première, 'Miss Nilsson, we would be honoured to have you buried in Bayreuth!' In defence of the official, the ground of Bayreuth contains the remains of some very distinguished people, Liszt, Jean Paul, the Wagner family and many great performers. Richard and Cosima Wagner lie in the grounds of their villa, Wahnfried.

Legendary Tristans have included Wolfgang Windgassen[13] and the Canadian Jon Vickers. As well as Nilsson, who made her debut at the New York Met in the role, legendary Isoldes have included Kirsten Flagstad whose co-star was often Lauritz Melchior, a huge Dane. He appeared over 200 times as Tristan.

Without the support of **King Ludwig II of Bavaria** (1845–1886) we may assume that the composition of *The Ring* and Wagner's later works *Die Meistersinger* and *Parsifal* would never have been completed. Ludwig was passionately fond of music, although Wagner, probably unfairly, reckoned he was totally unmusical and endowed only with a poetic temperament.

The ancient Wittelsbach family had recently created the new Munich and restored the family castle of Berg fifteen miles to the south, and also the 'castle of Lohengrin' at Hohenschwangau, on the edge of the Alps. When only twelve, Ludwig heard about a production of Wagner's *Lohengrin*; he began to study Wagner's writings and soon he knew the libretti of *Tannhäuser* and *Lohengrin* by heart.

Ludwig called his steam-launch for cruising on Lake Starnberg, twenty miles south of Munich, *Tristan*.

To the consternation of his ministers, Ludwig began to build his own magical castles, shrines to German chivalry and in particular Tannhäuser, Lohengrin and Parsifal. The castle at Neuschwanstein – which has been described as 'one of the most fascinating toys in the world' – was begun in 1869, Linderhof in the following year, and Herrenchiemsee in 1878. The overall cost was little more than the indemnity Bavaria paid to Prussia after backing the losing side in the Austro-Prussian War in 1866.

---

[13] Windgassen was a soccer fan and supporter of Germany. During a performance of *Tristan*, he managed to be kept informed of the results of a big match. In Act 3, the inconsolable King Marke went up to him and said 'You lost 4–2 to Sweden', meanwhile Tristan had been kept informed by stagehands holding up placards in the wings. The love duet had been rather platonic because he was thinking about the placards rather than about the performance.

But Ludwig's eccentric behaviour and his support for Wagner led eventually to his deposition. He and his doctor drowned in Lake Starnberg, next to the castle of Berg, when out on an evening walk. What exactly happened remains a mystery. 'The King was not mad; he was just an eccentric living in a world of dreams,' said his relative, Elisabeth, Empress of Austria.

More on the ancient sources

Gottfried von Strassburg's epic, on which Wagner based his poem, was one of the early literary versions of a story whose origin is in Celtic antiquity, and was handed down orally.

The poem of 20,000 lines is full of tales of treachery, lies, deception and fraud. It seems to us to be thoroughly immoral. The lovers lead their wretchedly suspicious king up many a garden path before he finally discovers the truth. As all their actions can be attributed to the love potion, the misbehaviour seems to be justifiable, somehow.

Gottfried's lovers consummate on board ship. They find an easy way to get round the difficulty that their relationship provided for the nuptials of King Marke with his wife: they get the virgin Brangäne to lie with Marke. Isolde then worries that she will have too much fun and will not vacate the bed before dawn. So after the couple break for a post-coital glass of wine (in the dark), Isolde takes over. To the lustful King, 'one woman was like another ... both paid him their dues, one way and another, so that he noticed nothing amiss.' In case Brangäne might reveal what has happened, Isolde tries to have her murdered, and her would-be murderers killed.

In the poem, there are three Isoldes, the mother, her daughter Isolde the Fair, 'the wonder of Ireland ... an ultimate unsurpassable perfection', and a third 'Isolde of the White Hands' from Arundel.

After Tristan has to flee Cornwall, he does some soldiering overseas. In another slightly earlier source, Thomas of Britain, Tristan then takes up with Isolde of the White Hands, whom he marries. But he does not consummate the marriage, and makes various clandestine trips back to Cornwall to have his pleasure with his former flame,

Isolde the Fair, the Queen. When discovered, he is wounded with a poisoned sword, and returns to Britanny, where he sends for his sweetheart. He orders that a white sail should be hoisted when her ship is seen, and a black one if she is not on it. Isolde of the White Hands arranges for a black sail to be hoisted despite the fact that the Queen is on her way. Tristan dies. The Queen arrives and dies.

One suspects that the French or Italian composers, had they been writing an opera based on the same material, would have retained some of the more colourful material. It probably would not have passed the censors, however. They might have included Isolde's trial by ordeal with a hot iron – in which she avoided perjuring herself by swearing a formal oath which was strictly accurate even if wholly misleading. They might have included Tristan's second trip to Ireland in which he slew the dragon in County Wexford, and also the Cave of Love episode wherein the two nourished themselves on nothing but love, but at the crucial moment ensured that they were discovered lying on an altar divided by a sword. Wagner cut away all these inessentials.

Darkness and Light: the philosophical stuff

Wagner fancied himself as a philosopher. And he was highly proficient, even if Nietzsche, who he knew well, rejected his views.

Views which are false, which wither and die (as all 'philosophies' tend to do), are particularly hard to explain. In order to enjoy *Tristan*, we do not need to understand Wagner's complex metaphysical viewpoint, or delve into the various interpretations of it which compound what may already seem confusing. But it helps to have an inkling of what is being sung about on the *Tristan* stage – especially in Acts 2 and 3 when there are many references to Darkness, Light, Night, Day and so on.

Metaphysical philosophers like Wagner and Schopenhauer[14] are concerned with what actually exists, how we know it exists, and

---

[14] Wagner, never one to underrate himself, believed that he and Schopenhauer arrived independently at similar philosophical conclusions. The summary given here is of course just one of many interpretations.

whether there is anything beyond our direct experience (for example, a god, a heaven). Many philosophers have stated that things beyond our experience may well exist, although we will never know for certain – for Christians, such items (e.g. God, Heaven) then become a matter of faith.

For Wagner, there is indeed an additional world to the world we experience. That parallel world is reality, the eternity where we all belong. We yearn to enter that world. We might perhaps expect Reality to be a bright, celestial place, suffused with light, such as we would expect to encounter in a heaven. But, for Wagner, it is the Romantic world of 'Darkness'.

The world which we experience and perceive is merely a representation of this world of 'Darkness', the other side of the same coin. An analogy (albeit not Wagner's) could be the bright and dark sides of the mirror, one side of which is generally brown or black. The dark side and the reflective side are inseparable; you cannot have the one without the other. We (on the bright side) are just the temporary manifestation of this other, dark, place, 'the unconscious eternity, the Beyond.'

So far, so good, perhaps. But with the next proposition, the opera enthusiast is easily lost. It is this: one way by which we can access and reach that Reality is through the will, a key feature of which is the sexual drive to reproduce.[15] This, next to the love of life, is 'the ultimate goal of almost all human effort',[16] and, for Wagner, is consummated in the *Liebestod*.

To propound his viewpoint, Wagner sought to produce a musical art-work analogous to ancient Greek theatre. In that, music and drama were combined to present the author's story and, more importantly, proclaim his beliefs to his fellow citizens. *Tristan*, especially Act 2,

---

[15] Despite one chapter having the titillating heading 'The Metaphysics of Sexual Love', *The World as Will and Representation*, Schopenhauer's magnum opus of nearly 1,200 pages, is not recommended pre-opera reading. This chapter mainly argues that nature dupes the individual into confusing physical desire with the overriding imperative, which justifies anything, of propagating the species appropriately.

[16] It follows that the urge to procreate and sustain the species overrides the individual's needs or duties: Tristan's treachery and betrayal of his King is thus wholly justifiable.

displays the sensuousness of Greek Dionysiac drama, surging, intoxi-cated, sinking into eternal rapture, wholly absorbed and sublimated in it, wholly dissolved into it – *ewig einig, ohne End', ohn' Erwachen, ohn' Erbangen*. This leaves the audience almost prostrate, virtually insane. 'Good performances of *Tristan* must make the listeners go mad,' said Wagner. Other philosophers might say the same.

The term *Liebestod* (love-death) can be applied just to certain parts of the opera, or, alternatively, to a specific Wagnerian concept exemplified within it.

Wagner used the term to describe the love music in Act 2, but it is also applied to Isolde's oration which concludes the work, and which is sometimes combined with the Prelude in concert programmes.

Wagner's almost unique concept defies concise verbal expla-nation: it is best conveyed, as he thought, through music, or in literature. (It has parallels with the nirvana found in Buddhism, which he had studied.)

Love-death can easily be confused with routine Romantic suicide: but it is not 'death through love'. It is more like passing into eternity for the sake of love. We move towards it in the scene with the love potion at the end of Act 1. In Act 3, *Liebestod* is proclaimed by Tristan, even if perhaps not clarified. It is exempli-fied in the opera's conclusion, by which time most audiences are, perhaps fortunately, so overwhelmed by the beauty of Wagner's work that they forego a credible explanation. *Liebestod* is utter unification, 'united, undivided', but it is not physical or sensual: using the words of a great 20th-century Italian novelist, it might be described as the 'annihilation of one's own personality, that sub-limation in renunciation, without which there is no love.'

The Tristan motif and chord

The cellos begin the overture and are immediately joined by the woodwind. The sad opening notes seem to relate to the 'trist' of

Tristan[17]; then the music soars 'ecstatically upwards' in a way which, for one authority, depicted 'the woman yielding unquestioningly to the rapture of requited love.'

The quiet discord of F, G#, B, and D#, resolves itself into further discords rather than resolving in the normal classical way. The chromatic chord progressions and shifting keys left contemporary listeners with a novel feeling of the absence of key.

The motif and chord has 'spawned countless analyses'. It recurs as a leitmotif, the motif of the love-potion, longing or yearning. It has been quoted, for example, in works by Debussy, Schoenberg and Berg, and by Wagner himself in Act 3 of *Die Meistersinger*. The style was adopted in Puccini's *Manon Lescaut*, when portraying passionate love.

For many, things 'went wrong' with music after Wagner's *Lohengrin*. Contemporary twelve-tone composers can be traced directly back to the *Tristan* idiom and its 'ambiguous kind of tonality.' It was contentious at the time: the eminent critic, Hanslick, complained that the Prelude reminded him of 'a martyr whose intestines are slowly unwound from his body on a reel.'

'Modern' productions

After Wagner died, his widow Cosima, the daughter of Liszt, saw it as her duty to recreate his own productions as faithfully as possible, 'rather than to establish her own theatrical style.' Wagner left explicit instructions for his productions, which were essentially depictions of Viking-like and medieval characters performing against a background of painted scenery flats.

Meanwhile, in the early 1900s, there was a move towards symbolic representation, especially after technical developments in theatre presentation, notably lighting, opened new avenues. Symbolic representation was cautiously promoted by the director of the Imperial Opera in Vienna, Gustav Mahler, the great composer. He welcomed a stage

---

[17] The story goes that when he was born, the priest who baptised him recommended the name Tristan. *Triste* means sorrow: he was an orphan who had been conceived in sorrow, born in sorrow and indeed would live in sorrow.

on which 'everything is only intimated.' He appointed Alfred Roller, whose skill at 'painting with lighting' provided a breakthrough in the style of production. He was followed in style by Adolphe Appia, for whom 'the designer's task was to paint with light in an empty space', and who valued the power of suggestion rather than literal depiction.

As Birgit Nilsson remarked in a later context, 'the provocative stage directors had not yet, thank God, begun their devastating interventions.' Mahler certainly did not issue a licence for anarchy: his overriding concern was to achieve unity between music and its visual manifestation on the stage. He was not prepared to give up his overall control to another person, a designer or producer. He only gave consent for revolutionary designs after much thought had convinced him of their relevance to the work's musical shape. And his successor in his endeavour, Otto Klemperer, was concerned to make 'not avant garde theatre but good theatre.'

But Mahler opened the floodgates. Wagner's grandson Wieland, in his productions after the Second World War, gave the modernist approach the imprimatur of the Wagner family. The tide continues to flow. A literal depiction, say, in the style of 'Vikings', would hardly be reviewed enthusiastically today.

Wagner's poetry

Wagner mainly wrote his own poetry for his operas. Up until *Lohengrin*, he had usually written 'conventional' poetry. Later, he became greatly influenced by the distinctive Nordic poetry in which lines are linked together by alliteration or *Stabreim*.

This provided an alternative to the rhyming or blank verse which suited the arias and recitatives of conventional operas, but which Wagner found constricted the rhythms of his free-flowing musical declamation. In *Tristan*, he still used end rhyme, but there is considerable use of alliteration.

The rhythm of Wagner's music complements the stresses in his poetry.

When we become tired of looking at the static stage in Act 3, and 'when our ears begin to buzz with the almost senseless alliterations, all we have to do is to sit back and listen to the music.' *Tristan*, with its sexual lust, this 'passionate symphonic orgy', carries the sensuous expressiveness of music to its ultimate limits.

ACT BY ACT

Act 1

A ship on the Irish Sea

Isolde's angular and truly violent music underscores her conflicting and confused emotions: her love-hate of Tristan; and her sense of guilt for having failed to kill him when she had the opportunity, thus betraying the memory of Morold, her dead fiancée, and her Irish compatriots.

Tristan has collected her from Ireland to take her to Cornwall to marry King Marke. Tristan is on the prow of the ship, together with his retainer, Kurwenal. Isolde is also on stage, in her own quarters, with Brangäne, her lady-in-waiting.

After the well-known Prelude, the act opens with a sailor singing a cheeky song about a 'headstrong, beautiful Irish girl'. This ignites Isolde, who, apart from her deep sense of guilt, is furious at being taken away as a kind of trophy bride. She calls on storm and tempest to destroy the lot of them. Brangäne desperately tries to calm her down, and asks her to confide in her. She does not know Isolde's guilty secret about having foregone the opportunity to revenge herself on Tristan, and cannot understand why her lady left Ireland noticeably pale and anorexic and is so unenthusiastic about her forthcoming nuptials to a celebrity husband, even if he is a bit elderly.

The sailor's cheeky song is heard again. Isolde eyes Tristan with love-hatred, and commands Brangäne to require him to attend her and pay homage. When Brangäne goes to fetch Tristan, Kurwenal jauntily greets her with 'Watch it, Tristan, here's an emissary from Isolde': *Hab' acht Tristan, Botschaft von Isolde*. Tristan[18] however replies

---

[18] The conductor Sir Thomas Beecham was rendered speechless when he insisted that the Tristan should bear himself in a more dignified way. 'Don't you know who Tristan is supposed to be?' he asked. The Tristan, a Yorkshireman, replied 'E's only a sailor, isn't he?'

that they will reach land before sunset; he cannot come to Isolde because he must steer the ship, and it would not be seemly or customary for him to meet Isolde before he formally presents her as bride to his King. Kurwenal, who is annoyed by Brangäne's disrespect, reminds her of Tristan's heroic status, and how Morold was sent home in a coffin. These sentiments are echoed by the sailors. The atmosphere is as bad as it can possibly be.

Brangäne reports back to Isolde. But the Princess has been eavesdropping and is already contemptuous of Tristan's curt response. She tells Brangäne about the story of the splinter, how she cured the pathetic 'Tantris', and she disparages this conceited man who she had desisted from killing: *Er sah mir in die Augen* ('He looked me in the eyes'). In a mocking way, she describes how she is being brought to Cornwall as a trophy bride. She curses Tristan: *Fluch dir Verruchter.*

Brangäne desperately tries to calm her down, reassuring her that she will be Queen. That does not help: Isolde mutters that she will be unloved, while the noblest man will be near her. Brangäne does not understand her or her love-hatred of Tristan. She assures her that if there is any difficulty arising from the fact that she will have an old man for a husband, she has the remedy: Isolde's mother has given her a box of potions including the necessary cure for such a situation. Isolde commands her to bring it. Rather than an aphrodisiac, Isolde has poison in mind: the death drink, *Der Todestrank.* At this moment, the sailors give the order to shorten sail as they are close to land.

Kurwenal arrives and jocularly orders the ladies to get ready for landing: *Auf! Auf! Ihr Frauen!* Isolde dignifiedly announces that she wont budge unless Tristan comes and craves pardon for an unexpiated wrong. She bids the horrified Brangäne farewell and orders her to prepare the drink of atonement, *Den Sühnetrank,* by which, to Brangäne's horror, she means the poison.

Tristan comes to Isolde and coldly and formally asks what she wishes: *Begehrt, Herrin, was Ihr wünscht.* When she admonishes him for earlier refusing to come – custom, and respect are his excuse – she informs him that there exists a *Blutschuld* ('blood-feud') between them.[19] Tristan says that he thought that this was all sorted out before they left Ireland. She tells him about the healing of 'Tantris' and her unfulfilled commitment to avenge Morold, and blames herself for not having struck Tristan there and then. 'OK,' replies Tristan, calmly, 'here's my sword.' She replies that she can hardly turn up to her wedding having killed the best man. She says that the wrong should be expiated by them drinking the drink of atonement (which is of course poison): *Nun lass uns Sühne trinken.* For her, they have reached the end, and not just of the journey: *Wir sind am Ziel.*

The sailors are heard taking in the sails. Isolde mockingly presages Tristan's introduction of this trophy bride to his liege lord and uncle (King Marke): a nice girl, well-brought up, whose betrothed (by the way) he happened to slay; they have settled their scores by taking the drink of atonement.

Tristan grabs the cup. She stops him drinking it all – 'half is mine.' Contemptuously, she declares *Verräter, Ich trink' sie dir!* ('Faithless wretch, I drink to thee!')

The effect is immediately clear. Brangäne has in fact given them the love potion, the *Liebestrank.* Having drunk it, they fall rapturously into each others' arms as the ship comes in to Tintagel to land. The act concludes with some sensationally erotic music.

Act 2

Garden of Marke's castle in Tintagel, Cornwall

Isolde awaits Tristan, with whom she has arranged an assignation at a time when King Marke has gone off on a hunt. This act provides some of the greatest and most erotic love music ever composed.

First, Brangäne urges Isolde to be careful: the horns still sound too close. She fears that Tristan's enemies have 'stitched them up'. It had been obvious that something was up between the two of them, from the state of utter confusion in which they disembarked from the ship.

---

[19] Birgit Nilsson wrote that Isolde's 'lips speak of humiliation and revenge but her heart speaks only of love. Over Isolde's entire persona must be written, "I love you! I love you!"'

Isolde is not worried. Brangäne tells her that she is deluded by desire, and tries to get her to call the assignation off. She particularly fears Melot, Tristan's best friend, and bitterly regrets having given Tristan and Isolde the wrong potion.

Isolde tells her to stop being so pathetic: Melot is party to the plan for the assignation. She orders her to quench the torch, the light, and thereby signal the all-clear to Tristan. Isolde, having explained how she must obey the goddess of love, *Frau Minne*, who wrenched the lovers back from death, herself quenches the torch and orders Brangäne to go to the look-out tower and keep watch.

Tristan arrives and the lovers fall ecstatically into each others' arms. In the surging music, with two high Cs for the excited Isolde, Tristan describes how he could hardly wait until the Light was extinguished (*Das Licht, Das Licht*): Isolde has defied the Day, (*Der Tage, Der Tage*) and they will be plunged into Darkness. Isolde could never be his in the bright light of Day. She had longed to draw him into Darkness, the Night. Hail to the potion *O heil dem Tranke*, declares Tristan, which revealed to him the wondrous realm of Night for which he has yearned and longed; holy Night, where eternally true love's delight smiles at him.

They sink down for the great love duet, *O sink hernieder, Nacht der Liebe* ('Descend upon us Night of Love').[20] Brangäne intersperses warnings from the lookout tower[21]: *Habet acht, bald entweicht die Nacht* ('Take care, soon Night [Darkness] will give way to Day'). But Tristan and Isolde, united, undivided, just want to enter into oblivion, to 'die', never to awake, and be united in love for eternity: *Ewig einig,*

[20] The first performance of this section was given privately in the music room in Paris of Pauline Viardot, the leading mezzo-soprano of the mid-19th century. Tristan calls for the last glimmer of light to be extinguished: *Verlöschen nun die letzte Leuchte*. It has been known for this to coincide with all the fuses blowing, or even for stage and house lights to come up in a sudden blaze.

[21] Between the wars, scenery in provincial theatres could be somewhat amateur, although it was to their enormous credit, in days before the widespread dissemination of recordings, that they put on works like *Tristan*. Having given instructions for a tower in Act 2, Beecham arrived in Kings Lynn, Norfolk and was surprised to find 'our old friend the set for the second act of *Iolanthe*, with Big Ben in the background.'

ohne End' namenlos in Lieb' umfangen. So far as the lovers are concerned, let Day give way to death.

It does. Kurwenal rushes in ahead of King Marke and his retainers. As dawn breaks, the lovers are found *in flagrante delicto*. Melot, Tristan's best friend, has betrayed them. This is no comfort for King Marke, who is appalled. He laments[22] that Tristan, his heir and most loyal subject, should have betrayed him: *Tatest du's wirklich?* How could he do it, after so much trust was placed in him? Tristan cannot find an explanation, other than that he is about to return to the land of Darkness, the wondrous realm of Night, from whence his mother brought him at birth. Isolde pledges to follow. Melot and Tristan fight. Tristan does not defend himself. He simply looks pityingly at him, because those who have experienced 'Night' see 'the demands of friendship and marital loyalty' as illusions of the 'Day'.

The leitmotifs

Wagner unifies the opera, and to a great extent tells the story musically, by means of leitmotifs. These are snippets of melody, each 'a sort of musical label' associated with a particular person, thing or idea, such as the motif of the love-potion, longing or yearning. There is a motif for the Day and a motif for the Night. The motif, which is woven and blended into the musical fabric to underpin the context, is usually sounded at the first appearance of the item and repeated, in some form or another, when it recurs or is relevant.

Act 3

A courtyard in Tristan's ancestral castle, Kareol

Kurwenal has taken the dying Tristan to his own castle in Brittany. While a shepherd boy plays in the background, he tends Tristan. He

---

[22] The music of the last twenty minutes of the act, which includes the King's Lament, is magnificent. However, it can come as an anticlimax to an audience emotionally exhausted by the love music.

has sent to Cornwall for Isolde, because he knows that she alone has the healing powers to save his lord.

The extraordinary dialogue between Kurwenal and Tristan becomes more comprehensible if one appreciates that Tristan has been so mortally wounded that he has actually entered Death, the Darkness, the Night into which he and Isolde in their earlier love music were yearning to be united. But they are inseparable, as the love duet has explained, united as 'Tristan *and* Isolde'. Isolde has however called him back out of the Night into the Day. So he is drawn relentlessly back to the world of Light. Tristan longs for her arrival so that by their joint death, *Liebestod*, they will quench the light and together enter into Darkness, where they will be united blissfully in eternity, nirvana, a *Liebestod*. All this is in total contrast to the hearty, well-intentioned, worldly outlook of Kurwenal who just hopes that by fetching Isolde, the medical expert, Tristan can be healed in the physical sense that we all understand.

The act opens with the shepherd boy playing a sad tune on his pipe (a cor anglais). Kurwenal tells him to sing a jolly one when he sees the ship (with Isolde in it) on the horizon. When Tristan awakes, the joyful Kurwenal explains how he brought Tristan back to Kareol in Britanny after the fight with Melot. Tristan, who we might regard as having been to Purgatory and back, recalls how he has entered the nether-world of Darkness – *im weiten Reich der Weltennacht* – but his yearning for Isolde has driven him back to seek her in the Light of Day.

Kurwenal explains that, once Isolde arrives, they will be able to live happily ever after. Tristan says that this is not so: he has entered the realm of universal Night, whence, if only Isolde would come and release him, he would be able to stay. Burning love, yearning, drove him back to Light, the false bright Light that still shines on Isolde. He has already heard death's door (*des Todes Tor*) crash behind him: Isolde has however called him back out of the Night into the Day. Curse the Day![23]

---

[23] His dramatic curses are directed 'at the torment of living in the absence of the beloved.'

Kurwenal in his matter-of-fact way informs Tristan that he has sent for the best doctor he knows, and that she is about to arrive. Tristan thanks him profusely and thinks that he sees the ship: *Das Schiff! Das Schiff!* Deprived of Isolde, yearning for her, he cannot find peace.

But there is no ship yet. The shepherd boy's mournful tune haunts Tristan, reminding him of the death of his parents, which determined his own fate: to yearn and die, *Sehnen und Sterben*. In a sequence of great complexity, his mind wanders to his going to Ireland to be healed by Isolde, how she failed to kill him, and the potion which cast him back into the Day, the dreadful Day from which he seemingly cannot escape.

Kurwenal is relieved that he is still alive and tries to calm him. But Tristan is surprised that he cannot see her coming. Surely Kurwenal can see the ship! He eventually sees it, and, with Isolde clearly on deck, it comes in to land. They are exultant.

Kurwenal goes to fetch Isolde. She arrives, and Tristan expires in her arms. Isolde, cheated of an hour's happiness on earth, declares, 'United, let the Light of life be quenched for us both.'

But there is a second ship. King Marke arrives with Brangäne and Melot. Kurwenal assumes that it has come to attack them. He attempts to fight them off and kills Melot. Kurwenal goes for Marke and is himself killed.

Brangäne tries to explain that they are all mistaken. With the stage littered with bodies, Marke laments that they are all dead: *Tot denn alles! Alles tot!* He explains how as soon as he learnt about the love potion and that Tristan was guiltless, he hurried to Britanny to wed Isolde to Tristan. But Isolde is already in another world. The opera concludes with Isolde and Tristan sinking, unconscious, into supreme bliss, *höchste Lust*, transfigured in death. The Liebestod is some of the most glorious music ever written, indeed 'the scene all Wagner lovers wait for.'

VERDI: *RIGOLETTO*

THE OPERA AND ITS COMPOSER

Debauchery, seduction and rape by a king. Regicide, kidnap, murder. It is not surprising that the police and censors in Venice gave Verdi a hard time over his proposed opera for their 1850/51 carnival season. The libretto, by Francesco Maria Piave,[1] was based on *Le Roi s'Amuse*, a play by the towering French literary figure, Victor Hugo (1802–1885), who we know particularly for *Les Misérables* and the *Hunchback of Notre Dame*. The play had been banned in France after the first night.

Even in the 1920s, the audience at New York's Met found the rape sufficiently shocking that some women turned their backs to the stage when Gilda, deflowered, emerged from the royal bedroom.

Towards the middle of 1850, Verdi had contracted with La Fenice to produce a new show for the carnival season in the New Year. For some time, he had been pondering the operatic potential of Hugo's play, which is set in the luxurious dissipation of the French court of King François 1er, consummate lecher and debauchee, contemporary of the English King Henry VIII.

The proposed libretto proved unacceptable to the authorities, who regretted that Verdi had chosen to base his opera on a play which displayed 'repulsive immorality and obscene triviality.' True to character, Verdi 'passed the buck' and threw the blame onto Piave.

Delegations from Venice, and emasculated libretti, went backwards and forwards to Verdi's farm, where he was trying to work, as well as to deal with business aspects and recover from a stomach upset. He was also in the middle of a domestic crisis, expelling his parents,

---

[1] Francesco Maria Piave (1810–1876) was born at Murano (Venice) where his father owned a glassworks. At first, he trained to be a priest but instead he became a proofreader and then a librettist. Although he wrote for other Italian composers, he worked principally for Verdi, starting with *Ernani*. His libretti include *La Traviata* and *Simon Boccanegra*. Sometimes Verdi brought others in to assist, as in *Macbeth* and *La Forza del destino*.

with whom he was having a row about his mistress, and arguing even over rights to the produce of the chicken-yard.

Verdi

The Venetian censors had not allowed for the dour, determined composer who, although desperate, dug in. Verdi had a sure sense of what would be a success: his market was the audience, and he knew that they had to be entertained and that he could make this a winner. There was a stand-off until less than three weeks before the opera was due to be performed: at one time, it looked as if Venice would have no opera at all from Verdi. With intense pressure exerted by the composer and the theatre authorities, the censors' arms were twisted, with the result that we have an opera which must have been about as politically incorrect as was possible at the time. It is politically incorrect today, but in a rather different way, featuring as it does a disabled comedian, and generalising about women being fickle (*mobile*). It is surprising what can be done under cover of a good tune.

In the negotiations, the opera had been relocated from the Louvre in Paris to the ducal court in Mantua.[2] What the New York ladies would have done if the opera had shown the King breaking into the bedroom after Gilda had (unfortunately) chosen that room in which

---

[2] This was then considered an insult to the Gonzagas, the former dukes of Mantua, patrons of Titian and Monteverdi. Some members of the family still lived in Venice.

to take refuge, we do not know. Verdi had agreed to cut that bit. But when somebody later suggested adding another scene, he refused, and wondered whether they would like him to show the Duke and Gilda together in the bedroom.

The première at La Fenice on 11 March 1851 was a great success and the opera played for thirteen nights. Working from a complete sketch which he had prepared, the revised opera had been completed on 5 February, leaving the instrumentation to be done during the rehearsals. But in the rush, Verdi had made no compromise on quality. Even in late January, he had set about rewriting the Act 2 duet *Sì, vendetta* – now one of the very popular tunes – because he was unhappy with it.

Rigoletto has been compared in Verdi's output to Beethoven's revolutionary *Eroica* symphony, because both made a clean break with the past. In Verdi's opera, 'the barriers between formal melody and recitative are down as never before'; 'There is no formal precedent for it in the whole of Italian opera.'

The well-known quartet in Act 3 is the pièce de résistance of the opera. It has been described as one of the finest pieces of concerted music in Italian opera, an achievement comparable with some of Mozart's. In this, the Duke seduces the prostitute with the glorious *Bella figlia dell'amore* while Rigoletto and Gilda eavesdrop; she is appalled; her father is determined to take revenge. The four characters express four different feelings at the same time. This is 'something that can only be accomplished through the means of the music drama, for the music unites the outpouring of their various sentiments in a homogeneous constellation and lends it an accent of plausibility.' Words alone could not express this.

However, *La donna è mobile* is the tune which immediately caught on with the public generally, and has done more than anything to make *Rigoletto* one of the most popular of all operas. Musically, that tune is not up to the standard of, say, the quartet. One expert has regretted how, 'To the uninformed, *La donna è mobile* is *Rigoletto*.'[3]

---

[3] It has been suggested that this catchy tune is plebeian and not suited to the character of an aristocrat. Secondly, if anybody is fickle it is the Duke himself rather than women generally. Verdi's sense of theatre was such that he knew that *La donna è mobile* was going to cause a sensation

Within five minutes of the curtain rising, we hear the Duke's *Questa o quella*, and later, Gilda's *Caro nome*. But the wonderful music does not stop there: we also have the Duke's *Parmi veder le lagrime*, Gilda's *Tutte le feste*, Rigoletto's *Piangi! piangi fanciulla* and, not least, the final duet between father and daughter at the end. This is a feast.

Giuseppe Verdi, whose life spanned the 19th century, brought the development of Italian opera to its ultimate conclusion. He was born on 10 October 1813 in northern Italy, at Le Roncole, near Busseto in the Duchy of Parma. He died in Milan on 27 January 1901. When La Scala reopened after his funeral, the programme, conducted by Toscanini, included the quartet from *Rigoletto*, with Enrico Caruso as the Duke.

His studies in Milan were sponsored by a local businessman, Antonio Barezzi, whose daughter he subsequently married. But she died, as did their children, early on. After this, Verdi lived with (and eventually married) Giuseppina Strepponi, the daughter of the organist of Monza cathedral. She had an 'endearing person-ality', but also a 'reputation' for depositing unwanted children around the place. She was a star in the late 1830s and was the prima donna of Verdi's early opera *Nabucco*, best known for the Chorus of Hebrews yearning for freedom. From early on, Verdi (and his name) was associated with the Italian nationalism spear-headed by Mazzini and Garibaldi, and this relationship contrib-uted to his success.

By 1851, Verdi had composed or arranged eleven operas including the first of the three ground-breaking operas of the early 1850s *Rigoletto*, *Il Trovatore*, and *La Traviata*. He set himself up as a gentleman farmer on an estate he acquired at Sant'Agata, near his birthplace. It was a difficult time for the tactless, humourless and unforgiving workaholic. He felt he owed no thanks to the

and might be plagiarised. So he held it back and would not provide it to the Duke until the last minute. He pleaded with the whole orchestra and cast to keep it confidential.

people of his birthplace who did not hide their outrage at his living openly with Giuseppina. His house was robbed by the servants; his mother died; he had major rows with his father about finances and with his father-in-law about family matters. This was the context in which he was working on *Rigoletto*, *Il Trovatore* and *La Traviata*.

After the subsequent few years, which produced *Les Vêpres siciliennes*, *Simon Boccanegra*, *Un Ballo in maschera* and *La Forza del destino*, Verdi slowed up. Only four operas were composed in the last 38 years of his life. After *Don Carlos* (1867) and *Aïda* (1871), he had a long pause. However, at the end of his career, he was persuaded by the publisher Giulio Ricordi to compose the two operas for which Arrigo Boito contributed the libretti, *Otello* (1887) and *Falstaff* (1893). These considerably added to his greatness. *The Requiem* (1874) was written for the funeral of the writer, poet and novelist Alessandro Manzoni.

Towards the end of his life, he took up with Teresa Stolz, one of his prima donnas.

There was a great divide between the adherents and style of Verdi and of Wagner. Bruno Walter, the conductor, tells of how, in the reign of Cosima Wagner, daughter of Liszt and Wagner's widow (who lasted 47 years beyond his death), it was forbidden to mention the name of Verdi. Bruno Walter said something to her about the astonishing development in Verdi's work between *Ernani* and *Aïda* and finally *Falstaff*. Frau Wagner went icily frigid: 'Development?' she asked. 'I can see no difference between *Ernani* and *Falstaff*.'

WHO'S WHO AND WHAT'S WHAT

The story below is based on the libretto. Certain directors may amend opera stories to suit their production.

In the 16th century, the oversexed **Duke** of Mantua[4] rules over a licentious court. The courtiers dislike the hunchback[5] court jester

---

[4] Mantua (Mantova) is around 100 miles south-east of Milan.
[5] Rigoletto's hump has been known to slide down his back.

Rigoletto. Unknown to everybody, Rigoletto has a beautiful, innocent sixteen-year-old daughter, **Gilda**, of whom he is very protective. He confines her to her lodgings, and she knows nothing about her background or about him. The courtiers **Borsa** and **Marullo** are fed up with Rigoletto's jibes and biting sarcasm, as is Count **Ceprano**, whose **Countess** the Duke is in the process of bedding. They discover that the ugly jester has a mistress (actually Gilda), and conspire to get their revenge by abducting her and presenting her to the Duke.

The Count of **Monterone**[6] complains about the seduction of his daughter by the Duke. The Duke has him arrested, and Rigoletto mocks him. Monterone places a **curse** (*la maledizione*) on both, in particular Rigoletto, for laughing at a father's grief.

On the way to visit his daughter, Rigoletto is stopped by **Sparafucile**, a cut-throat. Rigoletto is haunted by the curse and his low position in life. He may need Sparafucile's services, but not yet.

Rigoletto does not know that Gilda has been followed to church by a man, for whom she has fallen. Rigoletto interrogates **Giovanna**, her companion, about security. Thinking he has heard a noise, he rushes out into the street to look. As he goes out, the Duke slips in behind him.

Inside the house, the Duke, disguised as a poor student, 'Gualtier [Walter] Maldè', declares his 'love' for Gilda. She resists him. But she sings of her love for him and his name – ***Caro nome*** – as she walks upstairs in full view of the conspirators.

The house is next to Ceprano's palace. When Rigoletto returns, the courtiers/conspirators pretend they have come for Ceprano's wife, as Rigoletto himself has suggested the Duke should do. They blindfold him and get him to hold the ladder while they climb into his own house and abduct Gilda. When he discovers that she has been taken, it is the curse: *la maledizione!*

---

[6] Monterone is based on the father of Diane de Poitiers, who became the influential mistress of the son of King François 1ᵉʳ. Her father had conspired against the King, but, with his head on the block, was pardoned. The King had enjoyed his daughter and could hardly execute his 'father-in-law'.

In his palace, the Duke is annoyed that the object of his desire has been kidnapped, but delighted to hear who she is. He does not waste time before going off to have her. The courtiers taunt Rigoletto, who soon senses that Gilda is with the Duke. Only when he demands her back, do the courtiers realise that Gilda is not the jester's mistress but his daughter. They are all against him.

Gilda rushes out, having been raped. She tells her story to Rigoletto, who tries to comfort her: *Piangi! piangi fanciulla.* She, however, is in love with the Duke. Monterone passes on the way to the dungeons. Rigoletto assures him that he will be avenged: *Sì, vendetta, tremenda vendetta.*

Rigoletto takes Gilda to see her lover in action. The Duke has gone, disguised as a soldier, to an inn to have Sparafucile's sister, Maddalena, who has lured him there. He comments to himself on the character of women: ***La donna è mobile***.

In the famous **quartet**, *Bella figlia dell'amore*, the four express their feelings. Gilda is appalled at what she sees and hears; the Duke just wants Maddalena, but she plays 'hard to get'; Rigoletto will take revenge. He does a deal with Sparafucile: half now, half on completion at midnight.

A **storm** brews. The Duke goes to his room and goes to sleep. Meanwhile, Maddalena has fallen for the Duke and wants his life spared. Her brother eventually agrees that anybody else who comes before midnight will be killed instead. Love drives Gilda back, and she determines to die for her lover. As she comes in, she is murdered.

Rigoletto returns at midnight. Sparafucile gives him the body in a sack. As he heads for the river, he hears *La donna è mobile* and knows something is wrong. With another flash of lightning, he recognises Gilda. She still has enough life left to ask her father for forgiveness. When she dies, Rigoletto recalls the curse: *Ah! la maledizione!*[7]

---

[7] Tito Gobbi has described how he used to rise with the ascending chromatic scale on the strings, silhouetting his deformity against the light of dawn. With all the strength left he would hurl '*Ah! la maledizione.*' The score does not indicate that he dies, but 'the last thing one could wish the poor Jester is that he should live to tear his hair fruitlessly. Better death – and our compassion.'

Le Roi s'Amuse

We are less familiar with Victor Hugo's drama *Le Roi s'Amuse*, written in 1832, than with his novels *Les Misérables* and the *Hunchback of Notre Dame*. Verdi called Hugo's play about Triboulet, the deformed jester, 'a creation worthy of Shakespeare', 'the greatest subject and perhaps the greatest play of modern times.'

Triboulet is not so much a source of humour as one of biting sarcasm and contempt, 'the means of laughter to an idiot court.' He has procured a mistress for the King, Diane de Poitiers. The opera follows the play closely. The King even sings a song similar to *La donna è mobile*: 'Women are fickle. They blow around like feathers, the sport of every puff of wind.'

The play was banned after its first performance because the French censors thought that it contained insulting references to the French King, Louis-Philippe. Some of Hugo's descriptions were bound to cause trouble. The jester says, 'Let not that vicious monster contaminate this abode of innocence with his pestilential breath.' And he describes the King as 'this monster of infamy and lust.'

The lawsuit that Hugo brought to permit the performance of the play propelled him into celebrity as a defender of freedom of speech. He lost the suit, however, and the play was banned for another 50 years.

Verdi knew that he was on to a winner. 'Turn Venice upside down to make the censors permit this,' he wrote. He felt it was the most effective subject he had so far set to music. Certainly the opera seems even more effective than Hugo's play. 'Verdi's music fills in the gaps in the action and animates the moments when the figures in the drama do not have anything to say.' The title *Rigoletto* was taken from a parody of Hugo's play, and was only determined around eight weeks before the first performance of the opera.

THE INTERVAL: TALKING POINTS

Rigoletto, the lead part in the opera

Tito Gobbi, the baritone, regarded the title role as the greatest of all Italian baritone parts. The part is 'murderously high … one of the roles that all baritones aspire to sing at some point in their career.' Verdi's Rigoletto was Felice Varesi, who had also been his Macbeth and was subsequently to be a less successful Germont at the première of *La Traviata*.

The role calls for great stamina and very wide emotional range. 'Dramatically it is as three-dimensional as nineteenth-century opera ever becomes.' In a short space, Rigoletto may move from a snarl to a biting speech-song, to a heart-rending legato.

The role of Gilda

Gilda and the Duke are given most of the 'pretty' tunes to sing. Their roles have been sung by Patti, Melba, Callas, Domingo, Pavarotti, and so forth. These days, we would not support a critic contemporary of Verdi who described Gilda's part as 'cold, childish, puerile'; or claim that in 'the Quartet of the last Act her share amounts to little more than a chain of disconnected sobs.'

In the dénouement at the end of Act 3, Gilda's propensity to survive long enough has always been a source of humour. But the staging can cause a difficulty if she is substantial. Occasionally, the Sparafucile has not been not strong enough to give the sack to Rigoletto: he may have to be assisted by some of his 'brothers' who have been brought along for the task. And it has even been known for the lady herself to arrange for her feet to protrude so that she can tiptoe along behind him.

For the staging to be convincing, the protruding boots need to be soldier's boots, boots which Rigoletto takes to be those of the Duke. At the end of a 19th-century performance in Liverpool, he laboriously hauled on stage a vast heavy sack, with policeman's boots protruding, and purporting to contain a petite Gilda. The cast and the conductor came to a halt laughing. Fortunately the orchestra kept playing. The audience was none the wiser, but were 'deeply moved, thinking all was as it should be.' Maybe the boots were those worn today by the mounted police who lead in the Aintree Grand National winner.

The place of *Rigoletto* in Verdi's oeuvre

Verdi's best-known pre-*Rigoletto* opera is probably *Macbeth* (March 1847). With *Rigoletto*, which was quickly followed by *Il Trovatore* and *La Traviata*, he marked the start of a new phase in his career. Despite their gestation being hectic and in quick succession, they are far more effective than his earlier works.

Unlike to the north, where Wagner developed a completely new musical style, Verdi essentially evolved the styles of his Italian predecessors, Rossini, Bellini and Donizetti. The result was his own, a style which represents the culmination of Italian opera.

Rigoletto demonstrates immense dramatic power, an example being the orchestral build-up to the finale of Act 1, 'rising chromatically as if coming to the boil.' Not all listeners have liked his 'violent music'. One mid-19th-century critic considered that 'in Signor Verdi's operas, the hysterical element is as sure to have a large place, as are the incitements for the singer to use the utmost force of his voice.'

But we can enjoy Verdi's incredible sense of theatre, and some most unusual sounds – some far from violent or hysterical – in *Rigoletto*: for example, when the jester is first accosted by the cutthroat assassin, a muted solo cello and double bass play a sinister melody at the top of their range, above a deep accompaniment of woodwind and strings.

Verdi also makes use of recurring musical themes, an obvious one being the theme of Monterone's curse. In the last few minutes, he brings together the melodies of *La donna è mobile*, the storm theme, and the Duke's seductive *Bella figlia dell'amore* theme.

ACT BY ACT

Act 1

At first, in the Duke's palace in Mantua; then a back street

After the sinister Prelude, there is a complete contrast: merrymaking is at its height in the palace, with music at first provided by an on-stage band.[8] The predatory Duke tells a courtier, Borsa, that he intends to seduce a girl he has been eyeing in church for the last three months. He has followed her to a back alley where she is visited by a mysterious man every night.

Meanwhile, he will have the Count of Ceprano's wife. But he never gives his heart to any of them: the women around him are all the same, objects to be had, one after another. Fidelity is nonsense and jealous husbands are ridiculous: *Questa o quella per me pari sono.* During a minuet, also played by an on-stage orchestra, he makes a pass at Ceprano's wife. Despite her protestations and her husband's rage, he takes her off briefly, presumably for a kiss.

Rigoletto is part of the court fixtures and fittings. He has exhausted his resources and descends to insult instead of wit. He taunts Ceprano.

Another courtier, Marullo, excitedly gives the amazing news that Rigoletto has a mistress himself.

Rigoletto suggests to the Duke that he should abduct Ceprano's wife that night, and get rid of her husband by imprisonment or banishment, or even by chopping off his head. The Duke warns Rigoletto that he may go too far: the wrath he provokes could backfire. The courtiers all loathe the jester, but he knows that nobody dares touch the favourite of the Duke. Nevertheless, Ceprano conspires with the others: they will meet at his palace that night, and take action.

The jollifications are interrupted by the Count of Monterone, who demands an audience to complain about the seduction of his daughter by the Duke. Rigoletto imitates Monterone, whose arrest the Duke orders (not least because he is already tainted with having

---

[8] There are three separate 'orchestras' at work: an on-stage band, an on-stage string orchestra and the main orchestra in the pit. What there is not is a female component to the chorus, which is entirely male.

led a conspiracy). Monterone curses them both. In particular, he fingers Rigoletto, the serpent who laughs at a father's grief: *tu che d'un padre ridi al dolore, si maledetto!* While the Duke orders Monterone to be taken away, and the courtiers suitably express their disapproval, Rigoletto shudders at the curse.

* * *

The scene changes to a back alley with, on one side, Ceprano's palace; and, on the other, Rigoletto's modest dwelling, which has an outside staircase visible from the street.

Rigoletto, disguised in a cloak, creeps home muttering about the old man's curse, which haunts him: *Quel vecchio maledivami!* He is approached by Sparafucile, a cut-throat, who he fears may be about to mug him but who is actually seeking business. They converse, in what is called a duet but is in fact a continuous flow of conversation: they discuss terms, and Sparafucile describes how his pretty sister is used as a prostitute to decoy the person to be assassinated.

Rigoletto observes that they are both two of a kind: *Pari siamo!* Sparafucile kills with his sword, he wounds with satire. Still haunted by the curse, and with a premonition of disaster, he laments his role and status, his absurd jester's outfit. He is employed to laugh, and not allowed to weep.

The atmosphere suddenly lightens. He has reached his door where his daughter Gilda greets him. She, his only possession, brings him joy. He has kept his job and his name secret from her. He has kept her 'locked up' for the three months since she arrived from her foster parents in the country. He admonishes her never to leave the house, except to go to church. She wants to know about herself, who her mother was. He forbids her to speak of her dead mother, the only person, the angel, who was prepared to love him: *Deh non parlare al misero.*

Before leaving, Rigoletto interrogates Giovanna, who is Gilda's companion, about security. He seeks assurance that nobody has followed Gilda to church, and that she would not open the door, even for the Duke, if it came to it: *Veglia, o donna, questo fiore* ('Watch over this flower entrusted, pure, to your keeping; be vigilant, that nothing may ever sully its purity'). Gilda is surprised by his concern (and expresses it on top B flat).

Thinking he has heard a noise, Rigoletto rushes out into the street to look. As he goes out, the Duke, incognito, slips in behind him, throws Giovanna a purse, and hides.

After Rigoletto has gone, Gilda expresses remorse to Giovanna that she did not mention the young man who she saw in church. The Duke rushes forward and interrupts her when she tells Giovanna that she is in love with him, and declares his 'love' for her. Gilda calls out to Giovanna, who, conveniently for the Duke, has disappeared. She demands that the young man leave. But he declares his ardent love. He explains that love is like the sunshine of the soul, it is life itself: *È il sol dell'anima – la vita è amore.* He demands that she repeat that she loves him: *Che m'ami, deh! ripetimi.*

She wants to know her young man's name. The Duke gives his alias, 'Gualtier [Walter] Maldè', a poor student. Giovanna returns to say that she has heard footsteps outside, where, little do they realise, Count Ceprano and the other conspirators are congregating outside Ceprano's palace. The Duke, furious at this interruption, nevertheless thinks it is best to go: *Addio, addio.*

The woodwind introduces the glorious *Caro nome*, in which Gilda usually soars to top E: she contemplates her beloved's name, 'Walter Maldè': *Gualtier Maldè!*[9] She climbs the outside staircase, in full view of the conspirators in the street. They are astonished to see that Rigoletto has such a beautiful mistress.

Rigoletto returns, worried that things are not right, and still haunted by the curse. In the dark, Ceprano wants to kill him, but the others have a better plan. Marullo invites Rigoletto, who is greatly relieved, to join in the abduction of Ceprano's wife for the Duke. To reassure Rigoletto, he hands him the key to Ceprano's palace, which is recognisable in the dark by the feel of the crest. Rigoletto is given a mask, secured with a blindfold. So, he does not realise that

---

[9] Two muted solo violins depict her fluttering heart.

he is steadying the ladder to afford access into his own house, rather than into Ceprano's palace. The conspirators' trap is closing; they will kidnap his mistress, and in the morning have a good laugh: *Zitti, zitti.*

Gilda is kidnapped, while Rigoletto thinks he is enjoying the fun. After he hears her scream, he realises that he has been duped. Ripping off the blindfold, he sees that his gate is open. Gilda's scarf is on the ground where she has dropped it. He realises that she has been taken. It is the curse: *la maledizione!*

Act 2

The Duke's palace

Back in his palace, the Duke is none too pleased with having his tryst interrupted and the latest object of his desire stolen from him. *Ella mi fu rapita!* He was actually very taken with Gilda: she is so pure that even he could be tempted to lead a virtuous life (so he tells us). He can recall her tears, and her calling out his name, when the kidnap took place: *Parmi veder le lagrime scorrenti da quel ciglio.* But he could not run to her assistance.

The courtiers report that Rigoletto's mistress has been kidnapped. They, in unison, explain to the disgruntled Duke how they found her in a back street. They were about to abduct her when Rigoletto came along. They convinced the fool that they were going for Ceprano's wife. They used him, blindfolded, to hold the ladder and climbed in and abducted the girl. To their surprise, the Duke's mood changes to delight as he realises who she is. He will now have her, and hurries off to take his quarry.

The courtiers taunt Rigoletto when he arrives, and he tries to hide his anguish: *La rà, la rà.* He is looking for Gilda. When a page, sent by the Duchess, is given transparently false explanations about where the Duke is, Rigoletto suspects that she is with the Duke. He demands his daughter back. The courtiers for the first time appreciate that they have in fact abducted Rigoletto's daughter. He lashes out at them, vile, venal courtiers, demanding what price they were paid for his treasure: *Cortigiani, vil razza dannata, per qual prezzo vendeste il mio bene?*

He demands to be admitted to the Duke's room, but they bar his way. He pleads desperately with them.[10]

They are all against him. He begs them to give an old man back his daughter. Gilda rushes out, having been raped, and expresses her shock, her shame and, not least, her amazement at seeing her father: *Mio padre! ... Ah l'onta.* Rigoletto intones an order telling the courtiers to go. They realise it is best to get out of sight.

With the strings augmented by an oboe solo, Gilda tells how she was visited by the handsome young man, a poor student, who she saw in church: *Tutte le feste al tempio mentre pregava.*[11] Then she suddenly found she was abducted. For the father, it is a disaster. He tries to comfort her: *Piangi! piangi fanciulla.*

Count Monterone enters under guard on the way to the dungeons. When Monterone thinks that his curse has been in vain, Rigoletto assures him that he shall be avenged. *Sì, vendetta, tremenda vendetta.* Gilda pleads with her father to forgive the Duke. The orchestra conveys his urgency for vengeance and her concern, because, despite everything, she is in love with him. With a bit of luck, she will make this clear on top F.

Act 3

Sparafucile's dilapidated inn, by the river Mincio

The Duke's affair with Gilda has continued: he loves her still, apparently. Her father is about to demonstrate the Duke's true character. He has taken her to see him in action. The Duke is out womanising, disguised as a soldier, in boots and spurs. He arrives at the inn, where he recalls having seen a pretty girl. He orders a room and a bottle of wine. He observes that women are as fickle as feathers in the wind

---

[10] Verdi reinforces Rigoletto's desperate lament with the cor anglais, and colours the strings with a solo cello. The orchestration is most unusual.

[11] Verdi uses the oboe solo for describing how the disaster began, but throbbing pizzicato strings to underline her growing love for the young man. He scores the woodwind, with a cello bass figure, to support Rigoletto's voice in one of the most emotional moments in the opera, for *Piangi! piangi fanciulla.*

– simple and lovable, but don't get too attached to one or you will regret it: *La donna è mobile qual piuma al vento.*

Gilda, looking through the window, is distraught to see her lover seducing Sparafucile's sister, Maddalena: *Un dì, si ben rammentomi, o bella, t'incontrai.* Rigoletto asks her whether she has not seen enough. In the famous quartet,[12] *Bella figlia dell'amore*, the Duke declares that he is a slave to Maddalena's charms, but she plays hard to get; his amatory vocabulary is only too recognisable to Gilda, who is appalled at what she sees and hears. Rigoletto tells her to disguise herself as a man and leave for Verona, where he will join her tomorrow. Meanwhile, he will take revenge.

Rigoletto does a deal with Sparafucile: ten scudi now, ten on completion, at midnight. He insists that he himself will dispose of the body in the river. When Sparafucile asks the names of his client and the victim, Rigoletto says that the victim is Crime and he is Punishment: *Egli è Delitto, Punizion son io.*[13]

A storm brews in the background. Sparafucile offers the Duke his room. The Duke, whose drink is spiked, goes upstairs and falls asleep. Sparafucile orders Maddalena to remove his sword.

Meanwhile, love has driven Gilda back to the inn. She is in the alley, wearing her disguise: that of a soldier, in boots and spurs. She overhears Maddalena pleading with her brother to spare the Duke's life and urging him to kill Rigoletto instead, when he returns with the final payment. Sparafucile declares that he is a man of honour, who does not cheat his clients. Eventually however, he agrees that if someone else comes to the hovel before midnight he will kill him. There is still half an hour left.

Gilda determines to die for her lover. She knocks on the door. Maddalena encourages her brother – she is keen to save one life with another. As the storm rages (with a thunder machine on stage), she opens the door and lets Gilda in, where Sparafucile awaits her.

---

[12] Gilda reaches high D flat. This is where the four characters express four different states of mind at the same time.

[13] Dostoyevsky's novel *Crime and Punishment* was written fifteen years later, in 1866.

The storm reaches its height then subsides a bit, and the chorus produces a sound like the sighing of the wind.

The lightning continues. Rigoletto arrives. He has waited 30 days for this vengeance: *Della vendetta alfin giunge l'istante!* Midnight sounds. When Sparafucile (going away on a bottom G flat) gives him the body in a sack,[14] Rigoletto can feel the spurs – *Ecco i suoi sproni* – so he presumes it must contain the Duke. It does not cross his mind that it could contain his daughter dressed as a man. He is exultant. As he heads for the river – *All'onda All'onda* – he is horrified to hear the sound of *La donna è mobile.* (For the avoidance of doubt, the Duke is instructed to appear on stage.) Rigoletto realises he has been duped. In a flash of lightning, he thinks he has seen his daughter, but it cannot be: she has left for Verona. Another flash, and he knows it is her.

Gilda is not quite dead. She is able to tell him she loved the Duke too much: it's her fault; now she is dying for him. She pleads with her father to forgive him and bless her. With high violins and a flute accompanying her (standard for a Verdi death scene) she tells him that she will be up in heaven with her mother: *Lassù … in cielo, vicina alla madre.*[15]

'Do not die' – *Non morir* – begs the distraught jester. When she does, Rigoletto remembers the curse: *Gilda! mia Gilda! è morta! … Ah! la maledizione!* He falls on her body.

[14] Covent Garden dancers always got a bit extra when they had to do something that was not dancing. The body in the bag got 3s 6d, a privilege reserved usually for the assistant stage manager's wife.

[15] The celestial sound is provided by flute arpeggios and trills above four violins and two violas.

VERDI: *IL TROVATORE*

THE OPERA AND ITS COMPOSER

Within its first few minutes, the story of *Il Trovatore* ('The Troubadour, or The Gypsy's Vengeance') transpires as one of the more absurd plots in the operatic repertoire. It starts with a relatively minor character recalling a confusing tale of two babies, a nurse, a gypsy, her daughter, the daughter's child, and a bonfire. This story is 'of the most paltry quality ... next to unintelligible', according to the leading English critic when it arrived in London in 1855. But he also observed that it was 'the favourite Italian opera of today.' Indeed, the aria *Il balen* was then as much a 'top of the pops' for the street barrel organ players as Rossini's *Di tanti palpiti* had been earlier.

The première at the Teatro Apollo in Rome, on 19 January 1853, had been a resounding success, far beyond Verdi's expectation. He was led back in a torch-lit procession to his hotel; beneath his window a band played music from his operas throughout the night. *Il Trovatore* became the most-loved Verdi opera in his own day.

Two years previously, by the end of March 1851, Verdi had the composition of *Rigoletto* behind him. It had been a major landmark in his development and in the history of music. He was busy. Apart from running his increasingly large business as a composer, he was distracted by managing his farm, and also by domestic problems, difficulties with his father, and his neighbours' negative attitude to his mistress Giuseppina Strepponi.

For more than a year, he had been considering the operatic potential of *El trovador* ('The Troubadour') by Antonio García Gutiérrez.[1]

---

[1] Another play by Antonio García Gutiérrez (1813–1884), a leading Spanish Romantic, provided Verdi with the subject for *Simon Boccanegra*. Gutiérrez came from Cadiz. Having studied medicine, he moved to Madrid to become a poet. In the early 1830s, two Spanish Romantic dramas were very successful, so Gutiérrez decided to write one. *El trovador* was staged in 1836. In all, he wrote some 60 plays.

Giuseppina Strepponi

This was a play about passionate love which conflicts with fate. It was the most popular and successful drama of the Romantic period in Spain. Set against the background of civil war, we can understand why its ingredients – suicide, infanticide, vengeance, hatred, honour, shame and sacrilege – were effective on the stage.

It seems that Giuseppina promoted the idea of developing the play into an opera. Verdi himself provided the outline of scenario to his librettist Salvatore Cammarano.[2] But the highly experienced Neapolitan was unenthusiastic, and even anxious, about the drama's potential as an operatic libretto, and therefore delayed putting pen to paper. Also, he was worried about the censors' likely reaction to nuns being shown praying on stage while the protagonists organised

[2] Salvatore Cammarano (1801–1852), the official poet at Teatro San Carlo, came from a prominent artistic family in Naples. By the time he wrote his first libretto for Verdi, *Alzira*, he had written texts for many of the 19th-century composers, including *Lucia di Lammermoor* for Donizetti. His operas for Verdi include *La Battaglia di Legnano* and *Luisa Miller*.

an abduction. The reluctant librettist became ill and died in July 1852; however, by then, he had completed most of the work. Leone Emanuele Bardare, a young teacher and journalist, was delighted to complete and polish it.

The story of mistaken identity has been satirised by many, consciously or unconsciously, albeit often with happier consequences: Gilbert and Sullivan's *HMS Pinafore* is an example. And at one time, *Il Trovatore* became the most frequently performed opera in Western Europe. It was soon the most popular work in the operatic repertoire of practically every country, and it is still among Opera America's 'twenty most-performed operas'. It has been performed by a galaxy of stars. In later years, Maria Callas, Renata Tebaldi and Joan Sutherland have starred as Leonora. Manrico has been sung by Placido Domingo and Luciano Pavarotti.

The opera's success may be attributed to two characteristics. Firstly, its 'almost unbroken melodiousness', which for us is a reminder of the importance of good tunes if an audience is to be pleased. Secondly, Verdi compensates for the weaknesses in the plot by taking the opera at a relentlessly hectic pace. *Il Trovatore* is 'Verdi of forty working at white heat.' It displays those characteristics that people particularly noted when they met him: his 'energetic air which inspired respect', his 'rough' manner. The libretto is thus an irrelevance. The music, which is like a box of chocolates, can result in indigestion, but, at home at least – if metaphors may be mixed – the volume can be turned down.

In the opera house, these characteristics put enormous pressure on the quality of performance and, especially in modern times, the production. At the end of the 19th century, George Bernard Shaw, the Irish playwright and music critic, observed that *Il Trovatore* is 'capable of producing a tremendous effect if heroically performed. But anything short of this means vulgarity, triviality, tediousness, and failure; for there is nothing heroic to fall back on – no comedy, no spectacle, no symphonic instrumental commentary, no relief to the painful flood of feeling surging up repeatedly to the most furious intensity of passion; nothing but love – with hate, jealousy, terror, and the shadow of death throughout.'

This opera is not the sort to generate tears. But the audience can be confident of leaving the house having heard a relentless succession of good and famous tunes.

(More on the life of Verdi can be found on pages 210–211.)

WHO'S WHO AND WHAT'S WHAT

The story below is based on the libretto. Certain directors may amend opera stories to suit their production.

The story is set the early 1400s in the Basque country and Aragon in the north of Spain.

Ferrando, the hearty henchman and captain of the guard, rouses the sentries and other retainers of the **Count di Luna**. To stay alert, they ask to be told the dreadful story about what happened to the Count's brother some fifteen years earlier.

Then, a gypsy was convicted of bewitching the younger brother of the Count, and she was burnt at the stake. That night, her daughter **Azucena** took instant revenge by kidnapping the child and casting it into the embers. We will later hear that she made a terrible mistake: the infant she destroyed was her own and not the Count's. But she took pity on the surviving child – the one she had meant to kill – and brought him up as her own son, **Manrico**, who is now a troubadour.

Unknown to each other, the two brothers, the Count and Manrico, are competing for the love of **Leonora**,[3] the Queen's lady-in-waiting. They are politically opposed to each other.[4]

Leonora walks in the garden with her companion, **Inez**. She longs for the victor at the recent tournament, the troubadour, who had subsequently serenaded her on a lovely moonlit night: *Tace la notte*. The serenade begins again, just as the Count himself comes to woo her.

---

[3] The name can be confusing because the prima donna of Beethoven's *Fidelio* is also a Leonore.
[4] These were turbulent and unstable times, with the royal succession often disputed. Rival families and factions jostled for power. The Luna family was one of the great noble families in Aragon at the time. The opera depicts Manrico as fighting for the rival Urgel family.

In an extraordinary gaffe, Leonora mistakes the Count for the troubadour and falls into his arms, only to turn aside to Manrico. The Count is more than put out. He recognises Manrico as a rebel who is already condemned to death. He challenges him there and then and the two men go off to fight a duel. We will later hear that Manrico won, but, guided by a call from heaven – 'Don't strike!' – he has spared the Count's life.

Some time later, Manrico, still on the run, is with his mother, the gypsy Azucena, in the Basque country. The gypsies sing of love and wine in the **Anvil Chorus**. But Azucena relates a horrific story about the crowd rejoicing at the burning of a witch.

After an **old gypsy** leads the others away, Azucena tells Manrico the story of her mother's agonising death and call for vengeance. She describes the incident muddling up the babies. Since then she has always behaved as a mother to Manrico, even though he is not her son.

Manrico's colleague **Ruiz**, another rebel, arrives to tell him that he is to take charge of Castellor, a castle which has fallen to the rebels. He also reports that Leonora, thinking Manrico died in recent fighting, is about to enter a convent. Manrico rushes off, despite Azucena's vehement protests.

The scene changes to night-time in the cloister of a convent. The Count intends to abduct Leonora before she takes the veil. He thinks that Manrico has been killed. Burning with passion, he sings one of the most beautiful baritone solos of Italian opera:[5] *Il balen del suo sorriso d'una stella vince il raggio!* In the background, the **Nuns' Chorus** indicates that the service has begun.

Leonora appears, comforting Inez, who is distraught. The Count bursts in as Leonora asks to be led to the altar. 'The only altar for you is the nuptial altar,' he declares. At this dramatic moment, Manrico also appears. Ruiz arrives, in support of him, with the other rebels. They disarm the Count. Manrico rushes away with Leonora.

[5] There is no respite for the singer in this aria, which is viewed with dread by most baritones. It ends with an aggressive flourish, so demanding at this stage that baritones often simplify it. Throughout this section, the orchestra supports the Count's 'underlying brutality'.

The soldiers entertain themselves, gambling and so on, in the camp of the Count, where they are besieging the castle. They sing the famous **Soldiers' Chorus**. A gypsy has been found wandering around the camp. She is interrogated and is identified as Azucena. The Count now has the chance to avenge his brother and claim Leonora. Azucena is dragged off.

Meanwhile in the castle, Manrico, Leonora and Ruiz await the morning attack. Leonora and Manrico enjoy a brief moment of love. When they see Azucena being dragged off to the stake, Manrico rushes to save her. The call to arms is announced.

His rescue attempt fails, and the castle falls. Manrico and his mother now await execution. With the bell tolling for the dead, monks inside chant the *Miserere*. Leonora, who wears a ring containing poison, and Ruiz, hear Manrico, accompanied by the harp, singing his farewell from the tower where he awaits his fate.

When the castle fell, there was no sign of Leonora. Now she appears and pleads for mercy for Manrico. The Count refuses, until she agrees to give herself to him. While he instructs the guard to delay the execution, she sucks the poison from the ring.

Meanwhile, the condemned couple, Manrico and Azucena, await their end. Leonora arrives to say that she has come to save Manrico, who must go immediately. But it is too late: the poison takes effect. The Count appears. Once she has died, in the last 37 hurried bars of the opera,[6] the Count orders Manrico to the block, where he is beheaded (with a thump); then Azucena informs the Count that Manrico was his brother. 'Mother, you're avenged,' she screams to the horrified Count, as the curtain falls.

---

[6] If the conductor follows the metronome marking, the time between the Count ordering Manrico to the block and the axe falling is ten seconds. This may sound fast. But Pierrepoint hanged a man within seven seconds of him leaving the condemned cell – the record.

THE INTERVAL: TALKING POINTS

Verdi's skill and craftsmanship

Gutiérrez's play is conventionally, but unfairly, blamed for the virtually unintelligible plot of *Il Trovatore*: it has been said that it is 'as impenetrable as it is improbable', 'the acme of absurdity.' Cammarano, the librettist, followed the construction of the drama and its story extremely closely. However, the compression and the submergence of language in music have the effect of obfuscating detail and explanations which words alone render quite plausible.[7]

In other hands, this could have been disastrous. But Verdi has the artistry, skill and craftsmanship to sweep aside the unintelligibility and create an effective opera. This exemplifies the power of music to override the problems of an unsuccessful libretto. He does this by driving the rhythm of the work relentlessly forward with intense energy.

The score is littered with instructions for fast and urgent tempos such as '*allegro assai agitato*', '*allegro vivo*', '*poco più animato*', '*più mosso*'. Indeed, in Act 2, when Manrico rushes off in search of Leonora, and Azucena tries to restrain him, the score is marked '*Velocissimo*'. The final prison scene may start slowly, '*Largo*'; but not for long: soon the tempo is more lively, '*Allegretto animato*'.

Much of the vitality is provided by the obsessively vengeful Azucena and the obsessively enraged Count. This allows the score to be punctuated with some lyrical 'best tunes', such as Manrico's Act 3 love song *Ah si, ben mio* and Leonora's Act 4 air *D'amor sull'ali rosee*. And, although the Count is normally overpoweringly forceful, he too

---

[7] Weak aspects of the opera plot read convincingly in the play. Here are some examples. (1) In Act 1, we may be surprised that Leonora can confuse the Count and Manrico. In the play, the Count, who we may reasonably presume looks like his brother, tries to abduct and seduce Leonora under cover of darkness, so her confusion appears plausible. (2) The notorious mistake whereby Azucena throws the wrong baby into the bonfire reads credibly in the play: it takes place a few days after the execution, rather than immediately; and Azucena is so emotionally overcome by her recollection of the cruelty to her mother that she has a seizure, which causes her not to appreciate what she is doing. (3) Leonora's suicide can appear unconvincing in the opera. In the play, the dramatist uses this, alarmingly and disturbingly, to expose convincingly the very essence of romantic passion.

has a slow and glorious love song in Act 2, *Il balen*. And Azucena has her final dream of returning to the mountains, *Si la stanchezza*.

Much colour is provided by Verdi's powerful choral writing, particularly the gypsies' Anvil Chorus, the Nuns' Chorus in Act 2, the Soldiers' Chorus which starts Act 3, and the Miserere of Act 4.

Backsliding?

Verdi has been accused, in *Il Trovatore*, of 'backsliding into vulgarity after the prodigious advance shown in *Rigoletto*.' In that opera, 'the barriers between formal melody and recitative came down as never before.' In *Il Trovatore*, he took orchestra back to its traditional role of accompanying voices. Until the final scene, the music is organised as a series of formal numbers. But, in the final scene, he 'gathers up the threads in a continuity approaching that of *Rigoletto*.'

The characters are weak: only the old woman Azucena is 'sculpted in depth'. Indeed, one can feel that Manrico is a fool for not having taken advantage of two opportunities to rid himself of the other brother, who is such a nasty piece of work.

The challenge for the singers

Caruso said that a production of *Il Trovatore* requires the four greatest singers in the world.

Verdi himself wrote that Azucena 'is a leading role – even the very most important role, more beautiful, more dramatic, more original' than that of Leonora, who in the playwright's drama is the central figure. To his librettist, he called Azucena 'a woman of very special character' with two overwhelming passions, filial love and maternal love. Acting this part convincingly provides a great challenge. The role also demands a secure tone at the very extremes of the contralto's vocal range: when she describes her mother calling for vengeance, and when she says that it was her child who was burnt, Azucena is on top A, the top territory of the soprano; when, a few bars later, she describes her horror, her hair standing on end, she is two octaves lower on the deep A below middle C.

There have been few similar leading female roles for a contralto written since *Il Trovatore*. One of its greatest interpreters was Pauline Viardot, the 19th-century opera star who took part in the London première in May 1855, and whose portrayal of the role was described by a contemporary critic as one of the most remarkable interpretations of the period.[8] A few years earlier, she had portrayed a similar role, Fidès in Meyerbeer's *Le Prophète*.

Pauline Viardot

Manrico's role requires the skill and artistry of both the lyric tenor and the dramatic tenor. After Act 3's demanding *Ah! sì, ben mio*, the love song in which he briefly imagines that Leonora might be his, the applause normally enables him to recover and gather strength for *Di quella pira*, in which he rushes to the aid of his mother who is being dragged to the stake. Placido Domingo has called this 'the killer cabaletta', observing how difficult it would be to bring off in a venue where applause does not conventionally take place in between numbers, as was the case in London.

---

[8] Viardot's range, like that of her equally famous sister Maria Malibran, was extraordinarily wide and enabled her to sing contralto and soprano roles. On one night, she filled in for an absent singer by performing both the mezzo-soprano and soprano parts. (An account of this can be read in the author's *Enchantress of Nations: Pauline Viardot, Soprano, Muse and Lover*.)

The Count's role is also very challenging. In his *Il balen del suo sorriso*, well over half of the notes lie at the top of the vocal range, from B flat to high G. Even when the aria is transposed down, as is often the case, the strain on a normal baritone is considerable.

Troubadours

In the Age of Chivalry, that is, around the time of the Crusades, from the end of the 11th century to the end of the 13th, troubadours could be found in the various courts of Europe. They were poet-musicians, and came mainly from Provence. They were people of rank: Richard the Lionheart, later King Richard I of England, was one.

The essence of their poetry was the knight's courteous striving for the grace and favour of a respected but unreachable lady, which is very much the tone of Manrico's Serenade in Act 1: *Deserto sulla terra* ('Lonely I wander, always at war with fate and fortune, sighing for a heart to bless the troubadour') The historical troubadour's relationship with his lady was spiritual, almost religious, not physical. The knight would wallow in the lady's unattainability, and the masochistic suffering that arises from it.

On the face of it, the relevance of the opera's title 'The Troubadour' is not entirely clear. The love of Manrico and Leonora is sexual. It would remove much of the piquancy of the opera if it were not. '*Il Trovatore*' is of course a consequence of '*El trovador*', and presumably its marketing power at the time. It is very important to the playwright Gutiérrez's drama that Manrico is a troubadour. Without this, Leonora might appear as insubstantial as a photograph in a glossy magazine. Wandering around with his lute, Manrico is presented in Gutiérrez's play as being of an inferior social class to the lady-in-waiting and the aristocratic Count. As a consequence, Leonora is wrenched between her social duty to her family to marry the Count and her potential *mésalliance* with the man she truly loves. The opera skates over this central aspect of the play, Leonora's relentless conflict between love and duty, a thoroughly Romantic conflict, which is the rationale for her behaviour.

In Verdi's work, the conflict between love and duty is however the rationale for Azucena's behaviour. She could save Manrico by disclosing his identity before it is too late. But, under extreme pressure, her allegiance is to her mother and her dying call for vengeance. Maybe Verdi should have called his opera 'Azucena' – but it would have been a less colourful and commercial title than 'The Troubadour'.

Witches

For centuries, the accusation of witchcraft was levelled at women who were deemed to have power to produce effects other than by natural causes. A witch was thought to have entered into a bargain with an evil spirit, that the spirit should do what the witch desired of it. It included conjuration, sorcery, incantation and divination. Today, witches appear in relation to Halloween, eccentricity or marketing.

Witchcraft was legally punishable as far back as the Roman period. An accusation of witchcraft, as of treason, rendered any person, regardless of rank, liable to torture. In a textbook on the subject, written in Germany in the 15th century – a period when prosecution became particularly vigorous – it was explained that witchcraft is more natural to women than men on account of the inherent wickedness of their hearts. Joan of Arc is possibly the most celebrated individual to be convicted.

King James I of England was a notorious expert and specialist in the matter and attended trials when he was King of Scotland. At his accession to the English throne in 1603, he passed a special law, which applied throughout the 17th century, the most vigorous and hysterical period of prosecution in England; it was only repealed in 1736. In Lancashire in 1634, seventeen witches were condemned on the evidence of one boy. The last trial in England was at Hertford in 1712, in which Jane Wenham was convicted but not executed; the last execution in Scotland was in 1722. The trials of the witches of Salem in Massachusetts in 1691–1692 are particularly notorious: nineteen people were executed, and one man suffered death by the *peine forte et dure*, being crushed under the weight of stones, for refusing to stand trial and plead.

ACT BY ACT

Act 1

The Duel

It is the 15th century, at the 'Troubadour tower' in Saragossa in northern Spain. There is no time for an overture.

It is almost midnight. With a drum roll, a flourish, a few calls on the horn, Ferrando, a henchman of the Count of Luna, orders the sentries and servants to look sharp. The Count is a-wooing and has a rival in love, a troubadour. To keep the retainers awake, Ferrando tells them the dreadful story about the Count's brother.

The Count's father had two sons. Their nurse awoke to see a gypsy fortune-teller in the room. One of the children went into a decline, and had obviously been bewitched: *Abbietta zingara*. After the hag was found and was burnt at the stake, her daughter took revenge. The Count's child disappeared, and seemingly was dead because a child's skeleton was found in the embers. The surviving son, now the Count, had been enjoined to keep searching for his brother, in case he is still alive. Meanwhile the witch is occasionally seen in various forms. Indeed, one soldier had died of fright when she appeared to him in the form of an owl at midnight. We hear the midnight bell ring.

* * *

Leonora, the Queen's lady-in-waiting, walks in the garden with her companion, Inez. She regrets that another night has gone by without her seeing the unknown man in black armour to whom she had awarded the victor's prize at the tournament. She subsequently heard him, a troubadour, serenading her on a lovely moonlit night: *Tacea la notte placida e bella in ciel sereno*.[9] He had mentioned her name! And she had felt ecstatic, as is indicated by her cadenza starting on high C and dropping almost two octaves, to be sung 'slowly and evenly'. Inez

[9] One commentator observed, 'For concentration of lyrical poetry *Tacea la notte placida* is unsurpassed in all Verdi's music, while as a tour de force of melodic craftsmanship it is without parallel anywhere.'

is worried by this and tells Leonora to put him out of her mind. But she cannot. Such love is irresistible. She vows to be his.

The young Count heads towards Leonora, with whom he is obsessively in love. He is appalled to hear her being serenaded by another man. In the background, to a harp accompaniment, his rival, the troubadour Manrico, sings a lament: *Deserto sulla terra*. Alone on earth, at war with fate, the troubadour's only hope is in one heart, which, if he possesses, makes him greater than a king.

Leonora runs towards the Count. In the darkness (and presumably because the Count and Manrico – who, unknown to everybody, are brothers – look very alike), she has made the unfortunate 'gaffe' of mistaking him for the troubadour. But the moon comes out from behind a cloud and reveals Manrico, at whose feet she now falls and to whom she declares her love. This about-turn not surprisingly enrages the Count, who demands to know his name, and gets the answer, Manrico. The Count recognises him as an opponent, a rebel who has already been condemned to death. Despite Leonora's protests, he challenges him there and then. With Leonora and Manrico singing in unison, albeit different words, it is clear which side she is on. She asks him to kill her rather than Manrico. But the two men go off to fight their duel, and she falls senseless.

Act 2

The Gypsy

Some time later. Dawn is rising on a mountain in the Basque country. Manrico is with his mother, the gypsy Azucena. There is an 'uncouthness, a bar or two of Oriental drawl' before the gypsies, tinkers by trade, hammer their pots and pans on their anvils. In the well-known Anvil Chorus, they sing of love and wine: *Vedi! Le fosche notturne spoglie*. The orchestral sounds include the triangle, hammers on an anvil, and a high, shrill woodwind.

Verdi has cleverly already introduced the audience to Azucena through Ferrando's description at the outset of the opera. In a well-known aria, *Stride la vampa!*, she describes the crowd rejoicing at the burning of a witch: the flame crackles!

When the gypsies, led by one of their number, have gone off to work in the nearby villages, Manrico, who has heard Azucena's strange words before, asks her to tell the story. She gives her version of the story of his grandmother's bitter end, after the Count's father had accused her of witchcraft – the story we have already heard: *Condotta ell'era in ceppi*. To the accompaniment of a sinister solo oboe and first violin, she tells how she had followed her mother as they took her to the stake. In the flames, the condemned woman shrieked in agony, and called with a weird cry for vengeance, a cry which Azucena has never forgotten. She had immediately kidnapped the Count's son and brought him to the fire. His cries, depicted on the flute and piccolo, had moved her heart. But she recalled the cry 'Avenge me!' and pushed the baby into the embers, only to realise, too late, that it was the wrong baby. Azucena had murdered her own child, not the Count's.[10]

Manrico realises that he cannot be Azucena's son after all. She regrets her disclosure, and maintains that she was confused and he is indeed her son: has she not always been a tender mother to him? Did she not save him, wounded, from the battlefield of Pelilla[11] when the Count di Luna had attacked him? In the duet *Mal reggendo*, she reproaches Manrico because, in the duel, he had the Count at his mercy, but, guided by a cry from heaven – *Non ferir* ('Don't strike!') – he had spared him. Next time, Azucena tells him, he should do the job properly, and Manrico swears to do so.

A horn is heard and Manrico's colleague Ruiz arrives with two pieces of news: Manrico has been ordered to take charge of Castellor, a castle which has fallen to the rebels; and Leonora, thinking Manrico is dead, is about to enter a convent. Manrico calls for a horse and rushes off despite Azucena's vehement protests: *Perigliarti ancor languente*. The score is marked '*Velocissimo*' and, towards the end, '*Tutta forza*'.

* * *

[10] She ends mournfully on A.
[11] Pelilla is near Salamanca, close to the Spanish border in the North-East of Portugal. Although *Il Trovatore* may not display Verdi's skills at characterisation at their best, the 'grizzling and grumbling of a rather pathetic old woman' contrasts very well against the lyricism of Manrico.

The scene changes to night-time in the cloister of a place of retreat (a convent) near Castellor. The Count, with Ferrando and a few retainers, enters cautiously. They are wrapped in their cloaks. The Count believes that he has killed his rival, but now a further obstacle has arisen to his conquest of Leonora: she is to take the veil. He intends to abduct her before she takes her vows. Burning with passion, he sings one of the most beautiful baritone solos of Italian opera: *Il balen del suo sorriso* ('The flashing of her smile is brighter than the ray of a star').

Even at this fatal hour, the Count is determined to seize her. Then he hears the bell[12] and the chanting of the nuns, in the Nuns' Chorus. These indicate that Leonora is about to be received into the convent.

* * *

Leonora appears, comforting a distraught Inez. She sings *O dolci amiche* ('Sweet friends, earth no longer has for me any laughter, hope, or flower'). As she asks to be led to the altar, the Count bursts in: 'The only altar for you is the nuptial altar.'

At this dramatic moment, the troubadour also appears.[13] While Leonora is overcome with joy – *È deggio e posso crederlo?* – the Count and Manrico argue vociferously. The Count, surprised to see Manrico alive, tells him that if he wants to live he had better go. However, Ruiz arrives, in support of Manrico, with the other rebels. They disarm the Count. Manrico rushes away with Leonora.[14]

Act 3

The Gypsy's Son

In the camp of the Count, the soldiers entertain themselves, gambling and so on. The attack on the rebels at Castellor is to begin at dawn. Ferrando tells them that there is rich booty to be won. The soldiers

---

[12] Verdi, who at this time loathed La Scala, which 'massacred' and 'slaughtered' his operas, was appalled that there a frying pan covered with a cloth was used for the bell.

[13] Domingo recalls a performance at the Met in which he leapt down seven feet, sword in hand, by swinging from a tree. This gave way, and he fell. Instead of singing *Se tu dal ciel disceso* ('Have you descended from heaven?'), the Leonora sang *Sei tu dal ciel cascato* ('Have you fallen out of the sky?').

[14] In the play by Gutiérrez, Leonora has already taken the veil, adding to the piquancy.

sing the famous Soldiers' Chorus, *Squilli, echeggi la tromba guerriera*, one of the best known of Verdi's choruses.

The Count is haunted by the thought that Leonora is in his rival's arms: *In braccio al mio rival!* At this moment, Ferrando comes to tell him that a gypsy has been found. Azucena is dragged in. When asked where she is going, she says she does not know. Gypsies just wander from place to place. She is wandering in search of her adored son who has deserted her.

When she says that she is from the Basque country, Ferrando and the Count interrogate her about the child who was stolen all those years ago. Ferrando, observing her terrified reaction, recognises her (the music stops for a bar). He accuses her of burning the child. As they bind her, she calls for Manrico and derides him for not coming to her aid. At the mention of this name, the Count realises that she is Manrico's mother; he senses his opportunity to avenge his brother and claim Leonora. The soldiers and Ferrando tell her she will soon be brought to the stake, and she is dragged off.

* * *

Meanwhile in Castellor, Manrico, Leonora and Ruiz await the morning attack. Leonora and Manrico enjoy a brief moment of love – *Amor, sublime amore: Ah! sì, ben mio, coll'essere io tuo* ('When you are mine and I am yours'). Even if he now has to die, his last thoughts will be with her, and death will seem as if he is just preceding her to heaven. The organ (or, alternatively, a wind band) is heard as they approach the chapel. But at this moment, from the ramparts they see Azucena being taken to the stake. Manrico is appalled and tells Leonora that it is his mother. The blaze burns and inflames all of his being: *Di quella pira l'orrendo foco tutte le fibre m'arse.*[15] Manrico rushes to save Azucena. The call to arms is announced.

---

[15] The high C in this aria was inserted by the tenor Tamberlick, and it has remained standard ever since. Gustav Kobbé, the music critic and author, observed that 'The tenor who sings the high C without getting red in the face will hardly get the credit for having sung it at all.'

Act 4

The Execution

The rescue attempt has failed. An unusual combination of clarinet and bassoon begins a sequence of great beauty.

Beneath the tower of the palace where Manrico and his mother await death, Leonora, with Ruiz, thinks of her lover: *D'amor sull'ali rosee*. (She reaches top D at the end of this, although a lower alternative is provided.) She purposively fiddles with a ring on her right hand.

With the bell tolling for the dead, monks inside chant the *Miserere* for those about to die.[16] The orchestra accompanies them with a distinct rhythm evoking death and fate which will recur in many of Verdi's operas. In what used to be 'the best known of all *Trovatore* melodies in the days of the barrel organ', Manrico, from the tower, and accompanied by the harp, sings his farewell to Leonora – *Ah che la morte* – and hopes she will not forget him. She responds suitably: never was there a stronger love than hers, she declares. She drops from top C to conclude a sequence which a leading English critic in the mid-19th century, who regarded *Il Trovatore* as 'dismal', had to concede was 'captivating'.

The Count tells his men that at dawn the son goes to the block and the mother to the stake: he may be exceeding his judicial powers,[17] but too bad, it's Leonora's fault! When Castellor was taken there was no sign of her. Where is she? At this moment, she appears and pleads for mercy for Manrico. The Count is amazed; vengeance is all he is interested in. He would like Manrico to die a hundred deaths and suffer a thousand agonies. The more she loves him, the more determined and enraged he is.

Finally, she agrees to yield to him in return for mercy: let Manrico go, and she swears that she will be the Count's. As the Count is giving instructions to the guard, she sucks the ring, which is poisoned: *Vivrà!*

---

[16] For a long time this competed with the intermezzo from *Cavalleria rusticana* as 'the most popular of all melodies from opera.' The *Miserere* was sung at Verdi's memorial service. Manrico usually has to be let out of jail temporarily to take the applause.

[17] It is odd that, in this era, the Count should have had any concern about 'human rights'.

... *contende il giubilo* ('He'll live! Words of joy to me'). The Count, irritated but delighted and excited, just wants her to give herself to him.

* * *

Meanwhile, the condemned couple await their end. Manrico comforts his 'mother' and urges her to sleep. She cannot; she is terrified of the fire, the stake. She raves about a horrible vision, a reminder of her mother's death: *Un giorno turba feroce*. Manrico calms her. In a tear-jerking duet, she talks of returning to the mountains, where he will sing with his harp, and she will sleep: *Ai nostri monti*. Eventually, she does fall asleep.

At this moment, Leonora arrives to say that she has come to save him. He must go; but she is not coming with him. He is horrified that she has done a deal with the Count, and curses her. She desperately tries to persuade him to leave, because she knows that her time is quickly running out: the poison she has taken will soon have its effect. Once it does, there will be no hope for Manrico. Azucena thinks again of returning to the mountains. Leonora starts to falter: her hands are freezing. Manrico now reproaches himself for cursing her. The Count appears, and, realising what has happened, softens as she expires.

Once she has died, Verdi wastes no time. In the last 37 hurried bars of the opera, the Count orders Manrico to the block; he shouts farewell to his mother and is beheaded (with a thump on the big drum). Azucena informs the Count that Manrico was his brother: *Egli era tuo fratello!*; *Sei vendicata, o madre!* ('Mother, you're avenged!'). *E vivo ancor!* ('But I still live'), cries the horrified Count, as the curtain falls.

VERDI: *LA TRAVIATA*

THE OPERA AND ITS COMPOSER

A fiasco. That was Verdi's own description of the première of *La Traviata* ('The Fallen Woman') at La Fenice in Venice on 6 March 1853.[1] The performers were apparently not up to their parts and the leading tenor was hoarse – they excused themselves by claiming that the music did not suit them.

Most of the blame is usually heaped on the Violetta, Fanny Salvini-Donatelli (1815–1891). She had been very much a second choice, because Verdi's first choice was ill. For his prostitute dying of consumption, Verdi wanted a prima donna who was 'young, had a graceful figure and could sing with passion.' Fanny actually sang very well indeed. But, at the age of 38, she was obviously no longer the *nuovo ed ardente sirena* of her youth. And there was a worse, insuperable problem: she weighed 286lb, or over 20 stone.

For Verdi, the singer was expected to provide a 'near perfect union of music and drama', the one complementing and supporting the other, in perfect balance. *La Traviata* is a reminder of the importance of the singer, as a minimum, looking credible in the role – a matter usually, but far from invariably, attended to today.

At the première, the Prelude with which the opera starts was greeted with great applause. From the beginning of Act 2, though, the reception took a turn for the worse, and the audience began hooting. However, the production ran for nine nights and actually did quite well at the box office. Verdi withdrew it for fourteen months. After this, it was performed to great acclaim. Today, it is at the top of the list of most-performed operas.

---

[1] The great fiascos of the century are sometimes said to be the disruption of Rossini's *The Barber of Seville* in Rome in 1816, the 1861 Paris production of Wagner's *Tannhäuser*, and the first night of Bizet's *Carmen* in 1875.

Verdi had composed *La Traviata* under great pressure. He had been in Rome working hard on *Il Trovatore*, which was premièred there only seven weeks before. However, we should not be too surprised: this was a time when operas were produced like shelling peas – Donizetti had assembled *L'Elisir d'Amore* in about a fortnight.

Verdi had first encountered the story of *La Traviata* around a year earlier. During a visit to Paris,[2] he went to a performance of an immensely popular play by Alexandre Dumas, *La Dame aux Camélias*, which was based on a novel of the same name. This romance features Marguerite, 'a virgin who some accident had made a courtesan', and who is always to be seen carrying a bouquet of camellias, 'a pale, scentless, cold flower, but sensitive as purity itself.' The 25-year-old Armand falls in love with her, but their affair ends in tragedy.

Over a hundred years earlier, Abbé Prévost had shown in his *Manon Lescaut* how a novel about a love affair between a young man and a courtesan/prostitute can attract a wide readership. And Dumas's soft porn[3] enabled the prurient to peep yet again behind the curtains of Paris, that 'great mother-city of scandal'. It was a bestseller. The part of Marguerite has been played by great actresses such as Sarah Bernhardt and Vivien Leigh, and the lead roles have been danced by legendary ballet dancers such as Fonteyn and Nureyev. It has been filmed and made into musicals, and adapted as a modern play.

Verdi, having seen the play, immediately began to toy with its possibilities as an opera, but the following months were taken up with business and domestic matters, including the health of his father. Even in midsummer, he had not yet agreed a subject for the opera he had undertaken to have ready for Venice early in 1853. It was only in October that he settled on Dumas's story. With one of his librettists, Piave, he put together a rough draft in about five days. Piave's work has been called 'a lesson in condensation'.

---

[2] Paris at the time was reeling from the coup in which Louis-Napoleon, the nephew and step-grandson of Napoleon I, transformed himself from President to Emperor Napoleon III.
[3] Not everyone would agree with one translator who has claimed that Dumas's tale may be 'contemplated with a good conscience because of its prevailing tone of moral fervour.'

In December, Verdi had to be in Rome to prepare for *Il Trovatore*. It looked at one moment as if the *La Traviata* venture would have to be called off, with Verdi citing illness as the justification. It was very frustrating: he could not get the singers he wanted, and he did not like the production. Verdi wanted it staged as a contemporary drama, in modern clothes. But to get round the rigorous censorship, the opera had to be staged as a period piece around 1700 during the reign of Louis XIV.[4] By the time of his arrival in Venice in late February, he knew it was going to be a disaster. But he had to comply with his contract so he could not cancel.

When *La Traviata* was revived in Venice in May 1854, Verdi made some considerable modification to the detail. The reception was completely different. In another theatre, with a different cast, there was 'an uproar of indescribable applause'. Verdi famously commented, 'Then it was a fiasco; now it is creating an uproar.'

A canon from Bologna duly censored it to make it suitable for the Papal States and Naples, and the critic of *The Times* denounced its 'foul and hideous horrors' at the London première in 1856. But two years later, on 25 May 1858, all three musical theatres in London – Her Majesty's, Covent Garden and Drury Lane – were performing *La Traviata* at the same time. When you have a compelling story, you have a hit as well. It has been like that ever since. Handkerchiefs are a necessary accessory.

As Tito Gobbi pointed out, 'it is Violetta's evening or it is nothing.' She has been sung by such legendary stars as Christine Nilsson, Adelina Patti, Nellie Melba and Tetrazzini. It is not a role for which every star is ideal: Victoria de los Angeles, Kiri te Kanawa, yes; Elisabeth Schwarzkopf, no. When Maria Callas tried to create a sickly quality in the voice of Violetta, the critics said, 'Callas is tired.' Some stars sensibly confine themselves to recorded excerpts, such as Joan Sutherland.

[4] The first performance in contemporary dress was not given until 1906, in Milan. There may have been further reasons for the original failure. Dumas's own version *La Dame aux Camélias*, on which it was based, was playing at another theatre in Venice at the time.

Melba as Violetta

Pavarotti sang the role of Alfredo in his early years, but subsequently he had too much in common with that first soprano, Fanny, to make him a sensible choice. Placido Domingo made his debut as a lead tenor as Alfredo, in Mexico, aged 20. He later conceded that he 'had not yet learned to control his emotions'. He accepted that he was not technically ready, and he found it a difficult role subsequently. He starred with Teresa Stratas in a highly acclaimed film version directed by Franco Zeffirelli.

Because Verdi's characters 'are not make-believe, but are real', this opera is enduringly successful.

(More on the life of Verdi can be found on pages 210–211.)

WHO'S WHO AND WHAT'S WHAT

The story below is based on the libretto. Certain directors may amend opera stories to suit their production.

Violetta Valéry, a courtesan, is throwing a party in her Paris mansion. **Alfredo Germont**, from a provincial family in Provence, arrives with his friend **Gaston**, a Viscount. Violetta is always seen with a bouquet of camellias, and is suffering from the deadly disease of the lungs, consumption. Her **doctor**, Dr Grenvil, is at the party.

Violetta has been installed in the mansion by her protector, the **Baron** Douphol. The guests include her friend, another courtesan, **Flora** Bervoix, who is with her admirer, a **Marchese** (Marquis).

The wild party-goers join in Alfredo's '**Brindisi**', a toast to pleasure and love. Violetta falls for him.

Five months later, the couple are living together in a house in the country, running out of cash. **Annina**, the maid, has returned from Paris where she has, unknown to Alfredo, been to sell Violetta's possessions. When Alfredo discovers this, he rushes off to Paris to sort out the finances.

The servant **Giuseppe** brings an invitation to a party at Flora's that night. Alfredo's father, Giorgio **Germont**, comes to stop him disgracing the family. Germont tries to persuade Violetta to sacrifice herself in order to avoid tarnishing the marriage prospects of Alfredo's sister, and to return to her Baron.

In the pivotal dramatic moment of the opera, Violetta capitulates and agrees. She accepts the invitation from Flora, and writes a message for Alfredo (that she is leaving him). He returns as she is finishing it, but he only grasps its significance when a **messenger** brings it to him after Violetta has left for Paris. The distraught Alfredo is comforted by his father, who reminds him to think of the family at home in Provence. Alfredo sees Flora's invitation and rushes out to seek revenge.

At Flora's party, gypsies dance and tell fortunes; others arrive dressed as matadors. Violetta arrives with her Baron. Alfredo turns up. Unlucky in love, he is in luck at cards. He flings his winnings at her, as he sarcastically puts it, to repay his debts. His father arrives and admonishes him for his insult to a woman. Alfredo pleads for her forgiveness. Violetta declares that even in death, she will always love him. The Baron challenges him to a duel.

The following month, Violetta, attended only by Annina the maid, is on her deathbed, and virtually penniless. The doctor says she has only a few hours to live. We hear that Alfredo has wounded the Baron and had to go abroad.

Alfredo returns to her. His father also returns to fulfill a promise he made to embrace her as his child. She gives the despairing Alfredo a locket for his future wife, and asks him to tell her that she is with the angels praying for him in Heaven. She seems to recover. Then a spasm chokes her and she dies.

THE INTERVAL: TALKING POINTS

Alexandre Dumas and *La Dame aux Camélias*

Alexandre Dumas *fils* (1824–1895) was the son of a seamstress. His father was Alexandre Dumas *père*, whose literary mass-production line extruded great novels such as *The Count of Monte Cristo* and *The Three Musketeers* among some 1,200 other volumes (40 were produced in 1844 alone). In so doing, the father made a fortune but died penniless, having fallen out of favour during the Second Empire. President Chirac had his remains reburied in the Panthéon in 2002.

The son's far more carefully crafted writings were influenced by his illegitimacy, by the grief of his mother at his being wrested from her when his father took custody of him, and by his ancestry – his great-grandmother was a slave from Santo Domingo.

He is best known for his novel of 1848, *La Dame aux Camélias* ('The Lady with the Camellias' or 'Camille'). This told the tale of Marguerite Gautier and Armand Duval. Dumas adapted it into a play which was staged a few years later and which was translated into many languages. As is so often the case with stage and screen adaptation, the book is much better: even though the play was accompanied by incidental music available from a shop in the rue Montmartre, it seems pedestrian. Although Verdi and Piave used the broad structure of the play[5], they enlivened the party scenes and sharpened the tragic

---

[5] There are perhaps two really notable differences between the book and the opera: in the book, Marguerite dies before any final reunion; and, although in life she experiences cash-flow problems which only the richest of admirers can alleviate, the auction of her effects after her

conclusion. Modern versions of the play spice up the sexual content considerably.

The novel was a precursor of D.H. Lawrence's *Lady Chatterley's Lover*. It helped that its sexy story was described by a distinguished critic as a real 'domestic tragedy', which had actually been experienced by its author. It had to be censored,[6] even though today the excisions may seem relatively tame. The original edition, for example, is more explicit about Armand's success, and also explains a deliberately surprising fact of life: it is far more difficult to be loved by a hardened courtesan than by a young virgin – it gives a titillating explanation as to why sixteen-year-olds are easy prey, despite the hopeless efforts of their mothers to protect them. Through the bars of their 'prison', they are desperate to learn the secrets of life: *'Plus la jeune fille croît au bien, plus elle s'abandonne facilement.'*

The book's reader can participate in the realistically described exhumation of Marguerite (Violetta) in Montmartre cemetery, and in a posthumous auction of her effects, a social event at which mingle ladies both of sententious and easy virtue.

Consumption (tuberculosis)

It is hard today to imagine the concern with which, in earlier times, a friend or relative heard a cough or noticed a blood-stained handkerchief. The rapid emaciation which characterised tuberculosis led to it being known as consumption. Although still a common disease around the world today, pulmonary tuberculosis was incurable until around 1944, when the drug streptomycin was identified. Galloping consumption was terrifying: death in around three or four months, from exhaustion by coughing, or from a sudden haemorrhage; for others, life might be more prolonged, with termination perhaps in two to eight years. (In Dumas's novel, Marguerite's exhaustion was

death leaves a substantial surplus after payment of her creditors, a surplus which accrues to her gobsmacked relatives.

[6] Some of the cuts are short but pregnant. When Armand makes his second visit to Marguerite's bed, his predecessor, a count, has just been in it. Armand notices that the linen is unsoiled. Equally thrillingly, Marguerite is already in her dressing-gown: *'Malgré moi, je jetai les yeux sur le lit. Il n'était pas défait: quant à Marguerite, elle était déjà en peignoir blanc.'*

aggravated by the doctors bleeding her.) The end was often accompanied by a surprising 'buoyancy of spirits' or optimism, known as the *spes phthisica*. We see this portrayed in the last moments of *La Traviata*.

The disease at the time was thought primarily to affect people aged between fifteen and 30, perhaps 35. Various therapies were popular: fresh air, improved hygiene, long sea voyages, even singing. Health resorts and sanitoria were recommended such as those at Bournemouth, Hastings, Torquay, Ventnor and Penzance. For the more affluent, the Alps or the Rockies were recommended. Opium was prescribed to sooth the cough.

Staging an opera depicting a death from consumption was a sensitive matter – perhaps similar to putting one on today about sexually transmitted diseases. George Bernard Shaw, the Irish critic and playwright, suggested that a plump soprano can at least mitigate 'the painful impression which the last act produces whenever there is the faintest realism[7] about it.' But it is that realism which provides the drama. From Violetta's conversation with her doctor at the outset of the opera, from the first cough, the audience can guess the inevitably tragic outcome. As the drama unfolds, the characters on stage desperately try to resist what we know is inevitable. Verdi heightens this tension by contrasting revelry with illness, carnival with death, wild pleasure and excruciating emotional and physical pain.[8] This provides the drama, the momentum; this is what moves us to compassion and makes us unobtrusively fumble for our handkerchiefs. It also makes us channel our emotions into applause, which if we were less transported, we would realise contrasts so inappropriately with the tragic scene we have just been presented with on the stage. That is art.

[7] The source of the operatic realism (verismo) found particularly in some of Puccini's operas (e.g. *Tosca* and *La Bohème*), and in *Cavalleria rusticana* and *Pagliacci*, is usually dated back to Bizet's *Carmen* (1875). *La Traviata* however may perhaps be regarded as an earlier and 'more poetic' source. Puccini's own *La Rondine* is sometimes described as the 'poor man's *Traviata*'.
[8] The father Germont, who faces a very difficult situation and is far from a rogue, highlights the contrast between provincial and metropolitan attitudes, between sexual and parental love, between Alfredo's passionate love and his Provençal sister's domestic love.

The courtesans

The character of Violetta was based on Alphonsine Plessis, who called herself Marie Duplessis. She was a *grande horizontale* with whom Liszt is reputed to have had an affair. Dumas met her at his father's neo-gothic mansion; he helped her at a party at which she had had to retire to cough up blood, and had a 'stormy and unhappy' affair with her. But he could not keep her in the style she demanded.

A tinker's daughter, Marie was successively a maid at an inn, a laundress, a milliner, and a prostitute. She was picked up by a duke, then by a viscount by whom she had a son. A baron set her up, on the condition that she gave up prostitution. In Kensington Registry Office in 1846, she was married to an impecunious count, who then left her with no money. In the following year, aged only 23, she died in her lavish apartment. Various former lovers, rivals for her favours, kept watch by her bedside. As a prominent critic wrote, 'Her death proved a kind of event; people talked about it for three days, which is a great deal in this city.' So when Dumas wrote a novel based on her, it was not surprising that it was a bestseller.

For many, the oldest profession was the only escape from sheer economic desperation and starvation, as Fantine in Victor Hugo's *Les Misérables* found out. Around the time of *La Traviata*, there were 240 registered brothels in Paris. As one would expect in France, the official trade was regulated. Those who did not register ran the risk of imprisonment, as Manon Lescaut had earlier discovered. Quotations varied from 50 centimes for a visit with the common prostitute who walked the streets with a bare bum under her silk skirt, to 40 francs for the 'standard time' of between twelve and twenty minutes with a very high-class tart, or even 100 francs when more adventurous tastes were catered for.

At the top of the remuneration structure, the really successful prostitute, the courtesan, had the beauty, character, or opportunity to select her clients, to whom she would sell her warmth and award the trophy. The cash flow would be used to finance her luxurious life-style. The bed for business of one of Marie's competitors was said to have cost 100,000 francs. This was at a time when a skilled laundry-girl, who might carry on work until three in the morning, might earn 3 francs a day. The cost of a box at the opera could buy bread for a family for six months. It is not hard to find shocking stories. We hear of the little girl who solicited for her fourteen-year-old sister, her own role being 'to breathe on the windows of the carriage so that the police could not see inside.'

Dumas's Marguerite handled one of the practical aspects of her lifestyle by wearing white camellias, except during the last five days of every month when she wore red ones. In some editions, this information is expurgated.

The notion of a courtesan actually falling in love with one of her men was not new: in Shakespeare's *Othello*, it was said of a courtesan: ''Tis the strumpet's plague to beguile many, and be beguiled by one.'

Immorality

It is not difficult to see why – as with *Carmen* later – respectable people, particularly the English in their High Victorian period, found difficulty with *La Traviata*, even though one theatre manager justified it on the footing that it 'conveyed a salutary warning to the young men of our times.'

A death scene would have been normal and appropriate; indeed it would have been perceived as introducing a desirable level of serious-ness into an opera. But *La Traviata* with its courtesans, its gambling, went too far. Even its nocturnal parties were criticised at the time for being in the nature of 'orgy rather than of sprightly revel.'

A leading critic called the opera 'distasteful and feeble'. The prima donna for the Paris and London performances of May 1856 (who was either fortunate or unfortunate to be the niece of a cardinal) seems to have acted the part of a willing 'grisette' rather too successfully.[9]

---

[9] Marietta Piccolomini, the Violetta who popularised *La Traviata* in London, Paris and New York, had a notoriously poor voice, and little idea of how to sing, but, with her wonderful ankles, teeth, smile and hair, she was far from piccolo when it came to sex appeal or the demonstration thereof. Her formidable mother kept males at bay until a marquis married her and took her off the stage.

Another soprano, who characterised Violetta as a woman who bad luck had driven into fitful recklessness, was considered more acceptable. Maybe the view of the critic – the distinguished Henry Fothergill Chorley – was tainted by his Quaker background.

The negative reception was such that even Chorley was prepared to concede that some of the fulminations against *La Traviata* were ridiculous. The opera house has never been considered as 'a place in which our art has been devoted to the service of only that which is high and pure and righteous,' he observed. The French were clearly at fault: 'That there is an unwholesome interest in the story, is evident from the fact of its having been the first of a series of bad dramas which have since taken possession of the Parisian theatre – for the exhibition of female frailty.'

The music

The moral issue maybe led 19th century critics to become unduly critical of the music. Chorley wrote about the 'trashy music of *La Traviata*', obviously relishing his alliteration. It is 'a story untenable for music,' he expostulated. 'Consumption for one who is to sing! A ballet with a lame Sylphide would be as rational.' For him, in the second and third acts, 'there is little or nothing worth the trouble of singing.' He also disliked Verdi's 'bad tunes', his 'violent music', the 'hysterical element' and the requirement for the singer to use 'the utmost force of the voice'. Act 1 'is almost the solitary act of gay music from the composer's pen,' he wrote.

How wrong critics can be, and how unenviable is their task when looked at in retrospect! We cannot dismiss so lightly the glorious melodies, the great ensembles, such as at the end of the Act 2 finale, in which the principals combine to sing melodic lines ideally suited to their individual emotions. We can point to earlier moments such as the searing chromatic lines when Violetta tells Germont that she would rather die than make the sacrifice of leaving Alfredo.

And it is not just the vocal line. Verdi uses his orchestra to very great effect. One can be misled by the simple, sometimes thin, orchestration, and apparently superficial dum-de-dum accompaniment.

The scene in the country is masterly. A figure on the cellos and basses depicts Violetta's mind wrestling as she yields – the score marked *con estremo dolore* ('with immense sorrow') – to the pressure put on her by Alfredo's father. We can hear how the orchestra, simply but through rhythm, builds up the tension, to almost hysterical levels, when Alfredo comes in and finds her writing the letter before that wrenching emotional climax of the opera, her outburst *Amami, amami, quant'io t'amo*.[10] Verdi also uses the orchestra to build the tension, with a distinctive rhythm and low clarinets, in the Act 3 card scene.

That said, the effectiveness of *La Traviata* derives from a combination of factors: the design of the work, the music, the story and the libretto. It represents a team effort, the team led by Verdi. We should not forget that the stars at the time regarded themselves as being more important than the opera itself. *Plus ça change, plus c'est la même chose*.

Verdi was developing a new type of opera with which the critics were unfamiliar. With *Macbeth*, he had begun to demand a new kind of voice, a 'harsh, stifled, dark' sound, which was no longer limpid. The emphasis was now on power rather than prettiness of sound. Singers required colossal stamina, vocal lines were broader and more sustained, roles were longer and heavier and darker tonal colour was required.[11] We see this not just with the ladies: Germont goes up to G flat *con forza*, right at the top of the baritone range, in the *Di Provenza* in Act 2.[12]

But, perhaps surprisingly, Verdi himself recognised that *La Traviata* 'while inevitably attracting the great, can make its effect with artists of the second rank'. When looking for a Desdemona for *Othello*, he

[10] Other examples are the agitated semiquavers, when Violetta remains behind when the others go in to dinner. In Act 3, the weaker Violetta becomes, the more diaphanous the scoring.
[11] Verdi was unusually demanding with his music. Act 1 demands a bright coloratura. In amongst the runs and scales of the *Sempre libera* which concludes the act, Violetta jabs away at top C several times. The second act has more recitative, and is more lyrical. And for the duet in Act 3, when she is joined with Alfredo, she requires great power and energy – indeed, a power unexpected in a consumptive (this has been a source of considerable irritation to the critics).
[12] One Alfredo, Giuseppe Di Stefano, was so annoyed that the Germont was encored after this aria that he threatened (in the middle of a performance) to withdraw. He was told that there was a young understudy by the name of Domingo waiting in the wings who would take over. Di Stefano changed his mind and carried on.

wrote to his publisher Ricordi: 'even a mediocrity could possess the right qualities to shine in *La Traviata*.'

ACT BY ACT

Act 1

Violetta's mansion in Paris, August 1700

A short prelude gives us a premonition of the tragic end, with sounds which will be heard again at the beginning of Act 3, and also the theme of Violetta's love for Alfredo.

The curtain rises on a party in the salon of a Paris mansion where the courtesan Violetta has been installed by the Baron, her protector.[13] Violetta's conversation with her doctor is interrupted by the arrival of guests, whom she welcomes and who are already well lit up: they have come from an earlier party at Flora's. She is another courtesan who is financed by a Marquis.

Gastone, a Viscount, arrives with his friend Alfredo Germont.

At Violetta's invitation, the party sits down to dinner. Gastone explains to Violetta that Alfredo is obsessed with her: during her recent illness, he came daily to enquire after her. She chides the Baron for being unattentive, which irritates him.

Alfredo is invited to sing a drinking song. All join in his 'Brindisi', a toast to pleasure and love, *Libiamo ne' lieti calici*. Violetta joins in, and emphasises the need to enjoy life while you can. She then invites the guests to dance to the accompaniment of the band next door (on stage).

During this, she has a coughing fit. She protests that it is of no consequence – she felt a sudden chill, but it passed. However the mirror tells her the truth. Alfredo advises her to take care of herself. But she cannot afford to give up this lifestyle. When he says that he will look after her, she doubts his sincerity. But he protests that he has secretly loved her for a year, *Un di felice*. We hear the first strains

---

[13] Violetta appears straightaway. Frequently in operas, the entry of the star soprano is delayed so that she can make a dramatic entry later.

of the well-known tune as he sings of that love, the mysterious unattainable love: *Di quell'amor, quell' amor ch'è palpito*, ending with a cadenza. (This tune recurs throughout the opera as a reminiscence of the love that they have for each other.) She gives him a flower, which he should bring back when it has faded. He persuades her that this will be tomorrow.

After Alfredo goes, the guests return from the ballroom; the chorus and soloists join in a large 'Verdi' chorus, which is almost a trademark of his. Dawn is breaking and they must leave. When they have gone, Violetta bursts forth: she has never known such joy, actually to be loved and loving! *Ah, fors'è lui che l'anima solinga ne' tumulti.* Alfredo is the man she has been longing for. Then suddenly she realises the folly of it all. She is an unfortunate, lonely woman, abandoned in Paris; she must be free to enjoy pleasure and desire: *Sempre libera degg'io folleggiare di gioia in gioia.* She has felt love throbbing in her heart, a mysterious sensation of pain and ecstasy! We hear the tune of *Di quell'amor* again. In the street beneath her balcony, Alfredo echoes this famous melody, to the accompaniment of a backstage harp, as he leaves. And she reaches top C several times, and even D flat.

Act 2 Scene 1

A country house outside Paris, the following January[14]

We learn from Alfredo, who has been out hunting, that Violetta has given up the fast life to live in the country with him, in considerable luxury.[15] It has been marvellous: *De' miei bollenti spiriti.* But Annina the maid has, unknown to Alfredo, had to go to Paris to sell Violetta's

[14] Audience concentration can sometimes sag in a second act, and one without a lively chorus. But the beauty of the melodies, the cleverness of the orchestral writing which underpins so much of the emotion conveyed by the singers, Violetta's dramatic outburst, Germont's perhaps familiar predicament, all combine to make it truly memorable.

[15] In the novel, Marguerite and Armand set up in Bougival which 'despite its frightful name [possibly because the word *bouge* in French connotes a pigsty] is one of the prettiest places that can be imagined.' Bougival, where Impressionists resided and painted, was the location in the 1870s for the *ménage à trois* between the Russian novelist Ivan Turgenev, Pauline Viardot and her husband. Viardot was one of the most distinguished opera singers on the 19th-century stage. More can be read about her, and about Turgenev, in the author's *Enchantress of Nations*.

possessions. They are running out of cash and they need 1,000 louis, indeed an enormous amount of money. Alfredo determines to go into Paris himself, and sort out the finances. He expresses his horror at the shame the situation has brought upon him, *O mio rimorso! O infamia!*[16]

After Alfredo has gone, Violetta opens an invitation from Flora to go to a party that night. Meanwhile, she awaits the arrival of the financial adviser she is expecting. Instead, Alfredo's father Giorgio Germont walks in unannounced. Although initially somewhat taken with her, he accuses her of ruining his son, and being a fortune seeker. He ignores her order to leave. He admires the luxury; she says she lives just for Alfredo. She says she is selling up and shows him some papers. He asks a sacrifice from her and pleads for the future of his two children. He has a daughter, pure as an angel, whose marriage is at risk because of the scandal Alfredo has caused, *Pura siccome un angelo.*

Violetta appreciates that she must give up Alfredo temporarily. But Alfredo's father insists that it must be forever. She resists: Germont does not appreciate her immense love for Alfredo, *Non sapete quale affetto vivo.* She would rather die than make the sacrifice of leaving Alfredo. But Germont persists:[17] *Un dì, quando le veneri* – in years to come, when passion has subsided, they will realise that their union is not blessed by God. (We hear the three-note rhythmic motif which is to be associated with her death.) A repeated figure in the cellos and basses tells us how she is wrestling with the quandary she is in. She eventually undertakes to separate, in the exquisite *Dite alla giovine sì bella e pura* ('Tell the pure and beautiful maiden, that an unfortunate woman, crushed by despair, sacrifices herself for her, and will die'), of which one expert has claimed 'nowhere in Italian opera is grief more beautifully transfigured than here.' Germont, who greatly appreciates

---

[16] In the next scenes, the listener can easily appreciate what set Verdi apart from other 19th century composers of Italian opera. He demonstrates a masterly use of the orchestra to balance, and create, the mood of the singer, and, *inter alia*, depict the agony going through Violetta's mind.

[17] In the novel, Armand's father accuses him of having a vocation to rescue prostitutes. While this may sound sarcastic, that mission attracted a number of distinguished people in the 19th century, Gladstone and Dickens being perhaps two of the most noteworthy.

her sacrifice, consoles her: *Piangi, piangi.* He tells her to say to Alfredo that she no longer loves him. Death will be her memorial, she answers. She asks Germont to embrace her as his daughter. They bid each other farewell and Germont goes out into the garden.

Violetta, accompanied sadly by a mournful clarinet, writes an acceptance to Flora's invitation. Then, while she is writing to Alfredo, he comes in. He asks to see the letter but she refuses to show it to him. We again hear the rhythmic triplet which is later to be associated with her death. He says his father is coming, and is confident that he will like her. She, however, is almost hysterical. She says she must get out of the way and rushes off, but not before having implored Alfredo, in an outburst marked in the score *con passione e forza* by Verdi, in those searing tones presaged in the Prelude at the start of the opera, always to love her: *Amami, Alfredo, quant'io t'amo* ('Love me Alfredo ... Goodbye').[18] And she rushes into the garden.

At first, Alfredo does not realise what has happened, and relaxes: Violetta has set off for Paris. Giuseppe, the servant, tells him this; but Alfredo only appreciates the significance when a messenger arrives with her letter for him.[19] As he starts to read, 'Alfredo, by the time you read this ...', he is confronted by his father and they embrace. Germont asks him to think of the happiness at his home in Provence: *Di Provenza il mar.* But Alfredo is distraught, and thinks that the Baron has been undermining him. Germont tells him to come away with him, but Alfredo sees Flora's invitation and rushes out to seek revenge.

---

[18] There are many stories about buxom Violettas unsuited to the consumptive role. The slightly built Tito Schipa (1889–1965) was, at the outset of his legendary career, playing Alfredo to a portly Violetta. When in Act 2 she uttered the passionate '*Amami Alfredo*', she grasped Schipa to her bosom with such forcefulness that a protest was heard from the Gods, 'Don't hurt the poor boy, we want to hear him sing.'

[19] Unfortunately, in Placido Domingo's début in the lead role, the messenger did not appear, so there was no answer to 'Who's there?' Domingo had to answer his own question by singing, 'No one.' Luckily, there were some sheets of paper on the table where Violetta had written her note, and he picked up one, and sang, 'From Violetta!' Domingo comments, 'You have to be prepared for absolutely everything in this business.'

Act 2 Scene 2

Flora's mansion in Paris

Flora's party, for which her Marquis has paid, is in full swing, as she awaits the arrival of Violetta and Alfredo. She is told that they have separated: but, in fact, Violetta is coming with her Baron.

The entertainers include gypsies who perform the customary ballet:[20] *Noi siamo zingarelle*. They read fortunes: when the Marquis's infidelity is identified, Flora is furious. Guests arrive dressed as matadors and sing of love: *È Piquillo un bel gagliardo*. They tell of Piquillo, the handsome matador, hero of the bullring, who comes from Biscay. He floors five bulls and beds his lady. (Unusually, the score specifies that the picadors bang their goads on the ground in tie to the music.)

Alfredo arrives and goes to the tables. When Violetta ces in on the Baron's arm, she is shocked to see Alfredo, and, to elf, she prays God for mercy. Alfredo may be unlucky in love, be is in luck at cards. The Baron challenges him to keep playing fry high stakes. To the entertainment of the others, he keeps dog and continues to win. Dinner is called. The Baron asks for a tch, as they all go into the dining room.

Violetta remains behind. She sends for Alfredo and w 'him to go, because the Baron will challenge him to a duel. (We a hear a portentous rhythm Verdi associates with death.) Alfredo ases her of being worried that, if he wins, she would lose both her 'er and her protector. She refuses to leave with him. She pretends hat she has committed herself to the Baron. Alfredo calls in the guests and announces that he foolishly allowed Violetta to waste all her money on him; but he is now repaying his debts. With this, he flings his winnings at her, to the outrage of everyone. At this moment, his

[20] Composers provided a ballet in Act 2 with an eye to the regulation in Paris that works staged at the Opéra should include at least one ballet. The rakes from the Paris Jockey Club came almost as a gang, late, although in time to view the ballet dancers in the customary second act. Six years after *La Traviata*, there was the notorious riot when Wagner refused to provide a ballet in the second act of the Paris production of *Tannhäuser* because it would have been a dramatic absurdity.

father comes in and agrees that Alfredo has behaved disgracefully to a woman. It is behaviour unworthy of his son.

Although Alfredo is full of remorse and shame, Violetta reassures him of her love: *Alfredo, Alfredo, di questo core non puoi comprendere tutto l'amore!* Some day God will forgive him and he will be remorseful. But even in death, she will always love him. As his father takes him away, the Baron challenges him to a duel. The act ends with another great 'Verdi' chorus, in which all the participants express their feelings.

Act 3

Violetta's bedroom, a month later, 7am

Violetta wakes. Coughing, she asks Annina her maid, who has dozed off, to open the curtains. The doctor arrives to see Violetta. The priest has visited and she feels better; she has slept quite well. The doctor says he will come back soon; but as he goes, he tells Annina that Violetta has only a few hours to live.

Close, we hear the preparations are being made for the carnival. Violetta tells Annina to go and give half their remaining money to the poor.

Violetta reads a letter from Germont. This is spoken (the normal convention for reading a letter) rather than sung, but it is underpinned by echoes of the famous love tune from the end of Act 1. We hear that the Baron was wounded in the duel but not badly. Alfredo is out of the country but will return to seek her forgiveness.

Violetta sees in the mirror how dreadfully she has changed. But she takes comfort from the doctor's words of hope. Yet we hear the sad oboe as she explains that her only hope is death: *Addio del passato bei sogni ridenti* ('Farewell past memories. My rosy cheeks are pale'). She misses Alfredo. A fallen woman, she seeks God's forgiveness. *Ah, della traviata sorridi al desìo.* The noise of the carnival *baccanale* is heard outside.

Annina returns excitedly to say that Alfredo is coming. The lovers fall into each other's arms. Violetta feels rejuvenated. He craves forgiveness. They will live happily together forever. They will leave Paris and she will recover. *Parigi, o cara, noi lasceremo.*

As she prepares to go to church to give thanks for his return, she has a spasm. He calls for the doctor. She so desperately wants to live, but recognises the cruelty of her position, to die so young, to have suffered so much, when there is hope of such happiness. *Ah, Gran Dio! Morir sì giovane.* He says they must never give up hope.

Germont and the doctor arrive. The repentant and remorseful Germont says that he is fulfilling his promise to embrace her as his daughter, as he said he would when they parted in the country. She gives the despairing Alfredo a locket, telling him that, when he marries, he must tell his wife that this woman loved him and is now with the angels praying for him in Heaven. Against the love tune, she seems to recover, to everyone's surprise. Then a spasm chokes her and she dies (on top B flat).

VERDI: *AÏDA*

THE OPERA AND ITS COMPOSER

The Grand March from *Aïda*, Verdi's 'farewell to Grand Opera', is one of the most popular and ubiquitous of opera tunes. It raises the roof at the Royal Albert Hall. It can be heard outdoors at Verona, or on parade in Whitehall, or even on a squeaky harmonium at a small wedding. In the opera house, we have the magnificent spectacle of Egypt over 3,000 years ago. The principals, the chorus, the full orchestra and the stage band let rip. Because of the quantity of music in the last couple of minutes, a particularly small font has to be used to print those pages of the full score.

In November 1869, the Suez Canal was officially inaugurated by Empress Eugénie of France. A few days earlier, Cairo celebrated the opening of its new opera house with a production of Verdi's *Rigoletto*. Verdi had been asked to write a hymn for the celebrations, but that type of composition did not appeal to him. Anyway, he was focussing on his farming and other activities, and besides, the tough businessman was not too impressed by the terms of the offer.

So he was asked by the Khedive (viceroy) of Egypt to compose an opera for the following season, and to name his own terms. He was reluctant, but, tempted with a fee of 150,000 francs for the Egyptian rights alone, at a time when 10 francs a day might be regarded as an exceptionally good wage, he agreed. He signed the contract in August 1870. As well as delivering the score, with his fee he was to pay for the libretto and for the producer and conductor for a première in Cairo in the following January. There were various stipulations should the arrangements be disrupted by the Franco-Prussian War, which had just broken out.

Verdi led the preparation of the libretto, but others were involved, including an outstanding Egyptologist, Auguste Mariette,[1] and possibly also the librettist of Verdi's early opera *Nabucco*. The Khedive is sometimes, improbably, credited with creating the original story; it actually seems to date back to Heliodorus, a Greek in the third century AD. The Italian libretto was written in verse by Antonio Ghislanzoni.[2]

Verdi was 'working like an animal' during October, and the opera was virtually complete by mid-November. Premières had been envisaged for Cairo and Milan early in the New Year. But in the autumn, the scenery, the costumes and the Egyptologist were trapped in Paris during the 130-day siege by the Prussians. This lasted until the end of January. All the work on the sets was suspended through lack of workmen. Verdi heard the news of this from a message flown out of Paris by balloon.

In the event, the world première was delayed until around a year later. Verdi accepted that it had to be in Cairo, and the opera got a good reception there on Christmas Eve, 1871. He did not attend. However, just over a week later, he was in Milan to prepare for the very important first performance at La Scala,[3] on 8 February 1872. There, the tickets were being traded on the stock exchange.

Aïda was a sensational success. At a time when unification of Italy was reaching its climax, *O patria mia* ('Land of my fathers') was bound to send the audience ecstatic. The occasion was 'a gratifying personal triumph' for Verdi, and he was called out 32 times. He was presented with an ivory baton, and a diamond star with 'Aïda' and his own name set in rubies and other jewels. The opera also proved to be a gold mine for La Scala and other opera houses.

---

[1] Auguste Mariette (1821–1881) had worked at the Louvre. He was involved in the exploration of many of the antiquities on the Nile familiar to modern tourists (Memphis, Thebes, Karnak, Denderah). He discovered the Temple of the Sphinx and bared the Sphinx itself to rock level. He began his career as a teacher of French and drawing in Stratford-upon-Avon. His tomb is outside the Egyptian Museum building at the side of Tahrir Square in the centre of Cairo.

[2] Antonio Ghislanzoni (1824–1893) was a failed priest, failed doctor, baritone and poet. He was librettist of about 85 librettos and author of 2,162 articles. He was a pro-nationalist journalist who also worked with Verdi on the libretto for the second version of *La Forza del destino*.

[3] He wrote a separate overture for Milan but withdrew it.

Normally Verdi would finish the scoring of an opera during rehearsal. But he never intended to go to Cairo. The delay allowed him time to work on *Aïda* at home during 1871. It is astonishing how, just sitting at his desk, he succeeded in depicting the Nile. While he worked on the score, he was also closely involved in the casting and scene design.

One member of the La Scala cast was Teresa Stolz, who had incensed him and his publisher by initially demanding an exorbitant fee. But when she came for rehearsals at his house during September, they not only made it up, but he prised her away from her fiancé, a leading conductor with whom (as so frequently happened with his friendships) Verdi had fallen out.

By the time of the first performance in Naples just over a year later, 'ugly rumours were circulating' about Verdi's passion for Stolz.[4] She was originally intended to be the Amneris in Milan, but he switched her to Aïda. The significance of this may not have been lost on Verdi's wife Giuseppina, who was to feel some of the same jealous emotions felt by the Pharoah's daughter.

At first, Verdi refused to allow a performance in Paris: he particularly disliked the arrogance of the Opéra orchestra, and he did not much care for the French. He had stormed out of a production there of his *Les Vêpres Siciliennes*. So, in 1880, the Parisians made a considerable effort to make *Aïda* at the Opéra a success. He conducted himself. The President of France gave a banquet in his honour and presented him with the Légion d'honneur. The expanded ballet that he composed for the Paris production was incorporated into all future editions of the vocal score.

Today, we can overlook the fact that the characters are, to an extent, stereotypes like those in 18th-century opera; and that Radamès, with his 'pillow talk', is another of those male fools who have a tendency to frequent opera. We can be astonished by Verdi's use of the orchestra

---

[4] Stolz, in her mid-thirties, was from Bohemia. She had sung for Verdi in *Don Carlo* and *La Forza del destino*. She had 'a phenomenal dynamic range and was sensitive to every nuance of Verdi's thought.' When Verdi died in a Milan hotel nearly 30 years later, she was there too, in a state of collapse.

to underpin their feelings in the dialogue, and particularly to portray the jealousy and anguish of Amneris. We can enjoy the beauty and modernity of the Nile scene, the great moments such as *Celeste Aïda* and *O patria mia*, and the extraordinary double scene and music of the last act. We can leave the house agreeing that *Aïda* indeed has 'one of the most magical endings to any opera.'

(More on the life of Verdi can be found on pages 210–211.)

WHO'S WHO AND WHAT'S WHAT

The story below is based on the libretto. Certain directors may amend opera stories to suit their production.

At Memphis, near modern Cairo, **Ramfis**, the High Priest, confirms to **Radamès**, captain of the Egyptian army, that he will support his appointment as commander of the Egyptian forces against the Ethiopians. Radamès is in love with **Aïda**: *Celeste Aïda, forma divina*. She is an Ethiopian and the slave of **Amneris**, the fiercely jealous daughter of the **King** (**Pharoah**).

Amneris is passionate about Radamès. Aïda's emotional response to the news about the forthcoming war confirms her suspicion that Aïda is indeed her rival in love.

The Pharoah orders a **messenger** to report the latest news: the Ethiopians have attacked Thebes (modern-day Luxor). Radamès's appointment as supreme commander of the Egyptian forces is announced. The people respond with a bellicose chorus *Su! del Nilo al sacro lido*. Aïda joins in the rousing *Ritorna vincitor*. But she is torn between **love and patriotic duty**: On the one hand, she loves Radamès; on the other, she owes duty to her own country and family. She pleads with the gods to let her die: *Numi pietà*.

The consecration of Radamès is held in the Temple of Vulcan. The priests and priestesses invoke their god: *Possente, Immenso Fthà*.

As it transpires, the Ethiopians are defeated by Radamès. By pretending to Aïda that he has been killed in battle, Amneris tricks her into revealing her relationship with him. From Aïda's response to this news, and its subsequent correction, Amneris knows for certain that she is pitted against Aïda. However, the Pharoah's daughter versus her slave should be an unequal contest. The crowd prepares for the victory ceremony. Aïda is miserable and wants to die.

The victory parade with the **Grand March** – *Gloria all' Egitto* – takes place outside the Temple of Ammon at the gates of Thebes (Luxor).

Radamès, the victor, is promised anything he wishes. He asks first that the prisoners be led in. They include Aïda's father, **Amonasro**. Disguised as an ordinary soldier, it is not known that he is in fact the enemy king. Radamès secures clemency for the prisoners. The Pharaoh gives his daughter to Radamès.

On the banks of the Nile, Amneris arrives in her boat on a starlit night and enters the Temple of Isis to pray before her marriage. The **High Priestess** with her priestesses can be heard invoking the goddess. Aïda has an assignation with Radamès, and fears that it is to be a farewell: *O patria mia.*

Amonasro gets there before Radamès. War has broken out again; he pressurises his daughter to wheedle out of Radamès the route by which the Egyptian army is going attack. She persuades Radamès to flee with her and start a new life together. As they go, and within earshot of Amonasro, Radamès blurts out the military secret. His betrayal is overheard by Amneris. Although Aïda gets away, Radamès is arrested.

In the palace, the fiercely jealous Amneris laments her plight. She is about to lose Radamès, but, as the Pharoah's daughter, she has the power to save him. Despite her efforts at persuasion, Radamès will not renounce Aïda, and goes for trial and certain death.

The trial and condemnation can be heard. He is to be buried alive under the altar. Amneris is aghast.

In the '**double scene**', the Temple of Vulcan is above, and, below, the crypt where Radamès is being entombed. He finds that Aïda has already secretly hidden herself there. She is too lovely to die. But she is ecstatic. The lovers die in each other's arms. Above, Amneris, in mourning, is prostrate on the stone which seals the tomb.

THE INTERVAL: TALKING POINTS

The big roles

The four principal roles in *Aïda* have attracted countless great singers; names such as Patti, Callas, Domingo, Pavarotti …

Aïda herself inevitably gets the limelight. Her part is somewhat static and it needs a great singer and actress to bring it off.

Much of her music is located in the upper notes of an exceptionally high voice. Even Callas sometimes had difficulty with the very high notes. Thereby, she confirmed George Bernard Shaw's conclusion: 'Verdi's worst sins as a composer have been sins against the human voice.' She and Radamès have to be able to soar effortlessly above a full chorus.

It requires skill, at the start of the opera, to avoid Radamès, the great soldier, appearing stilted and comical. He has been compared with a 'school captain' – 'And school captains are usually too well-adjusted to be interesting as people.' The final sustained note in his *Celeste Aïda* has proved to be a challenge for tenors. Verdi subsequently provided rather a limp alternative.

Tchaikovsky found himself unmoved by the characters of Radamès and Aïda.

Radamès might have done better with Amneris, despite her ruthlessness. She has a part which is at least as large, if not more so, than that of Aïda. She uses the full range of the mezzo-soprano, reaching top A, and, within a couple of bars, ranging from top A flat down to bottom B flat. Her gorgeous deep rich sound portrays a real person, whose character is underpinned most effectively by the evocative orchestral music that accompanies her. She is a dangerous competitor to the sorry Aïda, not only musically but emotionally, especially in Act 4. It is not surprising that Verdi originally envisaged Teresa Stolz in the role.

Amonasro demands some expert acting: although a prisoner of war, he has also to appear to be a born leader of men.

Don't be a disgruntled opera-goer

After the Milan première, Verdi not quite 60, rushed around to performances, first in Parma, then in Naples. He used the time, as he travelled, to deal with correspondence on subjects varying from politics to a recipe for cooking a shoulder of pork. One of the letters he received came from an opera-goer who so disliked the performance in Parma that he asked for his money back, for both his ticket to get there and his dinner. Verdi reimbursed him for the ticket provided the complainant undertook never to go to a Verdi opera again. But he refused to reimburse him for his dinner – after all, he could very well have eaten at home. Verdi had the story released to the press. All hell broke loose on the individual, who got letters threatening decapitation.

The Suez Canal

Egypt was a province of the decomposing Ottoman Empire, and so the viceroy, who in 1866 was granted the regal rank of Khedive, was nominally a vassal of the Turkish Sultan. The spendthrift Khedive's grandfather, Mehemet Ali, had dominated early 19th-century Egypt, such that it was relatively independent.

There had long been an intention to build a Suez canal. In pre-Christian times, there had been a water route connecting the Mediterranean and the Red Sea. An overland rail route from England to India opened in 1837. From the mid-1850s, M. de Lesseps master-minded the construction of the canal.

In view of its strategic importance on the route to India and the Far East, Egypt was the source of considerable friction between France and England. French money was used to develop Egypt's cotton-growing industry.

A few years after *Aïda*, Disraeli, the British Prime Minister, seized the opportunity to buy from the Khedive, who was virtually bankrupt, a large block of The Suez Canal Company shares for £4 million, using a loan from Rothschilds.

French and British involvement caused resentment, which culminated in a nationalist uprising in the 1880s. French failure to participate in the bombardment of Alexandria further weakened French influence.

Gods: *Numi*

Numi is the Italian word for deities, gods. It appears many times in the libretto, as in *Numi pietà*.

The gods are an odd mixture, but have no significance other than to add colour to an already colourful opera. Vulcan, in whose temple Ramfis presides (according to the libretto), was a Roman god, the divine blacksmith and god of fire who forged thunderbolts for Jove on Mount Etna in Sicily.

Three gods specified in *Aïda* were gods of immense importance in the complex and shifting pantheon of sun worship in Egypt: Ptha, the creator god from Memphis (Cairo), who is invoked in *Possente, Immenso Fthà*; Amun, outside whose temple at Thebes (Luxor) the victory parade takes place; and Osiris, whose vast statue is specified to support the ceiling of the crypt in which the lovers are buried alive.[5]

The status of Ptha, Amun Ra and Osiris is evident in the colossal temple at Abu Simbel, the southernmost attraction for a modern tourist to Egypt. It was the creation and glorification of the mighty Ramesses II (1279–1213BC), who, deified, joins these three gods in the innermost sanctuary.

Musicians recognise Osiris from Mozart's *The Magic Flute* in which the High Priest Sarastro sings the well-known aria *O Isis und Osiris*, in which he prays that the gods will grant the lovers wisdom and endurance.

---

[5] Isis, whose temple Amneris enters at the beginning of Act 3, was the consort, or even the female form, of Osiris. The Mysteries of Osiris were performed annually, re-enacting the god's kingship, death and resurrection. Four thousand years ago, participation in these became a lifetime goal for many Egyptians, comparable to a pilgrimage to Mecca or Jerusalem today.

Franco-Prussian War and Commune

The Franco-Prussian War came out of the blue and proceeded at great speed. The vacant Spanish throne was offered to a German. This rattled France, which was increasingly neurotic about the growing strength of Prussia. War was declared on 15 July 1870. Napoleon III was penned in at Sedan in the Ardennes, where he capitulated on 1 September. The German armies reached Paris, which was then still a fortified city, surrounded by a wall.

There were no contingency plans for a long siege. Famously, Paris survived on horsemeat, cats, dogs and rats. It capitulated at the end of January, after a siege of 130 days.

During the siege, 65 balloons left Paris: they carried nearly eleven tons of official despatches, including around 2.5 million letters, one of which contained the information that the Egyptologist, the scenery and dresses were stuck there. Ballooning was a risky business. The crew were liable to be shot as spies. Only five balloons fell into enemy hands, but many were simply blown off course.

Soon after the end of the siege, there was an uprising, in which some generals were butchered. The government moved from Paris to Versailles. At the end of March 1871, a municipal council, a motley collection of Jacobins, old socialists, anarchists, intellectuals and Bohemians installed itself as the 'Commune de Paris'.

In early May, a proclamation was issued warning the Commune that Paris would be attacked. In less than a fortnight, the Versailles troops broke in. The destruction of property and lives was terrible. Hostages, including the Archbishop of Paris were shot. When his corpse was found, 147 men were taken to Père Lachaise cemetery and shot. This was only the beginning of the vengeance and bloodletting.

ACT BY ACT

It was normal for a prelude to open quietly and atmospherically. The muted violins express the repressed yearning, to be associated with Aïda throughout the opera. Verdi's craftsmanship in this '*preludio*' has been praised for surpassing that in any instrumental piece that he had previously composed.

Act 1

The opera opens in a hall in the palace of the Pharaoh at Memphis, the ancient city founded in about 3100BC, near to modern Cairo. Through a great door can be seen the Pyramids, and temples and palaces.

Ramfis, the High Priest, converses with Radamès, captain of the Egyptian army. He confirms a rumour that Ethiopians, to the south, have renewed their attacks. Ramfis hints that he is going to inform the Pharaoh that the goddess Isis has signified that Radamès should be appointed commander of the Egyptian forces. Radamès knows that this would give him the chance to win glory for himself, and for his adored Aïda to share his laurel crown: *Celeste Aïda, forma divina.* (In this famous romanza, the final note is the sustained top B flat; Verdi refused to allow it to be transposed down.)[6]

Amneris, the Pharoah's daughter, hopes that Radamès's radiant look indicates his love for her. She checks flirtingly (the oboe gives a slight waggle of the hips) whether any other attraction in Memphis might be making him appear so happy. Radamès (the agitated orchestra betrays his concern) worries that she has guessed that he is in love with Aïda, who is an Ethiopian and her slave. Amneris expresses her jealous fears. Aïda enters to the sound of the clarinet playing the theme that started the Prelude. That Radamès and the slave are in love is confirmed by Aïda's emotional response to the news about the forthcoming war. Amneris is agitated.

Amneris asks ingratiatingly why she is emotional: *Vieni, o diletta,* Aïda betrays reasons more personal than the war alone. The two women are clearly opposed to each other: Amneris is driven by jealousy, Aïda by her concern at her precarious and servile status as

---

[6] In *Celeste Aïda*, Verdi indicates quiet dynamics so as to ensure that Radamès 'does not open the evening by merely raising the roof.'

a conquered Ethiopian, and, as we will shortly hear, by being no less than the daughter of the Ethiopian King.[7]

The Pharoah and his entourage enter to a fanfare. He orders a messenger to announce that the Ethiopians have attacked Thebes, and are led by Amonasro (who Aïda, in an aside, tells us is her father). War is declared, and Radamès is proclaimed supreme commander. The Pharoah leads a bellicose chorus *Su! del Nilo al sacro lido*, during which the High Priest reminds everyone that the gods alone determine the outcome. Amneris presents Radamès with the standard. Aïda joins in the rousing chorus *Ritorna vincitor*, which is led by Amneris.

Aïda echoes *Ritorna vincitor* ('Return as conqueror'). She recognises the desperate predicament she has found herself in. She is caught between her love for Radamès on the one hand, and for her king, country and family, on the other. She suddenly realises, on a sustained top B flat, that she is calling for them to defeat the man she so much loves. She thinks of him, accompanied by a clarinet playing the opening theme of the Prelude again. In a beautiful cantabile, she pleads the gods to let her die: *Numi pietà*.

* * *

In the Temple of Vulcan at Memphis, the Pharoah's daughter attends Radamès's investiture and consecration. Ramfis and his priests and priestesses invoke the god Ptha – *Possente, Immenso Fthà* – to grant them victory. In the evocative opening, distant priestesses are at first accompanied by a harp, and the priests chant their invocation. The priestesses dance a sacred dance.

When Radamès joins the ceremony, Ramphis reminds him that Egypt depends on him. With his priests he prays the gods to support him. Radamès is invested with the consecrated armour. The music recedes to a pianissimo to allow the act to conclude dramatically with two colossal shouts of '*Immenso Fthà*'.

---

[7] The orchestra underpins the dialogue and the trio *Trema che il ver m'apprenda*, as the three realise the mess they are in. The climax is almost hysterical, ending with Aïda on top B.

Act 2

In Amneris's apartment, the harp accompanies the slaves as they perform her toilette. She longs to possess Radamès. There is a dance by
the little Moorish slaves.

When Aïda brings Amneris her crown – the motif from the start
of the prelude being played again – Amneris is plagued by doubt and
jealousy. She is patronising towards Aïda, whose people have been
defeated, and who does not know the fate of her brothers and father.

In order to find out the secrets of Aïda's heart, Amneris at first
pretends that Radamès has been killed in the battle. Aïda's immediate
grief betrays her emotions. When Amneris reveals that she was just
pretending, Aïda is overjoyed. With the score marked *massimo furore*,
and with the clarinets giving 'a ferociously sarcastic smile', she tells
Aïda, her base slave, that she, the Pharoah's daughter, is her rival in
love: *son tua rivale … trema, o vil schiava*. She will take part in the
victory ceremony and she will destroy her.

The crowd can be heard preparing for the ceremony. Aïda, who has
no joys in life, just wishes for death (reaching top B flat and top C).
She calls on the gods to let her die: *Numi pietà*.

* * *

This is the scene of the victory parade[8] outside the Temple of Ammon
at the gate of the city of Thebes (Luxor). The Pharoah takes his place
on the throne, with Amneris beside him, looking imperiously down
on her slave. The Grand March, or Triumphal March, *Gloria all'*
Egitto,[9] 'the most celebrated tune in the opera', follows. It features
two groups of three 'Egyptian' trumpets playing in different keys

---

[8] This is sometimes presented (especially at open-air productions in Italy) with a circus of animals of African origin. The staging is of course fraught with problems. It has been known for the
animals all to relieve themselves at the same moment. The music is often used at weddings, where
the bride, who is clearly unfamiliar with its origins, would presumably prefer not to be likened
to a camel, let alone an elephant – or even a slave. It has also led to some cruel comments: after
a performance by Callas, early in her career, one of the critics said that it was impossible to tell
the difference between Callas's legs and those of the elephants.

[9] The Khedive of Egypt wanted to adopt this theme as the Egyptian national anthem.

and when one group takes over from the other there is a memorable change of key.[10] Thereafter there is the ballet.

The Pharaoh receives Radamès, the victor, and asks Amneris to present him with the laurel crown. Radamès can ask whatever he wishes. He asks first that the prisoners be brought in.

They are paraded, with Amonasro, at the back, disguised as an ordinary officer. When Aïda sees him, she famously blurts out *Mio padre!* ('My father!'). He quickly tells her not to betray who he is. But Amneris scents an opportunity, and the Pharoah asks Amonasro who he is. He pretends that he saw the dead King, who was mortally wounded during the battle. Amneris notices Radamès's loving expression towards Aïda, who reaches top C.

Radamès asks for the prisoners to be spared, but Ramfis and his priests warn against this. The people ask for clemency. Ramfis demands that, at the very least, Aïda and her (still unidentified) father should remain as hostages. The Pharaoh gives his daughter to Radamès. Only Radamès and Aïda can forsee the disaster that lies ahead. All the others are pleased with the ostensibly happy outcome, as they duly repeat the *Gloria all' Egitto*. Amonasro tells his daughter that there is still a chance for vengeance.

Act 3

This act is 'among the most dramatic as well as the most atmospheric that Verdi ever wrote.' Indeed, the atmosphere changes completely, and uniquely; Verdi evokes the river gently rippling as Amneris, accompanied by the High Priest, arrives in her boat on a starlit night to visit the Temple of Isis, on the banks of the Nile. Amneris is coming to pray for the success of her marriage. The High Priest receives her, dropping to low F sharp as he explains that Isis can see deep inside all hearts.

The string sound for the first sixteen bars is the note G played on various instruments and on different strings. The flute adds a melody

---

[10] Halfway through the march, Verdi gets the Egyptian trumpeters to exchange their instruments tuned to A flat for trumpets tuned to B natural – and the music lifts up accordingly. All the different emotions of the sections of the crowd and the main players are musically expressed.

also based on G. Later, we hear from within the temple the distant but growing sound of the priestesses, led by the High Priestess. They invoke Isis, the consort/mother of Osiris.[11] One can hear the sound of the crickets. It is 'supremely beautiful'.

Aïda appears quietly, to the theme heard at the opening of the prelude. Radamès has asked her to meet him. If it is to be a last farewell, the Nile will be her grave and she will never see her fatherland again. *O patria mia* ('Land of my fathers' – a phrase which will have excited many Italians at a time when unification of Italy was reaching its climax) begins to the mournful accompaniment of a solo oboe. The surging violins leave no doubt about what it would feel like to be swallowed up in the waters. Her emotional adieu reaches top C.[12]

She is suddenly interrupted by Amonasro. Their duet brings to a climax the tension between love and patriotism, private emotion and public duty. The critic and author Gustav Kobbé wrote that this 'is and will remain one of the beautiful dramatic efforts of the Italian repertory.'

Amonasro knows exactly what is going on. He tells her that she must betray the route which Radamès and the invading Egyptian forces will take, and then they will be able to avenge their defeat. He holds out the hope of her seeing her country again: *Rivedrò le foreste imbalsamate*. When she tries to resist, the orchestra leaves no doubt of his fury. He depicts the carnage, the murder of her people, for which she will be responsible. Her mother's shade will rise up and curse her. He threatens her: *Non sei mia figlia, Dei Faraoni tu sei la schiava* ('You're not my daughter, you're the slave of the Pharoahs').[13] She is appalled. He says it all depends on her. She whispers, *O patria. Quanti*

---

[11] The priests sing in E minor, and the priestesses in G minor. There is a suggestion of bitonality. This passage shows Verdi 'reaching out far beyond the limits of traditional composition.'

[12] Birgit Nilsson suggested that the beautiful Nile aria with its high C may be a reason that relatively few sopranos try to sing Aïda.

[13] In the duet with Amonasro, Nilsson had an unfortunate experience when her 'father' threw her vehemently across the stage and she fell over. For various reasons, mainly to do with her tight-fitting dress, she was not wearing underwear. So not only did she disclose more than she intended to, but, because the normally visible parts of Aïda are usually covered with black make-up, the disclosure was partly black and partly white.

mi costi? ('How much you demand from me'). He hides among the lotus plants and reeds when Radamès comes to court Aïda.

* * *

What hope has she? Radamès must go and marry Amneris. But he holds out a different prospect. War has been resumed; he is optimistic that, when he is victorious, he will successfully claim Aïda: he is confident that the Pharoah will grant her to him. She sensibly says that Amneris would not allow this; and she suggests that they flee and start a new life together. Radamès is horrified at the idea of fleeing, but, in a beautiful duet, she softens him up with an appealing top B flat: *Fuggiam gli ardori inospiti* ('Flee with me'). When he hesitates, she suggests that he does not love her. He does, and they will flee: *Sì, fuggiam da queste mura.* The vast desert shall be their bridal bed. They are ecstatic.

As they flee, the orchestra suddenly sounds an unrelated chord, pulling them – and the audience – up: which route will they take to avoid the Egyptian army? she asks. He replies: until the attack takes place tomorrow, the Napata[14] gorges will be unguarded.

Amonasro immediately emerges to say that, if so, he will put his troops there. Radamès is horrified when he discovers that he has been overheard by the Ethiopian King himself, and that he has thus betrayed his country. Amonasro assures him that it is fate which has led to this, it is not his fault; and they should flee with him.[15]

Amneris appears and accuses Radamès of treachery. He stops Amonasro from killing Amneris and tells him and Aïda to flee. He surrenders himself to the priests. Verdi enhances the drama by concluding the act with around 25 repeated chords of D minor.

---

[14] Aïda's question is devious. His answers are unnecessarily informative and traitorous: 'the route the army will take, but which it will not reach until tomorrow.' She presses him to be more precise, and he reveals, 'The Napata gorges.' Napata was the capital city of Kush, an area in Upper Nubia, rich in gold, part of 'Ethiopia' in ancient times, but today in the Sudan, north of Khartoum.

[15] Amonasro could easily have kept quiet; or, instead of fussing about dishonour, Radamès should have killed him there and then. This is fiction.

Act 4

In the Pharaoh's palace, in a room next to the judgement chamber, Amneris realises that she has not scotched Aïda but is certainly about to lose Radamès. She is still passionate – *disperato, insano* – about him and orders the guards to have him brought up from his subterranean cell. With a bass clarinet and cor anglais accompaniment, she reminds him that she has the power to have him reprieved. He maintains that although he disclosed the route, his honour is intact.[16] He welcomes death. She declares her unbounded love for him.

Amneris informs him that the Ethiopians have been defeated again and Amonasro has been slain. But Aïda has escaped. Amneris repeatedly calls on Radamès to renounce Aïda. But he will not, and is led away. She is desperate: who can possibly save him from the fate he is facing? *Chi ti salva, sciagurato?* With the background of the second theme from the prelude, played on the cellos, the anguished Amneris laments her fate, the result of her own jealousy, and is horrified to see the priests preparing for the trial and execution.

The High Priest can be heard in the subterranean judgement chamber calling on Radamès to defend himself and justify his betrayal and treachery. He accuses him of revealing secrets and also of absenting himself from the army the day before battle. Thus he is a traitor. Radamès is silent. The priests condemn him to be buried alive under the altar of the god Vulcan.

Amneris is aghast. To herself, she rounds on the priests for being the bloodthirsty agents of the beneficent gods.[17] She tells them that Radamès is guiltless. However, the judgement is irreversible: Radamès is a traitor and must die. The orchestra goes wild.

* * *

In the so-called 'double scene', which apparently Verdi himself suggested, we see, above, the brightly lit Temple of Vulcan, and, below,

---

[16] His justification seems to be that he betrayed military secrets unintentionally, and thus is innocent.

[17] Verdi's dislike of priests is palpable throughout this opera.

the subterranean dark crypt, where the ceiling is held up by a vast statue of the god Osiris.

The priests seal Radamès in the crypt, his tomb. Just as he hopes that Aïda will never hear of his ghastly fate, but laments that he shall never see her again, a groan (that is, a solo flute and oboe) is heard in the shadows. Aïda anticipated his fate and secretly hid herself in the tomb. He tells her that she is too lovely to die: *Morir, si pura e bella.* But she is ecstatic, as she sees the angel of death approaching – *Vedi? di morte l'angelo* – and the gates of heaven opening to receive them.

The priests perform a dirge to the god Ptha: they dance, accompanied by the harp, above. Radamès tries, in vain, to move the stone. Against the sound of the chanting to Ptha, the lovers die in each other's arms: *O terra addio.*[18]

Above, an anguished Amneris, in mourning, and prostrate on the stone that sealed the tomb, prays to Isis to receive Radamès in heaven, as the chorus sings *Immenso Fthà*. It is surely right that Amneris should have 'the last word'.

---

[18] The rhythm, with its unusually sustained upbeat, creates the character of what otherwise might be a commonplace melody.

GOUNOD: *FAUST*

THE OPERA AND ITS COMPOSER

In the late 19th century, the music critic, wit and playwright George Bernard Shaw said that he had heard *Faust* not less than 90 times within the last ten or fifteen years. He was fed up with spending ten years out of every twelve of his professional life listening to it.

Faust had been a sensation, 'one of the most successful operas ever written', 'the glory of the opera houses of the world.' Berlioz, himself the composer of *La Damnation de Faust*, had approved of it.

Like the composer of a modern West End or Broadway musical, Gounod caught the mood of the Paris public. Here was something new, a lighter and brighter style, more intimate and poetic than the massively staged grand operas that people were used to, such as the grandiose operas of Meyerbeer, the German-born composer of *Les Huguenots*.

Gounod provided a succession of popular tunes such as 'Even bravest heart may swell' (the *Dio possente*), the Song of the Golden Calf, the Waltz, *Salut! Demeure chaste et pure*, the Spinning-wheel Song, the Jewel Song, the duet *O nuit d'amour*, the Soldiers' Chorus. The ingredients were perfect: on the one hand, love, involving a fallen woman (it was only just over two years since Paris had enjoyed *La Traviata*); on the other, religion, which was about to go into a period of considerable growth. Besides, the prurient public were fascinated by the subject matter: unwanted pregnancy, infanticide, the scaffold.

Faust's success was assured. It ran for 59 performances in its first year. In 1944, the Paris Opéra staged its 2,000th performance. In the first decade of the 20th century, *Faust* was performed nearly 3,000 times in Germany. It became Queen Victoria's favourite opera. After its London première in 1863, it was performed in every Covent Garden season until 1911. Performances of Balfe's *The Bohemian Girl* and Gounod's *Faust* on Saturday nights kept many provincial operas solvent in the early 20th century. But the popularity waned. In London, during the inter-war years, performances were less frequent. After the Second World War, it was being described as 'a worn-out old chestnut of an opera.' In 1938, Covent Garden gave it up for 36 years. *Faust* had given way to *Carmen* as the most popular of all operas in London. That was by Bizet, who, to earn a crust, had done hack work for Gounod.

Back in the mid-1850s, the librettist Jules Barbier[1] wanted to do an opera based on Michel Carré's drama *Faust et Marguerite*. He offered the idea to Meyerbeer, who, being a German, was reluctant to mess around with Goethe's masterpiece, and turned the idea down. Léon Carvalho[2], the director of the Théâtre-Lyrique, now wanted Gounod to write it.

At the time, Gounod was essentially a composer of religious music, but he was trying to break into opera, where the money was. His first attempt had been a disaster.[3] But *Faust* provided a suitable topic for somebody with a tendency to hover, as he did, between the sacred and profane.

However, it was learnt that a rival 'Faust', with music interspersed, was about to be staged. So the plan for an opera was postponed. Meanwhile, Gounod composed an opera based on Molière's *Le médecin malgré lui*. This, in January 1858, was a great success.

---

[1] Jules Barbier (1825–1901), with Michel Carré (1821–1872), adapted literary works into libretti for several of Gounod's operas including Molière's *Le Médecin malgré lui* and Shakespeare's *Romeo and Juliet*. They were prolific, and their other adaptations include Ambroise Thomas's *Hamlet* and *Mignon* (another Goethe adaptation). Barbier also wrote the libretto for Offenbach's *The Tales of Hoffmann*.

[2] Léon Carvalho (1825–1897), a distinguished and highly influential opera director, came from Mauritius. He was married to Caroline Miolan (1827–1895), who, after singing Marguerite, took the lead in Gounod's *Mireille* and *Roméo et Juliette*. She mutilated the music of composers such as Mozart, but fitted ideally into Gounod's roles, and he complied with her demands. Many years later, Léon was imprisoned for negligence after the theatre in which his company was performing burnt down and 131 people were killed.

[3] Gounod's operatic career was launched by the influential diva Pauline Viardot, for whom he composed *Sapho*, which was not a success. An account of this may be found in the author's *Enchantress of Nations: Pauline Viardot, Soprano, Muse and Lover*.

Gounod

His *Faust,* based on Part 1 of Goethe's drama, was eventually premi-èred in the Théâtre-Lyrique, Paris, with spoken dialogue, on 19 March 1859. Gounod supervised the rehearsals, during which he made considerable cuts, not least in response to the demands of the Marguerite, Léon Carvalho's 'terrible wife – Oh! Yes, terrible,' as one Parisian composer called her. An early example of the prima donna (in the worst sense), Caroline Miolan-Carvalho was adored by her fans, and unstoppable when she had her husband's influence behind her. When, during the *Faust* rehearsals, she thought she might be upstaged by another singer's aria, she simply got Gounod to delete it.

Gounod's success with *Faust* made his name with the wider public. Unfortunately for him, the score was sold to the publishing house Choudens for 10,000 francs; thus the vast revenues went to Monsieur de Choudens, who was only interested in the profit on the work and was contemptuous of the work itself – if his children misbehaved, he would make them sit through *Faust.*

Charles Gounod (1818–1893) was the son of a Parisian art teacher with good connections at court. Charles was an infant prodigy and won the coveted Prix de Rome. During his studies there, he became an adherent of an influential priest. When he returned to Paris and became a church organist, he continued his religious activities. He styled himself 'Abbé', although he never actually took Holy Orders. He excused himself by saying that he did not think he had the moral strength to take confession from women.

As his mixture of religious compositions and opera showed, he tended to fluctuate between sacred and profane love. He was sometimes to be found at Passy in Dr Blanche's fashionable clinic for the mentally unstable.

His *Ave Maria* of 1859 was very popular in the salons, and helped his popularity enormously.

His recognition of the important interaction between commerce and aesthetics was possibly reflected in his marriage to the daughter of a piano professor at the Conservatoire, whose father was the piano manufacturer Zimmermann.

After *Faust* came *Mireille* and his extremely successful *Roméo et Juliette* produced at the time of the Exposition Universelle in 1867. He was awarded the Légion d'honneur.

During the Franco-Prussian War of 1870 and the Commune, he took refuge in London. There he fell under the spell of a 35-year-old Welsh lady, Mrs Georgina Weldon. She ran a 'National Training School of Music', a combination of an orphanage and a music school located in Dickens' old house in Tavistock Square. Gounod moved in with her and turned down an offer to become head of the Paris Conservatoire. (Bizet jested that it would be unsafe to assign to him the direction of a school for young girls.)

When the relationship with Georgina broke up, she successfully sued him for an enormous amount, which he refused to pay. To avoid imprisonment, he could not visit England, where his religious works, such as *Mors et Vita* and *La Rédemption* were extremely popular. He had an amazing facility to compose: 'masses, prayers, motets and canticles dripped from him as the rain from heaven.' He was offered, but did not accept, a million francs to go on tour to the USA. He died on 17 October 1893.

Ten years after the première, it was staged at the Paris Opéra. For this production, Gounod, who was amenable to making amendments such as inserting an extra aria for a prominent English singer at his request, had to comply with its rule that the libretto of operas performed there should be completely set to music, with no spoken words.[4] Also, there had to be a ballet – the Paris Opéra audiences particularly enjoyed ogling the corps de ballet, even to the extent that the place had been called 'the great brothel'.

Gounod's *divertissement* did not disappoint. Three historic beauties, Cleopatra, Helen of Troy and Phryné,[5] danced by three star ballerinas, were summoned to encourage Faust to forget Marguerite. The sensationally fascinating Eugénie Fiocre is reputed to have lived up to her reputation and stripped in a kind of dance of the seven veils, as she brought the bacchanal to its conclusion.

Another Eugénie, the Empress, was so excited that she even suggested that Gounod and she should write a ballet together. Given the proclivities of the composer – the *prêtre érotique* – this was a most interesting proposition. Sadly, we are not aware that anything came of it.

---

[4] When the Théâtre de la Monnaie in Brussels tried to use its roster of sung-version singers to perform the spoken version, and vice versa, there was such a rumpus that the production had to be withdrawn for a year.

[5] Phryné's sex trade in ancient Greece was so profitable that she offered to rebuild the walls of Thebes provided a notice was put up declaring that whereas Alexander destroyed them, Phryné the prostitute rebuilt them. A precedent for the 1869 divertissement, although rather less sensational, had been had been set nearly 40 years earlier with Meyerbeer's *Robert le Diable*, in which a diabolical character conjures up nuns before there is an orgy.

WHO'S WHO AND WHAT'S WHAT

The story below is based on the libretto. Certain directors may amend opera stories to suit their production.

In Germany (possibly Nuremberg) in the 16th century, **Faust**, an elderly Doctor of Philosophy, has despaired of discovering the secret of life and wishes to die. He is about to drink a fatal draught, but hears women and men enjoying themselves. He curses the world, whereupon **Méphistophélès,** the Devil, appears and tempts him with a vision of the beautiful **Marguerite** at her spinning-wheel. Faust bargains with Méphistophélès, pledging his soul in exchange for youth. He is transformed into a youthful, lusty man.

* * *

At the funfair, the '**Kermesse**', the people watch the world go by. **Wagner**,[6] a student, leads the drinking. Marguerite's brother **Valentin**, a soldier, is off to war, and worries about who will look after her: she has given him a medallion as a charm. Her boyfriend, **Siébel** reassures him. Valentin sings, 'Even bravest heart may swell in the moment of farewell', known as the ***Dio possente***. Wagner begins a drinking song about a rat, but Méphistophélès intervenes with the **Song of the Golden Calf**.

Méphistophélès tells fortunes. He predicts that all Siébel's bouquets of flowers will fade. Valentin and Méphistophélès have a fight, in which Valentin's sword shatters against the magic circle with which the Devil is protected. The students drive Méphistophélès away.

The youths and girls dance the famous **Waltz**. When Marguerite appears, Faust approaches Marguerite, but she rebuffs him.

* * *

In the **Flower Song**, Siébel collects flowers for a bouquet to present to Marguerite. But all the flowers he picks wither until he dips them in

---

[6] Faust's assistant in Goethe's poem, Wagner, is cast as a leading student in the opera. This, of course, has nothing to do with Richard Wagner, the composer.

holy water. Méphistophélès persuades Faust that a jewel case will out-bid Siébel's flowers, and goes to fetch one while Faust apostrophizes Marguerite's house: ***Salut! Demeure chaste et pure***.

Marguerite wonders about the man who approached her. She sings the **Ballad of the 'King of Thulé'**. She sees the jewel case and is tempted by it. She admires herself in the mirror and sings the **Jewel Song**, a complete contrast to the ballad.

While Faust is wooing Marguerite, Méphistophélès dallies with **Martha**, her neighbour and elderly companion, a war-widow. After some beautiful love music, notably ***O nuit d'amour***,[7] Marguerite eventually gives herself to Faust, who, urged on by Méphistophélès, leaps through the open window to possess her.

* * *

Marguerite, now pregnant, has been deserted: she sings the **Spinning-wheel Song**. Although Siébel supports her, she is still in love with Faust.

In church, where she prays, Méphistophélès conjures up demons to torment her. He tells her that she is condemned to everlasting damnation.

The soldiers return to the welcome of the crowd, and the well-known **Soldiers' Chorus** ('Glory and love to the men of old') is sung. Valentin cannot find Marguerite.

Faust and Méphistophélès reappear. Méphistophélès sings an offensive song, and Valentin breaks his guitar. Valentin demands sat-isfaction; he and Faust fight. Valentin dies cursing his sister.

* * *

Marguerite has killed her child and is condemned to death. Méphistophélès tries to distract Faust with a **Witches' Sabbath, Walpurgis Night**. During the ballet, Méphistophélès conjures up the courtesans of antiquity. Faust has a horrifying vision of Marguerite, as

---

[7] This is not to be confused with another famous tune, the barcarolle (gondolier's song) from Offenbach's *The Tales of Hoffmann*: *Belle nuit, ô nuit d'amour*.

if she has been executed. Méphistophélès takes Faust to her. Faust tries to persuade Marguerite to escape, but she resists. She calls on God to save her, and the angels to bear her to God above: the repentant sinner dies and is wafted up to heaven.

THE INTERVAL: TALKING POINTS

Lèse-majesté

The story of Faust has been considered and used by many composers. Beethoven planned a setting of it. His contemporary Louis Spohr wrote a *Faust* opera in 1816. Schubert wrote the song *Gretchen am Spinnrade* ('Gretchen at the spinning wheel'); Berlioz's Opus 1 was entitled *Eight Scenes from Faust* and he tried to 'extract the musical essence' in *The Damnation of Faust*. Schumann wrote a *Faust* oratorio, one of his last lucid works. In mid-century, Liszt wrote his *Faust Symphony*, with its mystic-religious elements (in the last movement), and his *Mephisto waltzes*. Mahler used elements of Faust in the *Symphony of a Thousand*.

Even Wagner wanted to write a 'Faust Symphony', but only got as far as a *Faust Overture*, which was supposed to be the first part of it: he realised then that instrumental music was not his forte and dropped the idea.

It is not surprising that Meyerbeer balked at the idea of writing an opera, the most ambitious of musical forms, based on Faust. However, Gounod, a *Faust* enthusiast – he carried a copy of Goethe's work around with him when doing his studies in Rome - was presumptuous in taking the project on. Goethe himself said, 'Mozart should have composed Faust.' For a Frenchman such as the then relatively junior Gounod, messing around with a German icon was particularly high-risk. For performances in Germany, it was re-badged 'Margarethe'.

The lack of respect, the 'lèse-majesté', particularly annoyed Germans[8]. One expert on music in the Romantic era has asked

---

[8] Tchaikovsky's use of Pushkin's *Eugene Onegin* met similar criticism in Russia.

what this pantomime demon with his hocus pocus has to do with Méphistophélès: 'What does Mademoiselle Marguerite have to do with Goethe's Gretchen? It is but decorative Romanticism, or Romantic decoration. Gounod's music, replete with excessively soft lyrical passages, aspires to nothing more lofty than the achievements of many lucky song-writers.'

Wagner was particularly dismissive. He refused to listen to Gounod's opera even once. He regarded it[9] as 'a repellent, nauseously vulgar, affected concoction, with the music of an inferior talent who would like to make something of it and desperately grasps at any means.'

Goethe

In fairness to Gounod, he and his librettist 'should not be condemned for failing to reflect the range of ideas in a literary masterpiece.' That was not what they set out to do. Besides, the *Faust* libretto is closer to Goethe's masterpiece than the play on which it was based.

[9] One presumes that he read the score.

Johann Wolfgang von Goethe (1749–1832) was one of the greatest poets of all ages ranking with Homer, Dante and Shakespeare. He was at first destined to follow in the footsteps of his father, who was an imperial councillor in the formal, old-fashioned city of Frankfurt.

Goethe studied law at Leipzig University, but as a polymath, a painter and scientist, he preferred literature and to move in intellectual circles. For his doctorate, he went to Strasbourg University where he met Herder, the distinguished philosopher, who introduced him to the works of Shakespeare and other writers. This is often said to have given rise to the 'Sturm und Drang' movement in which freedom of expression broke through the bounds of classicism.

Goethe's fame was made with his tale of the medieval knight, *Götz von Berlichingen*. This 'ran like wild-fire through the whole of Germany.' An actual case of a disappointed lover committing suicide led to *The Sorrows of Young Werther*, the immensely influential novel which quickly spread around the world, even as far as China. This 'opened up the floodgates of pent-up sentimentalism which had been stirred by the philosophy of the time.'

Goethe himself was always in love. At the age of fifteen, it was Gretchen, an innkeeper's daughter. Then there was Kitty in Leipzig, Frederike and Lili in Strasbourg, Lotte in Wetzlar (the scene of *Werther*, near Frankfurt), and Charlotte von Stein in Weimar. He eventually married Christiane, who had been his mistress for some time. She was a shadowy figure who remained behind the scenes, but their union lasted 30 years.

He settled in Weimar, where J.S. Bach had once worked as court musician and organist. Until recently, German culture had been French. But the smaller courts, shut out from the great world of politics practised in the courts of Vienna and Berlin, welcomed the German authors and artists. Goethe became a bosom companion of the young Duke, who employed him as a councillor and ennobled him. After an eighteen-month Italian journey, which had a considerable influence on him, he returned to Weimar to concentrate on art. He began his friendship with Schiller, the poet and playwright, a relationship which led to Goethe's *Wilhelm Meister's Lehrjahre*, and *Hermann und Dorothea*.

Goethe's preliminary work on *Faust* dates from the time he wrote *Werther*. But *Faust* Part 1 was not published until 1808; he finished at the age of 80 a plan which he had conceived 60 years before.

He had a sad old age as everyone died around him. He died in March 1832.

The music

Gounod believed that 'melody alone counts in music', and he has attracted a torrent of adverse criticism.[10] Commentators have wallowed in their denigration of his music. Bernard Shaw said of it, 'If you will only take the precaution to go in long enough after it commences and to come out long enough before it is over, you will not find it wearisome.' A modern critic calls *Faust* 'sentimental, saccharine', but concedes that some scenes are very effective.

As against this criticism, Gounod's neat and graceful style, his delicate orchestration, represented a complete contrast with his contemporaries and immediate predecessors. He distinguished himself from the 'excess, pretentiousness, disproportion, long-windedness', which he doubtless attributed to the Germans. Although the Song of the Golden Calf and the church scene are reminiscent of grand opera, there are none of the spectacular stunts, horses on stage, prima donnas leaping into Vesuvius, that characterised grand opera.

Gounod's music cleverly delineates the different characters. Arguably, Marguerite herself has a 'finely chiselled musical personality', and her portrayal is the main reason for the work's success.

[10] The Soldiers' Chorus reminded one critic of the polished faces of boys 'marching up to the rostrum to receive their prizes on speech day.' When someone suggested that the Soldiers' Chorus and the Waltz attracted undue applause compared to the rest of the opera, Gounod responded, 'Operas are not born like men, head foremost; operas are born feet foremost.'

The sequence beginning with the Ballad of the 'King of Thulé' is 'infused with girlish excitement' and 'conveys her awakening sensuality.' In the quartet with Martha which follows the Jewel Song, the various characters are distinctively portrayed.

Act 3 has been particularly praised for its unprecedented variety, for the lyricism of *Salut! Demeure chaste et pure*. The love music *O nuit d'amour* set a standard that influenced composers of love music for the rest of the century, as did the expressive weight Gounod gave to his orchestra. Bizet's Act 1 duet between Don José and Carmen, and his opera *The Pearl Fishers*, are obviously based on Gounod's style. He had an enormous influence on Fauré and Saint-Saëns, and on Massenet (the timpanist at the *Faust* première and subsequent composer of *Manon* and much besides), who would acquire the pejorative nickname 'La fille de Gounod' – the daughter of Gounod.

The Faust story

An English-speaking audience's first encounter with Faust may have been *The Tragical History of Doctor Faustus* by the wild and colourful contemporary of Shakespeare, the dramatist Christopher Marlowe (1564–1593). This play, 'which contains some of the finest dramatic poetry in our language', may have appeared shortly after the standard version of Faust's life, based probably on many centuries of tradition, was published in Frankfurt. By the early 17th century, Faust was a stock piece, extemporised on the boards of German puppet theatres, a tradition which lasted well into the 19th century.

Goethe's lengthy *Faust*[11] totally transformed the tale from its origins as a vulgar fairground show. His *Faust* was the closing masterpiece of his life, and 'the summit of German literary classicism.'

A colourful 19th-century writer, Oscar Browning, observed that Goethe's *Faust* was 'founded on, and indebted for its interest and pathos to, incidents of universal experience. It deals with the deepest

---

[11] Part 1, on which Gounod's opera is based, moves from Heaven to Hell; In Part 2, in which the heroine Helena marries Faust, he returns through the world to Heaven. It ends with the complete regeneration of the soul of Faust, happy that he has not lived in vain.

problems which can engage the mind of man.' The innocence and the fall of Gretchen 'appeal to every heart; the inward struggles of Faust, like those of Hamlet, and the antagonism of the sensual and moral principles, interest the reader just in proportion as his own mind and nature have been similarly stirred ... Deeper meanings are opened up at every reading.'

Gounod's opera does not probe these philosophical, timeless aspects.

Morality and the English

However fascinating they may be, the loss of virginity, unmarried pregnancy and infanticide were tricky subjects to deal with in Victorian England.[12]

There, *Faust* was sung in Italian[13], which probably helped most in the audience to lose their way, unless they bought the Book of Words for one shilling[14] or 'the words with the principal airs' for eighteen pence. The text had been translated by the critic, writer, poet and *Faust* enthusiast, Henry Fothergill Chorley, who combined his personal friendship with the notoriously promiscuous Napoleon III with having a Quaker background. With Arthur Sullivan, of Gilbert and Sullivan fame, he was responsible for the English vocal score.

This English vocal score plays down the misbehaviour of Marguerite, and omits her hankering after Faust. It omits the Spinning-wheel Song, in which she longs for her lover to return, and the declaration to Siébel that she will always love Faust, a sentiment in which

---

[12] In France, Marguerite's behaviour was probably more acceptable. Legend had it that St Mary Magdalen, the penitent sinner who had outraged the Pharisees by washing and anointing Jesus's feet, was French property: she had spent her latter years penitently near Marseilles, from where she had been wafted up into heaven by the angels.

[13] Sometimes the performance involved a mixture of languages. Melba, whose 'type of beauty', according to the critic Gustav Kobbé, 'was somewhat mature for the impersonation of the character', was known to sing in French, while Méphistophélès tempted Faust in Italian, and Martha flirted with him in French.

[14] With an advertisement on the front for Epp's cocoa (for breakfast); on the back, there was an advertisement for Eno's Fruit Salt, 'the greatest blessing the human mind can conceive.'

Siébel rather wetly acquiesces. As might be expected, it also omits the Walpurgis Night scene, the ballet with the courtesans, and Wagner's drinking song.

The English version is quite pleasing. Marguerite shows loyalty to her lover (so the heroine is not promiscuous), she receives due punishment by demons for her misbehaviour. She demonstrates true repentance and therefore ultimately achieves salvation, as her soul rises to heaven. Indeed, it is all very appropriate and instructional.

ACT BY ACT

Prelude

The first section of the Prelude creates the feeling of 'mystery, world-weariness, but then collapses into a non-descript tune.'

Act 1

Faust's study

Faust, a Doctor of Philosophy has tried to fathom the secrets of creation and existence, but in vain. Of his own free will, he now seeks death. As he is about to drink a fatal draught, he hears the joyful sound of young girls and labourers hailing the morning and praising God. He holds back. However, God has been useless, so he curses the world and all it stands for, and calls for the assistance of Satan instead.

At this, Méphistophélès, the evil spirit, instantly appears. 'Don't be surprised that I look quite normal,' he declares. However, he hopes he is not wasting time. Does Faust want gold, or glory? To which he gets the response: youth, and sex (*Je veux la jeunesse, les jeunes maîtresses*) The cost? Trivial: *Ici, je suis à ton service Mais là-bas, tu seras au mien!* ('I'll help you up here, but down below you'll help me').

To encourage Faust to sign the contract selling his soul, Méphistophélès conjures up a vision of the beautiful Marguerite at her spinning-wheel: *O Merveille*. Faust signs, and toasts the vision with the draught, which, instead of poisoning him, turns him into a youthful, lusty man.

Act 2

The fun-fair, the 'Kermesse'

The students, led by Wagner, drink to Bacchus.[15] The soldiers rejoice at their sexual prowess; the girls eye the boys; the burghers enjoy the safety of being at home and drinking, but regret their shrewish wives; the wives reckon they are still attractive and disdain the girls who are out for the quick chance.[16]

One of the soldiers, Valentin, has received a charm from his sister Marguerite, which he hopes will bring him good luck in the war: *O sainte médaille.* He worries about who will look after her when he leaves. Marguerite's boyfriend, Siébel assures him that their friends will do so. Valentin sings one of the most popular numbers in the opera, especially written for Santley, the first Valentin at the Royal Italian Opera in London: 'Even bravest heart may swell in the moment of farewell'.[17]

Wagner starts to tell a story about a rat and a cat. This has the effect of conjuring up Méphistophélès, who sings the Song of the Golden Calf: *Le veau d'or est toujours debout!* He tells Siébel's fortune, and forsees that every flower he touches will wither. He annoys Valentin by taking Marguerite's name in vain. But Méphistophélès has drawn a magic circle around himself and when Valentin fights him, his sword shatters. The students use the cruciform hilts of their swords to drive him away.

Méphistophélès is left with Faust who asks to meet the lovely girl of the vision. The youths and girls sing the famous Waltz, *Ainsi que la brise légère Soulève en épais tourbillons* ('Light as the air at the dawn of the morning'). When Marguerite appears, Méphistophélès chases

---

[15] Once, the wine flowed from the statue of Bacchus, but would not stop; nobody could turn it off. So the members of the chorus had to keep filling and refilling their mugs with red-dyed water. Fortunately a stagehand soon found the tap; otherwise the stage would have been flooded.
[16] Note how Gounod's music characterises the different groups of people, for example, the toothless chatter of the old men (in high falsetto).
[17] Sir Charles Santley, the distinguished English baritone, wrote in his reminiscences, 'I would have preferred being an actor of moderate fame to being the most renowned singer on earth.' Performances in English-speaking countries were usually given in Italian, so 'Even bravest heart may swell' became known as 'the *Dio possente*'.

Siébel away. Faust propositions her, but receives a rebuff: *Non mon-sieur! Je ne suis demoiselle, Ni belle, Et je n'ai pas besoin qu'on me donne la main!* - which just increases his ardour. Méphistophélès reassures him. The chorus continues the waltz: *Valsons! valsons! valsons! Valsons encor! Valsons toujours!*

Act 3

Marguerite's garden

Siébel asks the flowers to assist his endeavours: *Faites-lui mes aveux, Portez mes voeux!* But the flower he picks immediately withers: the devil is at work again. When he dips his hand in a stoup of holy water (where Marguerite usually prays), the flowers recover. The flowers will enable him to steal a kiss from her.

Faust and Méphistophélès see what Siébel intends to do. Méphistophélès tells Faust he will outbid Siébel's flowers with jewels. Faust is overwhelmed with love for Marguerite: *Salut! Demeure chaste et pure*. He is apprehensive, but Méphistophélès tells him not to worry: the jewel case will do the trick.

Marguerite appears. She has been fascinated by the man who approached her. She sings the Ballad of the 'King of Thulé', *Il était un Roi de Thulé*, who made a gold goblet in memory of his fair lady. When he drank from it, he would weep. As he lay dying, he called for the cup, and drank the wine for the last time.

Marguerite notices the flowers, obviously from Siébel, foolish boy. But then she sees the jewel case, and is amazed and attracted by the contents.[18]

Decorated with jewels, she admires herself in the mirror and sings the Jewel Song, a complete contrast to the ballad which preceded it:[19] Is it really her, Marguerite? She wishes her love could just see her, a

---

[18] In one performance of this, a soprano was criticised for going through the contents of the casket 'as though going through the week's laundry.'

[19] This provides 'one of the most effective scenes in opera for a soprano who can rise to its demands: the chaste simplicity required for the ballad, the joyous abandon and faultless execution of elaborate embellishments' for the Jewel Song. This is the first time that, apart from a very brief episode in Act 2, the high soprano has been heard.

princess worthy of a king: *Ah! je ris de me voir Si belle en ce miroir …
Est-ce toi, Marguerite, est-ce toi?*

Her neighbour Martha arrives and is amazed. Méphistophélès
appears and introduces himself to Martha: *Dame Marthe Schwertlein,
s'il vous plaît?* He informs her that her husband is dead, persuades her
that she needs a replacement, and serenades her while Faust is wooing
Marguerite. Marguerite tells Faust about herself.

While Méphistophélès goes off with the excessively enthusiastic
Martha, Faust and Marguerite are left together to make love. At first
she dismisses him: *Il se fait tard, adieu!* But then she acquiesces. Yet he
must go. He presses: *Laisse-moi contempler ton visage*; and then *O nuit
d'amour* ('O night of love').

She promises to meet him tomorrow, and rushes inside, where
she opens the window and rejoices in her love: *Il m'aime! il m'aime!
Quel trouble en mon coeur!* As Faust is about to leave, Méphistophélès
upbraids him for weakening. As Marguerite wishes the night away,
and wants Faust to come, he does; and they fall into each others' arms.
Méphistophélès roars with laughter.

Act 4

Marguerite's room, then the church, then the street.[20]

Following an entr'acte, Marguerite, now pregnant and deserted, sings
the Spinning-wheel Song. She has been cast out. Love led her astray.
She is condemned in the way that she used to condemn. Where can
he be? When will he return?

The faithful Siébel comes to support her, and threatens revenge.
But she is still in love with Faust. She goes to church to pray for him
and her unborn child.

In church,[21] Méphistophélès conjures up demons to torment her.
He tells her that she is condemned to everlasting damnation, while
priests pray God for mercy: *Seigneur, accueillez la prière Des coeurs*

---

[20] Sometimes the order is changed: the soldiers' return and Valentin's death precede the church
scene. Subsequent to the première, Gounod switched them round and back again.

[21] The French government was worried that this scene would cause a diplomatic incident with
the Vatican, but it was allowed through.

malheureux! The *Dies irae*, from the Requiem Mass, about the Day of Judgement, is heard on the organ.

Outside, the soldiers return to the welcoming crowd. They sing the well-known Soldiers' Chorus, *Déposons les armes*, glory and love to the men of old.[22] Valentin looks for Marguerite but cannot find her. When he hears she is in church, he assumes that she is praying for his safe return. Siébel disabuses him and implores him to forgive her.

Faust and Méphistophélès reappear. Méphistophélès serenades Marguerite with a guitar: *Vous qui faites l'endormie*. The substance of this offensive piece is 'Don't open your legs until you have a ring on your finger': *N'ouvre ta porte, ma belle*.

Valentin rushes out. Having broken Méphistophélès's guitar, satisfaction is demanded. He throws away the charm which Marguerite gave him; he fights Faust, and falls.[23] The others arrive and blame Marguerite for this. As Valentin dies, he curses his sister: *Ecoute-moi bien, Marguerite.*

Act 5
The Witches' Sabbath and the prison scene

Méphistophélès takes Faust to the Harz mountains in Saxony for Walpurgis Night, the May Day Witches' Sabbath. The demons sing: *Dans les bruyères Dans les roseaux*. This is followed by a ballet, which a 21st-century dance critic noted that some consider to be the 'sole opera ballet worth seeing.'[24] In this scene, which Gounod radically shortened during rehearsal, Méphistophélès conjures up the courtesans of antiquity. The ballet depicts the powerful female prowess of

[22] The Soldiers' Chorus was added after Gounod played at a party an item from an opera of his about Ivan the Terrible, which had not been performed. The excerpt delighted everybody so much that Gounod was persuaded to replace one of Valentin's arias with this.
[23] Santley's daughter had her first visit to a theatre to see her father perform. She was warned in advance that the duel scene was not real and only 'fun'. When it began, she started to tremble, but persuaded herself that it was indeed only fun and not real. When her father received the 'fatal wound', she let out a terrified shriek, and had to be taken from the theatre, not to return. 'She was not satisfied until she saw me safely seated at dinner,' recorded her father.
[24] Another writer has observed that Gounod's music is 'so unterrifying' that, when the ballet is cut, the whole episode is also often cut.

Cleopatra, the coquetry of Helen in the *Variations de Miroirs*, and the fiery eroticism of the final *bacchanal* of Phryné. As this ends, Faust has a horrifying vision of Marguerite, with a red line around her neck, like the wound of an executioner's sword.

Méphistophélès takes Faust to the prison where Marguerite awaits execution for having killed her child. The scaffold is ready. Méphistophélès tempts Faust to save Marguerite, and he tries to. But she resists. She recalls their first meeting – she was neither a lady nor a beauty: *Je ne suis demoiselle, Ni belle.*

Méphistophélès urges them to hurry. She will not flee; she demands that Méphistophélès is cast out. Faust tries unsuccessfully to claim her. She calls on God to save her, and the angels to bear her to God above: *Anges purs, anges radieux, Portez mon âme au sein des cieux!* Faust implores her, but to no avail: *Va! tu me fais horreur!* 'Damnation,' (*Jugée*) says Méphistophélès. The heavenly choir however declares 'Salvation' (*Sauvée*). In the apotheosis, her soul rises to Heaven: *Christ est resuscité!*

Johann Strauss: *Die Fledermaus*

The opera and its composer

This operetta with its 'sparkling brilliance, tunefulness and rhythmic piquancy' is a winner for everyone. The audience loves the melodies, the jaunty rhythms and the audience participation. The management anticipates a considerable boost to bar sales after Prince Orlofsky's invitation to everyone to enjoy the Champagne. For the cast, it provides an end-of-term spoof in which staid, and often aging, opera singers can let their hair down. Besides, Rosalinde is 'a smashing role for a prima donna with a touch of class' and Eisenstein good fun for a baritone with bags of personality and acting ability.[1]

Being an operetta, over a third of it is spoken. The dialogue, which in places is often adapted to modern circumstances, will certainly be enjoyed by devotees of Wienerschnitzel, even if the gourmet devotee of nouvelle cuisine may not relish it quite so much. However, as the Prince points out, in French of course, the language of the upper classes, *Chacun à son goût* ('Each to his own taste'). Hopefully, the director will have cut or changed much of the dialogue, not least the section lasting over eight minutes. Otherwise the audience may find itself laughing at, rather than with, the antics of trained singers purporting to be professional comedians, especially if their gags are in a language foreign to them. The musical numbers will be entertaining too, so long as the diction is clear and the words can be heard.

Many people were involved in bringing *Die Fledermaus,* 'one of the few masterpieces of Viennese operetta', to the stage. Its origins are in a vaudeville, a farce with songs, in which the police mistakenly arrest

---

[1] Strauss wrote the role of Eisenstein for a tenor, but it is usually sung by a baritone. Frank is cast for a high baritone but usually sung by a bass. The original cast was far more 'all-purpose', similar to singers in today's West End musicals, rather than opera stars.

the wife's lover when they come to apprehend the husband.[2] Henri Meilhac and Ludovic Halévy, who had written many of Offenbach's successful libretti in the 1860s, notably *La Belle Hélène* and *La Vie Parisienne*, wrote their own version of this, called *Le réveillon* (The Midnight Supper). It was a 'resounding hit' in Paris and was staged in London, where W.S. Gilbert, of Gilbert and Sullivan fame, even based one of his plays on the same subject.

Viennese theatre management did not like the first Germanised version.[3] So it fell to Richard Genée, who was experienced in Viennese vaudeville, to write a libretto with which to tempt Johann Strauss. In the process, various changes were made: the more risqué aspects – the party scene had included courtesans – were toned down. The blue-bird, the extraordinary fancy-dress which had led to the original call for revenge, was replaced by a bat. Bats were a costume routinely worn at the dances held at the Viennese Shrovetide carnival, the Fasching.

Strauss wrote the score for his 'comic operetta in three Acts'[4] in six weeks.[5] It was premièred on Easter Sunday, 5 April 1874 in Vienna's Theater an der Wien. It was generally well received. One of the more traditional critics dismissed it as 'a potpourri of waltz and polka motifs.'[6] But it quickly spread to Berlin and Paris where it was acclaimed. Mahler, who was 'enchanted by its guileless gaiety', later championed it in matinée performances in Hamburg and evening performances in Vienna, where, at the turn of the century, it had become the most frequently performed and most profitable work. Although Strauss was concerned that an opera house company would not show the light touch he wanted, *Die Fledermaus* entered the mainstream opera house repertoire. Indeed, it hardly counts as an operetta

---

[2] *Das Gefängnis* (The Jail), 1851, by Julius Roderich Benedix (1811–1873).
[3] This had been assembled by Carl Haffner, an East Prussian, who was on the staff of a Vienna theatre.
[4] The production is sometimes divided into two halves, with an interval in the middle of Prince Orlofsky's party. Genée had an incentive to write the operetta in three acts rather than two, because he was remunerated by the act.
[5] For the Hungarian Csárdás (in the style of a gypsy folk dance) which Rosalinde sings at the party, Strauss used an item he had already written for a charity concert.
[6] The waltz has three beats in a bar; the polka (a Bohemian dance) has two.

any more, 'so hallowed has it become as every opera house's gesture to the Lighter Music.' One may feel that Gilbert and Sullivan have a right to be envious.

Johann Strauss

The first run in Vienna had only been sixteen performances, possibly because people could not afford to go to it. The confidence of the Viennese middle class had recently been inflated by a tremendous economic boom, driven by a 'mushrooming financial sector willing to invest in the economy', especially in new technology, the railway sector. The boom was crowned by a World Exposition held in Vienna. A few days after this opened, there was 'bust'. The stock market crashed on 'Black Friday', 9 May 1873. Panicky crowds mobbed the banks, frauds were exposed and 152 people committed suicide.

At the time of the première of *Die Fledermaus*, six years of severe depression had just begun. The entertainment industry was hit hard: attendance was down 60% at one of Vienna's main ballrooms. Champagne consumption dropped by 95%. But the *bürgerlich*, *gemütlich* Viennese enjoyed seeing themselves lampooned. And the great party at the centre of the operetta enabled them to forget reality and have a laugh, to spin around in a waltz, to enjoy vicariously the glass of frothy Champagne which was no longer affordable, and to return home humming a happy tune.[7] Not just *Chacun à son goût*, but perhaps *Plus ça change, plus c'est la même chose.*

Johann Strauss the Younger was the 'King of the Waltz', the composer of *The Blue Danube*. His father Johann Strauss, who died in 1849, is well known for his famous *Radetsky March*. The father was a partner of Josef Lanner. He led the waltz craze in the beer gardens and dance halls of Vienna. He toured abroad, and played at the celebrations for Queen Victoria's Coronation.

Johann the Younger was born in Vienna in 1825. His father provided him with an up-market education, and hoped that he would become a banker. But he wrote his first waltz when he was six, and surreptitiously learnt the violin from the leader of his father's band. He united Lanner's soft melodies and his father's vigorous rhythms in a vast number of dances. His anti-Habsburg sympathies delayed his appointment as Court Dance Music Director.

His performances ranged from dubious taverns and casinos to a monster concert in the USA in which he coordinated around 100 sub-conductors who were controlling 30,000 musicians. His work was exhausting so, at the instigation of his wife, he took up writing Viennese operettas of the kind with which Suppé had succeeded in the 1860s.

Indigo in 1871 was the first of Strauss's sixteen operettas, but 'operatic' success only came three years later with *Die Fledermaus*, the music of which was 'full of grace and wit.' He is now best known for that and for *The Gipsy Baron* (1885). None of his colleagues or successors could match him. In his later years, he had an ambition to compose a serious opera (like Offenbach with *The Tales of Hoffmann*). He wrote *Ritter Pásmán,* but this was 'a glittering social occasion, a sell-out and a flop.'

[7] One former millionaire, who was reduced to cooking his own meals, would still ring the bell before putting his food on the table. 'It's not so bad,' he said, 'I get prompt service. I ring and I come.'

At the end of the century, in 1899, on the 25th anniversary of *Die Fledermaus*, Strauss conducted the overture vigorously at a special performance. He cooled off walking home, and caught pneumonia. In less than a fortnight, he was dead. One of his visitors during those last days was the American author Mark Twain.

Who's who and what's what

The story below is based on the libretto. Certain directors may amend opera stories to suit their production.

Doctor Falke has concocted a practical joke to take revenge on his friend, the wealthy Gabriel von **Eisenstein**. Three years ago, after they both got drunk at a fancy-dress party, Eisenstein deposited Falke outside the town still dressed up as a **bat**. He had to make his own way home, looking an absolute idiot. When Eisenstein is about to be jailed for assault and verbal abuse – **Dr Blind**, his lawyer, has failed to get him acquitted – Falke seizes his opportunity.

The operetta begins with **Alfred**, a Russian Prince's singing teacher, coming (at Falke's instigation) to seduce his former girlfriend **Rosalinde**, now Eisenstein's wife. To get **Adele**, the saucy soubrette maid, out of the way, Falke inveigles her to ask for time off, ostensibly to visit an aunt, but actually to go a party at which her sister **Ida** is going to perform in the ballet.

Falke easily persuades Eisenstein to delay turning himself in to serve his sentence. That night, there is to be a fancy-dress Champagne ball. This will give Eisenstein the chance to use his standard ploy when he wants to seduce a girl: he offers his chiming (lady's) 'repeater' **watch** (which strikes the hour when required to do so). This facilitates the question 'Is the time right?' – hopefully, the answer is both positive and instantaneous.

When **Frank**, the prison governor, comes to Eisenstein's villa to arrest him, he mistakenly arrests Alfred, whose departure is marked by the **Drinking Song**.

We now meet the eighteen-year-old **Prince Orlofsky**, an eccentric and languid Russian (a trouser role). The **Champagne party** which Falke has organised takes place that night at Orlovsky's palatial villa, with Adele's sister performing in the ballet. Various well-known **waltzes** and **polkas** are danced and sung. There Eisenstein, disguised as the 'Marquis Renard', is disconcerted to find someone looking uncannily like Adele; she responds with the **Laughing Song**. Frank, disguised as 'Chevalier Chargrin',[8] also goes to the party, where he befriends Eisenstein.

The masked Rosalinde is inveigled to attend, disguised as a **Hungarian Countess**. There, she is astonished to find Adele, attired in her own best outfit – and her husband ogling the ladies. She pockets his watch as 'Exhibit A'. Rosalinde sings the **Csárdás**, a gypsy dance.

Often the Champagne party will include entertainment provided by (real) star **celebrities**. The cast includes a variety of attendees and ballet girls, whose names are amended to suit the location and time of the production.

Increasingly drunk, chummy and sentimental, Eisenstein and Frank leave at six; they head in their respective directions, which turn out to be the same place, the jail.

By now it is dawn, and **Frosch** (Frog),[9] the jailer (a speaking role), keeps watch over the wretched Alfred who has called for Dr Blind to provide legal aid. Adele and Ida come looking for 'Chevalier Chargrin' who has promised Adele a new job. Rosalinde arrives, veiled. By dressing as Dr Blind, Eistenstein discovers what has been happening. He is furious and wants revenge. However, Rosalinde produces his watch as evidence that he himself has been up to no good.

Orlofsky and the other guests appear, and all is revealed. It is 'the bat's revenge', just a big joke conceived by Falke. Adele goes off with Orlofsky. Eisenstein asks for forgiveness. Besides, it can all be blamed on the Champagne.

---

[8] The French word *chagrin* means melancholy, sad. It is deliberately misspelled in the score.

[9] There are three 'F's. It is easy to confuse Falke (the 'bat') and Frank (the governor). Frosch is the jailer.

THE INTERVAL: TALKING POINTS

Vienna in Strauss's time

Vienna in the 19th century was in the throes of 'the gradual but relentless asphyxiation of the Habsburg monarchy.' Strauss provided a means of escape from reality. 'Behind the froth lay a civilization in decline.'

Once upon a time the Habsburgs, that 'global family property concern, whose managers were focused on growth and on passing the group of subsidiaries and related companies to the next generation', had ruled Europe, from the Russian empire to the Mediterranean, from the Turkish empire to the Atlantic. Charles V, the mid-16th-century Holy Roman Emperor, who appears in the last act of Verdi's *Don Carlos*, also controlled large portions of America, Spain and Italy, and even married his son into the Tudor family in England. No wonder France, surrounded by Habsburgs, developed a lasting inferiority complex. The centre of the world was in Vienna.

By the 1870s, the Habsburgs' German base had shrunk considerably, but the family portfolio still included Bohemia, the Balkans, Hungary, and their own little Archduchy of Austria. However, after the First World War that finally finished them off, Austria was left with a land area about two-thirds the size of England, and today its population is less than twenty per cent of England's.

At the time Strauss wrote *Die Fledermaus*, the regime was spluttering to a halt as an imperial force. Its armies had recently been decimated by the French at Solferino in Italy in 1859, and by the Prussians at Königgratz in Bohemia in 1866. As against this, their Austrian subjects derived confidence from their industrial boom. But that came to an abrupt halt with the stock market crash of May 1873, when the boom sectors of finance and heavy industry and the related building trade were worst affected. It led to the 'distrust of laissez-faire liberalism, and caution being exercised by the banks who contented themselves with cultivating relationships with already successful businesses.'

Strauss provided a counterpoint to the death march of this doom-laden outfit. Austria might be consistently defeated on battlefields, its stock market might crash, but it could still produce Strauss; just as Great Britain, increasingly overshadowed by the United States, could a century later contribute a galaxy of film, pop and sporting celebrities. Gabriel von Eisenstein, for all the grandeur of his title, is no aristocrat, but a Viennese bourgeois, a 'nouveau', posing as one. The Habsburgs were 'eager to co-opt a newly confident bourgeoisie in their survival campaign.' They threw titles around to those who were as brittle – and even as dodgy and doubtful – as some modern-day celebrity peers, knights and dames.

As the pressure on the regime developed, there was a nasty surge in anti-Semitism. At the turn of the 19th century, half of Vienna's doctors, lawyers and journalists were Jewish, although Jews were only some ten per cent of the population. So audiences in the mid-1870s would probably have associated the stuttering and absurd Dr Blind with those lawyers. Ironically, Strauss himself had Jewish ancestry – something which the Nazis tried very hard to conceal – and his third wife was Jewish.

Die Fledermaus and alcohol

Operas frequently feature celebratory drinking songs or choruses. One can think of Bellini's pirates in *Il Pirata*, or Gounod's students in *Faust* singing *Vin ou bière, bière ou vin!* The title role in Verdi's *Falstaff* is a sot. And most famously, in the 90 seconds of his so-called Champagne aria (*Fin ch' han dal vino*), Mozart depicts the wild, dangerously rapacious character of Don Giovanni.

The approach to alcohol in *Die Fledermaus* is rather different. The drinking duet between Rosalinde and Alfred in Act 1 envisages alcohol as a palliative, as a means of drowning sorrows: *Trinke, Liebchen, trinke schnell* ('Drink, darling, drink quickly'). *Giebt der Wein Dir Tröstung schon durch Vergessenheit* ('By getting sloshed, wine will enable you to forget things'). Adele in Act 2 even advocates the governmental encouragement of Champagne consumption in order to anaesthetise the population from the realities of a collapsing society. At the end of the operetta, while the chorus applauds Champagne – the 'King of

Wines' – Rosalinde praises it for facilitating her discovery of the truth about her husband's infidelities.

Audiences enjoy a drink in the interval, even a glass of Champagne. So this may not be the ideal time to raise issues regarding lager louts, or alcoholics, or the appropriate level of regulation for the drink industry or its sales outlets.

The music

Some commentators speak eloquently about the music in *Die Fledermaus*. 'Something that all subsequent operetta composers could not understand, the dramatic in the dance, is presented here with consummate artistry,' wrote one leading expert. 'The dance becomes a dramatic mood most convincingly presented in the masterly musical pantomime melodrama of the prison warden Frosch which is a worthy counterpart to the Beckmesser scene in the *Meistersinger*.'

We may raise eyebrows at this comparison with Wagner, but, again, *Chacun à son goût*.

One point of view is that *Die Fledermaus* is first and foremost 'an entertainment that – at least for the duration of the performance – no one would want to analyse too much.' Strauss's music is less subtle than that of Offenbach: the Viennese wanted humour rather than subtle satire; they wanted romance and sentimentality, and some cross-dressing. They liked the erotic thrill of holding a partner tightly while they whisked her around.

Strauss's textures and harmonies are almost simplistic, as is the standard pattern to which his waltz adheres, five sections with an introduction and coda. But it is wise not to underrate his music. We can admire his use of music to underpin the features of the different characters, the melody and rhythm, the way in which he dispels the 'tyrannical monotony' of the standard 'one-two-three' waltz accompaniment. His secret ingredient was probably the 'one-two-maybe three' beats in the bar.

A more positive point of view would be held by those who instance, among other subtleties, the Act 1 trio involving Rosalinde, Adele and Eisenstein. In this, Rosalinde quickly and (for us) humorously, moves from sadness at the forthcoming separation, in the minor key, to the joyous and famous polka. Thus we experience her initial sad emotion, followed by the realisation of the potential it unleashes – the famous tune is topped by her lively arpeggios. The characters pull themselves together and then let go with a great crescendo into the polka again.

Other examples of Strauss's artistry include the use of a short-short-long rhythm, associated with Eastern Europe, to introduce Orlofsky and his *Chacun à son goût*; Rosalinde's Hungarian gypsy 'Csárdás' dance being so authentic that we can infer that her disguise must be perfect; and the use of the piccolo and the trumpet to give the Champagne Chorus a sparkling quality.

Chacun à son goût. Brahms enjoyed Strauss's music and went to beer-garden concerts to listen to it. He is said to have given Strauss's wife a signed photograph on which he had jotted down the first bars of *The Blue Danube* and had written, 'Alas, not by Johannes Brahms.' But Brahms could afford to be condescending. Strauss was not a competitor; they were not in the same class. Massenet, not obviously the most discerning of composers, probably summed it up when he said, *Brahms est l'âme de Vienne; Strauss en est le parfum* – Brahms is the soul of Vienna, Strauss its perfume. Whatever the point of view, *Die Fledermaus* is good fun. Remember to pre-order the interval Champagne.

Strauss and Brahms

Russian boredom

Orlofsky is, of course, a grotesque caricature of a Russian noble. He is aged eighteen, but feels like 40. This class was depicted in the 19th century as idle and bored. Indeed, in St Petersburg, far from their estates, the Russian nobility had to cope with 'the long and unendurable day', especially during the winter. There was little to do, and life on one's lonely country estate was even worse.

The notion that the nobility were all fabulously rich was misconceived. Wealth was skewed: four-fifths owned fewer than 100 serfs, whereas Liszt's mistress, Princess Carolyne, had 30,000. For many of this class – 'landed gentry' would be a more realistic term with which to describe them – life was an uphill struggle.

Tchaikovsky's Eugene Onegin exemplified this boredom, although he has none of the emasculated characteristics of Orlofsky. Although *Eugene Onegin* followed three years after *Die Fledermaus*, the concept of the bored, 'superfluous man' was already entrenched in literature. Pushkin's poem, on which Tchaikovsky based his opera, was written early in the century.[10]

ACT BY ACT

Act 1

A villa by an Austrian spa town, summertime, late 19th century

In the overture, we get a taste of the melodies which will recur later, including the well-known waltz. Then Alfred is heard outside, serenading his former girlfriend. Gabriel Eisenstein's wife, his lovely Rosalinde, is Alfred's little dove who has flown away: Come quickly and be caught again: *Täubchen, das entflattert ist.*

---

[10] The 'superfluous man' is to be found in the work of several Russian writers, notably Ivan Turgenev (1818–1883) who spent much time in Western Europe, in Paris and Baden, where he lived in a *ménage à trois* with the famous soprano Pauline Viardot and her husband. One of his characters declares, 'People are bad, good, clever, stupid, pleasant and unpleasant; yet not usually superfluous. But in my case nothing else can be said about me. I'm superfluous and that's all there is to it.' At the end of one novel, the leading character shoots himself. When he briefly regains consciousness, he has just the time to exclaim, 'Failed again.'

Adele, the maid, bursts in with a terrific coloratura, reading a letter ostensibly from her sister Ida. If she can get the night off and get hold of a suitable dress, she can come to Prince Orlofsky's party. If only she was not a maid, chained to her job, but was like the little dove and could fly around!

Although she throws the singer a coin to shut him up, she realises that he is no street-singer, but a lover serenading Rosalinde, her mistress.

Rosalinde comes in, in a high state of excitement. She recognises Alfred, a cheeky fellow who was her lover four years ago, before she was married. Adele asks for a night off 'to visit her sick aunt', but Rosalinde refuses: she needs her at home – her husband starts his five days in jail today, convicted for assault and verbal abuse to the court usher. Adele realises that she, a mere maid, is stuck: *Ach, ich darf nicht hin zu dir!*

When Rosalinde sees Alfred, she is very worried in case her husband suddenly returns home and finds them *à deux*. But she finds his high B flat makes him irresistible. Alfred makes her swear that she will receive him when her husband is in jail. When she hears her husband coming, arguing vociferously with his stuttering lawyer Dr Blind, the omens are not good.

Eisenstein comes in, raging at the useless Dr Blind: *Nein, mit solchen Advocaten*. As a result of the latest hearing, his five-day prison sentence has been increased to eight. Rosalinde and Blind try to calm him.

When Adele appears tearfully, Eisenstein thinks she is sorry because he is going to jail. He is surprised when she explains that she is sad because her aunt is sick, because he has recently seen the aunt riding a donkey. He asks her to fetch in some supper, and get his old clothes: he does not want the other jailbirds thinking he is rich.

Dr Falke arrives and congratulates Rosalinde for getting rid of Eisenstein for eight days. When Rosalinde has gone, he invites Eisenstein to a party at Prince Orlofsky's: *Komm mit mir zum Souper* ('Come with me to the supper party'). It will feature the alluring ballet girls.

He can pretend to Rosalinde that he is going to jail, but in fact go to the party. This will divert him from thinking about his sentence. Provided he reports there in the morning, it will be time enough.

Falke will introduce him as the Marquis Renard. Eisenstein recalls an earlier party when he went as a butterfly and Dr Falke as a bat. On such occasions, Eisenstein's chiming repeater watch is the bait with which he habitually lures the girls. He promises it to each one (but has never given it to any of them).

Rosalinde returns with the old clothes. She is a bit surprised when her husband now asks for his evening dress instead. Adele brings in food, and he tells her to give it to her aunt.

Rosalinde realises that if she wants to entertain Alfred, she had better get rid of Adele, so she gives her the night off after all. Eisenstein has an emotional farewell with his wife: *So muss allein ich bleiben.* But privately, he reflects on the fun he is going to have: *O je, o je, wie rührt mich dies* ('Oh dear, oh dear, how this arouses me!').

After Eisenstein has gone, Alfred reappears. Rosalinde is horrified when he settles in for the evening, and she tries to get rid of him. He continues to sing a love song to her. He calls on her to be cheerful, lie back and enjoy it. She tells him not to sing, because his singing arouses her too much.

He pretends to be Rosalinde's husband. He puts on Eisenstein's clothes and helps himself to the food and drink and sings the 'Drinking Song': *Trinke, Liebchen, trinke schnell* ('Drink, darling, drink quickly'). They might as well enjoy themselves. He tells her to drown her sorrows; there is no point in trying to resist the impossible: *Glücklich ist, wer vergisst was doch nicht zu ändern ist.*

When Frank, the prison governor, arrives to arrest Eisenstein, he apprehends Alfred instead. To avoid scandal, Rosalinde insists he must go quietly: *Mein Herr, was dächten Sie von mir* ('Sir, what would you think of me if I were found sitting here with a stranger dressed like a Pasha?') Frank is sure that her man must be her husband: *Nein, nein, ich zweifle gar nicht mehr* ('No, no, I no longer have any doubt'). Someone so bored and so blasé can only be a husband. He orders them to take a farewell kiss. Alfred comments that if he has to serve time on behalf of her husband, he might as well enjoy a kiss.

Frank is in a hurry. His carriage awaits him and he invites 'Eisenstein' to free lodging in his nice big birdcage: *Mein grosses, schönes Vogelhaus.* One more kiss and he'll have courage. He and Rosalinde are victims of fate. Sadly, there is no time for supper and Alfred is led away.

Act 2

In Orlofsky's villa, just before 10pm

The chorus eyes the magnificent spread, organised by Dr Falke: *Ein Souper heut uns winkt* ('A supper beckons us today'). They are going to have a great evening's entertainment. But the Prince has not arrived yet: he likes his guests to warm up first.

Ida is amazed to see her sister Adele as a guest at the party, dolled up to the nines; equally, Adele is surprised at her surprise. There seems to have been some confusion: it appears Ida did not write the note after all. They agree that they had better play their designated parts, one the ballet girl, the other an actress.

The languid and bored Orlofsky, all of eighteen years old, comes in with Dr Falke who assures him he will have a laugh tonight with his comedy 'A Bat's Revenge'. Ida introduces Adele as Olga, an actress. Just before Eisenstein arrives (alias the Marquis de Renard), Falke warns Orlofsky that Olga is in fact the chambermaid. Meanwhile, Eisenstein is surprised that the Prince is so small, as he thought all Russians were as big as bears. Falke suddenly remembers to invite Eisenstein's wife, and sends a servant off with a letter.

Orlofsky tells Eisenstein how he likes to throw parties: *Ich lade gern mir Gäste ein* ('I like to invite guests'). He may be bored himself, but he cannot tolerate boredom in his guests, who he will kick out if they appear bored and do not keep drinking: *Chacun à son goût!* ('Each to his own taste!'). He himself has lost his taste for everything, including love.

Adele returns, having gambled and lost the contents of a purse which Orlofsky gave her. Falke introduces her to Eisenstein who is surprised to see her. When he observes her resemblance to his chambermaid, Adele calls him impertinent and scolds him for his faux pas.

The Marquis's mistake in thinking the lady is a chambermaid sends Orlofsky and Falke into paroxysms of mirth. The assembled company also roars with laughter: *Ach, meine Herr'n und Damen* ('Ladies and gentlemen'). While Eisenstein splutters, Adele tells the Marquis that a man of his class must really do better: *Mein Herr Marquis, ein Mann wie Sie*[11] (the Laughing Song). Could her hand, her foot, her waist, her Grecian profile really be that of a ladies' maid?

Frank, the prison governor arrives, disguised as 'Chevalier Chargrin'. He is introduced to Eisenstein, and they converse in French, much to Eisenstein's annoyance, before reverting to the local language. They get on famously and look forward to seeing more of each other.

A Hungarian Countess appears, wearing a mask. Meanwhile, Eisenstein has a go at waving his repeater watch at Adele (and asking the seductive question 'Is the time right?'), and goes off with her.

Overjoyed with his watch and with his bosom companion 'Chargrin', in whose company he again finds himself, the returning Eisenstein sees the Countess and immediately sets to work on her with his watch. He compliments her beauty and deportment: *Dieser Anstand, so manierlich*. He asks her to remove the mask, while she seethes at his cooing and flirting and plans revenge: *Wie er girret, kokettieret*. He presses on with his watch. She is intent on getting this as evidence of his infidelity; he just wants to seduce her. She suggests that he should count her heartbeats, while she counts the tick-tock of the watch. During this she manages to pocket the watch.

The assembled company also asks her to remove her mask, but Orlofsky excuses her. Adele says that she cannot be Hungarian because, if she were, she would have such fire in her veins that she would have exploded by now. To convince them of her authenticity, Rosalinde sings the Csárdás, a gypsy dance about her country, which starts slowly and accelerates – *Klänge der Heimat* ('Sounds of my homeland') – and toasts her fatherland. It ends on top D, which they applaud.

When the ballet girls ask Dr Falke to tell his story about the bat, Eisenstein claims that the joke is his, so he must tell it. It happened three years ago, when Falke was already a lawyer and Eisenstein was still unmarried. There was a masked ball: he went as a butterfly, Falke as a bat. Falke got extremely drunk and Eisenstein took him to a

---

[11] In which Adele should hit top C at the end.

wood out of town and left him there. When he woke up, he had to return and walk into the town dressed as a bat, much to the derision of all and sundry. Has Falke ever taken revenge? No, the Marquis has been too careful for that. They all go in to dinner. Eisenstein presses the Countess to drop her mask. When a chorus girl asks him how his wife allows him to be at the party he says his wife is an awful old bag. Orlofsky leads a toast in Champagne, the 'King of Wines', *Im Feuerstrom der Reben.*

Eisenstein and the prison governor (alias Chevalier Chargrin) both get increasingly inebriated. *Herr Chevalier, ich grüsse Sie!* ('I salute you, Chevalier!') In a sentimental vein, and led by Falke, the cast sings the well-known sentimental song expressing brotherhood: *Brüderlein, Brüderlein und Schwesterlein* ('Little brothers, little brothers and sisters'). In the famous and nostalgic *Du und Du* waltz, they swear to address each other with the familiar 'Du' for ever. Tomorrow can take care of itself. There is a ballet, a polka.

Orlofsky calls for a waltz. They sing another very famous waltz: *Ha, welch ein Fest, welche Nacht voll Freud'!* ('Ah, what a party, what a night full of joy!')

When Eisenstein and Frank come together in the dance, the others observe what a happy reunion they are about to have in prison. Frank looks at his watch; Eisenstein has lost his, and calls again on the lovely Countess to remove her mask. She won't, she has a pimple on her nose: *Hab' ein Wimmerl auf der Nase.* They hear the clock strike six. It's time to go. Eisenstein and Frank go off together.

During this act, some further light entertainment is added, ostensibly to amuse the guests.[12]

Act 3

In the jail

The drunken jailer Frosch, who, like his boss, is new to the place, imagines he hears music from the prisoner in cell 12. It is none other

---

[12] In a Cologne production, this was to be a piano recital. When the instrument was pushed on to the stage, it gathered pace. As the stage was raked, it landed in the pit. Fortunately there was time for the players to move and the only casualties were the piano itself and two squashed tubas.

than the wretched Alfred singing his serenade to Rosalinde. Frosch tells him to shut up: singing is against the regulations.

Frank, the prison governor, returns. He is still very drunk and reminisces about the party, whistling bits of the waltz, and calling for Olga, Ida and the Marquis. He collapses into his chair with his newspaper and falls asleep. Frosch wakes him up, to make his report: the prisoner in number 12 wants a lawyer, so he's sent for Dr Blind. For Frank, the whole world rotates: he curses the Champagne.

The doorbell rings. There are two women, but he could be seeing double. It is Adele and Ida who are looking for 'Chevalier Chargrin'. Adele confesses she is just a chambermaid, to Frank's horror. She asks him to put in a good word for her with Eisenstein, who recognised her last night at the ball. She is anyway going to become an actress under the protection of the Chevalier. She tries out her piece for her audition: *Spiel ich die Unschuld vom Lande ... eine Königin ... 'ne Dame von Paris* ('When I play the innocent from the country ... a queen, a lady from Paris'). Has she got talent? Of course. She demonstrates it, reaching top D.

The bell rings again. This time, it is 'the Marquis'. Frank gets Frosch to take the women to cell 13, out of the way. Eisenstein simply cannot believe that Frank is not the Chevalier but the prison governor. Similarly, Frank cannot believe that Eisenstein is not the Marquis, but his prisoner come to serve his eight-day sentence: besides, he cannot be Eisenstein because he personally arrested Eisenstein at 10pm last night, sitting cosily with his wife, and he is now reposing in cell 12.

Frosch announces the arrival of a veiled lady. But she is preceded by Dr Blind, the lawyer. Eisenstein suggests that he and Blind exchange clothes so that he can investigate the chap in cell 12. While they do this, Alfred appears as does Rosalinde. He tries to be romantic, but she is not too keen on it. She is scared that her husband will appear and find Alfred wearing his clothes: *Ich stehe voll Zagen.*

Eisenstein reappears dressed as the lawyer and tells them that he must be told the full story about what happened. Alfred describes how he was arrested: *Ein seltsam Abenteuer* ('An unusual adventure'). Rosalinde expresses concern that she could become compromised and her husband could be furious. They are a bit surprised at the lawyer, because he is supposed to be defending them. Rosalinde accuses him of sympathising with her husband. Her husband is a monster who spent the whole of last evening chasing the girls; she is going to divorce him, having first scratched his eyes out. Alfred asks their lawyer's advice on how to give the husband his comeuppance.

This is too much for Eisenstein. In a rage, and with appropriate theatrical drama, he reveals his identity to Rosalinde: *Ich selbst bin Eisenstein!* ('I myself am Eisenstein!') It is he who they have betrayed: *Ja, ja! Ja, ich bin's, den ihr betrogen.* Husband and wife, and Alfred, shout at each other, demanding revenge.

Rosalinde then produces the watch, and asks 'the Marquis' if he wants to count her heartbeats. It dawns on Eisenstein that she was the Hungarian lady. Alfred presses for Eisenstein to be taken to his cell.

Frosch returns to say that the two women in cell 13 are raising hell. Adele and Ida come in protesting at having been locked up, and are amazed to see that Frank, their Chevalier, is in fact the governor. He asks Adele to identify Eisenstein.

Falke calls for further witnesses. The door opens: Orlofsky and the other guests appear. *O Fledermaus, o Fledermaus, Lass endlich jetzt dein Opfer aus* ('O bat, O bat, let your victim go'). It is 'the bat's revenge'. It was all just a big joke conceived by Falke. Alfred demurs at this description, but reckons that it is better to say nothing. Eisenstein is reconciled with his wife.

Adele is left wondering what is going to happen to her. Frank tells her that she should stay with him in the prison; he will have her trained for the stage. But Orlofsky chooses her for himself.[13] As a patron of the arts, such talent cannot escape him. It is his custom: *Chacun à son goût!*

Eisenstein asks for forgiveness. It was all the fault of the Champagne: *Champagner hat's verschuldet.* In a rip-roaring finale, they all applaud the 'King of Wines', in a 'bouquet of the most memorable tunes of the evening'.

---

[13] The audience will have guessed that more typically she is heading towards high-class prostitution. There is not much morality to this story.

BIZET: *CARMEN*

THE OPERA AND ITS COMPOSER

Carmen is both a masterpiece, and 'the most fantastic success in the annals of Opera.' Films have been made of it; there have been jazz and rock ballet versions. It has been updated into an African-American setting in the Broadway musical *Carmen Jones*. A Russian has done a version for 47 percussion instruments and an American has done one for solo kazoo and symphony orchestra. A sound extravaganza has been produced called *The Naked Carmen*.

It is possibly the most colourful and exotic of operas. It was sexually explicit in advance of its time. Indeed, before a regular performance, the cleavage has to be sorted out, so that, to the audience, its possessor appears to be sexy but not sluttish.

It has been known for a prima donna to object vociferously to the little piece of black fabric she was expected to wear as a dress. On the other hand, one who seemed she might burst out of her bra earned 'the undying devotion of stage hands and cognoscenti alike.'

The first night, at the Opéra-Comique in Paris on 3 March 1875, was a historic failure and the attendance was poor at subsequent performances during the first run. At the première, the opera went reasonably well up to the tuneful Toreador Song in Act 2, but, after that, it was mainly 'received in glacial silence.' The venue and its bourgeois-dominated clientèle were not receptive to a sensational groundbreaking work such as this. But there was an amazing reversal of fortune. By 1959, the Opéra-Comique had chalked up its 2,942nd performance of it.

The failure of the première plunged Bizet back into chronic depression, thus aggravating his already poor health, sapping his resistance and leading to his death exactly three months later.

The libretto is very loosely based on an 1845 short story by a distinguished French writer, Prosper Mérimée. This was adapted by a well-tried and highly successful combination of librettists, Henri Meilhac and Ludovic Halévy.[1]

Bizet

Had it not been for *Carmen*, Bizet today might be remembered merely for the 'best tune' *Au fond du Temple Saint*, which comes from his *Les Pêcheurs de Perles*. He would hardly have ranked among the great composers. How and why he produced *Carmen*, this ground-breaking opera, is a mystery. Tchaikovsky thought *Carmen* was a masterpiece 'in the true sense of the word': it was 'one of those rare works which reflect the aspirations of an entire era.' Brahms, not someone one would automatically think of, was a considerable admirer and got his publisher to supply him with the full score. Later, Vaughan Williams 'went to scoff but remained to pray.'

Indeed, its influence on other composers was immense: in particular, the composers of earthy, realistic 'verismo' opera – for example, Mascagni in *Cavalleria rusticana* – built on 'its low-life ambience, and its moments of brutal passion.' But 'the elegance, the light-fingered, brilliant scoring and the clear, sometimes astringent harmonic palette also left its mark on Verdi.'

[1] Henri Meilhac (1831–1897) and Ludovic Halévy (1834–1908) were librettists of several Offenbach operettas, including *La Vie parisienne* and *La belle Hélène*. One of Bizet's teachers was Ludovic's uncle, the celebrated Fromental Halévy, the extremely rich composer of the highly successful grand opera *La Juive*, which appeared in the mid-1830s. In 1869, Bizet married Fromenthal Halévy's daughter, Geneviève.

On 3 June 1875, **Georges Bizet**, a very disappointed man, died of quinsy, a throat abscess. He was aged only 36. Earlier, he may have had rheumatic fever, which may have been connected. He was also a chain-smoker.

Bizet was born in Paris on 25 October 1838. He showed prodigious talent. He was so keen on books that his parents had to hide them to avoid him neglecting his musical career. He was admitted to the Conservatoire when he was ten. Liszt thought him one of the three best pianists in Europe. He won the coveted Prix de Rome. But enduring success eluded him and he spent his time doing hack work, often for Gounod, for whom he had a great regard. Bizet's opera *Les Pêcheurs de Perles* (1863) was a failure. 'There were neither fishermen in the libretto nor pearls in the music,' wrote a critic at the time. *La Jolie Fille de Perth* (1867) and the incidental music for Daudet's play *L'Arlésienne* (1872) fared little better.

Bizet was a wild character. He had little respect for his superiors. He fought with a gondolier; he frequented prostitutes; he had a child by his mother's maid; he set up house with a famous courtesan, Elisabeth-Céleste Venard, known as Mogador.

Bizet joined the National Guard for the Franco-Prussian War, and remained in Paris during the Siege. He and his wife Geneviève escaped from Paris at the beginning of the Commune which followed. He parted from her in 1874, but loyally supported her and his mother-in-law, despite both women being seriously unhinged. After Bizet's death, Geneviève recovered and married a rich lawyer. She ran a distinguished salon and provided a source of inspiration for Marcel Proust and the basis for one of his characters, La Duchesse de Guermantes.

Bizet died at Bougival, near Paris, in the house on the Seine where he had finished composing *Carmen*.

One of the challenges in performing Carmen (and indeed *Carmen*) is to avoid vulgarity and sensationalism. As the great conductor Sir Thomas Beecham observed, 'any singer who fails to make her portrayal of Carmen in accordance with the refinement of the music is doing something that is an aesthetic offence ... to make a harridan of Carmen is at complete variance with the fact, for the people of Spain have the best manners in the world.'[2]

Fundamentally, she is a capricious Romany, and José is a man possessed by love. However, she is also a harlot and he is a man driven to commit a *crime passionel*. Around a century and a half later, placing their characterisation at the right point on the spectrum remains a compelling challenge and makes every performance unique.

WHO'S WHO AND WHAT'S WHAT

The story below is based on the libretto. Certain directors may amend opera stories to suit their production.

From the crash of percussion which opens the Prelude, we know that we are in colourful Seville, in southern Spain, renowned for its bullfights. The strings announce, and then the full orchestra thunders out, *Toréador en garde!*, that famous tune which **Escamillo**, a toreador, will be associated with throughout the opera. **Carmencita (Carmen)**, a whore who works in a tobacco factory, will fall for this celebrity.

But the mood of the Prelude suddenly changes and we hear a searing, baleful, fate-loaded tune which will end the opera and mark the complete disintegration of the character of **Don José**, a conscientious corporal ('brigadier' in French), who becomes infatuated with Carmen, and ultimately kills her.

Meanwhile, dragoons under the command of **Moralès**, another corporal, keep guard outside the factory. They try to flirt with **Micaëla**, a nice country girl with whom Don José is in love, and

---

[2] Beecham, renowned as a humorist, may have deliberately chosen the wrong word. Dictionaries define a harridan as a haggard old woman, an old jade, which nobody would dream of portraying Carmen as. But his point is well made.

whom Don José's mother has sent in the hope that he will marry her. The dragoons inform her that Don José will come when the guard is changed. We soon hear that this is about to happen, preceded by a chorus of street-boys.

It is break time in the factory. But Don José is not interested in the girls who emerge, smoking. They include Carmen, who particularly fascinates the young men. But she is irritated that Don José is not immediately captivated by her charms. She flaunts herself and flings a flower at him at the end of the well-known *Habanera*.[3] He is shocked and very disturbed by this sorceress, and is unable to give Micaëla the welcome she deserves when she returns to find him. However, he decides he will marry her, as his mother wishes.

There is an interruption. In the factory, there has been a fight and it is not clear whether Carmen went for **Manuelita**, another worker, or vice versa. The officer, Lieutenant **Zuniga**, sends Don José in to sort it out.

Carmen tries her charms on Zuniga. He has her arrested. She then entices Don José with the *Seguidilla*,[4] about a place of assignation, the bodega of **Lillas Pastia**. He loosens her bonds and she seizes the opportunity to escape. Having failed in his duty, he himself is imprisoned.

A couple of months later, Carmen, and **Frasquita** and **Mercédès**, two gypsy girl friends of hers, are in Lillas Pastia's bodega, the haunt of Seville's demi-monde of smugglers and prostitutes. The leading smugglers **El Dancaïro** and **El Remendado** recruit her.

Lieutenant Zuniga is also there, and fancies Carmen. She however falls for Escamillo, the celebrity toreador.

Don José, having served his sentence, returns to woo Carmen. Her flower had been his comfort in prison. She tries unsuccessfully to persuade him to disobey orders by ignoring a roll call. But they are interrupted by the return of Zuniga, his superior, who has come to

---

[3] The habanera is a dance developed in Cuba. Its rhythm is similar to the tango. Bizet based his on what he thought was a folk tune, but in fact it was by a contemporary (but obscure) composer.

[4] The seguidilla is a dance in quick triple time, accompanied by guitar and castanets. It is from southern Spain, especially Andalusia.

take Carmen. They fight. After this, José has little option other than to disobey orders and to join the smugglers.

At the smugglers' camp in the mountains, the girls draw cards: these predict death for Carmen and Don José.

Micaëla comes in search of José: his mother is dying and wants to forgive him before she dies. When Escamillo comes looking for Carmen, he and Don José fight. Carmen intervenes to save the toreador, who invites them all to the bullfight. Having been told that his mother is dying, Don José goes away with Micaëla.

Later, outside the bullring in Seville, Carmen's girl friends warn her that José is in town. With the crowd in the bullring acclaiming the victorious Escamillo, Carmen and Don José confront each other. He has sacrificed everything for her, and, when she rejects him, he stabs her.

THE INTERVAL: TALKING POINTS

The first night failure: the audience

Although *Carmen* complied with the regulation that, at the Théâtre de l'Opéra-Comique, the performance had to be in French and comprise a mixture of music and spoken word,[5] it was an unsuitable venue for its première.

A show there did not have to be a comedy; but Opéra-Comique audiences were used to shows which were reasonably light, and pleasant. This made it a popular rendezvous for marriage interviews and family parties.

Roméo et Juliette had been performed there, so 'death' was not prohibited. But there was a world of difference between staging Gounod's sentimental tale and the realistic, sexy, violent *Carmen*. Although the audience might even be expected to welcome the retribution that Carmen brings down upon herself, the staging of her murder was

---

[5] If the opera had music throughout, the proper location for operas in French was the Opéra, with Italian ones being at the Théâtre-Italien. The rules were gradually being relaxed and *Roméo et Juliette*, which was performed at the Opéra-Comique, is actually composed right through.

totally unprecedented, frightening and horrifying, not least for young girls. The sexy seductress, the smoking chorus girls who scratched each other's eyes out – they could ruin the wedding business, which needed shows that were *'joli, clair, bien ordonné.'*

The Carmen was the leading mezzo-soprano[6] of the Opéra-Comique, the tiny, vivacious Célestine Galli-Marié (1840–1905). She was an excellent actress who had starred in Ambroise Thomas's successful, charming, but unpassionate *Mignon*. Galli-Marié possessed a 'cat-like grace' and a very distinctive timbre, with slightly harsh top notes which must have helped to convey her sensuality, and the impression that she possessed sexual knowledge. We owe the *Habanera* to her, because she insisted on having a solo at that moment.

Whereas female characters were normally kept towards the background, the Carmen of Galli-Marié was certainly neither respectable nor 'suitable'. She was criticised for exaggerating Carmen's vices, and for not tempering her passions. The 'heartless, faithless, lawless gypsy' was portrayed with a realism 'that would at best be bearable in an operetta in a small theatre.' The press notices described the opera as obscene. One critic wrote that Galli-Marié's interpretation 'deserved correction in the police court.'

During the five months of stormy rehearsals, the production team became aware that there would be difficulties. The chorus were unused to realistic acting, and the women disliked smoking[7] and having to flirt with the soldiers. Also, the musicians found the score exceptionally difficult.

Not surprisingly, morale sagged. One of the co-directors of the Opéra-Comique resigned; the other one foolishly told the press that he disliked the music. He was so concerned that, when a Government Minister applied for a box on the first night, he advised him first to attend the dress rehearsal and check it out. The librettists tried to

[6] Verdi had taken the female voice up to the high soprano. But 'operatic lust belonged primarily to the lower register.' So, where sexual experience was implied in younger women, as with Carmen, or Saint-Saëns's Dalila, the sensual, dark, lower tones of the mezzo or contralto were called for. And the higher notes, e.g. Carmen's B at the end of her *Seguidilla*, were used for attack. The contraltos got fed up that they were always allotted the roles of the unpleasant characters.
[7] Nothing in *Carmen* is found shocking today, other than the smoking.

get the realism toned down, but Bizet was not having it; nor was Galli-Marié. All this was public knowledge – the poster advertising it portrayed the final ghastly moments – so the audience was conditioned to expect a contentious production from the start.

The influential burgeoning bourgeoisie really just wanted 'caressing melodies, pleasant stories and plots which would help to obliviate the worries of daily existence.' That is why Donizetti, Saint-Saëns, Gounod and Massenet were so successful, and Bizet was not. The bourgeoisie did not want to endure the noise of those vulgar, unmusical Spanish castanets. Twenty years later, old Bernard Shaw would thunder that Emma Calvé (1858–1942), shocked him beyond measure. She was a 'superstitious, pleasure-loving, good-for-nothing' Carmen, 'with no power but the power of seduction, which she exercises without sense or decency.' It is no wonder *Carmen* is so popular today.

The first night failure: the story

There was another, separate reason for the failure: lèse-majesté towards a highly respected French author. Many people in the audience will have been familiar with Mérimée's short story. He had only died a few years previously. As a Senator and Member of the Académie-Française, he was very distinguished. He has been described as 'one of the great masters of French style during the nineteenth century' and 'at the very head of the French prose writers of the century.' Bizet's librettists showed little respect for Merimée's story: they merely picked some bits from it, and, for very good reasons, added some bits of their own.

The opening will have been unrecognisable. The opera misses out the first part of the book. And who is this woman Micaëla who dominates the opening? She is nice, unlike Carmen, but there is nobody in the book by that name, and no reference to such a person except possibly in a throwaway line in the death cell, when Mérimée's José, before being garrotted, asks for a locket to be delivered to a woman back home.

Who is Escamillo? The book refers to some useless picador, the whore's latest lover. He is injured in the bullring, but there is no victorious celebrity toreador.

And, as to the dénouement, Mérimée had the propriety to have José murder (and bury) Carmen in a lonely valley, not in public outside the bullring at exactly the moment Escamillo is proclaimed victor.

Members of the audience must have felt like a modern audience seeing a film adaptation of a book which plays fast and loose with the story, however necessary it may be to do so in order to render it effective in a very different medium.

Prosper Mérimée (1803–1870) is best known today for his short stories such as *Colomba* (about Corsica) and *Carmen*. He died three weeks after the surrender of Napoleon III at Sedan, which marked the collapse of the Second Empire. He combined being a civil servant, an archaeologist, and a man of letters. He started his literary career by publishing, as a hoax, works he claimed were authored by others, when they were actually by him. He was highly influential within the imperial family. He became a close friend of Madame de Montijo, Empress Eugénie's mother, who may well have been the source of his tale about Carmen (1845). Some said he was a hanger-on and toady. These impressions may have added to his unpopularity and his being regarded as a cold-hearted cynic. His style is naturalistic, using literature to depict local colour and exotic scenes. This was at a time when there were no films or TV, and travel was limited.

Recitative or spoken dialogue

The score for the première in March 1875 was far too long, even though it had been cut during rehearsal. The performance lasted for four-and-a-half hours. (Today it lasts less than two-and-a-half hours).

Nearly eight months after the première, for the Vienna production (in German) the dialogue was shortened and replaced with musical recitative, in accordance with Bizet's original intention. The recitative was composed by Guiraud[8], a close friend and class-mate of Bizet. Both versions are performed today.

Guiraud's recitatives have attracted much criticism. Saint-Saëns disliked them, although he was very enthusiastic about the opera. Some of the recitatives are regarded as good; others are 'undeniably second-rate' and are said to fall flat next to Bizet's music. One recent critic even called them 'inescapably third-rate', writing, 'every time they come thudding in, the dramatic temperature drops.'

Aside from their musical weakness, Guiraud's recitatives omit some useful background information which is given in the spoken dialogue, such as Don José's family background. This makes some of the narrative hard to follow for the attentive listener, assuming, of course, that the person is both listening to the spoken words and understands French. The recitatives also cut some humorous passages, such as when one of the smugglers refers to Gibraltar, the source of the contraband: he says that in Gibraltar you can see the English, masses of them, 'de jolis hommes les Anglais: un peu froids mais distingués.' The omission of such text offends those who regard Carmen as 'above all a comedy.'

There is no easy solution. Spoken dialogue has its own problems today. When describing a production at Covent Garden, Placido Domingo wondered just how sensible it is to 'have a New Zealander, an American, a Spaniard and a Belgian speaking French to a British audience.' Joan Sutherland stormed out of a rehearsal when told that they were going to use dialogue rather than musical recitative. She knew that her 'incorrigible' Australian accent did not suit the spoken aspects of Micaëla's role.

---

[8] Ernest Guiraud (1837–1892) was born in New Orleans. Like Bizet, he won the Prix de Rome. Indeed his father was the Prix de Rome winner who beat Berlioz in the contest. In later life, Bizet's friend was an also-ran: laid-back, absent-minded and ineffectual. His fame rests on the fact that he rescued Bizet during a fight with a gondolier. Six years later, Guiraud completed the orchestration of Offenbach's The Tales of Hoffmann after its composer's death. He taught a somewhat bemused Debussy. He also arranged one of the L'Arlésienne Suites.

Today, there is an obsession with authenticity, 'the authentic performance.' Here, as so often, it is misplaced.[9] Because of the need for cuts, and the difficulty over musical recitative, we are unlikely to get an authentic performance of the *Carmen* which Bizet himself would have wanted.

Why is *Carmen* so great?

Until *Carmen*, opera had tended to avoid depicting real, up-to-date contemporary situations. Historical subjects in period dress, and mythology, had been safer. Similarly, reigning monarchs did not object to sanitised comic opera – nobody would have dared depict the monarch as comic.[10]

Carmen's 'brutal force and naturalness … the overheated southern temperament, the dazzling and vital orchestra, the wonderful harmonies, the inescapable melodies' represented a breakthrough, new in Bizet's time (and new for the composer of *Les Pêcheurs de Perles*). It is a musical landmark.

The portraiture, for example, the gradual disintegration of Don José, is masterly. The opera is also full of examples of Bizet's use of music, particularly contrast, to create atmosphere. A good example is the well-known entr'acte before the scene in the mountains: after a short introduction on the flute and harp, the woodwind is joined by throbbing strings, reminding us that although at first sight this is seemingly a rococo paradise, it is actually a scene of serious romance. Shortly after this, the vacant gypsy girls tell their fatuous fortunes, their giggles depicted by staccato woodwind. Their pipe-dreams are interrupted by crude reality: Carmen, at first nervously, then with two harsh downward scratches on the strings, discovers her own fearful and fateful future. With the score marked 'simply and very evenly',

---

[9] Purists inevitably experience, but for some reason choose to ignore, a difficulty with roles written for castrati.

[10] The insubordinate aspects of *The Marriage of Figaro* did not represent any threat to an Emperor who actually wanted to shake up his Counts and Countesses. Contemporary subjects as in Verdi's *La Traviata* were never actually performed in modern dress until the 20th century.

she quietly faces up to the truth: *la carte impitoyable* relentlessly discloses one outcome for her: *la mort* – death.

Carmen provides an alternative to the 'workmanlike, clever, scented mixture of little character and much sentimentalism, the atmosphere of sighs, caresses, spasms and tears' that we hear so much in the works of Donizetti, Saint-Saëns, Gounod, Massenet and indeed the modern West End and Broadway musical. It also provides a completely successful alternative to the works of Bizet's contemporary, Wagner.

ACT BY ACT

Prelude and Act 1

Seville around 1820, in the square outside the guardhouse of a tobacco factory

We may be in colourful Andalusia, at the bullfight with the toreador, but the famous Prelude pulls us up sharply with a pause: we then hear the baleful and haunting 'fate' theme which will also conclude the opera. Bizet is warning us that he is about to present us with the unpalatable truth that, in real life, behind the superficial picture postcard scene which we all enjoy, we find the complex and deeply disturbing consequences of human emotions, the most basic of which is raw lust.

The curtain rises on the bored Corporal Moralès at his guardhouse outside the tobacco factory. A country girl, Micaëla comes in search of Don José, another corporal, but he is still off duty. The soldiers unsuccessfully try to entice her into the guardhouse, while she waits for him.

Don José's relief guard comes on duty, preceded by street boys. Moralès tells him that Micaëla has been looking for him. The lieutenant, Zuniga, observes that Micaëla is a different kind of girl to the cigarette workers. Don José says that he loves her.

The young men of the city come to ogle the cigarette girls having their break and puffing their fags.[11] Carmencita stands out

---

[11] In Mérimée's book, the cigarette girls work virtually naked because of the heat, adding significance to José's experience when he sent into the factory. When the Angelus sounds, the

among the girls; Don José ignores her but she notices him. The young men ask her when she will return their love. She says she does not know, maybe never. Love is untameable, like a bird, unpredictable: *L'amour est un oiseau rebelle* (the *Habanera*). Needled by Don José's manner, she takes a flower from her prominent bosom and flings it at him.

The bell rings for the new shift and the girls go. Don José stays behind, disturbed. Just as he is thinking about the sorceress's flower – its scent is strong, the flower pretty – Micaëla returns. She tells him his mother has sent her, with a letter, some money and to give him a kiss from her. Don José misses the point, and he confuses her by talking about some demon, some peril. The letter asks him to marry her, but she leaves to let him read it. He decides to put the sorceress out of his mind and marry Micaëla.

There is an interruption. There has been a row in the factory. Two of the girls, Carmen and Manuelita, have been fighting. The Lieutenant tells José to take a party to see what has been happening. Don José brings Carmen out. She insolently taunts them, *Tra la la la la*. The Lieutenant, himself quite taken with her, tells her she will go to prison and orders José to bind her hands.[12]

José and Carmen are left alone. She flirts with him. He is increasingly captivated by her, as she sings the *Seguidilla*, *Près des ramparts de Séville*, about Lillas Pastia's bodega, a place of assignation. She suggests that he loosen the rope and he complies. The Lieutenant brings the warrant, and she flashes her eyes at him. And, as José marches her off, she gives him a shove and runs away.[13]

girls come down to the river to bathe, giving much pleasure to the young men who congregate there at 6pm.

[12] The orchestra tells us, with a quite quick sounding of the 'fate' theme, that Don José has not put her out of his mind.

[13] She reaches top B, above the G and A which are generally top of the normal contralto and mezzo-soprano ranges respectively. In the Gypsy Song in the next act, she goes up to G sharp. And when she rejects Don José in the last act, she reaches bottom A. Frasquita and Mercédès, being sopranos, can reach top C at the end of Act 2, and also before they go off to deal with the customs men.

Act 2

Lillas Pastia's bodega

Carmen, with two gypsy friends, Frasquita and Mercédès, are in Lillas Pastia's bodega, where soldiers, including Lieutenant Zuniga, mingle with Seville's demi-monde of criminals and prostitutes. The gypsies dance and Carmen sings the Gypsy Song, *Les tringles des sistres tintaient* ('the jingles tinkled and the tambourines and guitars played ever more furiously, Tra la la la la'). As it accelerates, Carmen and her friends join the dance.

Just as Frasquita is asking for the soldiers to leave – it is time for business – the victorious toreador Escamillo[14] arrives and sings of the bullring, *Toréador en garde*. He makes a pass at Carmen and she is captivated. He tells her that, at his next encounter with danger, he would like to invoke her name. And then leaves.

Carmen, Pastia and two smugglers, El Dancaïro and El Remendado, agree that to pull off their next job they need deception, the skill of a woman: *Nous avons besoin de vous*. To their surprise, Carmen is reluctant to be involved, because she is in love. The smugglers suggest that she should combine crime and love. She explains that she is waiting for a soldier who was imprisoned for a couple of months for doing her a good turn. Don José is heard singing in the background 'The Dragoon of Alcala', a song in which the dragoon is off to visit his lover: *Halte-là! Qui va là? Dragon d'Alcala!* The smugglers tell Carmen to inveigle José into joining them.

Carmen dances with the castanets for Don José – *La la la la* – but he interrupts her because, in the background, he can hear the bugles announcing the roll-call, indicating that he must return to barracks.

She is stupefied. She taunts him: his priorities are all wrong. How could she have been so stupid as to dance for such a fool? In the Flower Song, he tells her[15] that the flower which she once threw

---

[14] Sir Thomas Beecham is often believed to have said of one candidate for the role of Escamillo, 'he thinks he's the bull instead of the toreador.' The remark is however more properly attributed to the distinguished American critic Irving Kolodin when describing Alexander Sved in the role of Escamillo.

[15] He reaches top B flat.

at him had been his comfort in prison. It had maintained his single obsession, to see her. She continues: if he really loved her he would carry her away on his horse into the mountains. He declares that he will not desert. They say goodbye. Just as he goes to the door to obey the call to barracks, there is a knock: Lieutenant Zuniga has come to have Carmen. He explains that he is rather better than a corporal, and tells José to clear off. José refuses, and they fight.

The gypsies return as Carmen tries to separate the two. In view of their plans, the gypsies need to detain the Lieutenant. Carmen asks if Don José is going to join them; he says he has no choice – a somewhat unromantic response. Carmen says that he will enjoy the wandering life, where there is no law, but freedom.

Act 3

A wild spot in the mountains

The evocative entr'acte, the harp first accompanying the flute, which is then joined by other woodwind, leads us into the wild mountains, to the hide-out of the smugglers led by El Dancaïro.[16] They know they have to be very careful. José, who is now among them, thinks of his mother, who believes that he is still a decent soldier. (We hear a few bars of the melody sung earlier by Micaëla.) Carmen, who has had enough of José, says he should return to Mum. (We hear the fate theme on the cellos and basses, and some ugly chords led by the trombones as she refers to separation and the possibility that she is predestined by fate to be killed by him.)

Frasquita and Mercédès cut cards and wonder about their future. They chatter about fortune, love, being a rich widow: *Parlez*. Carmen takes her turn. We hear the ominous fate theme. The card she draws predicts death for her and José. There is no changing what the cards predict; for her it is to be death.

---

[16] The third act has been beset with problems caused by animals. At a Covent Garden production conducted by Beecham, a horse was brought in to join the smugglers and add colour. Unfortunately, it turned its back on the audience and 'performed the ultimate indiscretion.' Everything came to a stop. Sir Thomas commented loudly, 'A critic, by God.' This was perhaps unexceptional, as a donkey has been known similarly to star in Act 1.

El Dancaïro and El Remendado tell José to guard the goods while they go through the valley and deal with three customs men. The women will seduce them while the smugglers get through: *Quant au douanier, c'est notre affaire.*

Micaëla comes in search of José, nervous but pretending to herself that she is not fearful about the smugglers, nor, for that matter, about Carmen: *Je dis que rien ne m'épouvante,* a glorious aria in which she reaches top B. She prays for strength.

Escamillo has also come, in search of Carmen: he knows that affairs for Carmen last no more than six months, and the one with Don José will now be over. Escamillo and Don José fight. Carmen returns and intervenes to save Escamillo, who José is about to kill when his knife snaps. Escamillo invites them all to the bullfight, and leaves. Don José tries to attack him but is restrained by the smugglers.

Micaëla is brought in. She pleads with José that his mother weeps for him. Carmen tells him he had better go to her. But, for José, who is furious, their two destinies are inextricably entwined. He is not leaving her. Only when Micaëla tells him his mother is dying and wants to forgive him before she dies, does José agrees to go with Micaëla. Ominously, to the sound of the fate theme, he warns Carmen that they will meet again. The toreador is heard singing. As Carmen tries to follow Escamillo, José bars her way.

Act 4

A square in Seville

The entr'acte, 'like some hyper-realistic fandango', leads us to the festival in Seville, with the music we heard in the Prelude to the opera. Outside the bullring, Lieutenant Zuniga is buying some oranges. The toreador's parade takes place. At the end of this is Escamillo, with Carmen on his arm: *Si tu m'aimes Carmen ... Ah je t'aime, Escamillo.*

Frasquita and Mercédès warn Carmen that José is in town, but Carmen is not afraid.

The crowd goes into the arena. Carmen and Don José are left confronting each other. Desperately, he begs her to start a new life with him. She says it is impossible; it is all over between them: *Non, je ne t'aime plus.* He will do anything for her, he says; he will stay a bandit. Carmen says she was born free and will stay free.

The sound of the bullfight can be heard in the background. Don José bars her way to the arena. Don José says he has given everything up for her. All she, infamous woman, can do is lie in Escamillo's arms and laugh at him. 'Carmen, you will come with me,' he shrieks, and tries to pull her away; 'No, no never': *Pour la dernière fois, démon, veux-tu me suivre? Non, Non!* She flings back at him a ring he once gave her. *Eh bien! Damnée!*[17] He stabs her. As the crowd emerges, he falls on her body. 'You can arrest me,' he declares. 'I have killed her, Carmen who I adored': *Vous pouvez m'arrêter; c'est moi qui l'ai tuée! Ah! Carmen! Ma Carmen adorée!*

[17] A cat once got onto the stage at this point. Being attracted to the singer, it rubbed itself against Don José just as he was singing 'Eh bien, damnée'.

TCHAIKOVSKY:
EUGENE ONEGIN

THE OPERA AND ITS COMPOSER

Tchaikovsky brooded over Pushkin's *Eugene Onegin*[1], a 'novel in verse', as a subject for an opera. He originally thought that the suggestion, which came from a star mezzo-soprano, was crazy, and possibly even foolhardy: Pushkin and *Eugene Onegin* are as familiar and sacred to Russians as Shakespeare, *Hamlet* and *King Lear* are to people from the West; so you tamper with them at your peril.

Tchaikovsky thought he might compose an Othello, or an opera based on a historical novel about a favourite of King Louis XIII of France. In the event, he composed *Eugene Onegin* between May 1877 and February 1878.

This was a momentous period in his personal life, which should have entered a reasonably stable and secure phase: he was now being helped with finance from the widow of a railway tycoon. But he had been unsettled when his friend and pupil Vladimir Shilovsky,[2] who he was particularly fond of, went off to get married.

Tchaikovsky started working with Vladimir's brother, Konstantin Shilovsky (1849–1893), on a libretto for *Eugene Onegin*. They evolved it into seven 'tableaux', being incidents selected from Pushkin's poem, which, with less than 400 stanzas, is actually quite short.

---

[1] Bernard Shaw, the Irish playwright and critic, gave an indication of 'the sound of the hero's name (pronounced O'Naygin, or to put it in a still more Irish way, O'Neoghegan).' The Irish pronunciation of Eugene, as opposed to the French Eugène, is probably more appropriate as well, that is, unless Evgeny, Yevgeniĭ or Evgenii is to be preferred.

[2] The wealthy Shilovsky brothers were stepsons of the repertory director of the Moscow Imperial theatres. Tchaikovsky taught Vladimir music from around the age of fourteen, and perhaps taught him a lot more besides. He frequently stayed on his estate, and also with him abroad in the south of France. He liked him so much that, on one occasion, he travelled non-stop from St Petersburg to Paris to visit him when he was ill (which he often was).

In May 1877, a bolt came from the blue. Tchaikovsky suddenly received a love letter from an unknown 28-year-old music student. He met Antonina Milyukova, for the first time on 20 May, and callously dismissed her suit. He seems to have thought that this rejection was analogous to Onegin's treatment of Tatyana in Pushkin's great work. Within a week, Tchaikovsky had returned to see Antonina, proposed, and been accepted with alacrity.

Tchaikovsky and his wife

He went away to the Shilovsky estate, where he finished the Letter Scene in Act 1 and sketched out much of the rest of the opera. On 18 July, only eight weeks after they first met, he and Antonina were married.

From the outset, from their train journey to go on honeymoon, the marriage was disastrous. He found her physically repulsive, even though their union was entered into on the basis that there would be no physical relationship. He escaped, and his brothers sorted out the mess he had left behind. He had to return to Moscow for the Conservatoire term in September. Before winter set in, he seems to have tried to commit suicide by wading into the Moskva river.

Peter Tchaikovsky was born on 7 May 1840. His father ran a mining works near the Urals, 600 miles east of Moscow. Their family life was disrupted when his father changed jobs, moving them first to Moscow and then further afield.

Peter was educated at the Imperial school at Tsarskoe Selo and destined to be a lawyer and civil servant. When he was passed over for promotion, he turned to music for a career. He studied at the St Petersburg and Moscow Conservatoires, where the composer Anton Rubinstein (of the *Melody in F*) and his brother Nikolai, both leaders in musical education in Russia, were the leading lights. He taught at the Moscow Conservatoire. Much of his time was spent on his beloved sister's estate, about 150 miles south of Kiev, in the Ukraine. (There, many years earlier, Pushkin had got together with various of the Decembrist revolutionaries.)

Around the time of the Fourth Symphony (May 1877), Nadezhda von Meck, widow of a railway tycoon, started providing him with money, which she did for fourteen years. There was an extraordinary condition: they were never to meet.

After the emotional upheaval of a disastrous marriage, Tchaikovsky settled near Klin, 60 miles from Moscow. There he wrote the Fifth Symphony, *Sleeping Beauty*, *The Queen of Spades*, and *The Nutcracker*. He went on conducting tours to England and the USA.

His death on 6 November 1893 is a mystery. Some believe that he was about to be denounced for his homosexuality: according to this story, fellow alumni of the Imperial School demanded that he commit suicide by drinking water that would result in him contracting cholera, the disease which seems to have been the direct cause of his death.

He resumed work on *Eugene Onegin*. After a trip around Europe, in January 1878 he finished scoring the Fourth Symphony. In February, *Eugene Onegin* was completed.

The first performance of *Eugene Onegin,* by Moscow Conservatoire students in March 1879, made little impact. It was only about five years later that the opera was staged in St Petersburg. There it received some poor reviews, not least from those who thought that supplementing and emasculating Pushkin's masterpiece was tantamount to blasphemy – a fair criticism, because Tchaikovsky bypasses some very well-known sections of the poem and much of the humour.

However, Tchaikovsky's *Eugene Onegin* soon became recognised as a self-standing masterpiece in its own right. It was the first of his works to appeal to a truly mass audience. It also provided the composer with his own financial stability.

We hear some memorable orchestral music, and choruses. The opera unfolds in a delightfully understated way, seeming almost inconsequential; and the ending, devoid of stage tragedy, suicide, or murder, is exceptionally clever. The music is a total contrast to the Tchaikovsky who we can often associate with bombastic (if popular) music, such as the *1812 Overture* and some of the movements from his symphonies. The understatement is particularly welcome because through his thin but colourful orchestration we can hear (even if we may not understand) the sound of the beautiful and musical Russian language.

Tchaikovsky

WHO'S WHO AND WHAT'S WHAT

The story below is based on the libretto. Certain directors may amend
opera stories to suit their production.

In the garden of the family estate, **Tatyana**, the shy, bookish, romantic daughter of the widowed **Madame Larina**, chats with her more extrovert sister, **Olga**. Their mother and the family nurse, **Filipyevna**, recall their past: Madame Larina put aside romantic ambitions and settled down to an ordinary, routine Russian life. Tatyana's pale complexion worries them, but it is only a consequence of the book she is reading.

They are visited by the young poet **Vladimir Lensky**, who is engaged to Olga. He is accompanied by his new neighbour, the Byronic and disdainful **Eugene Onegin**, with whom Tatyana instantly falls in love. Lensky pays attention to Olga; the sophisticated Onegin observes the simplicity and naivety of Tatyana.

* * *

In the well-known **Letter Scene**, Tatyana hears from her nurse[3] that love did not enter into her marriage. After being tucked up by the nurse, Tatyana goes to her desk to write a letter to Onegin, with whom she is now obsessed. In the morning, the nurse is relieved that she looks better after a good night's sleep, and agrees to get her grandson to deliver the letter, secretly.

* * *

Tatayana tortures herself with second thoughts about the wisdom of having sent it. Eugene arrives and lectures her about why she is not the right girl for him, and he counsels her to get her emotions under control.

---

[3] The nurse or governess was a standard item of furniture in the Russian household. Often just a serf, the nanny became sufficiently close to her charges that she could not just be jettisoned when they grew up; so she carried on. Tchaikovsky himself had had a fixation with his family governess, a foreigner brought in to educate his brothers.

* * *

Tatyana's name day[4] is being celebrated with a country-house dance. The music is being provided by the local soldiery, courtesy of its **captain**. Tatyana dances with Onegin. He is intensely annoyed when he overhears guests pitying her for falling for such a cad. He disrupts the proceedings, and upsets Lensky, by flirting ostentatiously with Olga. Tension is momentarily eased when **Monsieur Triquet**, a poet who lives locally, presents some celebratory (and contemptible) verses in honour of Tatyana.

Onegin continues to wind up Lensky. They have a row in public, so a duel becomes inevitable. After Onegin challenges Lensky, they go for each other. Lensky rushes out bidding Olga farewell forever.

* * *

At dawn, Lensky's pernickety second, **Zaretsky**, is keen to finalise the arrangements. The poet awaits his fate. Onegin arrives and (as a deliberate slight) appoints as his second his valet, **Monsieur Guillot**. Despite both duellists regretting that things have come to this, the duel goes ahead. Onegin fires first. Lensky falls down dead.

* * *

In a St Petersburg palace, a grand ball is taking place. The band plays the well-known polonaise.[5] Onegin has just returned from abroad. Now aged 26, he is still bored, without occupation, unmarried, an obvious misfit. He discovers that the simple girl he once lectured is now the fashionable wife of the elderly **Prince Gremin**, a highly decorated soldier. Onegin realises that he himself is now passionately in love with her.

* * *

---

[4] The name day was the feast day of the saint in whose honour a person was named. It was generally considered more important than the birthday. St Tatyana was (perhaps) martyred in AD 230, by the Roman Emperor Alexander Severus.
[5] A polonaise is a dignified Polish dance in triple time.

Onegin calls on Tatyana in her drawing room. For her, the flame of love briefly flickers. Despite her conflicting emotions, she turns him away. He is just looking for a trophy, she suggests. She will not betray her husband. Onegin tries to persuade her otherwise. She however is resolved; he must go. Tough, we feel no sympathy for him.

THE INTERVAL: TALKING POINTS

Pushkin's story

Tchaikovsky did not use the whole of the story in Pushkin's poem, but projected specific lyrical tableaux. As these were taken from a classic with which its audience would have been totally familiar, the resulting lack of continuity did not matter. The two ballroom scenes, one in the country and the other in St Petersburg, with the well-known waltz and the polonaise, add colour and momentum which might otherwise have been lacking. Tchaikovsky also provides some glorious solos, such as Lensky's love song to Olga and his lament before the duel, and Tatyana's husband's passionate song about his love for his wife. The letter scene, when Tatyana opens her heart to Onegin, has been described as 'Tchaikovsky's finest operatic tableau.' It includes the falling musical theme which pervades the rest of the opera.

Pushkin

343

Alexander Pushkin (1799–1837), Russia's greatest poet, was from the landed gentry near Pskov, close to Russia's border with Estonia. His maternal great-grandfather was an East African child slave, who was brought to the court of Peter the Great and rose to the rank of Major-General.

Pushkin led a dissipated youth and was greatly influenced by the romanticism of Byron. After being banished for his liberal political writings, he wrote *The Prisoner in the Caucasus*. He was fortunate to avoid being implicated in the 1825 political demonstration held by the 'Decembrists' in St Petersburg's Senate Square in 1825. Its ringleaders were executed.

Music lovers particularly associate Pushkin with his poem *Eugene Onegin*, which the critic Belinsky described as an encyclopaedia of Russian life. It was published in 1831, after Pushkin had worked on it for over eight years. We also associate him with Glinka's *Ruslan and Lyudmila,* with Mussorgsky's *Boris Godunov* and with Tchaikovsky's *The Queen of Spades*. After Pushkin married in 1831, his young wife's preference for the social whirl diverted him from his literary activity. He died early in 1837, aged 37, a few days after being mortally wounded in a duel.

We can see some of the difficulties which Tchaikovsky faced. Pushkin's story is not operatic: there is no great climax. Indeed, Tchaikovsky was uncertain how to complete the opera.

The opera omits various items. These omissions would have irritated contemporaries of the composer who were familiar with Pushkin's poem. Soon after Onegin rejected her love letter, Tatyana had a terrifying, seemingly 'Freudian', nightmare: she escapes a raging flood, only to be chased by a bear through the snow. The bear whisks her off to a hut full of deformed animals, in the middle of which sits Onegin, who seizes her.

Also, after the duel, when Onegin has gone away, Tatyana visits his house and finds it full of Byronic memorabilia. And towards the end, after the St Petersburg ball, Onegin suffers from bulimia as he follows Tatyana around. He writes a letter to her, which matches her earlier one to him; however, even after further letters he still gets no response.

One can see why some contemporaries and Pushkin aficionados were upset.

Duels

Gambling, drinking and duelling were standard features of the Russian upper-class life. Duelling was technically a crime.

The two duellists would approach each other, each starting at a similar distance from a barrier, a no-man's-land of a 10–12-pace length. Each could fire his one bullet when he wished to. After the first had fired, the other (assuming he was still capable) was entitled to call his adversary to the barrier, and fire at him from there.

Of four great Russian writers in the nineteenth century, the duel killed two, Pushkin and Lermontov. Turgenev and Tolstoy, who actually fought each other, survived.

Pushkin's fatal duel arose from his jealousy of his brother-in-law's behaviour towards his (Pushkin's) wife. After a normal day's work, on an icy winter's evening, the two men met. The first shot went through Pushkin's groin into the base of his spine. As he lay in the snow, he took two minutes to return the fire. He wounded his opponent, although not fatally. Pushkin was taken home, where he died, almost 48 hours later, after suffering in agony.

Lermontov, Pushkin's literary 'successor', was an experienced duellist. In mid-1841, he was killed at the age of 26. According to tradition, the duel imitated the one described in his book *A Hero of Our Time*. This was held, at only six paces, on a ledge jutting over a cliff where even a slight wound would result in the loser being dashed to pieces below. The contestants drew lots to decide who would fire first.

Duels were not uncommon elsewhere. In 1809, two British cabinet ministers, Castlereagh and Canning, settled a dispute by means of a duel.[6] Twenty years later, the first Duke of Wellington, then Prime Minister, fought a duel with Lord Winchilsea over a matter relating to Catholic Emancipation. The writer Marcel Proust was involved in duels at the end of the century.

Onegin's attitude – arriving late and appointing his valet as a second – shows surprising contempt for the ritual, and we can only presume that he thought the challenge so absurd that it would not proceed. Normally, the seconds should have attempted to reconcile the duellists, but, for some reason, they did not. And, once the duel went ahead, the most noble course of action for Onegin would have been to let Lensky take his shot, and then not return the fire. Thus, Lensky should have survived.

Boredom in Russia: the 'superfluous man' above

Onegin's life is characterised by idleness, boredom and yawning. That condition, called *ennui*, was familiar to his class, the 'nobility', or landed gentry.[7] They comprised the top one per cent of the population. Indeed, opera was encouraged in St Petersburg to enable them to dispel boredom and to while away 'the long and unendurable day', especially during the winter. There was little to do in the capital; however, life on one's lonely estate was even worse, as Onegin, who finds going to the country for the uncle's death so dreadfully tedious, exemplifies.

For many of the noble classes, life was actually an uphill struggle.[8] It was very hard to make ends meet and to convert the value of their crops into the hard cash which was essential to exist in either St Petersburg or Moscow. An estate was reasonably self-sufficient

[6] Shortly afterwards, Canning asked a couple of female relatives, 'Pray, young women, have either of you ever had a Ball pass through the fleshy part of your thigh? If not, you can scarcely conceive how slight a matter it is.' Possibly as a consequence, subsequent cabinet ministers have not considered duelling an effective means of settling their disputes.

[7] 'Landed gentry' may convey more to us than 'nobility', which sounds too exclusive and aristocratic. The wealth was very unevenly spread. Eighty per cent of this class owned fewer than 100 serfs, whereas Liszt's mistress, Princess Carolyne, had 30,000.

[8] For example, Pushkin's Larins had to go to Moscow in their own carriage, the cheapest, slowest means of transport.

when the owner resided on it. The yield from 300 serfs was enough, at least for a time, to finance a totally idle life and 'lie about like a piece of dough' but insufficient funds would be left over for maintenance and reinvestment. Decline was inevitable and terminal.

The inertia led to the notion of the 'superfluous man', who pervades much of nineteenth century Russian literature. He is 'the bird of no account', 'the living embodiment of the sickness at the heart of Russian society.' Pushkin's Onegin is an early example of a personality later caricatured in Prince Orlofsky in Johann Strauss's *Die Fledermaus*.

The 'superfluous man' is much to be found in the work of Russian writers such as Turgenev, Goncharov and Lermontov. In Turgenev's story *The Diary of a Superfluous Man*, he describes him as 'a man of often real talent, who can find no place for himself in the society of his time.' He is 'superfluous by virtue of his own failings as well as by virtue of the indifference of society to his personal inadequacy and his personal fate.' Sometimes, at best, he is a misfit, which is what Onegin discovered when attending the grand ball in St Petersburg.

At the end of Turgenev's final novel, *Virgin Soil*, the leading character shoots himself. When for a brief moment he regains consciousness, he has just the time to exclaim, 'Failed again.'

The serfs below

The Russian estates were peopled with serfs, who did the work. These comprised about eighty per cent of the population. They were hidebound with superstition. They were regarded by many gentry as being 'in the transitional stage of development between ape and man.' There are countless stories of floggings, conscription to the army or deportation to Siberia for the most trivial of offences – such as not working hard, looking surly or doffing one's cap reluctantly. However, not all serfs were treated cruelly – clearly Madame Larina's were not; they are a happy, jolly bunch.

The structure and the serfs, for all their deprivation, were remarkably resistant to change.

ACT BY ACT
Act 1
Introduction and Tableau 1

After a brief orchestral introduction, based on a four-note motif[9] (possibly drawn from *Carmen*) that pervades the earlier part of the opera, the curtain rises in the garden of the Larin family's country estate.[10]

Olga and Tatyana, the two daughters of the widowed Madame Larina, chatter away about love. This stimulates Madame Larina and the family nurse Filipyevna to natter about their youth, and about the romantic novels of Samuel Richardson[11] which they used to read. Of course, in reality, they had had to settle down and put up with dull husbands and routine Russian life. A chorus of serfs arrive to pay their respects and, at Madame Larina's request, sing a very lively folk song.

Olga and Tatyana chatter about their different characters. Olga, the youngest, is loquacious and down to earth, whereas Tatyana is a romantic, melancholy dreamer who shyly, silently, and sadly suffers, and personally absorbs, the torments of the lovers she reads about in the novels.

The serfs are sent off to be given some refreshment.

Tatyana is noticeably pale. The others are worried about her, but she reassures them that she is well; her pallor is just the result of emotions caused by the story she is reading. (Her reference to the pain and torment suffered by the fictional lovers is noticeably associated with the four-note motif that we heard in the introduction.) Her mother reminds her that the stories are only fiction; there are no heroes in real life.

---

[9] This four-note motif accompanies the phrase 'my fate' when Tatyana is writing her letter to Onegin in Tableau 2. It tends to be associated with fate.

[10] This is broadly the same summer tableau that opens Turgenev's play *A Month in the Country* and Chekhov's *Uncle Vanya*, with its garden seats and the table set for tea, the 'young girl, in a broad-brimmed straw hat, with a rose-coloured parasol over her shoulder.' We can almost hear the sound of the peasant strumming the balalaika (Tchaikovsky uses the harp).

[11] Samuel Richardson (1689–1761) was an important English novelist. He wrote of seduction in *Pamela*, of rape in *Clarissa* and of a glamorous gentleman chased by several women in *Sir Charles Grandison*. These tales were titillating and informative for young ladies, and thus (like modern glossy magazines) very popular.

The family is sent into a spin by the arrival of Olga's childhood sweetheart, the young poet Vladimir Lensky, who lives nearby. He is accompanied by his new neighbour Eugene Onegin, who has recently inherited his uncle's estate.[12] In a quartet, Tatyana immediately marks out the Byronic and disdainful Eugene; while in a discreet conversation with Lensky, Onegin is sophisticatedly surprised that his friend can have fallen for Olga, who he instantly sums up as characterless, rather like a Vandyke Madonna.[13]

For Lensky, it seems like an eternity since he has seen Olga (who, far more down-to-earth, reckons they saw each other only yesterday). Lensky expresses his poetic love to Olga in a passionate love song. For her, they were destined for each other by their parents.

Onegin opens conversation with Tatyana by presuming that she must be awfully bored having to live in the country. Tatyana, however, is not bored, because she reads and dreams, an activity which Onegin shrugs off. He used to dream once.

He tells her that his deceased uncle was highly regarded, but goodness it was frightful waiting by his deathbed.

With darkness falling, they all go into the house to eat. The nurse Filipyevna muses about her shy Tatyana and Onegin.

Tableau 2

This is the well-known Letter Scene. The orchestra plays the four-note motif as the scene opens on Tatyana's bedroom. She does not want to go to sleep. She wants to hear from Nurse Filipyevna, not about fairytales, but about her own love life years ago. The nurse tells her that love did not enter into her marriage, which was arranged by a

[12] The opera only starts at chapter 3 of the poem. Pushkin gives us much more background on Onegin, the 'débutantes' delight' who is overwhelmed by ennui. The uncle's fortune replenished the family coffers which had been depleted by his father. Onegin socialises till dawn, sleeps until midday, and spends three hours before the looking glass.

[13] Sir Anthony Vandyke (1599–1641) was the portrait painter who famously flourished at the court of King Charles I, with whose works Onegin, the (in his opinion) highly cultured urban dweller, is of course familiar. Presumably he regards Vandyke's religious pictures as beautiful but somewhat stylised and characterless.

marriage broker when she was thirteen. She was terrified, and wept when they removed her maiden plait[14] before going to the church.

Filipyevna may think Tatyana has a temperature, but no, she is in love, indeed on fire with love. After her nurse tucks her up, Tatyana goes to her desk to write a letter to Onegin, with whom she is now obsessed. The orchestra depicts her emotions. She cannot get the image of him out of her mind. She spends the whole night writing romantically to him about their shared destiny.

Why did he come and upset everything? She might have married another and developed into a good respectable wife. Another! No, it was fate. She recognised immediately when they met that they were destined for each other. Maybe he is just a tempter. But, whatever, Tatyana's future – as expressed in both the original opening four-note motif and the haunting six-note descending theme which will become prominent in the second part of the opera – is in Onegin's hands. She awaits him. He must speak 'the word', or shatter her dreams.

Dawn rises, as we are told by the shepherd playing on his oboe, followed by the bassoon. When the nurse returns to wake Tatyana up, she is relieved that she looks better after a good night's sleep. Tatyana asks her to get her grandson to deliver the letter, secretly. Filipyevna wonders for whom the letter is destined. It is for Onegin.

Tableau 3

Back in the garden, as they work, serf girls sing about fooling around with boyfriends, throwing cherries at them. Tatyana rushes in and collapses on a bench: Eugene has arrived. Having had second thoughts, she tortures herself by wondering miserably whether it was wise to write 'that letter'.

The insufferable Eugene pompously and woundingly holds forth: he has clearly thought carefully through how best he should handle this awkward situation. So he tells her that he would doubtless choose

---

[14] The unmarried girl's single plait was re-plaited as two before she entered the church for her wedding. Married women kept their hair covered in public.

her as his wife if he was just looking for domesticity (the last thing of course that she envisages). But marriage would be a torment (the very heartache which she longs for). He concludes by condescendingly advising her to get her emotions under control, because others may not understand her as well as he does: inexperience can lead to disaster.

The serf girls resume their song.

Act 2

Tableau 1

After the orchestra has reminded us of Tatyana's emotions, the scene opens in the month of January, on the feast of Saint Tatyana, and thus our heroine's name day. It is to be celebrated with a party. The guests congregate in delighted anticipation and thank the captain for providing the military band; a dance makes a welcome change from hunting.

At first, Onegin waltzes with Tatyana. He overhears onlookers pitying her, who they believe may be about to tie herself to such a conceited character. He is furious at this: he blames Lensky for getting him to come, and decides to disrupt the proceedings. He starts by dancing and ostentatiously flirting with Olga, a silly girl, who reciprocates, to the horror of her betrothed. After the end of the waltz, Lensky vehemently and jealously reproaches her.

When he asks her to dance again, they are about to be interrupted by Onegin. But there is a break in the proceedings when a Monsieur Triquet, a poet who lives locally, presents some celebratory (and contemptible) verses in honour of Tatyana. (The verses are, of course, written in French, the language in which the top layer of the Russian upper class conversed, just about intelligibly.[15]) Monsieur Triquet's audience applauds appropriately.

---

[15] Although this episode may seem irrelevant, it is perhaps 'a device of suspense' deployed to interrupt a big argument. The ubiquitous sponge, Monsieur Triquet, would have been familiar to Pushkin's readers, as would Onegin's French valet. The smartly dressed wives wore French gowns. 'The French are our Gods ... French dresses, French ideas, French feelings,' it was said.

During the cotillion which follows – a mazurka[16] – Onegin chides Lensky for sulking, and looking like Childe Harold, a melancholy character in a poem by Byron. Their conversation develops into a full-scale row in public. Lensky accuses Onegin of playing with the emotions of the young ladies, and calls him contemptible. Although Onegin attempts to cool things, Lensky challenges him. The guests are apprehensive.

Madame Larina is horrified at this scandal taking place in her house, where, as Lensky says, he enjoyed such happiness in his child-hood. She dreads the prospect of it leading to a duel. Lensky groans about life being no romantic novel, friendship being vacuous and women duplicitous. Onegin recognises to himself that he has been immature to precipitate this row; Olga feels she is not to blame; and Tatyana feels a mixture of jealousy and doom.

Onegin answers the 'insult' by challenging Lensky. When he responds by hurling further 'insults' at Onegin, they go for each other. The guests hope they can prevent it, but after this public display, a duel is inevitable. Lensky rushes out, bidding Olga farewell forever.

Tableau 2

It is dawn, by a mill-stream. Lensky waits for the duel. His pernickety second, Zaretsky, is annoyed that Onegin has not turned up. He goes off to make arrangements.

Lensky, alone, expresses a premonition of death, with the falling, lamenting musical theme very prominent. Where are the golden days of my youth, he wonders. If he dies, will Olga, who he loved so much, come to shed a tear on his grave?

Onegin arrives with his valet, Monsieur Guillot. Zaretsky, a pedantic character, is worried that Onegin has not appointed a second to deal with the formalities. So he appoints Guillot as his 'second': he may lack class (a deliberate slight), but he is honest. While final

---

[16] A mazurka was a Polish dance in triple time, with an emphasis on the second beat of the bar. The men usually stamped, clapped and clicked spurs. It is generally danced in groups of multiples of four. The cotillion is just a lively spirited dance, of any variety, often the last one of the evening; it usually involved couples imitating the movements of a leading couple.

arrangements are made, and the blood-red wintry sun rises, the duellists regret how things have come to pass: two old friends like them should be having a good laugh, not shedding each other's blood. (Tchaikovsky composed this in strict imitation, with Onegin half a bar behind Lensky. Thus he adds to the irony by implying that the duellists are both in agreement, and indeed they come together at the end, just as they go off to shoot each other.)

Pushkin comments that the nightmare in which they are caught up is a consequence of the absurd etiquette of the fashionable society in which they move. To step back from the brink and shake hands would be shameful: the duel must go ahead. Guillot takes refuge behind a tree. Onegin fires first. Lensky falls down dead.

Act 3

Tableau 1

In a St Petersburg palace, a ball is taking place. As Pushkin describes it, it includes the very cream of the capital's society: actual aristocracy, would-be aristocracy, celebrities, the usual idiots. There are ladies of riper years in flowery bonnets making snide comments; and old men, their old-fashioned witticisms seeming mere pomposity to the youth of the day. The band plays the well-known polonaise.

Onegin, now aged 26, has just returned from abroad and is already bored: he was bored on his travels. He has killed his best friend; he has no occupation, no wife. At the end of an écossaise,[17] he sees his elderly relative, Prince Gremin, a highly decorated soldier,[18] who arrives with his beautiful, expensively and fashionably attired young wife. The guests are lost in admiration. They confirm that the oddball melancholic is Onegin.

He suspects that she might be Tatyana. He checks with Gremin, who informs him, in a beautiful, well-known bass aria, of his marriage

[17] An écossaise is a quick dance with two beats in a bar. It was popular in the early nineteenth century, and does not seem to have had any particular connection with Scotland.
[18] In Pushkin's poem, Prince Gremin (who is not named) is an important General. Although Tchaikovsky makes him grey-haired, he was not necessarily old; but, for Pushkin, he was overweight.

to Tatyana two years earlier, and of the bliss which she, the brightest and most beautiful star in the firmament, has brought to him in his old age: 'Love has no respect for age'.[19] She shines like a star, he avers, high above all the second-rate people who comprise St Petersburg society.

Gremin presents Onegin to her, but she moves quickly away, and then leaves. He is amazed that this is the Tatyana whom he once lectured on the need to control her feelings. He now cannot control his: he is passionately in love with her, as the orchestra depicts. An écossaise concludes the tableau.

Tableau 2

In her drawing room, Tatyana, fashionably attired, awaits Onegin, who has made an appointment. Fate has once more brought them together.

She weeps with emotion and love for him. When he arrives, he falls on his knees. But she recalls the lecture, that sermon, and reproaches him for pursuing her now. Indeed, he was right then: the thought of her behaviour then horrifies her. But she suggests that now all he is after is a trophy: her fall would redound to his credit as a seducer. They weep in each other's arms. Happiness was almost within their reach. But now, she tells him, he must go. It is too late: she will not let her husband down.

Onegin tries to persuade her otherwise. She decides that he must go. He departs in despair.

[19] He ends on bottom G flat.

'CAV & PAG':
MASCAGNI'S *CAVALLERIA RUSTICANA* AND LEONCAVALLO'S *PAGLIACCI*

THE OPERA AND ITS COMPOSER

These immensely popular operas, each lasting slightly over an hour, are usually performed in a double bill.

Cavalleria rusticana,[1] which constituted 'an historical landmark in Italian opera of the nineteenth century', was produced at the Teatro Costanzi (now the Rome Opera House) on 17 May 1890. Its 'sensational success' inspired Leoncavallo's *Pagliacci*, which was premièred two years later at the Teatro dal Verme in Milan on 21 May 1892, under Toscanini. The intermezzo from *Cavalleria rusticana* was the third-highest placed operatic number in *Your Hundred Best Tunes*;[2] *Pagliacci* has ranked fourteenth in lists of the most-performed operas in the United States.

Cavalleria rusticana has also been combined with other one-act operas.[3] But today it is almost always the first half of an evening of 'Cav & Pag'. The atmospheric beginning of 'Cav' provides the ideal opening; and the tragic, violent ending of 'Pag' – *La commedia è finita!* – the ideal close.

A galaxy of stars has performed in these operas. Maria Callas made her debut in a student production of *Cavalleria*. Caruso was a

---

[1] Bernard Shaw pointed out that the stress is on the penultimate vowel: 'it is a mistake to suppose that Italians call it "Cavvlearea".'

[2] It is number nine overall. It ranks behind *Au fond du Temple Saint* from Bizet's *The Pearl Fishers* and *Va, pensiero*, the Hebrew Chorus from Verdi's *Nabucco*.

[3] *Pagliacci* was intended as a one-act opera, but the applause after *Vesti la giubba* led to its division into two.

legendary Turiddu, and, as Canio, his *Vesti la giubba* ('On with the motley') was perhaps the most celebrated of all his recordings. Tito Gobbi was a famous Tonio, Tito Schipa a great Harlequin. Gigli used to perform both Turiddu and Canio on the same evening. Placido Domingo, who has also done both roles together, has described how exhausting this feat is, not just because of the amount of singing involved, but because of the effort needed to flip over from one completely different and very demanding character to another.

Domingo also stars in Franco Zeffirelli's film version of both operas, which was partly shot in Vizzini, the village near Catania in Southern Sicily where *Cavalleria rusticana* is supposed to have taken place. It was the home of Giovanni Verga (1840–1922), the Sicilian author who wrote the novel on which the libretto is based.

That libretto, which has been described as 'first-rate, one of the best ever put forth', was the work of 'Nanni' Targioni-Tozzetti (1863–1934) and Guido Menasci (1867–1925), two librettists with whom Mascagni worked on other operas.

Leoncavallo wrote his own story and libretto for *Pagliacci*. An action was brought against him for plagiarism. He argued successfully that in his childhood at Montalto, his father, a judge, had presided over a case in which the events of *Pagliacci* had happened. The plagiarism suit[4] was withdrawn.

It is not difficult to appreciate why this double bill is so enduringly popular. The music may not be regarded as of the highest quality; nor will one shed too many tears for the duplicitous Turiddu, who gets his just deserts. But *Cavalleria rusticana* is packed with emotional tunes and colourful choruses, and is full of contrast, all of which must stir an audience. *Pagliacci* is less lyrical, but its confusion of illusion and reality is arresting. Canio, whose *Commedia dell'Arte* role is inherently cardboard, develops into a truly human and tragic figure. This stirs the emotions, and creates the tears.

---

[4] Catulle Mendès, a prominent Parisian literary figure who himself had earlier been accused of plagiarism, brought an action in Brussels against Leoncavallo for plagiarising his *La Femme de Tabarin*. Mendès's estranged wife Judith Gautier was a 'flame' of Wagner, in his last years. This caused considerable annoyance to Wagner's wife Cosima.

Pietro Mascagni (1863–1945), the son of a baker, was born in Livorno, which was then known by the English as Leghorn. His father wanted him to work in his business. Pietro managed to obtain funds to study at the Milan Conservatoire, from which he was expelled for not working hard enough. For a time, he shared lodgings with Puccini.

Mascagni

He survived as a double-bass player and third-rate conductor, and lived in straitened circumstances as a music teacher in a town in southern Italy, near the Adriatic. (A 20th-century English-speaking commentator noted that he had to survive on a plate of macaroni a day; this was before the days of global popularity for Italian food.) In 1888, he was working on his opera *Guglielmo Ratcliffe* when the publisher and newspaper proprietor Edoardo Sonzogno offered a prize for one-act operas. Mascagni's wife Lina surreptitiously put *Cavalleria rusticana* in the post without him knowing it. He was among the three who were awarded prizes. He was aged just over 25.

Sonzogno doubted whether *Cavalleria* would be effective on the stage. But when it was premièred, although the house was only half full, it was received with 'frantic enthusiasm'. Indeed, it was the biggest success since *Aïda* twenty years before. The fashion for *Cavalleria* in opera houses around the globe was unprecedented. Mascagni's other works were very demanding and were far less successful. Queen Victoria, after attending the comedy *L'Amico Fritz* (which Mahler said was a decisive advance), received the composer with, 'Signor Mascagni, I hope you will soon write another *Cavalleria*.' His *Isabeau* was about Lady Godiva, which worried its prima donna who feared that she might catch cold. *Le maschere* was ridiculed for being premièred in seven theatres at the same time. When Toscanini gave up La Scala at the time of Mussolini, Mascagni took over. He died in a shabby hotel in Rome, a victim of his early success, and with an image tarnished by his fascist connections. 'I was crowned before I was king,' he said.

Leoncavallo

Ruggero Leoncavallo (1857–1919) was born in Naples, the son of a police magistrate. He studied literature at Bologna University. The impresario who he subsidised to stage his early opera *Chatterton* ran off with the cash. So he became a café pianist as far afield as Egypt. Like Mascagni he faced hard times: when on his beam end, he appealed to Verdi for help, but was rejected. The baritone Victor Maurel introduced him to Ricordi the publisher, and asked him to write the libretto for *Manon Lescaut* for Puccini.

But Puccini fell out with him, and nothing came of it. Fired by the success of Mascagni's *Cavalleria*, he set to work for five months on *Pagliacci*. He took this to Ricordi's rival Sonzogno. Leoncavallo wrote around twenty operas and operettas, but despite travelling far afield to promote them, none apart from *Pagliacci* has lasted. Among these was a *La Bohème* which was 'raucous and capricious' compared to Puccini's. The Kaiser asked him to write an opera glorifying his family, but this was not a success.

Leoncavallo was fond of his food, overweight and good-natured. It is said that he was 'somewhat ponderous for an Italian.' He was involved with recording early on in its development. *Pagliacci* was the first complete opera to be recorded in Italy.

WHO'S WHO AND WHAT'S WHAT

The story below is based on the libretto. Certain directors may amend opera stories to suit their production.

Cavalleria rusticana (Rustic chivalry)

Easter morning in Sicily. **Santuzza**, a peasant girl, has recently had an affair with **Turiddu**, the soldier son of **Mamma Lucia**, the innkeeper. His previous girl, **Lola**, lost patience while he was away in the army, and married an older man, **Alfio**, a waggoner.

During the prelude, Turiddu sings a love song from behind the curtain. In this, he pledges Lola eternal love.

Santuzza suspects that Turiddu and Lola have got together again. He told her that he was going away on a job, but she knows he was actually in the village overnight. Alfio, who has heard about this, prefers not to go into the church for Easter Mass.

Santuzza and Turiddu have a blazing row. She also argues with Lola when she comes looking for Alfio.

Santuzza pleads with Turiddu to take her back. When he refuses, and rushes into church, she curses him. She 'spills the beans' to Alfio. He threatens to kill her if she is lying; and he swears revenge on Turiddu.

The famous **intermezzo** is played and the villagers come out of the church and into the inn. Turiddu joins ostentatiously in the jollifications.

Alfio confronts and challenges Turiddu. Turiddu knows that he is in the wrong. He worries for the future of Lola and Santuzza. He asks his mother to look after Santuzza. He rushes into the orchard where Alfio kills him.

Pagliacci

Tonio, the clown, in 'the prologue',[5] warns us confidentially that today's performance is not the usual clownish jokery, but a depiction of real life. *Commedia dell'Arte* actors dress up like cardboard figures, but like everyone else, they also have hearts.

It is a religious festival, and a hot summer afternoon around 1870. A travelling circus arrives at a village in Calabria, in the toe of Italy. **Canio**, the 'Punchinello' (or *Pagliaccio*) and leader of the troupe announces a performance that evening.

Tonio has his eyes on **Nedda**, the 'Columbine'. She is the wife of Canio, who adores her but suspects she is unfaithful. Indeed she is; but she is actually about to elope with **Silvio**,[6] a villager. **Beppe**, the 'Harlequin', tries to keep the peace.

Most of the troupe goes off to the tavern. Tonio stays behind. The villagers taunt Canio by suggesting that Tonio is staying behind in order to make love to Nedda. Canio's response leads everyone to think that something may really be amiss.

Nedda, left alone, thinks of love and fate. She sings the '**Ballatella**' that her mother taught her. Tonio approaches her. But she strikes him on his face and he swears revenge.

Her actual lover, Silvio, then appears. He persuades her to abscond. Tonio fetches Canio who overhears their plan to elope. Silvio escapes unidentified. 'Until tonight,' are the lovers' parting words. Canio tries to force Nedda to disclose her lover's name. Beppe separates them.

---

[5] The prologue was a regular feature of classical Greek drama. The score tells him to introduce himself *con autorità*.

[6] The parts of Tonio the clown and Silvio the lover are often sung by the same baritone.

Canio laments that in such a state he is unfit to act in the evening performance. However, if Columbine has indeed been stolen, he will have to laugh along with the crowd, and be a jester, not a man. He sings the famous *Vesti la giubba ... Ridi Pagliaccio*.

There is a brief **intermezzo**.

The stage performance takes place later that day. While taking the money from the audience, Nedda finalises arrangements with Silvio. The performance begins.

The Columbine (Nedda), whose husband Punchinello (Canio) is out, awaits her lover, Harlequin (Beppe). Taddeo the clown (Tonio) however arrives with a hen, tries to woo her but is rejected. Harlequin arrives, and kicks the clown out. He provides a bottle of wine and they sit down to dinner together. He also gives her a sleeping potion to give to her husband so they can abscond while he is asleep.

The clown warns them that Punchinello is coming back early; Harlequin just has time to escape – 'Until tonight!'

The opera now fluctuates between reality and fiction, such that the stage audience at first thinks the show is really great. Canio is horrified to hear Nedda's 'Until tonight!' – those same words he had earlier overheard. Tonio comes out of his hiding place and tries to calm him. Columbine continues with the show, and the gavotte *Suvvia così terribile*: she tries to persuade him her lover was Harlequin. She will not disclose her real lover's name. Canio takes his revenge by stabbing her. She calls to her real lover in the audience for help – *Soccorso Silvio* – and thus Silvio identifies himself, and also suffers her fate.

In one of the most famous of last lines, Tonio declares *La commedia è finita!* ('The comedy is over').

THE INTERVAL: TALKING POINTS

Verismo (realism) in Italian opera

When *Cavalleria rusticana* first appeared, audiences found its realism (*verismo*) was strikingly novel. The success of both operas is a consequence of their dealing realistically with the earthy, uninhibited, violent and excessive aspects of contemporary everyday life: passion, betrayal and retribution. Larger-than-life characters are 'swept along in a whirlwind of passions.' Sex becomes the driving force, and, when thwarted, it 'leads to acts of insensate jealousy and savage revenge.' These acts are 'almost invariably committed on the open stage so as to score a direct hit at the spectator's sensibility.'

With its stylistic origins in Bizet's *Carmen*, and perhaps earlier in Verdi's *La Traviata*, *Cavalleria rusticana* was a trailblazer for *Pagliacci*. Puccini adopted the same artistic techniques, especially in *Il Tabarro*. In these operas, 'climax follows climax in swift succession and moods are no sooner established than they are destroyed. And since excessive tension cannot be sustained for too long, the one-acter becomes the favourite form.'

Verismo is also seen in paintings, for example, depicting economic problems such as those experienced by starving weavers. As a trend in opera, it coincided with the beginning of the naturalistic epoch in literature, exemplified by Ibsen's *A Doll's House*, *Hedda Gabler*, and *An Enemy of the People*, and by the relentlessly realistic novels of Emile Zola (such as *Germinal*), whose aim was 'to register human facts, to lay bare the mechanism of body and soul.'

The music

Despite (or perhaps because of) the enormous popularity of Cav and Pag, experts are not quite so confident about the quality of the music. Fauré, the leading French composer who most of us know for being the composer of *The Requiem*, dismissed the verismo school of music for consisting of 'three or four chaps who have conjured up a neo-Italian art which is easily the most miserable thing in existence.' He regarded their operas as 'a kind of soup, where every style from every country gets all mixed up.' He despaired that 'everywhere, alas! they are welcomed with open arms.'

People thought that Mascagni was the long-awaited 'successor to Verdi'. (Verdi was aging; the Italians awaited his successor, almost as they awaited the return of the Messiah.) Verdi actually had some reservations about *Cavalleria rusticana*, although he foretold its success.

Bernard Shaw, the Irish playwright and music critic, also demurred. 'The people who say that Verdi has found a successor would really say anything. Mascagni has shewn nothing of the originality or distinction which would entitle him to such a comparison.' He added that he had 'read things about *Cavalleria rusticana* which would require considerable qualification if they were applied to *Die Meistersinger* or *Don Giovanni*.' For Shaw, Cav and Pag are successors to Donizetti, rather than Verdi; they are 'Donizettian opera rationalised, condensed, filled in, and thoroughly brought up to date.' And, he added, Mascagni 'is a man in a thousand, though not in a million.'

These operas are intensely dramatic, but *Cavalleria rusticana* is more lyrical than *Pagliacci*. Only the most desiccated musicologist can fail to admire, and be moved by, Mascagni's luxuriant tunes, the opera's 'continuous and passionate melody.' But the harmonies of his four-minute intermezzo in *Cavalleria rusticana* – one of the most popular pieces of music ever written – are actually only marginally more sophisticated than might be expected from a reasonably competent village church organist improvising while awaiting the entry of the vicar.

Leoncavallo's melody seems more angular, compared with the simple progression of Mascagni's. Leoncavallo 'took what was once considered a transition between recitative and fully-fledged aria and converted it into a moment of climactic utterance.' It has been suggested that he was less gifted than Mascagni, but a finer craftsman.[7]

The success of both these operas is also due to their tight construction, their impetus and the speed of the dénouement. There is no hanging about, especially when we reach the final climax, and in each the conclusion is reached with astonishing speed; the fact that they can both be staged in the same performance is a reason for their success.

---

[7] Leoncavallo found himself in a place where *Pagliacci* was being performed, so he went to it incognito. The woman in the next seat was annoyed because he did not seem sufficiently enthusiastic. He replied that it was the work of a dilettante – a kind of amalgam of Bizet, Wagner and Verdi. 'Do you really think this?' she asked. 'Yes,' he said. 'One day you will be sorry for it,' she retorted. The local newspaper on the next day carried an article headlined 'Leoncavallo on his own opera *Pagliacci*.'

In *Cavalleria rusticana*, religion and raw sex are run in parallel on the stage – a veritable *coup de theatre*. The irony of Leoncavallo's troupe acting their real lives on the stage, the stage within a stage, is the reason why his story is so effective. Not surprisingly, Zeffirelli's film version of both operas is gripping. Maybe that is why they are regarded as unhealthy in the artistic sense.

So, for all their popularity, not everybody is so enthusiastic about these operas. Bruno Walter, one of the great German conductors of the 20th century, told a story about *Pagliacci*, almost a parable. Early in his career, he was conducting it in Hamburg. He tried very hard: his conducting was sufficiently vigorous that he scorched his fingers on the hot chimneys of the gaslight at the side of the conductor's desk. But whenever he turned to the second violins, he could see a lady in the front row knitting a stocking. She would periodically, in the middle of the performance, lean across the rail and ask him in a friendly way if the performance would be over soon.

OPERA BY OPERA, ACT BY ACT

Cavalleria rusticana

The prelude includes themes that will be heard later, when Santuzza despairs that, despite everything, she still loves Turiddu, and implores him to stay with her.

Unusually during a prelude, from behind the curtain, we hear Turiddu, to the accompaniment of the harp, singing a Siciliana (a Sicilian love song). He pledges Lola, his latest girlfriend, eternal love.[8]

On Easter morning, the villagers congregate in the square of a Sicilian village and move towards the church. The women sing of springtime, the men sing of love. The women indicate that today is Easter and the men should rest.

---

[8] The orchestral music at the start is relatively lengthy, to convey the *couleur locale*. During this, the chorus sings a couple of 'Ahs' from behind. But the interposition of the Siciliana very effectively avoids it seeming to develop into an orchestral 'concert'. The Siciliana also reinforces the duplicity of Turiddu.

Santuzza, a village girl, approaches[9] Mamma Lucia, the owner of the tavern, to ask for Lucia's son Turiddu. Lucia thinks he has gone to fetch wine from Francofonte, nearby; but Santuzza knows he has been seen in the village overnight. She feels that she cannot enter Lucia's house, because she is a fallen woman.

Just as she is about to tell of her broken heart, Alfio, a jolly waggoner, is heard approaching. He sings happily of the joys of returning home to Lola, his lovely wife. He calls to Lucia for some wine, but she has run out and she says that Turiddu has gone to Francofonte to fetch some more. Alfio is surprised (the accompaniment on double basses is portentous), because, earlier, he saw Turiddu lurking near his own cottage. When Lucia also expresses surprise, Santuzza tells her to be quiet. In the circumstances, Alfio decides that he will not go into church.

Santuzza soars above the hymn *Regina coeli*, as the people enter the church to rejoice in the Easter Mass. Lucia and Santuzza however stay behind. Lucia asks why she silenced her. She reminds her of how Turiddu returned home after serving in the army to find that Lola had married Alfio. Turiddu had turned to her, Santuzza, and they had had an affair. But he has been courting Lola when Alfio is away. Lola has stolen Turiddu from her. Santuzza says that she is damned[10] and asks Lucia to go into the church and pray for her.

When Turiddu arrives, he expresses surprise that Santuzza is not in church. When he tells Santuzza that he has come from Francofonte, she accuses him of lying. He counters by accusing her of spying on him, which she denies. She accuses him of loving Lola, and curses her. Turiddu shouts at her that he is not the slave to her jealousy. Santuzza says she forgives him; she still loves him.

At this moment, Lola, who is heartless and cruel, is heard singing a jaunty love song. When she sees Turiddu, she asks if he has

[9] In a San Francisco production, Santuzza entered in a donkey cart. Unfortunately, her entry coincided with a minor earthquake, which frightened the donkey. Braying wildly, it charged around, thowing Santuzza out of the cart and crashing into the scenery.

[10] In Ponnelle's production, Santuzza was made up to appear pregnant. In Sicily, one would expect that, if she had been visibly so, matters would have come to a head much earlier.

seen Alfio; and she wonders why Santuzza is not in church. Santuzza replies that the only people who pray are those 'whose hearts are pure and unstained.' The two girls have a bitchy altercation, as Lola enters the church.

Turiddu tries to send Santuzza away, but she refuses, and, harking back to the beautiful themes in the prelude, she pleads desperately with him to take her back. But he says his heart is made of steel and he does not love her any more. He adds, callously, that the fact that she is angry does not bother him. Santuzza curses him as he rushes into the church. This is a most emotional passage and the score is variously marked *Grande con sempre crescente passione*, and *con suprema passione*; her curse is followed by a menacing array of trombones and tuba.

At this moment, Alfio returns and wonders if the service is still going on. Santuzza betrays Turiddu. She tells Alfio that Lola has been unfaithful while he has been away, and has stolen Turiddu's heart. Alfio furiously threatens to kill her if she is lying, and he swears revenge on Turiddu. Santuzza realises that she has said too much.

After this drama, there is a complete contrast, the 48-bar 'intermezzo sinfonico', an astonishingly simple but effective piece of orchestral music, mainly played in unison on the strings, accompanied on harp and organ, with the oboe (an instrument Mascagni favours) adding a bit of additional colour. 'No piece of serious music can achieve the world-wide popularity of this intermezzo and not possess merit,' it has been suggested.

The villagers, including Turiddu with Lola, pour out of the church and head into the tavern. Turiddu invites everyone for a drink. He pours the wine and, enjoying Lola's company, sings a drinking song (known as a 'brindisi'), *Viva il vino spumeggiante*. Turiddu and Lola toast each other. And he has too much to drink.

When Alfio returns, Turiddu offers him a drink. With the tuba, trombones and bassoons making threatening noises, Alfio declines the offer. 'The wine is poisoned,' he says. The crowd sense trouble, the double bass and drum throb, and the girls decide it is wise to take Lola away. Turiddu embraces Alfio and bites his ear. Alfio accepts the challenge to settle the matter with stilettos.

Turiddu confesses to him that the fault is his; and he requests that Alfio should not take it out on Lola. He then begins to worry about who will care for his abandoned 'Santa' if he is killed. Alfio goes to the orchard to await him.

Turiddu becomes increasingly pathetic as he admits to his mother that the wine has gone to his head, and asks her to bless him as she did when he left for the army. He also asks her to be a mother to Santuzza, who he was to take to the altar. When Lucia is surprised by his behaviour, Turiddu brushes it off. Again, he asks her to look after Santa, gives his mother a kiss and rushes into the orchard to meet Alfio.

The orchestra rises to a chord marked *ffff* in the score. A scream is heard: 'Turiddu is dead.' Santuzza and Lucia fall senseless, as the curtain quickly drops.

Pagliacci

The opera opens with the orchestra playing a theme which almost sounds as if it is being played on a fairground squeezebox, or accordion. We quickly hear on the horns the theme of the *Ridi Pagliaccio* in which the cuckolded Pagliacci later laments how, despite personal sorrow, the comic actor has to keep on laughing.

Tonio, the clown, comes from behind the curtain in the role of the 'prologue'. This time, he has not come to remind us that the play is fiction, but to assert that it is true. To the theme which is later used in the love duet, he explains that the actors will be seen possessing the human emotions of passion and love, anger and humour. They may be disguised in their costumes, but, like everyone else, actors have hearts.

Act 1

It is 3pm on a hot summer holiday, the Feast of the Assumption (15 August), around 1870. The location is Montalto, Calabria, down in the 'toe' of Italy.

An excited crowd of villagers greets the arrival of the travelling circus. Beppe (Harlequin) drives a donkey cart in which Nedda (Columbine) reclines. Canio (Punchinello) proclaims their arrival on his drum and out-of-tune trumpet. He announces that there will be a performance at 7pm that evening.[11] It will depict a strange combination of love and hate. It will feature Tonio the clown, and Punchinello's troubles and his revenge. When Tonio helps Nedda down from the cart, Canio, who suspects his wife is unfaithful to him, roughly pushes him aside.

The troupe is about to go off to the tavern. When Tonio stays behind to 'clean up the donkey', the villagers taunt Canio by suggesting that Tonio is staying behind in order to make love to Nedda. Canio explains that while that would fine on the stage, it would be entirely unacceptable in real life. He is so menacing that the crowd suspect something is amiss. He reminds the villagers that, after church, they must come to the show later that evening.

Nedda, left alone, at first worries about how threatening Canio sounded. But, 'forget it'; she asks the sun to shine upon her. Her heart is throbbing with love as she sings the 'Ballatella' which her mother taught her, *Hui! stridona lassù*. This is about the songbirds who, despite storm and tempest, spread their wings and soar relentlessly upwards, led by fate.

Tonio does indeed try to woo her. He explains that he may be a clown, but he also has a heart. Nedda tells him to say all this stuff tonight when he is playing the fool. But he persists in his advances, and lurches towards her. She savagely picks up the whip Beppe has left behind and strikes Tonio on his face. We may not be surprised that he swears revenge. As he leaves, she mercilessly declares that his heart is even more ugly than his body – 'Viper, be gone!'

Her actual lover, Silvio the villager, then appears. He says that Canio is safely drinking in the tavern. She tells him about Tonio's attempt to kiss her and how she struck him with the whip. Silvio despairs that after the show, the troupe will move on and she will be gone for ever. They should abscond. She resists: he must not tempt her (she reaches high B flat). But she assures him she will never forget him.

---

[11] During the football World Cup in Hamburg, when he would normally hold up a notice indicating the time of the performance, Domingo held up the football results instead: 4-3, Germany having beaten Sweden.

She has been overheard by Tonio, who rushes off threateningly. Silvio persists, and she yields. They arrange to meet at midnight: *A stanotte – e per sempre tua sarò* ('Tonight, my love, and for ever I am thine').

Tonio has crept back with Canio, who overhears the lovers. But by the time he reaches them, Silvio has escaped, unrecognised, over the wall. Canio tries to follow him, but Nedda bars the way. Canio tries to force Nedda to disclose her lover's name. The only reason he has not cut her throat is because he wants to get the name out of her. She refuses, and he raises the dagger, but Beppe separates them. He tells Canio to pull himself together; the church service is over and the audience is about to arrive. Tonio suggests that they will find out who the lover is later.

Canio approaches the curtain, lamenting that in such a state he is unfit to perform. But if Harlequin has stolen Columbine, he will have to laugh along with the crowd, and be a jester, not a man. *Vesti la giubba … Ridi Pagliaccio* has been described as 'one of the most famous numbers in modern Italian opera': 'On with the motley, the paint and the powder … Laugh, Punchinello, for the love that is ended; laugh for the sorrow which gnaws at your heart.'

There is a brief orchestral interlude, the intermezzo.

Act 2

Tonio beats his drum while the crowd, which includes Silvio, arrives for the show, and villagers rush to get the best seats. Nedda, as Columbine, holds the plate to receive the money and Beppe checks that everyone has paid. Silvio reminds Nedda of their assignation that night. The crowd calls for the show to begin.

In the play, Columbine observes that all is clear, and her husband will not return before morning. She hears Harlequin (Beppe) serenading her with his guitar. But Taddeo (Tonio) first arrives, falls on his knees and offers Nedda both himself and the hen in his basket. She asks how much she owes him for the hen and shoves him away. Harlequin enters and boxes Taddeo's ears. Taddeo withdraws as gracefully as he can.

Harlequin begins to make love to Columbine. She shows him the dinner, the hen she has bought him. He contributes a bottle of wine, and they settle down to eat. Columbine also gives her a sleeping potion to pour into her husband's wine, after which they will abscond together.

They are interrupted by Taddeo, who announces that Punchinello has returned early. Harlequin hurriedly escapes out of the window.

Normally in the *Commedia dell'Arte*[12] performances, Punchinello, the jester husband, would be thrown out of the room, to the delight of the audience. But in the opera, the action of the troupe now fluctuates between reality and fiction, with the stage audience vigorously applauding what it thinks is fiction, but gradually realising that it is laughing at something which is seriously real.

Canio, as Punchinello, is horrified to hear Columbine (Nedda) use the words he overheard earlier when she was with her lover: *A stanotte – e per sempre io sarò tua.* ('Tonight, my love, and for ever I am thine'). He demands to know who has been with her. She says he has been drinking. She concedes that it was Taddeo, and calls him to come out of the cupboard. Tonio shouts from the cupboard that Columbine is true.

Canio presses her to reveal who was with her. She says, as if still acting her part in the play, 'Punchinello'. He declares that he is no longer Punchinello (Pagliaccio) – *No! Pagliaccio non son* – but a man with human feelings and emotions, and is bent on vengeance. He regrets having sheltered her and loved her. (The stage audience observes how realistic the performance is; Silvio becomes uneasy.) Canio continues to say how he adored her, how she has broken his heart and how he now hates her: *Sperai, tanto il delirio.* If so, she answers, she had better leave him. He demands to know her lover's name. The audience finds it great entertainment.

Nedda continues to act the Columbine role. She sings a gavotte, *Suvvia così terribile* ('I never knew you were such a tragic fellow'). She

---

[12] The *Commedia dell'Arte*, of ancient origin, was a strolling theatre in Italy. The performances, which were usually improvised, were held in the open air. Punchinello and Harlequin were standard members of the cast; and regular topics included love, geriatrics and cuckolds.

tries to persuade him her lover was Harlequin. Canio loses his temper, and Nedda declares she will not disclose her lover's name, even at the cost of her life (she reaches top B). Canio picks up the knife, shouting *Il nome, Il nome* ('the name, the name'). Silvio now realises that the game is for real and raises his dagger. But by then Canio has stabbed Nedda, who just manages to shout *Soccorso Silvio* ('Help me Silvio') before she dies. Thus Canio realises who has cuckolded him; he lunges at Silvio and kills him. The orchestra plays the *Ridi Pagliaccio* as Tonio[13] utters the famous last line of this drama: *La commedia è finita!* ('The comedy is over').

---

[13] Some Canios, for example Caruso, have appropriated this line for themselves. To do this is to overlook its relationship with Tonio's prologue at the beginning of the opera, and the 'grim cynicism' of the pathetic but vicious clown.

PUCCINI: *LA BOHÈME*

THE OPERA AND ITS COMPOSER

The image of 'Bohemians'[1], students and their *grisettes* living in attics in the Latin Quarter of Paris, was established around 1850 by the writer Henry Mürger[2] whose series of sketches, 'Scènes de la vie de bohème', was based on his personal experience of bohemian life.

Mürger might have been lost to history had not Puccini half a century later transmuted him into Mimì's lover Rodolfo. *La Bohème* has remained one of the most popular operas. For many theatres, it is 'an old standby', which has been sung by all the star tenors and sopranos of Italian opera. There is a tendency for celebrities to regard themselves as the attraction rather than the opera, but arguably that is preferable to the focus being on the production itself.

Puccini created *La Bohème* with immense skill and artistry, using an unlikely and quarrelsome pair of librettists: one a former sailor, the rough, republican, quick-working Luigi Illica, who produced the structure and first draft; the other, the smoother socialite, the very highly regarded poet and playwright Giuseppe Giacosa, a perfectionist who painstakingly versified and polished it.

This 'Holy Trinity' (as the music publisher Giulio Ricordi called them) had been involved in Puccini's first big-hitting production, *Manon Lescaut*. After *La Bohème*, they went on to create *Tosca* and *Madama Butterfly*. Their stormy relationship was exacerbated when

---

[1] The term 'Bohemian', used to describe anyone who sets social conventions aside, originated from a misconception that such people came from Bohemia (just as Gypsies were supposedly from Egypt).

[2] Henry Mürger (1822–1861) was born in Paris. His father was a concierge and a tailor. He started work in a lawyer's office, but, with the help of an influential literary patron, became secretary to a Russian count. His literary activity was unfruitful until the publication in 1848 of his collected sketches entitled *Vie de Bohème*. Thereafter, his life was easier. According to the *Encyclopaedia Britannica*, his writings 'exhibit the same characteristics – an excellent descriptive faculty, lively humour in drawing the follies of youth, frequently pathos, and not seldom a tender and poetical melancholy.'

Illica suggested that versification was of no relevance in a libretto; Giacosa, on the other hand, was infuriated by Puccini's endless refinements and changes as the work progressed. At one stage, Giacosa threatened to pull out of the project. Shortly thereafter, it was Illica's turn to explode. 'Illica should calm down,' said Puccini. Acts 3 and 4 proved particularly intractable, and Giacosa again offered to disclaim responsibility and waive any remuneration.

Toscanini conducted the première at the Teatro Regio in Turin on 1 February 1896. This was the third anniversary of *Manon Lescaut*, and around seven weeks after Puccini had finished composing. The public liked the opera, but the critics were 'decidedly hostile' at first. The realism of the subject matter may have been too hard to swallow.

Puccini

Puccini's initial feeling of mortification was premature. The production ran well and a subsequent performance in Palermo was prolonged by encores beyond 1am; by then, half the orchestra had left, the cast had changed out of most of their clothes, Rodolfo had removed his wig and Mimì's hair was all over the place. The conductor decided to repeat the whole of the last scene.

La Bohème became very popular indeed. People started calling their babies Mimì. King George V told the conductor Sir Thomas Beecham that it was his favourite opera, because it was the shortest one he knew. It is now at the top of 'the charts'. Indeed, before the time of the long-running, highly marketed West End musical, the number of performances of *La Bohème* was probably the highest ever attained by any serious stage work, including plays.

When Puccini was secretly working away on *La Bohème*, he discovered that his contemporary Ruggero Leoncavallo, the composer of *Pagliacci*, was also composing an opera based on the same sketches and its dramatised version. The two composers had a blazing row in a Milan café and this was followed by announcements in separate newspapers that each was working on the same opera. Puccini's blunt response was, 'Let him compose. I shall compose, and the public will judge.' Leoncavallo's version premièred fifteen months after Puccini's and at first was actually the more popular of the two.

WHO'S WHO AND WHAT'S WHAT

The story below is based on the libretto. Certain directors may amend opera stories to suit their production.

It is Christmas time around 1830, in Paris. **Rodolfo**, a poet, **Marcello**, a painter, **Colline**, a philosopher, and **Schaunard**, a musician who is managing to make some money, live, in a rumbustious jolly male way, in a freezing garret. They are behind with their rent which their landlord **Benoît** comes unsuccessfully to collect. Rodolfo stays behind when the others go off to the Café Momus.

In total contrast, **Mimì**[3], a frail and undernourished seamstress who lives next door, comes to obtain a light for her candle. We do not have to wait long for Rodolfo's *Che gelida manina* ('Your tiny hand is frozen') and her response *Mi chiamano Mimì* ('They call me Mimì …'), followed by his *O soave fanciulla*.[4] Thus their love affair begins.

---

[3] Whereas the tendency in English is to pronounce Mimì with the accent on the first syllable, it should be pronounced with the accent on the second. Where the rest of the cast finds the Mimì uncooperative, she has been known to be called 'Moomoo', a bovine imitation.

[4] This is one of the best-known and best-loved sequences in Italian opera. English has no obvious words with which to translate the expression *O soave fanciulla* – 'Sweet young girl' is one approximation. Translating it 'sweet maiden', as is sometimes done, would seem technically incorrect for a poor worker in Paris in that era.

Marcello's ex-girlfriend **Musetta**, has left him for an elderly and rich protector, **Alcindoro**. But in a colourful scene at the **Café Momus** in the Latin Quarter, Musetta and Marcello come together again, having made the old man look an ass.

A few weeks later, in February, near the **Barrière d'Enfer**, a customs post on the walls, we hear that Mimì's romance with Rodolfo is not going so well, despite their love for each other. She is increasingly ill, suffering from consumption. She returns to the garret to die.

Consumption (tuberculosis or TB)

In the 1820s, almost half of all deaths in Paris were due to pulmonary consumption, pneumonia, pleurisy and intestinal complaints. The social disruption, and the prevalent social conditions of the time, were later immortalised in Victor Hugo's *Les Misérables*. Even in late nineteenth-century Europe, consumption was blamed for one-seventh of the death rate.

Although Chopin is one of the more famous examples of a sufferer from consumption, the disease was particularly prevalent among the poor, who suffered from bad nutrition, cramped conditions and lack of sanitation. The terrifying symptoms were coughing and blood-stained sputum. For years, there was a desperate attempt to find a cure. Even at the end of the nineteenth century, it was being suggested that long sea voyages, such as those to Australia or New Zealand, could be a means of arresting the disease.

Only in 1882 did the Nobel prize-winner Robert Koch (1843–1910) discover the bacillus that was the cause of the condition. And not until after the Second World War was immunisation widespread. The disease is still a significant cause of death worldwide.

The interval: talking points

Puccini's place as a composer

Puccini wrote *La Bohème* when music was undergoing a considerable revolution. Wagner was long dead, Debussy already had *Pelléas* in hand, Schoenberg was aged 21 and Stravinsky was thirteen. By the time Puccini died in 1924, and bequeathed us his twelve operas, his style was an anachronism. As a consequence, he tends to get a bad press from musical professionals.

Fauré, who many know mainly as the composer of *The Requiem*, called *La Bohème* 'a dreadful Italian work'. 'I know the composer Puccini. I met him twice,' Fauré wrote, a few years after attending a *Bohème* performance, 'I wasn't able to escape.'

If to be a great artist one must move the art forward, then Puccini, who was in many respects static, cannot be reckoned as one. But *Madama Butterfly* and *La Bohème* are numbers one and two in charts of top-performing operas. And, for that position, *La Bohème* does not even have the advantage of the American aspects to the *Madama Butterfly* story. Although popularity on its own is no measure of artistry, there comes a point where critics begin to look foolish and out of touch. Taunts about being bourgeois and commercial are more redolent of envy than objective criticism.

It is beyond doubt that Puccini, the 'full-blooded opera composer, more familiar than any of his contemporaries with the secrets of theatrical effect and success', was a consummate craftsman. We can point to his extraordinary sense of the theatre, such as the conclusion to the opera, reminiscent of Violetta's death in Verdi's *La Traviata*, at which moment most people in the audience are discomfited to find the lights are up before the handkerchief can be hidden away. This scene exemplifies Puccini's perfect sense of musical contrast and of pace. Thus, despite being one of the best-known dying scenes on the stage, it never becomes mawkish and its pace is sustained until the end. The audience suspects the truth and is warned by Schaunard. But Rodolfo does not realise that Mimì is dead until Marcello, with great anguish cries out '*Corragio*' ('courage!'). The scene is so effective that it has become notorious.

We can hum one of those incandescent lyrical phrases, brief, simple and thus so memorable, such as *O soave fanciulla*. And we can recall the entire glorious fifteen-minute *Che gelida manina* sequence which concludes the first act. With the tenor sustaining a B flat and reaching top C at the end of *Che gelida*, its place in any 'All-time Hundred Best Tunes' is surely secure.

Perhaps, however, there is an element of truth in the suggestion, by an eminent musicologist, that 'what was ardent passion on Verdi's stage is more like hysteria on Puccini's.' But it is that of a craftsman.

Detail in the libretto

Puccini took immense interest in the choice and development of his librettos, which are surprisingly criticised for being too sparing with words. In *La Bohème*, the mixture of laughter and passion is highly effective, as is the use of contrast as a means of reinforcing the drama. For example, in Act 3, the underlying true love of Mimì and Rodolfo is reinforced by its juxtaposition with the bickering of Musetta and Marcello. And the dying Mimì's entry during the mock-duel adds considerably to the dramatic effect.

Musetta, although second to Mimì, has a major role and is most effectively characterised. She may be a prostitute, through desperation, but is full of humanity. Her prayer while Mimì is dying in Act 4 is wrenching, just as her bickering with Marcello and her treatment of her protector Alcindoro are totally realistic.

It has been suggested that 'where erotic passion, sensuality, tenderness, pathos and despair meet and fuse, Puccini was an unrivalled master.'

Detail in the music

Puccini, together with his rivals Leoncavallo and Mascagni, used Bizet's *Carmen* as a model. So, the music provides us with wonderfully colourful and realistic scenes, for example, the crowd scene at Café Momus in Act 2, or dawn coming up over Paris at the beginning of Act 3. Surprisingly, those parallel fifths on the flutes and harp, suggestive of a spooky dawn, were castigated by critics following the première.

In Rodolfo, Puccini provided a means for great singers to excel, and *Che gelida manina* is the role's greatest challenge. Pavarotti said that its quiet, low notes need a 'steady pure sound that floods the opera house.' Despite being soft, they require behind them all the power that the singer possesses: 'they need the same amount of support from the diaphragm that you give to the big notes.'

The orchestration, which infuses the drama, will be absorbed by most audiences subconsciously. Thus most listeners are unlikely to be aware just how subtle and unostentatious it is: Puccini's leading biographer described 'the astounding sleight of hand with which he manages an incessant interplay of action, characters and atmosphere.' But listen to the effective use of the harp throughout the opera, and perhaps particularly in Act 3. Note also the slightly ponderous use of the woodwind to accompany the philosopher Colline as he sends off his coat to be pawned in Act 4. Rodolfo and Mimì are chiefly accompanied by strings, Musetta by woodwind.

The score was painstakingly prepared. It is unusually detailed and is littered with instructions on dynamics (and everything else). Just before the final two bars of Act 3, when Rodolfo and Mimì are reconciled, the dynamic is marked *ppppp*. There is no word for this unusual marking. It can be interesting to consider whether the conductor has realised the composer's intention and brought out the subtlety of this relative to other gradations of pianissimo, *pp*, *ppp*, and *pppp*. Puccini's response when Ricordi, his publisher, remonstrated with him was: 'As for the *pp*'s and the *ff*'s of the score, if I have overdone them it is because, as Verdi says, when one wants piano, one puts *ppp*.'

Puccini completed *La Bohème* around midnight on 10 December 1895. According to the mythology, his mates were playing cards next door, calling their hands and drinking. All this while Puccini was working away. Puccini then joined them for a binge and a shoot. Considering the painstaking detail and workmanship in the last few pages, this tale is hard to credit. The other tale, that when Puccini finished the last few notes he stood up and wept, is certainly credible – perhaps like the audience weeps when the curtain falls.

Giacomo Puccini (1858–1924) came from a musical family in Lucca, a city in Tuscany. He himself experienced the '*Vie de Bohème*' when a student at the Milan Conservatoire. The prominent Milanese music publisher Giulio Ricordi brought him together with his librettists Luigi Illica (1857–1919) and Giuseppe Giacosa (1847–1906).

Puccini modelled himself on Massenet, France's most popular composer, a mass-producer of pleasing operas including *Manon*. Puccini's first successful opera was in 1893, also based on Abbé Prévost's novel, *Manon Lescaut*.

At a time when the operatic heir to Verdi was being sought, the music critic and writer Bernard Shaw thought that Puccini, with his catching melodies, was the likely candidate. His main rivals, Mascagni and Leoncavallo, the composers of *Cavalleria rusticana* and *I Pagliacci* respectively, lacked sustainability.

La Bohème (1896) was followed by *Tosca* (1900), *Madama Butterfly* (1904), *La Fanciulla del West* (1910), and *Turandot*. *La Rondine* (1917) and *Il Trittico* (1918) were less remunerative.

Puccini was a chain-smoker, who lived a 'fast' life and chased women. He eventually settled down with Elvira, who could only be married once her husband, a schoolfriend of the composer, had died. Elvira was possessive and jealous, and hounded one of the household servants, with whom she thought Puccini was having an affair. This was Doria Manfredi, who had joined Puccini's household five years earlier, aged sixteen. She committed suicide, and Puccini and Elvira had to settle a very difficult lawsuit relating to Elvira's behaviour.

Puccini's great hobby was shooting birds, especially on nearby Lake Massaciuccoli near his villa, quite close to Lucca. He also had a passion for high-speed motor cars and was lucky to survive, with just a broken leg, a crash in which the car plunged down a 15ft embankment before turning over.

His unpatriotic attitude during the First World War made him unpopular. He developed throat cancer, and died in a Brussels clinic on 29 November 1924. *Turandot* was incomplete at the time of his death and was finished by Franco Alfano, a minor composer of operas.

ACT BY ACT

Puccini pointed out that the hardest thing is to decide how to begin an opera – 'how to find its musical atmosphere. Once the opening has been determined, there is nothing more to fear.' So it is not surprising that the music of *La Bohème* immediately grabs our attention and takes us straight into the Latin Quarter of Paris in the 1830s.

Act 1
Christmas, a garret in Paris

The garret is home to four impoverished 'artists': Rodolfo, a poet; Marcello, a painter; Colline, a philosopher; and Schaunard, a musician. It is Christmas Eve, freezing cold, and it has been snowing.

Marcello sits with Rodolfo. He is trying to paint a picture of the Red Sea, but it is too cold: it is as cold, he opines, as his girlfriend Musetta's heart. Rodolfo looks longingly out over the rooftops at the smoke emanating from the chimneys. Desperate for some warmth, they contemplate breaking up the furniture for the fire; instead, Rodolfo sacrifices the manuscript of his latest play, all three acts, one after the other. Colline, the philosopher, returns having tried unsuccessfully to pawn some of his books.

The fire is about finally to flicker out when they are all astonished to see Schaunard, the musician, coming in with food and money. While the others try to relight the fire, he explains that an eccentric Englishman employed him as a musician to play for three days. Besides which, he also succeeded in seducing the maid.

The others lay the table with a newspaper as tablecloth. But Schaunard insists that the food should be put in the larder. As it is Christmas Eve, they should dine out. They decide to have a drink first.

At this moment, Benoît the landlord, who is owed three months' rent, bangs on the door with his demand. They reluctantly invite him in. They get him drunk. They talk about chasing girls and he recounts his conquests. But when he admits to having a wife, they feign moral indignation and kick him out.

When they leave for the café, Rodolfo stays behind for five minutes to finish an article for a journal, 'The Beaver'.[5]

Rodolfo cannot work up any inspiration. He hears a knock at the door. A frail, pale and consumptive girl enters in a state of near-collapse, and explains that her candle has gone out.[6] She faints, dropping her candle and key. He revives her with a drink. She says it was just the effort of climbing the stairs. She asks him to relight the candle and makes to go. Then she remembers that she has forgotten her key. As she comes back in, the wind blows both candles out. In the moonlight, they try to find the key. When Rodolfo comes across it, he puts it in his pocket.

As they continue to search in the darkness, their hands touch: *Che gelida manina, se la lasci riscaldar*[7], in which great tenors linger on the high Cs. In this, perhaps the most famous sequence in all opera, Rodolfo tells her that he is a poet. She replies that her name is Lucia, but they call her Mimì: *Mi chiamano Mimì*.[8] She is a seamstress, who embroiders silk and satin with flowers which, of course, have no perfume. She lives alone in the next-door room.

The others wonder why Rodolfo is taking so long, and they call out for him. He tells them to go on to Café Momus and keep a table. In the moonlight, Rodolfo is overwhelmed with Mimì's beauty – *O soave fanciulla*. There are now just the two of them, and they sing the famous duet, with its theme that is to be associated with Mimì. They kiss – at first she resists, but soon she abandons herself to passion

[5] *Le Castor* ('The Beaver') was the name of a journal in which Mürger, the author of *Vie de Bohème*, wrote.

[6] Opera operates on the brink of the absurd, as the stout coloratura soprano who sings the role of the consumptive Mimì often illustrates.

[7] Caruso, who did not like Melba, is said to have placed a hot potato (or, some say, a sausage) in her hand at this moment when she was playing Mimì to his Rodolfo. Pavarotti subsequently took a dim view of this: 'To me it seems very unprofessional,' he wrote. In another staging, in a freezing theatre during the Second World War, when Rodolfo sang 'Your tiny hand is frozen,' she whispered, 'You're telling Mimì'.

[8] Puccini is very precise in his requirements. The score abounds with his instructions: for example, when Mimì describes 'the first kiss' of spring, she is instructed to sing *Con grande espansione*, and *Con espressione intensa*, indicating broadening out, and great emotional intensity. Such expressions are well beyond the routine ones found in general glossaries of musical terms.

– the score is marked *Con abbandono*. She reaches top C, and he, if not in unison, reaches top E: *Amor!* Puccini was never to surpass the delicate poetry of this love scene.

The real Vie de Bohème

It was not until the 1850s and 1860s that the town planner and Prefect of the Seine, Baron Haussman, bulldozed the quaint and medieval Paris and created the city we know, with its broad boulevards. At the time in which *La Bohème* is set, the city was housing over 40 per cent more people than at the turn of the previous century. The migration into towns of country people in search of work created overwhelming strain on living and working conditions (thirty years later, nearly 70 per cent of the population of Paris originated from elsewhere). By the mid-nineteenth century, only one in five buildings was connected to the public water supply. The tenements had collective lavatories, which were emptied by 2,300 night-soil carts.

Economic desperation and the temptation of higher earnings drove girls such as Mimì and Musetta to prostitution, which was among the most common occupations for single, working-class women. Those not registered to work in the 180–200 licensed brothels lived in abject poverty or in the Saint-Lazare prison, which had separate divisions for under and over thirteen years of age. In Paris in 1846, 13% of babies were abandoned.

The easygoing morality of the 'Vie de bohème' sketches was criticised at the time. Its apologists pointed out that Rodolphe (Rodolfo) is not presented as a hero, and the author does not disguise the folly of the bohemians.

Act 2

Later, in the Latin Quarter

Puccini depicts a colourful crowd scene in the street outside Café Momus, which is doing a brisk trade. Street vendors call their wares and the urchins, students and others mill around. Schaunard tries a horn; Rodolfo buys Mimì a bonnet; Colline is after a frockcoat and then an ancient runic grammar; Marcello just wants a woman. The mothers drag their children away from the itinerant toy seller.

The friends order supper and Rodolfo introduces Mimì. They enjoy their meal and the jollifications.

Musetta, Marcello's former girlfriend enters, expensively attired, with an elderly protector, Alcindoro de Mitonneaux, in tow. People think Musetta is beautiful – and she knows it. In the street, all eyes are on her: *Quando me'n vo soletta per la via.*[9] She treats Alcindoro like a dog and calls him 'Lulu', a name he wishes she would reserve for intimacies. The crowd sees the opportunity to fleece him.

Musetta has only recently split up from Marcello, who is deeply upset with her because she is like a weather-vane. To her annoyance, Marcello ignores her, so she throws a plate on the ground to draw attention to herself.

Musetta, who is really the star of Act 2, pretends to be addressing Alcindoro while in fact she is addressing Marcello. She pretends her shoe is hurting her and orders Alcindoro to run quickly to the cobbler: *Corri va corri! Presto, va, va!* Musetta and Marcello embrace. When the waiter brings the bill, they have run out of cash, but Musetta gets him to add their bill to Alcindoro's. Some soldiers on patrol march along, led by their drum-major. They all joyfully parade off with the soldiers, leaving the exasperated Alcindoro, who has returned from the cobbler, to pick up the two bills presented to him by the waiter.[10]

[9] Puccini got the idea for Musetta's waltz when he was out shooting in his boat, which was gently rocked by the waves.

[10] Opera-goers attending *La Bohème* at Covent Garden in May 2012 were dismayed to be told that the performance would be interrupted so that a TV station could film a celebrity attempting to conduct a rerun of Act 2. Opera-goers are increasingly used to productions which show little fidelity to the composer's intentions. Lengthy interruptions are however a new and disrespectful development. Puccini intended his opera to be performed as a single uninterrupted work (the story is, after all, very dramatic). Top performers might be allowed a bow, and an occasional encore.

Act 3

February, next to the Barrière d'Enfer, a customs post on the walls of Paris

It is February. Snow falls. Paris is waking up, and street-sweepers, milkmaids and peasants arrive through one of the Paris Barrières, or city gates, next to an inn sign painted by Marcello.

Mimì, distressed and coughing, comes searching for Marcello, who is lodging at the inn with Musetta (she teaches singing to the patrons, while he is painting signboards).

Mimì (reaching high B flat) asks for help with her relationship with Rodolfo, who is so jealous and possessive. Marcello suggests that Mimì and Rodolfo should split up. She hides when Rodolfo appears. Rodolfo criticises Mimì as a *civetta* – a coquette – who shows off her ankle to every dandy viscount. But he loves her. However, his freezing garret is totally unsuitable for someone as ill as her, and he is so frightened for her. Mimì overhears this and is horrified.

Mimì's coughing reveals her hiding place. Marcello hears Musetta flirting and rushes into the inn. Mimì tells Rodolfo that they must part, although without bitterness: *Addio senza rancor* (Puccini at first thickens her sound with a solo clarinet an octave below). She will return to her small room where she dreamt of spring. He should arrange for her possessions to be returned to her, but he may keep the pink bonnet as a souvenir. Ironically, while they sing poetically of love, their dreams and morning-rise – *Addio, dolce svegliar* – Musetta and Marcello have a rip-roaring row about her flirting. Mimì and Rodolfo are reconciled, to the sound of a solo violin, an octave above.

Act 4

The garret in Paris

The orchestra takes us straight back to the original garret, where Marcello and Rodolfo pretend to work, but talk of Musetta and Mimì. Schaunard and Colline appear with some bread and a herring. They fool around and pretend to have a feast and a ball. They drown their sorrows. Colline and Schaunard have a mock duel.[11]

Their antics are suddenly interrupted by Musetta. She says that Mimì is climbing slowly up the stairs, and is very ill. Musetta had heard that Mimì had left her protector, the viscount that she had taken up with, and she came across her in the street. There is nothing left to eat or drink in the garret. Mimì is frozen and coughing. Schaunard fears she will be dead in half an hour. Rodolfo tells her not to talk but to rest.

Musetta rips off her earrings and tells the others to pawn them and fetch a doctor. She goes to get a muff, which Mimì craves. Colline sadly, but generously, gives his old coat over to be pawned, with the music providing the right tone for the dénouement.

They sense that it is time to leave Rodolfo and Mimì to each other.[12]

Mimì pretends to be asleep so that she can be alone with Rodolfo: *Sono andati? Fingevo di dormire.* They have so much to talk about. (This has been described as 'sadness incarnate' and 'one of the most inspired melodies that ever sprang into Puccini's head.')

The musical themes of the earlier acts recur. The lovers recall their first meeting and how they held hands together in the dark: we hear echoes of *Che gelida manina.* Rodolfo shows Mimì the bonnet, the souvenir. She is convulsed with a spasm, coughing. Marcello and Musetta return with the muff and a cordial; they say that the doctor is coming. Musetta gives Mimì the muff and pretends it is from Rodolfo.

Mimì sinks and fades away. Musetta heats the cordial and prays. The others know what has happened. Eventually, it dawns on Rodolfo that Mimì is dead.

---

[11] The props in this scene can create problems. A stage hand, who was asked to provide a herring, forgot that he was boiling a fish on the stage doorkeeper's gas ring and overcooked it. When thrown around, the fish disintegrated, and showered the singers with powder. Likewise, an old cushion that Schaunard used to fend off Colline disintegrated when struck with the poker.

[12] Away from an audience, the company can be allowed some fun. In rehearsal, Sir Thomas Beecham once called for more volume from his dying Mimì. 'Don't you realise that it is difficult to sing lying down?' she asked. Beecham replied, 'I seem to recollect that I have given some of my best performances in that position.'

PUCCINI: *TOSCA*

THE OPERA AND ITS COMPOSER

Today, it is hopefully unusual for a terrorist threat to disrupt an opera première. On 14 January 1900, it was less so. In recent years, bombs had gone off in theatres in Barcelona and Pisa.

The Queen and members of the Government were expected for the first night of *Tosca* at Rome's Constanzi Theatre. There had been a rumour of an attack. Indeed, the conductor Leopoldo Mugnone,[1] who had himself experienced the Barcelona incident, was told to play the national anthem if there should be one. He did not. The noise of latecomers during the start so worried him that he left the podium soon after the curtain went up. Fortunately, it was only a hoax, and the performance resumed.

Puccini's opera is based on Sardou's 'blood and thunder' melodrama *La Tosca* (1884), which was written for the great actress Sarah Bernhardt. Although the sadism and brutality in Puccini's opera was frowned upon at the time – the critics gave it a rather lukewarm reception – it quickly became an outstanding success. The public flocked to it then, and have ever since. It is not often one gets, in one evening, torture, an attempted rape, a murder, an execution and two suicides; and a police chief fantasising during a 'Te Deum' in a church. It is not surprising that it has attracted more than its fair share of mirth.

Puccini had thought of making use of Sardou's play ten years before his *Tosca* première. He was prompted to return to it, largely because of the vogue for 'realism': Mascagni's *Cavalleria rusticana* had been a great success ten years before, as had Leoncavallo's *Pagliacci* subsequently. And the play would make a good opera. Verdi had indicated that, had he been younger, he would have been interested in using it.

---

[1] Mugnone was the distinguished conductor of several premières, including *Cavalleria rusticana*. Beecham thought him the best Italian conductor of his time.

The right to turn it into an opera had been given to another composer, Franchetti. But, with utter knavery and dishonesty, Puccini's publisher Giulio Ricordi, persuaded him that it was a totally unsuitable subject, so he relinquished his rights. Ricordi immediately signed up Puccini.

Victorien Sardou (1831–1908), a loquacious raconteur – Puccini found it difficult to get a word in edgeways – was a very successful French dramatist in the second half of the 19th century. His output of more than 70 plays has attracted mixed views: the music critic and dramatist George Bernard Shaw considered them lightweight, and invented the term 'Sardoudledom' to characterise them. A leading 20th-century authority on Puccini has described the ingredients of Sardou's *La Tosca* as 'sex, sadism, religion and art, mixed by a master-chef with the whole dish served on the platter of an important historical event.'

Sardou recommended 'torturing the women' as an important ingredient of a successful play. There are four corpses in *Tosca*, and Puccini suggested to his publisher that perhaps Sardou, who was known as 'the Caligula of the theatre', would insist on killing Spoletta too.

The opera took Puccini three years to compose. He collaborated with Luigi Illica and Giuseppe Giacosa, in the improbable and quarrelsome team which also created *La Bohème* and *Madama Butterfly*. Illica, who was a rough republican, and who connived in the deception of Franchetti, produced the structure and first draft. Giacosa, a smooth socialite, versified and polished it despite at first thinking that Sardou's play was very unsuitable, being 'a drama of coarse emotional situations ... all plot and no poetry.' In his view, Sardou's final act was 'one interminable duet.' Even when Puccini had finished, Ricordi panicked about the third act and Puccini had to calm him down.

It has been rightly suggested that 'where erotic passion, sensuality, tenderness, pathos and despair meet and fuse, Puccini was an unrivalled master.' As well as being profoundly moved, we can leave the theatre humming one of those incandescent lyrical phrases, brief, simple and thus so memorable, from arias such as *Vissi d'arte*, *E lucevan le stelle* and *O dolci mani*. *Tosca* is surely secure in its place in the top ten operas.

(More on the life of Puccini can be found on page 380.)

WHO'S WHO AND WHAT'S WHAT

The story below is based on the libretto. Certain directors may amend opera stories to suit their production.

Most unusually for opera, the action is set on a specific day at a specific time. It takes place in Rome, during sixteen hours overnight on 14 June 1800.

Cesare Angelotti, a high-profile political prisoner on the run, rushes into a church, seeking sanctuary. The **sacristan** has been cleaning brushes for the artist **Mario Cavaradossi**, who is painting a portrait of Mary Magdalen. **Floria Tosca**, herself a prima donna, is in love with Cavaradossi and is rightly extremely jealous and suspicious of the 'lady' he has depicted in the painting. He explains that art blends contrasting beauties: *Recondita armonia*.

By helping Angelotti's escape, Cavaradossi becomes implicated, and falls into the clutches of **Baron Scarpia**, the police chief, who is on the scent of the fugitive. Scarpia fancies Tosca. In the **Te Deum scene**, to the background of the religious ceremony, he relishes catching the prisoner and having the woman: for him, the rope, for her, bed: *Va, Tosca!*

He orders his henchman, the police agent **Spoletta**, to find, arrest and torture Cavaradossi. Angelotti is found and commits suicide. The sound of the preparations for the execution of Cavaradossi is too much for Tosca, who has lived for art and for love, as she explains in one of the most famous arias in opera: ***Vissi d'arte, Vissi d'amore***. She barters her body for her lover's life. However, Scarpia explains that there will have to be a mock execution, and he writes a pardon and a passport to enable her and Cavaradossi to escape after this. She then stabs him when he moves forward to rape her.

Before dawn at the Castel Sant'Angelo, a **shepherd boy** passes with his flock, and various church bells chime. With one hour left before the **execution**, Cavaradossi bribes the **jailer** in return for permission to write a letter to Tosca. At the moment of death, he has never been so much in love: *E lucevan le stelle*. Tosca arrives with the pardon and passport. Cavaradossi is amazed when he hears what she did with her sweet hands: *O dolci mani*.

Cavaradossi is brought out for what Tosca expects is to be a mock execution. But Scarpia has played this trick successfully before: the execution is real. After Cavaradossi is shot, and Tosca discovers the truth, she leaps over the battlements.

As well as a chorus of clergy, soldiers and so on, other members of the cast include a torturer, a judge and **Sciarrone**, a gendarme.

THE INTERVAL: TALKING POINTS

Italy in 1900, at the time of *Tosca*

Italy was politically unstable following its unification, which was only finally completed in 1871. The country comprised an uneasy amalgam of the industrial north and the feudal south, with the middle of the country predominantly agricultural. Political shenanigans were rife, involving sordid bargains between local interests, and promises of virtually anything if it would secure a parliamentary vote. There was a colonial failure in Ethiopia. A demonstration in Milan resulted in a massacre. Seven months after the *Tosca* première, King Umberto, who had survived various assassination threats and attempts, was finally shot by an Italian-American.

Tosca: the historical background

Like many dramatists, Sardou manipulated history and his characters to create an 'illusion of authenticity that still deceives many commentators.' The setting is an amalgam of the Roman and Neapolitan ('Parthenopean') Republics, two out of a series of short-lived constitutions which followed Napoleon's invasion of Italy in 1796.

The Republics were excessively revolutionary or just ineffective, and were largely a front for the French, whose domination was resented. An anti-revolutionary alliance of Crown, Church and peasantry overthrew them. There were fearful reprisals. Nelson, with his mistress Lady Hamilton, played a significant and far from creditable role in suppressing the Parthenopean Republic.

In Rome, Papal rule, as symbolised in *Tosca* by Scarpia, was restored. However, on 14 June 1800, the specific date of *Tosca*, Rome, far from being tyrannised by a Scarpia, was actually lawless and chaotic.

The battle of Marengo took place that day. In a lightning campaign in May–June 1800, Napoleon, who by then was First Consul and keen to build on his position, crossed the Alps. He got behind the Austrians, who for years had dominated northern Italy. He was attacked by them on 14 June at Marengo, near to Turin. The battle went badly for Napoleon at first – hence the news in Act 1 of *Tosca* – but in the afternoon the French recovered the position and won, as we hear in Act 2. There were no mobiles in those days.

The victory was fortunate for Napoleon, whose position in Paris would have been severely weakened had he lost at Marengo. He in fact strengthened his image of 'statesmanship' by not reinstating the Roman and Parthenopean Republics. Later, when he became Emperor he distributed kingdoms in Italy to his relatives and supporters. His young son was created King of Rome, while the Papal States continued to be ruled by the subservient Pope.

Puccini's place as a composer

Puccini wrote *Tosca* at the turn of the century, when music was experiencing a considerable revolution. This has resulted in his operas being criticised for not moving the art forward, and thus being anachronistic. Fauré, the leading French composer who most of us know for *The Requiem*, regarded the Paris première of *Tosca* in 1903 as an important event because 'of Sardou, the librettist, and the bizarre school of music to which the composer Puccini belongs. It consists of three or four chaps who have conjured up a neo-Italian art which is easily the most miserable thing in existence.' In a letter to his wife, Fauré condemned the output of Puccini and his contemporaries, the composers of *Pagliacci* and *Cavalleria rusticana*, for producing 'a kind of soup, where every style from every country gets all mixed up. And everywhere, alas! they are welcomed with open arms.'

And yet *Tosca* is in the top ten of top-performing operas. Although popularity (on its own) is no measure of artistry, there comes a point where criticism begins to look foolish and out of touch. Taunts about Puccini being bourgeois and commercial – *Tosca* has even been described as 'a shabby little shocker' – are sometimes more redolent of envy than objective criticism.

Perhaps because *Tosca* is as explicit and exciting as a piece of good television, with many of the same ingredients – it has been produced as a self-standing film several times – it cannot begin to claim the same stature as a piece of abstract instrumental music by (say) Beethoven, which is on a different intellectual level.

Puccini is modern in his extraordinary sense of theatre: the conclusion of Act 1, the Te Deum scene with its procession and chorus, has been 'reckoned one of the most impressive finali in all opera.'

There are lesser details: each act begins with an attention-grabbing orchestral phrase: you must put aside your glass of wine! And each act ends with a spine-chilling, devastating declaration: *Tosca, mi fai dimenticare Iddio!* ('Tosca, you make me forget God'); *E avanti a lui tremava tutta Roma!* ('All Rome trembled before him'); *O Scarpia, avanti a Dio!* ('Scarpia, let's meet before God!')[2]

---

[2] Callas told a pupil, 'You must give the public the shivers.' Enormous effort goes into making the production effective. For the Callas recording, Tito Gobbi had to sing his Act 1 music 30 times, working on colour and inflection even in individual syllables; and she worked on the phrase *E avanti a lui tremava tutta Roma* for half an hour. For Domingo's film, the filming of the first-act duet between Tosca and Cavaradossi took nineteen hours, from noon till 7am.

Puccini's attention to detail: the music and the score

It is beyond doubt that Puccini, the 'full-blooded opera composer, more familiar than any of his contemporaries with the secrets of theatrical effect and success', was a consummate craftsman.

This is seen in the musical characterisation of the cast, the atmosphere, and the changes of mood on stage. In an attempt to follow Wagner, he uses around 60 musical labels for situations and objects. But *Tosca* is 'musical drama', not Wagnerian music drama. This may account for its immortality.

Puccini's scores were painstakingly prepared. The audience is not expected to pick up the detail, but, for example, in the last minute of Act 2, following the stabbing of Scarpia, the cellos and basses are, within just six bars, instructed to play *con passione*, *con anima* and *col canto*. A few moments later the strings are told to play *il più piano possibile*, 'as quiet as possible' against a gong playing *ppp* and the bass drum *pppp*. A few bars later, the instruction *trattenuto* (holding back) precedes a *ritardando* (slowing up), and this is followed by *lontanissimi* (fading away) on the side drum. It can be interesting to consider whether the conductor has realised the composer's intention, and brought out these subtle gradations.

An opera for stars

In *Tosca*, Puccini has provided a means for great singers to star. Enrico Caruso was a famous Cavaradossi. Maria Callas, like her rival Renata Tebaldi, was a great Tosca;[3] Tito Gobbi was a memorable Scarpia. In films, producers such as Franco Zeffirelli created an unforgettable dramatic experience.

Audiences used to conventional grand divas in massive robes, walking sticks, gloves and feathered hats were captivated by Callas's sensuality and sexuality. At one moment, she could be torn with jealousy; in the next, she could also plumb new depths of tenderness. She 'revealed depths in the role that few suspected were there.' She made the *Vissi d'arte* into an integral part of the musical drama, not just the

---

[3] The first record Callas's mother bought her was of the *Vissi d'arte*.

showpiece about which Puccini himself felt uncomfortable, because he worried that it delayed the forward drive of the action.

Callas as Tosca

The physical requirements for males are rather different. In one production, Pavarotti was expected to be up on scaffolding painting a vast canvas. There was a logistical problem: how to get him down to perform the love duet with Tosca. (For Pavarotti, the problem was medical: he had a bad knee.) So the producer arranged for him to be on the ground painting a sketch of the much larger painting which was up on the easel. Pavarotti observed, 'Sometimes you must remind designers and directors they are working with human beings, not acrobats.'

Jinxed?

Because *Tosca* is so dramatic and effective,[4] it has attracted ribald mirth and has facilitated more legends than other operas.

---

[4] The reader can decide whether to be as enthusiastic as Gustav Kobbé who considered that Scarpia's death is 'a wonderful scene – one of the greatest in all drama.'

The firing squad is known to have 'shot' Tosca rather than Cavaradossi – much to the confusion of the unrehearsed soldiers, who, having been told to exit with the principals, all leapt over the battlements after Tosca. And Tosca has been known to mistakenly kick a pile of cannonballs on the battlements; being rubber balls painted black, they bounced slowly down into the orchestra pit and stalls.

The highly dramatic scene at the end of Act 2 lends itself to things going wrong, because of the candles. Tosca has been known to set fire to Scarpia's wig. Callas's wig also caught fire. Galina Vishnevskaya leant back against the table just before stabbing Scarpia and her wig touched one of the candles. She was surprised that instead of falling down dead, he went for her hair. He pulled off her wig, and Placido Domingo, who tells the story, and was waiting in the wings, doused it with the 'wine'.

Less seriously, a Scarpia found his trousers falling down, perhaps conveniently, when chasing Tosca around. Earlier in the scene, at the cry of 'Vittoria', Domingo flung his head back and broke the nose of a supernumerary behind him.

Maria Jeritza walked towards the sofa where she was supposed to sing the *Vissi d'arte*. She slipped and sang from a prone position. Puccini had said that that is how it was to be sung; that is, Tosca should address her aria not to Scarpia but to heaven.

ACT BY ACT

Act 1

The Church of Sant' Andrea della Valle

The opera opens in the church, where an easel with a large painting indicates that an artist has been at work. The scene is set with three ferocious chords, played as loud as the orchestra can. These, and the 'whole tone' scale on which they are based, are later to be associated with the sinister character of the police chief. A fugitive rushes in. He finds a key at the base of a statue of the Madonna, and quickly lets himself into a side chapel belonging to the Attavanti family.

The comic sacristan wanders in with the artist's brushes, which he has been cleaning; he prays as soon as the Angelus sounds. Mario Cavaradossi appears and reveals his painting, a portrait of a beautiful Magdalen. The sacristan observes that it is modelled on a blonde blue-eyed girl who comes regularly to pray and leave a basket of provisions. Cavaradossi compares the face on a locket with that in the painting. He reassures himself that when he is painting the Magdalen, his mind is actually thinking of the dark, black-eyed Floria Tosca, the celebrated singer: art blends contrasting beauties, *Recondite armonia*. His sentiments shock the sacristan who asks to be excused, but has his eye on the basket of food.

The fugitive emerges from his hiding place. Cavaradossi recognises him as Cesare Angelotti, formerly a Consul of the Roman Republic, and for a long time incarcerated in the Castel Sant'Angelo.

When Tosca is heard arriving, Cavaradossi tells the jailbird to hide and gives him the food. Tosca sees the picture and jealously concludes that Cavardossi loves the blonde woman. When he tries to kiss her, she protests that they should not do it in front of a statue of the Madonna. She arranges to meet him after her concert performance that evening. They can make love by the light of the full moon in his villa in the woods. She upbraids him for not being enthusiastic enough, and describes the romantic nature of their trysting place.

Cavardossi really wants to get on with his painting, but Tosca continues to take exception to the picture. She recognises that the model for the Magdalen is a member of the Attavanti family. She is annoyed by the eyes and, before leaving, insists that he should paint them black like hers.

As soon as she is gone, Angelotti emerges again and explains that his sister has hidden some clothes for him to use as a disguise. Cavaradossi now understands why the woman used to come to pray so fervently: it was the love of a sister. They describe the evil nature of the vicious, but ostensibly pious, chief of police, Baron Scarpia. Cavaradossi tells Angelotti to get out through the chapel to his villa and, if necessary, hide in the well. He will accompany him.

To celebrate a defeat of Napoleon, the sacristan says that there is going to be a Te Deum, and that evening Tosca will sing at a gala concert at the Palazzo Farnese.

A gun sounds, indicating that the prisoner's escape has been discovered. At this moment, there is a hush: the fearsome Scarpia, who has designs on Tosca, arrives with Spoletta, his police agent, in search of the prisoner. He discovers a fan and the basket, notices the Attavanti coat of arms on the fan, and the lady in the picture. When told by the sacristan that Cavaradossi painted it, Scarpia concludes that he, Tosca's lover, must have assisted the escaper. When Tosca herself returns, Scarpia knows that, just as Iago used a handkerchief (to deceive Othello), he can use the fan to trap Tosca into revealing the whereabouts of his prey.

First, Scarpia conceals himself behind a pillar. Tosca has returned to tell Cavaradossi that on account of the forthcoming gala they cannot have their tryst. She is surprised to find that Cavaradossi has gone.

Scarpia approaches her, *Tosca Divina*. With the fan, he taunts her that the Marchioness of Attavanti, the lady in the painting, is Cavaradossi's lover. At this, Tosca vows revenge: the Marchioness shall not have Cavaradossi tonight. Scarpia, feigning to be shocked at such thoughts being given expression in a church, tells his henchman to follow her. As the procession sings the Te Deum for the supposed victory over the armies of Napoleon, Scarpia relishes catching the prisoner and seducing the woman: for him, the rope, for her, bed: *Va Tosca* ('Go Tosca, there is room in your heart for Scarpia'). He concludes dramatically, *Tosca, mi fai dimenticare Iddio* ('Tosca, you make me forget God').

Act 2

The Farnese Palace

At supper in his apartment, Scarpia reckons that, with Tosca as his bird of prey, both Cavaradossi and Angelotti will have been caught and despatched by dawn. The sound of the gala performance in honour of the Austrian victory can be heard in the background. Scarpia muses on his personal preference for sadistic conquest rather than tender courtship.

His henchman Spoletta reports that they followed Tosca to a cottage. They picked up a defiant Cavaradossi but lost Angelotti. Cavaradossi is brought in and refuses to admit any complicity. The gala, now with Tosca performing, continues in the background. Scarpia demands to know the whereabouts of Angelotti.

Tosca rushes in, in time to hear Cavaradossi being tortured in an adjacent chamber. Despite the blood spurting at every twist of an iron ring on his head, Cavaradossi refuses to answer, and orders Tosca not to do so. But the horrified Tosca eventually reveals that Angelotti is in the well. Cavaradossi is brought in in a state of collapse[5] and reproaches Tosca for submitting.

The news that Napoleon has actually won, and not lost, the battle (of Marengo) is announced. Cavaradossi shouts 'Vittoria' in Scarpia's face, but is sent off to be hanged.

Tosca is left with Scarpia, who sits down to supper. She asks him his price to save Cavaradossi: *Quanto?* The police chief has been aroused by her behaviour, and her loathing just increases his determination to have her. The march to the scaffold is heard, and Scarpia says that preparations for the execution are in hand.

In one of the best-known arias, in which she reaches top B flat, the forlorn Tosca sings 'I lived for art. I lived for love': *Vissi d'arte. Vissi d'amore.* She tried to be religious; why has the Lord repaid her in this ghastly way? Spoletta returns and announces that Angelotti killed himself when they found him in the well.

---

[5] This moment of drama is prone to disaster. Pavarotti was reassured by the director that the antique stool on which he was expected to collapse had been reinforced with steel. On the night, the Tosca was so involved that, instead of rushing to embrace him, she landed on top. The stool caved in, to the dismay of cast and stage management; fortunately the audience thought that the mid-stage heap was intentional. Occasionally a Cavaradossi has been so enraged by Scarpia's sadism that he has gone for him. One, Tito Schipa, had to be restrained by Spoletta from attacking him: 'Hold him down,' the Scarpia yelled. Indeed, Tosca herself has been known to draw blood when she skewers Scarpia: Callas stabbed Gobbi, and unfortunately the blade of the knife did not retract. He gasped a horrified 'My God' and carried on.

Tosca submits to Scarpia's demand for her, but insists on assurance and a safe conduct for herself and Cavaradossi, on the road to Civitavecchia.[6] Scarpia says that it will be necessary to have a sham execution and gives an order for Cavaradossi to be shot, significantly, 'as they did with Count Palmieri.' While Scarpia is writing out[7] the safe conduct, Tosca gets hold of a knife from the table. As he gives her the safe conduct, he lurches forward to take her: *Tosca, finalmente mia!* ('Tosca, at last you are mine!'). *Questo è il bacio di Tosca!* ('That is Tosca's kiss!') she replies as she drives the knife into him.

While he suffocates in his own blood, she taunts him. All Rome trembled before him! *E avanti a lui tremava tutta Roma!*

She calmly tidies herself, and takes two candles from the table and puts one on either side of Scarpia's dead body. She takes a crucifix from the wall and places it on his breast. She goes out and shuts the door.

Act 3

Castel Sant'Angelo

It is before 4am. A shepherd boy passes with his flock, and various church bells call matins. Cavaradossi, under escort, is brought up to the platform on the ramparts. He gives the jailer his ring in return for his last wish: to write a letter. At the moment that he must die, his mind is on Tosca: he has never been so much in love. The orchestra depicts his thought processes, which he himself expresses in the famous, 'emotionally charged' aria, *E lucevan le stelle* ('When the stars were shining brightly').[8]

Spoletta brings Tosca, who has come with the safe conduct. She tells Cavaradossi about Scarpia's demise, reaching top C in the process. He is amazed that she killed him with her sweet hands: *O dolci*

[6] Civitavecchia is around 50 miles from Rome, for which it has long been the main port.

[7] Some Scarpias take this opportunity to write messages. Sigurd Björling once wrote to Birgit Nilsson, 'Today you are, if that is possible, better than ever. Your Scarpia', making it rather difficult for her to continue loathing him.

[8] Puccini was virtually wholly responsible for this famous aria, 'for composing the music, for causing the words to be written, and for declining expert advice from his librettists to throw the result into the waste-paper basket.'

mani. She explains that there is to be a mock execution. After this, they will escape to Civitavecchia, where a ship awaits them. They sing of love and freedom; reaching top B, she tells him he must act the part very realistically, as she would on stage, and lie still until she calls him.

The bell sounds 4am. The firing squad prepares. Tosca is nervous. The soldiers fire. Spoletta stops the sergeant from delivering the coup de grace. While the squad departs, she worries that Cavaradossi will move. Then, leaning over the body, she is horrified to find that he is actually dead.

People are heard below shouting: Scarpia's murder has been discovered. Spoletta roars that she will pay for his life. She retorts 'with my own', as she shoves him away. She hurls herself over the battlements, crying *O Scarpia, avanti a Dio!* ('Scarpia! Let's meet before God!').[9]

---

[9] This is the famous moment when the fat soprano has been known to bounce on the mattress and reappear above the battlements several times. One soprano was so disliked that the New York stage crew deliberately substituted a trampoline in the place of the mattress, thus ensuring fifteen bounces in various positions. There have been more serious health and safety issues: Kiri te Kanawa badly hurt her back when making the leap.

PUCCINI:
MADAMA BUTTERFLY

THE OPERA AND ITS COMPOSER

Early in Puccini's opera, we hear that Cio-Cio-San is called 'Madame Butterfly' because she possesses all the delicacy, lightness and transparency of the fluttering tiny creature. In her early years, Maria Callas was invited to sing the part for her début at the Metropolitan Opera. To everybody's amazement, she turned the opportunity down: she reckoned that at nearly thirteen stone it would not work. How wise she was.

Much later, when a slimmer Callas sang in Chicago, a member of the audience commented, 'I never want to hear her Butterfly again … I'll end up liking this dreadful opera.' We can wonder whether it was Butterfly, the geisha,[1] which the individual did not like, or whether he was offended by Puccini's subtle portrayal of the arrogant cultural superiority assumed by 'the West'. It is surely amazing that music which quotes several times, and most disrespectfully, 'The Star-spangled Banner' can be found at the very top of lists of much-loved and most popular operas in the USA.

The libretto of *Madama Butterfly* is based on a story, almost certainly a true one, published in an 1898 magazine.[2] The author was a Philadelphia lawyer, John Luther Long. The Far East had opened up to Western trade in the second half of the 19th century. Japan was

---

[1] Geishas are traditional entertainers performing various Japanese arts, such as music and dance. The confusion with prostitutes particularly arises from the use of the term 'geisha girls' by American soldiers during the Occupation of Japan after the Second World War. Prostitutes wear the bow of the sash in front of their kimono whereas geishas wear it at the back. During the nineteenth century, there was a curious custom whereby visiting foreign naval officers were permitted to enter into temporary marriages with geishas, an arrangement which would terminate when the period of leave was up.

[2] The story has been traced back further, to 1887, to the French writer Pierre Loti's romance *Madame Chrysanthème*.

401

now topical, sufficiently so for Gilbert & Sullivan to produce their operetta *The Mikado* in the mid-1880s.[3]

Puccini, who was most careful in his choice of opera libretti, had for some time been searching for a suitable subject to follow *Tosca*. He had even had a serious look at the possibilities of Victor Hugo's novel *Les Misérables* but rejected the idea. A one-act stage version of Long's story, by David Belasco[4], was seen by the stage manager of Covent Garden who suggested that Puccini should come and see it. Thereafter, the negotiations with Belasco took nine months.

Luigi Illica, who was a rough republican, produced the structure and first draft of the libretto; Giuseppe Giacosa, a smooth socialite, versified and polished it. This improbable and quarrelsome team, the 'Holy Trinity' (as the music publisher Giulio Ricordi called them), had also created Puccini's *Manon Lescaut*, *La Bohème* and *Tosca*.

The première of *Madama Butterfly* took place at La Scala on 17 February 1904. Rosina Storchio was Cio-Cio-San, Giovanni Zenatello was Pinkerton, and Giuseppe de Luca was Sharpless. Puccini was very confident of its success. But complete pandemonium broke out in what was to be one of the sensational failures in the history of opera. Puccini withdrew it and revised it. He cut some of the material dealing with the wedding in Act 1, and also provided for an interval, which some today regard as a mistake, between the night and the dawn in Act 2.

Three months after the première, a revised version was staged with great success at the Teatro Grande in Brescia, a large city between Milan and Lake Garda. This was received with tremendous acclaim: *Un bel dì*, the letter scene, the flower scenes, and the Humming Chorus were encored; Puccini was called ten times. The opera has been a triumph ever since.

On the surface, the story is a very ordinary tale about typical behaviour

---

[3] In 1868, the Emperor or 'Mikado' was reinstated as supreme authority in Japan. For 650 years, real power had been vested in the Shogun, a military dictator, who operated from modern-day Tokyo, and the Mikado, who was housed in Kyoto, held a largely titular position.

[4] David Belasco (1853–1931) was born in San Francisco, of Jewish origin. At first a clown, he became an actor, prolific writer, director, producer, and impresario. Puccini later used his *The Girl of the Golden West* for *La Fanciulla del West*.

in a seaport. The drama, however, is created by the use of a technique familiar to the ancient Greeks, known as 'dramatic irony'. From the outset, the audience is 'in the secret of what is inevitable', first, that Pinkerton will desert Madame Butterfly, and then that he has deserted her. This should be apparent to her, but she does not understand, and does not want to understand. Apart from its melody[5], the effectiveness of *Un bel dì* is attributable to this dramatic irony. And later, Puccini underlines the irony by providing the beautiful Humming Chorus (at the end of Act 2 Part 1), as an interlude to enable the audience to be able to sit and contemplate, unencumbered by words, the inevitable drama which is about to unfold, and compare the vulnerability of one protagonist and the heartlessness and insensitivity of the other.

Puccini's sense of theatre is unsurpassable. The thinness and simplicity of his orchestration, designed to enhance the exotic atmosphere of Japan[6], can lead a listener to underrate the music, but those listening carefully will appreciate the quality of his craftsmanship. The Chicago resident completely failed to appreciate these aspects when he called *Madama Butterfly* 'dreadful'.

(More on the life of Puccini can be found on page 380.)

WHO'S WHO AND WHAT'S WHAT

The story below is based on the libretto. Certain directors may amend opera stories to suit their production.

At a residence high above the harbour of Nagasaki,[7] **Goro**, a marriage broker and pimp, arranges a sham 'Japanese' wedding between

[5] The listener can hear how the melody moves by very simple intervals, generally a feature of good tunes. Only one melodic leap is complex, a 7th when Butterfly says that, when Pinkerton sails in, she will not go down to the harbour to meet him, but will proudly await him in the house.

[6] Puccini quotes tunes from Japan, and evokes sounds and tunes in the 'Japanese manner', especially with bells, woodwind and the use of high-pitched timbres.

[7] Nagasaki, a natural harbour surrounded by hills of about 1,500ft, is well positioned as a seaport on the south-western coast of Japan. Having been virtually closed to foreigners for centuries, the port was opened in 1859 and grew enormously in the subsequent years. It was the subject of an atomic bomb attack on 9 August 1945.

the fifteen-year-old **Cio-Cio-San** (known as **Madame Butterfly**) and **Lieutenant Benjamin Franklin Pinkerton** of the US gunboat *Abraham Lincoln*.

Sharpless, the US Consul, can see that, in this case, the outcome will be disastrous.

The 'marriage' is conducted by the **Imperial Commissioner** and the **registrar**. It is attended by various relatives of Butterfly. Her uncle **the Bonzo** (a Buddhist monk) breaks up the ceremony and curses Butterfly because she has visited the Mission and converted to Pinkerton's religion. As a result, her people treat her as an outcast.

Meanwhile, to the glorious love duet *Ah! Dolce notte!* ('Oh Night of rapture, hasten to enfold us'), the happy couple retires to consummate the 'marriage'.

After Pinkerton returns to his ship, deserting her, Butterfly subsists alone with her servant **Suzuki**, and gives birth to a baby boy. It seems that Sharpless is providing limited finance, although he is unaware of the child.

Three years pass by. Goro tries to persuade Butterfly to marry the rich **Prince Yamadori** but, despite Suzuki's pessimism, she, now proud to be an American, is confident that her 'husband' will reappear one fine day: *Un bel dì*. He does eventually; but with his American wife **Kate**, who says she will take the child and look after it properly.

Butterfly agrees that Pinkerton can have the boy if he returns in half an hour. By then, she has stabbed herself with a dagger that was given to her father, on which is inscribed, 'Death with honour is better than life with dishonour.' Before doing this, in an emotional farewell, she gives the boy the US flag and a doll.

THE INTERVAL: TALKING POINTS

The first night fiasco

Puccini, who was still hobbling around as a consequence of a very serious motor crash, was supremely confident in the success of his opera, so much so that he uncharacteristically invited his close relatives along to witness the first night. However, *Madama Butterfly* was received with a crescendo of abuse which led, at the end of the evening, to complete uproar and chaos.

It seems probable that the disruption was organised by Puccini's opponents, using the 'claque' who were paid to applaud or hiss. Their boss was highly remunerated by actors and management, but Puccini habitually refused to participate in this racket.

After Act 1, there were hisses and catcalls. In the second act, Butterfly's kimono billowed up, and there was a shout of 'Butterfly is pregnant', a comment on Puccini's personal reputation.

Particular venom was reserved for an orchestral intermezzo at the end of Butterfly's vigil. This is omitted in the version we hear today. The producer Tito Ricordi had accompanied it with stage scenery which included twittering birds as dawn came up. The audience started imitating the twittering and eventually La Scala became more like a menagerie than an opera house. The end of the opera was greeted with hoots and howls. 'The opera is dead,' wrote one journalist.

Puccini cancelled the second night, withdrew the opera and returned his fee.

He made various changes, including slimming down Act 1. His earlier decision to compress the opera into two acts, the second lasting an hour and a half, had caused friction between him and his librettist Giacosa, who had regarded it as 'interminable, monotonous and boring', and had warned him of the consequences.

It was indeed far too long for the attention span of a La Scala audience: Verdi had appreciated the impatience of Italian audiences, and was concerned that the first act of his *Otello* lasted 42 minutes, as he said, 'two minutes more than is necessary.'

Puccini's achievement

Music was undergoing a considerable revolution at the time of Puccini. At the time of the *Madama Butterfly* première, Schoenberg was almost 30, and within ten years, Stravinsky's *The Rite of Spring* would be performed. By the time Puccini died in 1924, and bequeathed us his twelve operas, his style was an anachronism, and he tends to get a bad press from musical professionals. Fauré, who many know mainly as the composer of *The Requiem*, dismissed his music as 'a neo-Italian art which is easily the most miserable thing in existence ... a kind of soup, where every style from every country gets all mixed up.'

If to be a great artist one must move the art forward, then Puccini, who was in many respects static and eclectic, cannot be reckoned as one. But *Madama Butterfly* is in the hit parade of opera, and although popularity (on its own) is no measure of artistry, there comes a point where criticism begins to look foolish, out of touch, and redolent of envy rather than objective criticism. It has, after all, been described as 'a work of genius'.

It is beyond doubt that Puccini, the 'full-blooded opera composer, was more familiar than any of his contemporaries with the secrets of theatrical effect and success'. He was a consummate craftsman. Musicologists highlight his use of actual Japanese themes, and his use of exotic tone colour in the orchestra – woodwind, bells and gongs – to invent his own themes exhibiting 'the character which Japanese music has for Western ears.'

There is a world of difference between Puccini's opera and a typical Italian opera like Donizetti's *Lucia di Lammermoor*, which is set in Scotland but in which little is Scottish except the costumes. During Madame Butterfly's chattering Japanese wedding party, Puccini uses a musical form, the canon, with the singers imitating each other, note for note, a bar or so apart, so that the words they use appear jumbled and unintelligible.

The ultimate test of Puccini's achievement is surely this. The simple, almost naïve story of the gullible Japanese geisha singer is transformed by Puccini's use of music and dramatic irony into an opera of tear-jerking emotion and intensity.

The dominant role of Butterfly

Butterfly develops from being merely just one member of her chattering family to being the truly tragic woman at the end of the opera. Puccini put 'his whole resources into a musico-dramatic analysis of her shifting emotions and thoughts' (careful listening to the orchestra enables one to appreciate this). Thus, the story moves from an apparently perfunctory beginning to an overwhelming end. And the final chord[8] of the tragedy, provided the listener hears it through the applause, is in itself suitably disconcerting to match the tragic circumstances.

Once Butterfly appears, she is on stage for much of the opera, although she is allowed a brief rest in the early morning of the 'last day'. It is a colossal part, tougher than Tosca, and one which even a singer comfortable in a role such as that of Isolde has called 'one of the leading voice-killers.'

By comparison with her, all the other characters are perhaps peripheral. Indeed, it has been suggested that all that can be expected of Pinkerton is that 'he be a tenor, and sing the beautiful music allotted to him in the first act with tender and passionate expression.' Sharpless the Consul has no great aria to sing. But as a fundamentally decent chap, and increasingly compassionate, he has an enormous contribution to make in 'underpinning the emotional impact of the story.'

Placido Domingo has sung the role of Pinkerton in a 1974 film version of the opera conducted by Herbert von Karajan and directed by Jean-Pierre Ponnelle. But the stars generally avoid the male parts even if they may have filled them in their earlier years. They know that they will be eclipsed by the prima donna.

The clash of Eastern and Western cultures

Looked at today, the treatment in *Madama Butterfly* of the Japanese and the Americans can be considered, in their own different ways, to be in poor taste. Particularly in the wedding scene, the Japanese people are depicted in an unflattering light. And American people, personified in the arrogant, callous and 'colonial' Lieutenant Pinkerton, who is introduced with the United States

---

[8] The work ends in B minor. But the final chord is a chord of G major in its first inversion, with a cataclysmic effect.

national anthem 'The Star-spangled Banner', fare little better, albeit in a different way.[9]

It is surely almost blasphemous for Pinkerton's first names to be 'Benjamin Franklin' and his ship to be the *Abraham Lincoln*. It is no coincidence that this name symbolising American freedom is shrieked out by Butterfly at the pivotal moment of the opera, when, utterly destroyed by the news that she has been deserted, she suddenly sees through her telescope an image that she interprets as Pinkerton returning to her. Puccini again uses the moment to play a snippet of 'The Star-spangled Banner'.

The music critic Gustav Kobbé, who was born and died in New York, went so far as to write that the use of 'The Star-spangled Banner' was 'highly objectionable and might, in time, become offensive, although no offence was meant.' However, a Bucharest production in 1957 used Pinkerton as a propaganda figure against imperialism. This is perhaps not surprising given that in the original version of the love duet, Butterfly tells Pinkerton that her immediate reaction when Goro suggested him as a candidate for marriage was to regard him as a brute – *un Americano, un barbaro*.

Pinkerton was far more arrogant in the Belasco play and in the original version of the opera. Puccini and his librettists actually toned down both the anti-Japanese and anti-American aspects, especially in their revised version. From Act 1, they cut various rude remarks about Japanese food ('candied frogs and flies') and greed. Pinkerton's wife Kate had a more prominent role and was characterised as being more aggressive and heartless about taking the baby.

Some of the cuts can be regretted because they weaken the clash of cultures which Puccini was depicting. In retrospect, however, they were probably politically wise, not least when viewed from the 21st century.

---

[9] At the end, Pinkerton is given a brief arioso, *Addio fiorito asil* expressing farewell to his flowery bower, for a trysting place is all that, for him, it ever was. He expresses remorse. But this does not do much to dilute the heartless, cowardly impression he leaves.

Act by act

The short prelude is based on a 'Japanese' theme which runs through Act 1.

Act 1

Above Nagasaki harbour

The time is the present, that is, contemporary with the composition of the opera: the beginning of the twentieth century.

Goro, an obsequious marriage broker and pimp shows Lieutenant Benjamin Franklin Pinkerton, from the US Navy gunboat *Abraham Lincoln*, round a house high above the harbour of Nagasaki. Goro introduces him to the servants, led by Suzuki. Pinkerton is not too interested. The house is for Pinkerton to occupy with his bride Cio-Cio-San. Their marriage ceremony is about to take place.

The US Consul, Sharpless, arrives, somewhat breathless from climbing up the hill to the house. With an irreverent introduction, using the start of the tune of 'The Star-spangled Banner'. Sharpless and Pinkerton sit down for a drink: 'Milk-punch or whisky?'

Pinkerton jovially describes how he has bought the house for 999 years, with a monthly option to cancel the lease, rather like his marriage contract. Sharpless is disturbed to hear Pinkerton boast how he enjoys casual sex as he travels the world. His prospective 'wife', has only cost him 100 yen.

Pinkerton is intoxicated with her: she is like a butterfly. He felt an urge to rush after her and catch her, even though it might damage her wings. Sharpless has overheard her visiting his consulate and is concerned that she will get hurt. Pinkerton drinks to a proper marriage with an American girl sometime in the future.

Butterfly arrives with her girlfriends. Her outpouring of joy soars over the 'bridesmaids', to D flat if she can get there (Puccini provides a lower alternative).

She introduces them to Pinkerton. She tells how she is aged fifteen and has only a mother, her father being dead. Her relations appear, as do the Imperial Commissioner and the registrar. One of Butterfly's uncles[10] is in search of a drink. Pinkerton finds it all delightful and hilarious.

There is much chatter between Butterfly's relatives, some of it cleverly set by Puccini in the form of a canon, thus making the words unintelligible. Some claim that they themselves were also offered to Pinkerton by Goro; they express varying opinions of Pinkerton and of Butterfly. Sharpless continues to be disconcerted by it all.

Butterfly shows Pinkerton her few possessions. She withholds one, a sheath with a knife, which Goro explains that the Mikado (or Emperor) sent to her father with a message telling him to use it. Butterfly assures Pinkerton that she has been secretly to the Mission and has converted to his religion. She throws away the images of her ancestors.

With the Commissioner announcing Pinkerton of the *Lincoln*, to the horns playing an excerpt from 'The Star-spangled Banner', the marriage formalities take place. Afterwards, Sharpless, the Commissioner and the registrar leave. Before going, Sharpless warns Pinkerton to be careful.

When the party is about to resume, Butterfly's uncle the Bonzo (a Buddhist monk) is heard. He is furious because Butterfly has renounced her religion. He curses her, whereupon her relatives immediately desert her. Cast out by her own people, she collapses in tears, and is comforted by Pinkerton, who, being just interested in the coming night, does not take her concerns too seriously: *Viene la sera*.

Suzuki, her servant, prepares Butterfly for the night. Apprehensive that she may die of her love, she just wants to be loved: *Vogliatemi bene*. Pinkerton is ecstatic, but Butterfly cannot get the sound of her relatives out of her ears. When he calls her 'Butterfly', she has a premonition: she has heard that in his country, he who catches a butterfly will pierce its heart with a needle and leave it to die. True, Pinkerton says, but that is so that she cannot run away. He has got her! He catches her in his arms and they complete the glorious love duet *Ah! Dolce notte!* in which they

---

[10] In the original version performed at the première, this uncle's part was far larger, which increased the comedy but slowed up the action. The scene also involved a naughty little boy, who Puccini cut out in the revised version.

invoke the sweet night to enfold them in ecstasy. It does, as she reaches top C. In what has been described as the finest duet Puccini ever composed, they enter the house for the night, beneath the infinite, starry sky. For her, the stars laugh with endless joy.

Act 2 Part 1
Three years later

Butterfly is still in her house. Suzuki prays to her Japanese gods: *E Izaghi ed Izanami*. Their money is running out.

Suzuki is doubtful that Pinkerton will return, but Butterfly angrily reproaches her for her negative attitude: otherwise, why did he order the Consul to provide the house for them, and have it fitted with locks so that her frightful relatives could be kept out? He said he will return with the roses, and when the robins nest. One fine day, they will see a wisp of smoke and a ship on the sea: *Un bel dì, vedremo levarsi un fil di fumo*.[11] His ship will glide into the harbour. She will wait for him up in the house. They will see him in the distance, and hear him calling, 'Butterfly'. She will pretend to hide, and then he will embrace her with all the loving words he once used.

Goro arrives with Sharpless. Butterfly welcomes him, and is overcome with excitement at the sight of a letter that Sharpless has had from Pinkerton. She asks what time of year the robins nest in the United States – maybe in that country they nest less frequently than in Japan? Sharpless says that he does not understand ornithology. Sharpless eventually succeeds in conveying the contents of the letter to Butterfly.

Goro tells how he has been trying to persuade Butterfly to marry another man, the wealthy Prince Yamadori, who arrives, to a fanfare, to woo her. She dismisses the suggestion that she is divorced, and stands by the law of 'her country', the USA. Again we hear the

---

[11] There is a story about how Puccini heard *Un bel dì* being played far too slowly on a barrel organ outside his hotel window. He rushed out though the amazed guests and staff, admonished the organ grinder, grabbed the handle of the barrel organ and turned it like fury to get it up to speed. The next day, the organ grinder was there again, with displayed on his machine: 'Pupil of Puccini'.

strains of 'The Star-spangled Banner'. To Sharpless's desperation, Butterfly displays her optimism about her rights under US divorce law.

Pinkerton's ship has already signalled its arrival. But Butterfly delays Sharpless from telling her the bad news that Pinkerton does not want to see her. He begins to read the letter from Pinkerton; Butterfly interrupts him. Eventually, Sharpless asks her what she would do if Pinkerton were never to return. To her, this notion is like a deathblow. She responds that she would either return to her former life, or die. Sharpless urges her to marry Prince Yamadori.

They will surely not forget, she says, her baby, whom she now brings to show Sharpless (he has been unaware, until now, of its existence, as has Pinkerton). She shows him how the child has Pinkerton's features. She asks Sharpless to write and tell Pinkerton about the child.

She sings to the baby how the heartless Sharpless has implied that she should return to earn her living by taking the child into the town and by dancing and becoming a geisha again: *Che tua madre*. She would ten times prefer death – *Morta, Morta* – to that. Sharpless asks the baby's name: it is now Trouble, but when Pinkerton returns it will be Joy. Sharpless is overcome with emotion[12] and leaves, saying that he will inform Pinkerton.

In a complete contrast of mood, Suzuki rages at Goro, who has insinuated that, in the United States, a bastard child is treated as an outcast. Butterfly seizes the dagger and goes for Goro, who is lucky to escape. The cannon sounds, signalling the arrival of a ship in the harbour. She looks through her telescope and to her utter joy she can read the name *Abraham Lincoln*.

Butterfly is confident that the others were liars, her faith is to be rewarded, and Pinkerton is about to return to her. In the obverse of a

---

[12] Sir Thomas Allen has described how this scene provides the potential for 'one of the most moving half-hours in opera.' Unchecked, the performer's own emotional involvement, particularly at the moment when the baby is shown to Sharpless, could even have a detrimental effect on the performance: 'The lump in the throat is in danger of strangling one,' he wrote.

'mad scene', she and Suzuki scatter cherry blossom[13] all over the place, singing the 'flower song', *Scuoti quella fronda di ciliegio*. Suzuki helps Butterfly to dress in her wedding dress. They make little spy holes to see Pinkerton when he comes.

While night falls, an offstage chorus sings the Humming Chorus. The baby and Suzuki sleep, but Butterfly watches and waits, as does the audience, for whom this beautiful chorus provides a moment to contemplate the terrible dénouement about to unfold.

Act 2 Part 2

After the searingly sad interlude, sailors are heard in the very far distance. Their remoteness, and the paucity of the orchestration, emphasise the hopelessness of the situation.

There are sounds on the horns and bells as the world awakens: whistles depict birds beginning to sing. Suzuki urges Butterfly, who has been waiting up all night, to go and rest. She lulls her darling child to sleep, *Dormi, amor mio* reaching top B as she goes out through the door. Suzuki surely reflects the mood of the audience, a sense of profound, almost uncontrollable, sadness for Butterfly, as she despairs: *Povera Butterfly*.

Sharpless and Pinkerton creep in, telling Suzuki, 'ssh'. She tells them how Butterfly has watched every ship entering the harbour for the last three years, and how they scattered and arranged the flowers last night. She sees that they are accompanied by a woman and is horrified: it is Pinkerton's American wife.

Sharpless explains that they must secure the welfare of the child and asks for Suzuki's help. She must fetch Butterfly. Pinkerton, a contemptibly feeble character, can only look uselessly around at the strewn flowers and his photograph.[14] Sharpless reminds Pinkerton that he warned him to be careful.

---

[13] To provide the petals at a performance in Bristol, a box full of torn-up paper was shaken at the end of a long bamboo pole. The string broke, with the result that the box hit Butterfly on the head. She had to shuffle her way through paper, cardboard and string.

[14] At least Puccini gives him a couple of top B flats!

Pinkerton eventually, remorsefully, goes away, leaving some money behind. Kate Pinkerton asks Suzuki to explain the situation to Butterfly and tell her that she will take the child and look after it properly.

Butterfly appears before this can be done. She cannot be stopped from coming in. She is surprised to see Sharpless with Kate. She comforts Suzuki, who weeps uncontrollably. She checks that Pinkerton is alive. The truth dawns.

Kate admits that she is the cause of the trouble. She asks for the son. Butterfly congratulates her and agrees that Pinkerton can have him if he returns in half an hour. When the others go, Butterfly collapses. She recovers and orders Suzuki away to play with the child.

She goes to fetch the dagger which the Mikado sent her father, on which are inscribed the words, 'Death with honour is better than life with dishonour.' She is about to stab herself when the child comes in. She sings an anguished farewell to her darling child, her little god, *Tu tu piccolo Iddio*, 'possibly the most heart-rending music of Puccini's entire oeuvre', according to one of Puccini's leading biographers. She gives him a United States flag and a doll and urges him to play with them. She blindfolds him.

She takes the knife, goes behind the screen and stabs herself. She emerges, totters towards the child and embraces him: *Amore addio! addio! piccolo amor! Va, gioca, gioca!* ('Go and play'). The music in the orchestra, before the thump, tells us that her last thoughts are with '*tu piccolo Iddio*', with her little god, with her child.

The feeble Pinkerton is heard without. He appears with Sharpless just in time for Butterfly to gesture to the child, collapse and die. It is Sharpless who, sobbing, takes the child. The orchestra concludes the opera in unison with the theme heard earlier accompanying the word *morta* in Butterfly's great aria *Che tua madre*. And the orchestra ends the opera on a truly cataclysmic note. The structure of the final chord (G major in its first inversion) is surely without precedent as a closure to an opera.

Puccini: *Turandot*

The opera and its composer

Puccini's last opera *Turandot* is his 'greatest masterpiece and swan-song.' It appears in charts of the top twenty most-performed operas. And in particular, the aria *Nessun dorma*, sung by Pavarotti in the role of Calaf, the Unknown Prince, has provided one of the most famous recordings in classical music, two-and-a-half minutes of sheer melodic perfection.

Having reached his sixties, Puccini wanted to compose something different, something fantastic. He was not taken with the suggestion of doing an opera based on the story of *Oliver Twist*; so he took up the idea of Renato Simoni, a scholarly author, that he should use *Re Turandote*, a play by Gozzi, the Venetian 18th-century dramatist. Goethe had particularly liked this, and it had already attracted some composers. Seven years earlier, Puccini's contemporary Ferruccio Busoni had composed a two-act opera, and before that, Carl Maria von Weber had composed incidental music for it. Puccini actually used a version adapted by Schiller, the great German dramatist.

Puccini was most careful in his choice of libretti. He had the genius to see its operatic potential and to create a spectacle which grips audiences and accounts for the success of *Turandot* today.

The ghastly subject matter was a particularly improbable choice for the great womaniser Puccini. Gozzi's message is anti-feminist: male weakness allows female insubordination, and results in social disorder. Gozzi depicts the havoc caused by a stunningly beautiful Chinese Princess, 'the ultimate castrating female', who so abhors men that she gets the Emperor, her utterly pathetic father, to enact virtually certain decapitation for any man foolish enough to aspire to possess her: if the suitor fails to give the right answer to three virtually impossible riddles, his head will be chopped off, instantly.

The tale probably originates in The Arabian Nights, or earlier, and can also be found in the cultural heritage of many societies. In Shakespeare's *The Merchant of Venice*, each of the suitors for the hand of Portia must choose from three caskets, having first sworn, if he makes the wrong choice, 'never to speak to lady afterward, in way of marriage' – a rather less extreme fate.

With Simoni, himself an expert on Gozzi, and Giuseppe Adami, who had written the libretti for his less successful operas *La Rondine* and *Il Tabarro*, Puccini masterminded a libretto, a mixture of tragedy, grotesque comedy and 'the fantastications of a fairy-tale.'

Puccini had been concerned that he was growing out of touch with modern music. He told Simoni at one stage, 'Nobody sings in Italy any longer. Instead there are crashes, discordant chords ...' The exotic setting, and Turandot's horrible character, justified him in imparting modern, dissonant and exotic sounds which we might not otherwise expect, or like, from him. How he succeeded! Emotionally (not least in his creation of the slave girl Liù), he carries his audience, which might reasonably be disgusted, along with him. His music makes dramatically convincing some otherwise wholly incredible and dislikable protagonists. And peeping out among his frequently angular and shrill sounds, is melody which lingers in the mind, and which we hum, as we leave the theatre.

Puccini never saw *Turandot*, which he spent the last four years of his life struggling to compose. The première, conducted by the legendary Arturo Toscanini, was in Milan at La Scala on 25 April 1926, seventeen months after Puccini's death from throat cancer. He had only completed the score up to the death of Liù, the slave girl, in the final act.

At the time when he departed for the clinic in Brussels where he died, he left behind various sketches and 36 pages of continuous music in 'short score' indicating how the opera was to close. These were used by the unfortunate Franco Alfano[1] to construct and

---

[1] Franco Alfano (1875–1954), a Neapolitan, completed *Turandot*, rather like Süssmayer completed Mozart's *Requiem* after his death. Alfano composed several ballets and eleven operas, several of which were staged, including *L'ombra di Don Giovanni*, *Sakuntala*, and *Cyrano de Bergerac*. He spent much of his life teaching in various cities of Italy.

compose a conclusion to the opera. Toscanini gave him a hard time. At first, he rejected his work and then he cut it drastically. Alfano's final material still represents, roughly speaking, the last quarter of an hour of the opera.

It is one of the tragedies of music that Puccini did not live to finish the love duet near the end of the opera, in which the two protagonists were to be transformed through love and which was to have been the focal point for the whole work. This was the love which, with the help of the orchestra, would suffuse everybody on the stage.

At the première,[2] Toscanini did not perform Alfano's conclusion. He stopped with the suicide of Liù. He turned to the audience at this breathtaking moment and announced, 'Here Death triumphed over Art.' The audience left in silence.

In an infinitely less exalted way, the première featured a stand-off with Mussolini, the Italian dictator, who was in Milan for a political gathering. The La Scala management felt obliged to invite him. He refused to accept unless Toscanini performed the Fascist anthem at the start of the evening. Toscanani, who had had a brush with Mussolini about playing that anthem a couple of years before, refused to do this, so Mussolini refused to attend.

Turandot has been called the consummation of Puccini's creative career, blending elements such as the lyric-sentimental Liù, the heroic grandiose Turandot and Calaf, and the comic grotesque Venetian 'Masks', the court officials Ping, Pang and Pong. None of his other operas achieve this synthesis. But in doing so, *Turandot* is very different, and unique.

(More on the life of Puccini can be found on page 380.)

[2] Various celebrities starred in the première: the Polish soprano Rosa Raisa, who Puccini himself had in mind for the title role; Miguel Fleta, the Spanish tenor, as the Unknown Prince Calaf; and Maria Zamboni as Liù.

WHO'S WHO AND WHAT'S WHAT

The story below is based on the libretto. Certain directors may amend opera stories to suit their production.

The opera is set in legendary times in Peking (Beijing) where the walls are festooned with the severed heads of suitors who have failed to win the hand of **Princess Turandot**, the daughter of the ancient **Chinese Emperor** Altoum. The only man she will marry is a Prince who can solve **three riddles**. Any suitor who fails to do so will die.

The opera opens with a **Mandarin** announcing the latest casualty. Among the bloodthirsty crowd watching the spectacle, there is a slave girl **Liù**, the carer of an old man who falls in the crush and chaos. Also there is a fugitive, an **Unknown Prince**, who recognises that the old man is his father **Timur**, the deposed emperor. In earlier, better, times, the Unknown Prince had smiled at Liù.

The latest suitor, the **Prince of Persia**, goes to the block after Turandot, who does not sing at all in the first act, gives the thumbs down. When the Unknown Prince sees her, he is overcome with her beauty. He wants to risk his head and enter the contest.

Three comical court officials, **Ping** (the Grand Chancellor), **Pang** (the Purveyor General) and **Pong** (the Chief Cook), try to dissuade him, as does Liù. But he strikes the **gong** to signify his suit.

Ping, Pang and Pong, called collectively **the Masks**, long for this sorry business to come to an end. They go to the next ceremony of riddles predicting the inevitable outcome.

People congregate in front of the Imperial Palace during an orchestral interlude. The Emperor himself tries unsuccessfully to persuade the Unknown Prince to withdraw. The Mandarin announces the rules. Turandot appears (and sings for the first time after an hour of opera) and explains that she is the reincarnation of an ancestor who was raped and killed years ago by the Tartars. The bloodletting is her revenge for that.

The Unknown Prince answers correctly the first and second riddles, 'Hope', and 'Blood'. When he also answers correctly the third, 'Turandot', she is distraught. Her father insists she abide by the rules, but she asks the Unknown Prince whether he will take her by force. He nobly suggests that if, before dawn, she can state his name, he too will forfeit his life.

Overnight, she takes drastic action to discover his name. In the garden of the palace, **heralds** threaten torture and death if the Unknown Prince's name is not revealed before dawn. An offstage choir and the Unknown Prince echo the cry 'Nobody shall sleep', *Nessun dorma!*

Ping, Pang and Pong offer the Unknown Prince comely women and jewels if he will leave. Aware of their own fraught position, they offer to flee with him.

Unfortunately, the Prince's father and Liù were seen with the Prince, and presumably know his name. To prevent the old man being tortured, Liù declares that she alone knows it, but will not disclose it. Why? Turandot asks her. True love, she replies, which Turandot will eventually discover.

At the sight of the **executioner** Pu-Tin-Pao and his assistants, who have come to torture her, Liù plunges a dagger into her heart.

Alone with Turandot, who still resists him, the Unknown Prince grabs her and kisses her passionately. The kiss transforms her into a loving woman.[3] At dawn, Turandot is still reluctant but he claims her. He gives her the answer: he is **Calaf**, the son of Timur, King of the Tartars. At the ceremony, Turandot tells her father she knows the Prince's name: it is Love. They embrace passionately.[4]

THE INTERVAL: TALKING POINTS

'Dot' or 'doh'?

There is compelling evidence that Puccini pronounced the final syllable of Turandot as 'doh' rather than 'dot'. Rosa Raisa, the first

---

[3] Birgit Nilsson, the soprano, described how Domingo's kiss in Verona was so long that the audience began to shout *Basta, basta, adesso* – 'Hey, that'll do, thank you.' Unfortunately, in the process, he infected her with tonsillitis which nearly put her out of subsequent performances.

[4] In a Rome production, Calaf was on one side of a little Chinese bridge, and Turandot on the other. When she sings her final words, *Il suo nome è Amor*, Calaf was to charge over the bridge and embrace her. He forgot the bridge, tripped and fell into the stream.

Turandot, was emphatic that the 't' was not pronounced. Dame Eva Turner, herself a great Turandot, who attended the première and who sang the part shortly thereafter, pronounced it without the 't'. And the 't' was not pronounced in the early recordings. In particular, the recording conducted by Tullio Serafin, who knew both Puccini and Toscanini, does not sound it. Besides, in certain of the Prince's passages, it is extraordinarily difficult to sing the 't' effectively, especially in some of the high registers, just as enunciating the 't' can spoil the flow of the music in places.

The 't' seems to have crept in around 1960, with the recordings made then and the Metropolitan Opera production at that time. Perhaps the sounding of the 't' has something to do with Gozzi's play being named (in French) *Turandotte*, or with the German pronunciation of final consonants. Those who choose the silent 't' are certainly not wrong and are in good company, including that of the composer, even if today they may sound rather old-fashioned.

The 1990 football World Cup

Nessun dorma! ('Nobody shall sleep'), the 'best tune' in the opera, as sung by Luciano Pavarotti, and subsequently associated with him, was the theme song for the 1990 World Cup held in Italy. The recording reached number 2 in the UK singles chart, the highest rating ever achieved by a classical recording. It is the largest-selling classical recording ever, and demonstrates the enduring power of *pre-modern* classical music: this aria from the 1920s was welcomed globally as suitable to complement this most popular sport.

The first 'Three Tenors' concert, featuring Luciano Pavarotti, Placido Domingo and José Carreras, under the baton of Zubin Mehta, was on 7 July 1990. It was a celebrity occasion, held at the Baths of Caracalla, the outdoor opera venue in Rome, to celebrate the World Cup and Carreras's recovery from leukaemia. The singers were all football fans. The three stars performed for a flat fee, albeit not modest, which as Pavarotti said 'was not the smartest business deal any of them ever made.' Afterwards, as his agent put it, 'they didn't suffer in silence. The racket they made about it could be heard from Rome to California.'

When the concert was repeated in 1994 before the World Cup in Los Angeles, the terms were more lucrative. And then the Three Tenors went around the world, and kept going until the concept ran out of steam.

Pavarotti around the time of the 1990 football World Cup

In this aria, the Unknown Prince Calaf echoes the heralds who have proclaimed Turandot's edict that nobody shall sleep: unless his name is revealed by dawn, the city shall be put to the sword. He asserts that, at sunrise, he will win Turandot with a kiss: *All'alba vincerò*. It is presumably the *vincerò* – the 'winning' – rather than the kiss, which is more relevant to sport.

The *affaire* Doria

Puccini had a mistress, Elvira, for around twenty years, who he married after the death of her husband, in 1904. But he was bored with her: she had not kept pace with his success, and he was anyway a considerable womaniser. She was desperately jealous.

Elvira found him late at night chatting to the 21-year-old Doria Manfredi, one of the domestic servants at his house in Torre del Lago, near Lucca. Elvira became hysterical and started following Doria around the village, shrieking abuse. Doria was driven to commit an agonising suicide by drinking poison.

After this, the Manfredi family prosecuted Elvira, who was convicted, fined and sentenced to several months' imprisonment. The case was settled, so Elvira did not have to go to jail, but not surprisingly the whole matter caused Puccini enormous worry. Perhaps there is something of Elvira in the character of Turandot, and of Doria in the role of Liù.

Liù is entirely a creation of Puccini's. Her music is far more pleasing to the ear than Turandot's: for example, in *Signore ascolta*, she ends high on a gentle B flat, but does not shriek. She is the only character in the story who actually 'touches the heart.'

However, not only is Liù redundant to the drama, she also provides a dramatic problem. Her death is so final and so shocking that it provides a false close to the opera. It was where Puccini broke off before he died. It is particularly unfortunate that he was not alive to complete the subsequent final scene. It would have been interesting to see how he would have revived the drama and tension after such an apparently complete ending.

Turandot – her music

The part of Turandot is static and extremely difficult – even 'unsingable' – although fortunately it is short. Until the end of the opera there is little trace of lyricism. It can only be performed by powerful, imposing sopranos capable of singing 'throat-wrenching high tones', such as Birgit Nilsson (1918–2005). After the kiss, Turandot's 'tones like sharpened steel' at last transmute into 'warm sounds of love and pity.'

In her *In questa Reggia* in which she explains her actions, she sings at the top of the soprano range. There are various moments when

Turandot sustains a high C.[5] Perhaps the most dramatic is in Act 2, when, having sworn that never shall man possess her, Turandot reaches what has been described as 'probably the most dreaded high C of all.' She shrieks *Gli enigma sono tre, la morte è una* ('the riddles are three, death is but one'). At the same time, the Unknown Prince, in unison, reaching the top C of his tenor range, cries out *Gli enigma sono tre, una è la vita* ('the riddles are three, life is but one').[6]

They also reach high C, albeit separately, at the dramatic moment at the end of Act 2 when the Prince has solved the riddles and she protests, 'Will you take me in your arms forcibly?' and he replies, 'No, I want you ablaze with love.'[7]

The sustained high C can be an athletic achievement rather than an artistic one. Birgit Nilsson recalled that Franco Corelli 'could apparently sustain this tone for ever.' According to her, he had 'one of the most fantastic tenor voices ever.' But whether his sustained high C fitted with 'any style, or was in good taste, is another matter.' That question can usually be repeated today.

Turandot – the character

Turandot, 'the pathologically icy princess', the 'neurotic murderer' is a detestable woman, an 'inhuman monster'. Her cruelty and barbarism dominate the opera. Puccini deliberately exaggerated the ghastliness of Gozzi's Turandot.[8] For example, Puccini's answers to the three

---

[5] In Mozart's *The Magic Flute*, the Queen of the Night reaches D and F above high C. But that is sung as part of a coloratura run, and the notes are not sustained. The greatest sopranos such as Maria Callas and Joan Sutherland have found the E flats in the Mad Scene in *Lucia di Lammermoor* have provided a challenge.

[6] Nilsson suggested that 'there is probably no tenor who can dynamically overpower the high C of a soprano in his natural voice.' She described how one well-known tenor just spread his arms and opened his mouth wide and everybody thought that both he and the soprano had sung high C. She also infers that one great tenor ensured that he ducked behind Turandot for this purpose.

[7] For this, Puccini also provides the Prince with a less demanding alternative.

[8] Liù's equivalent in Gozzi's *Turandot* is Adelma, a conquered princess, now the slave of Turandot, and a rival to her mistress for the love of Calaf. Turandot's love-hate conflict makes her a far more complex character than in the opera. She is 'an 18th-century spokeswoman for modern woman's liberation', although she concludes the play by declaring that men are perhaps not so bad after all. The play contains the possibility of a lesbian relationship between the two princesses.

riddles are 'Hope', 'Blood' and 'Turandot'; whereas for Gozzi they were 'The sun', 'The year' and 'The Venetian lion'. Indeed, it might seem that the appearance of Turandot in Act 1 in a non-singing role was a deliberate attempt by the composer to avoid her character being compatible with the beauty of music.

We are told by enthusiasts that 'Puccini desired with all his heart and mind to glorify Love.' But he seems to have confused sex with love, a magazine image with a person. Nobody could possibly love this vengeful heroine, this 'flint-hearted beauty.'

Thus Calaf, far from displaying nobility and generosity, can appear to be a fool. He is a fool for falling for Turandot in the first place; then, having not lost his head literally, he loses it figuratively by releasing her from her side of the bargain. He takes yet a further risk by disclosing his name to her before dawn. Gozzi tells us, however, that 'the brightest intellect is no defence when love assails.' That seems clear in this case.

The Prince at times almost seems (unintentionally) comical. When Turandot claims that she is the daughter of Heaven, and her soul is on high, his response is hilarious: *la tua anima è in alto, ma il tuo corpo è vicino* ('Your soul may be on high but your body is down here'). He grabs her and kisses her passionately.[9] This is the climax of the opera.

Commedia dell'arte and chinoiserie

Ping, Pang and Pong are redolent of the *Commedia dell'arte* clowns, such as Harlequin and Pantaloon, which were a feature of the traditional strolling masked players who improvised their ribald humour, often featuring sex, disease, cuckolds and geriatrics. These 'Venetian Masks' were also modelled in Meissen 'Chinese' porcelain, and are predecessors to some of the characters in Mozart's *The Magic Flute*.[10]

They were central to the dispute between Gozzi and his contemporary Goldoni. Gozzi wanted to retain them as part of the

---

[9] This is reminiscent of the moment in Verdi's *Il Trovatore* when Leonora, about to become a nun, asks to be led to the altar. The bully-boy Count, her would-be lover, exclaims, 'The only altar for you, lady, is the nuptial altar.'

[10] Mozart's Papageno is derived from Gozzi's clown Truffaldino.

Carlo Gozzi (1722–1806) was a downwardly mobile Venetian nobleman, playwright, wit and satirist, and a contemporary of the lawyer Carlo Goldoni (who once wrote sixteen comedies in a year, and was the writer of many libretti).

Gozzi was a leading light in a group of literary wits who called themselves the 'Testicular Society'. The group's symbol was an owl and two testicles, and it chose as its president – the arch-testicle – an unfortunate dwarf who had pretensions to be a poet.

Gozzi and his friends were fiercely opposed to the new realistic style of writing introduced by Goldoni. To differentiate himself from his rival, Gozzi wrote fables, including *Re Turandote* and *The Love for Three Oranges* on which Prokofiev based his opera.

Gozzi's use of fairytales to convey his messages, including his misogyny, to a large audience was novel. Fairytales fascinate adults as much as children. Schiller observed that there was deeper meaning in the fairytales told to him in his childhood than in the truth that was taught by life.

At first, Gozzi was a tremendous success. Although Goldoni was driven away to France in 1762, where he remained until his death 30 years later, he finally won the day: Goldoni is today regarded as one of Italy's greatest playwrights.

historical legacy of Italian theatre, and he included them in his fairy-tales. Goldoni, the revisionist and modernist, thought these crude low-brow stereotypes had passed their 'sell-by date' and excluded them from his dramas.

Having chosen a fable by Gozzi as the basis of his libretto, Puccini was faced with how to incorporate these characters. Although at times Puccini and his librettists thought of eliminating them, in the end he adopted them fully. His sinister and sadistic Masks play a direct role and provide much Shakespearian light relief as a contrast to the awful-ness of the drama, whereas in Gozzi's play they just stand by as chorus.

Puccini gave them some delightful music, for example when Ping wishes that they could get away to their country homes, in *Ho una casa nell'Honan*.

From the outset the orchestra provides a 'Chinese' sound. The percussion is augmented with a variety of drums, cymbals, triangles and xylophones, along with bells and gongs of various sizes. Some of the tunes, including the final melodies, are actual Chinese tunes which Puccini possibly took from an old Chinese musical box belonging to a friend. He drew on Chinese folk songs for two of the themes associated with the Masks.

The outcome is, for European ears, highly exotic. Only time will tell whether Chinese people find this chinoiserie, not least the comic Ping, Pang and Pong, acceptable and politically correct.

ACT BY ACT

Act 1

The orchestra opens with a menacing four-bar fortissimo which leaves us in no doubt of the drama to come and the unpleasant character of Turandot. There is considerable bitonal dissonance, with various instruments playing in two different keys. The xylophone informs us that we are in the Far East.

We are at the walls of Peking (Beijing) in legendary times. They are festooned by spikes with severed heads on them. A Mandarin announces the edict that Princess Turandot will marry a Prince who solves three riddles that she has set. But he who tries and fails will be beheaded. At the rising of the moon, the most recent suitor, the Prince of Persia, is due to meet his fate.

The bloodthirsty mob[11] is so enthusiastic that it has to be repelled by the soldiers, and in the mêlée an Unknown Prince comes to the assistance of an old man and his carer, the slave girl Liù. The Unknown Prince recognises the old man as his father Timur, once the

---

[11] Puccini's use of the chorus throughout the opera is masterly.

Emperor, who was defeated, deposed and like him became a fugitive. Liù volunteered to accompany him because one day in the palace the Prince smiled at her: *Perchè un dì ... mi hai sorriso.*

To the encouragement of the mob, the executioner and his assistants oil and sharpen the sword with which the head of the Prince of Persia will be struck off. The mob eagerly awaits the rising of the moon, when the execution will take place: *Perchè tarda la luna?*[12] It looks forward to a succession of suitors who will strike the gong to enter the contest.

The moon rises and the march to the scaffold begins. At the sight of the wretched Prince of Persia, the mood of the crowd changes from bloodlust to pity. High on the battlements, Turandot appears, lit by the moon, *come una visione* – like an apparition – and, with a blast on the brass, gives the Persian Prince the Peking equivalent of a 'thumbs-down'. But she does not utter.

The Unknown Prince is overcome with the sight and beauty of Turandot, despite the protestations of his father and Liù. A distant last cry 'Turandot' from the victim on the scaffold can be heard. The Unknown Prince rushes to the gong, which he must strike three times if he wants to claim her.

Before the Prince can strike the gong, three imperial civil servants or courtiers intervene: Ping, Pang and Pong.[13] They are respectively Grand Chancellor, Purveyor General and Chief Cook. Although rather more concerned about their own survival than the Prince's, they urge him to leave: why waste a good life on one woman? If she is stripped naked, she is just flesh. There are many alternatives, in the form of Turandot's comely ladies-in-waiting, who now attempt to seduce him. And he is reminded of his fate by the spirits of former participants in the contest.

The executioner reappears and places the head of the Prince of Persia on a spike. In a complete contrast, Liù desperately (but the melody is beautiful, as is the orchestration with harp, woodwind

[12] To Placido Domingo, the chorus to the moon, when as a young performer he first heard it, was 'one of the most moving experiences of his life.'

[13] Their intervention is sung to a snippet from the imperial Chinese national anthem.

and muted violins) makes a final attempt to plead with the Prince – *Signore ascolta* ('Listen, Lord, listen') – but with no success: *Non piangere, Liù!* He asks her to look after his father, if he fails.

The stately climax builds as Ping, Pang and Pong again try to dissuade him, assisted by the spirits of former participants. To no avail. But the Unknown Prince strikes the gong three times, and the orchestra in a sudden and dramatic change of key blasts out the theme associated with Turandot. The crowd reckon they might as well start digging his grave.

Act 2

This is a contrast to the previous scene. The first scene in the act is devoted to Ping, Pang and Pong. And the detail in the score from the outset is considerable, especially in the percussion department. The three 'Masks' move from the serious to the comic, falsetto to natural, loud to soft and so on.

In a Chinese pavilion, Ping, Pang and Pong, having heard the gong, know that their job is to prepare either for a wedding or for a funeral. They look through the records and recall the executions. In the current Year of the Tiger, this suitor will be the thirteenth. In a change to a nostalgic mood, they wish they could get back to their country houses rather than have to organise all this: *Ho una casa nell'Honan*, which at first is principally accompanied by the celeste 'più piano possible'. They recall the fate of the Prince of Samarkand, the Indian, the Burmese and the Prince of Kirghiz. In a change of mood, they long for the nuptials of the royal lovers. They optimistically hope that they will serenade the Princess of China, who has become intoxicated by love, having previously been ice-cold and despising it: *Non v'è in Cina.*

They hear the sound of the palace awakening, and Ping brings them back to reality. They hurry off to the next ceremony of riddles.

During a beautiful orchestral interlude with the full orchestra, a colossal sound, the dignitaries congregate in the square in front of the Imperial Palace, and the crowd wishes the Emperor may live

10,000 years. The already ancient Emperor is on his throne at the top of a stairway; sages hold scrolls with the solutions to the three riddles. There is a great fanfare.

The monarch, so decrepit he can hardly utter, then unsuccessfully beseeches the virile Unknown Prince to withdraw: there has been enough blood. The Mandarin again proclaims the law that Princess Turandot will marry whoever of royal blood will solve the three riddles. He who tries and fails will be beheaded: *Popolo di Pekino*. From behind the scenes, boys sing a tune which Puccini seems to have heard on an old Chinese musical box belonging to a friend.

Turandot appears for the ceremony. At last, she sings. Her voice rages higher and higher as she recalls how thousands of years ago her ancestor had been raped and killed by the Tartars: *In questa Reggia*. This ancestor is reincarnated in her; she now avenges her ancestor's scream and death. She, Turandot, will never be possessed by man. After several Bs, her voice climaxes with a pause on top C as she threatens that the riddles are three, death is but one. The Unknown Prince declares, 'No, life is but one!' The crowd presses for the ceremony to begin.

The ceremony is orchestrated about as thinly as is possible: the tension is in the drama, and the orchestra does not distract from it. Turandot reads the first of the three riddles. The Prince's answer, 'Hope', is confirmed by the sages. The Prince slowly reaches the right answer to the second: 'Blood'. Like a bird about to seize its prey, Turandot screeches the third into the Unknown Prince's face: ice which gives him fire ... he has difficulty working it out, but, to Turandot's horror, he finds the answer: 'Turandot'. This is confirmed by the sages. To the Chinese theme, the crowd hails him the victor.

Distraught, Turandot then argues with her father whether she has to submit: *Figlio del cielo; padre augusto!* She swears that no man shall possess her. Her father will not release her from her vow, and the crowd is against her, so she asks the Prince (hitting high C) whether he wants to take her by force, a reluctant frigid bride. No, he replies, he wants her ablaze with love.

There is a complete pause, of almost a bar. He nobly releases her from her side of the bargain. She gave him three riddles to solve;

he will put to her but one: he challenges her to state his name.[14] If she finds it out before dawn, he will forfeit his life: *Tre enigmi m'hai proposto!* The Emperor hopes he will become his son-in-law. The crowd applauds the Emperor.

Act 3

It is night-time in the garden of the palace, conveyed with beautifully, almost perfumed, orchestration, with harp glissandos. The Unknown Prince hears eight heralds announcing Turandot's command: nobody may sleep; the stranger's name must be disclosed before morning, or the populace will be put to the sword. The desperate people, offstage, echo *come un lamento*. In the famous aria, which is so deliberately such a total contrast to the cold icy sounds we have heard before, the Prince also echoes their cry 'Nobody shall sleep' *Nessun dorma!* Yes, his name is his secret. But, her ice-cold frigidity will melt when he reveals it to her with a kiss. At dawn, he will be a conqueror: *All'alba vincerò!*

Meanwhile, Ping, Pang and Pong, desperate, greatly afraid for their own future, parade comely, veiled odalisques before the Prince. We hear that the maidens would look even more attractive with fewer clothes on them.[15] The civil servants also offer him jewels, also unsuccessfully; and, contemplating their own fraught position, they offer to flee with him. They remind him of her cruelty if he does not reveal his name; they threaten him. But the increasingly desperate Prince is adamant that all he wants is Turandot: *Crollasse il mondo, voglio Turandot*, even if the world falls apart, he wants Turandot.

There is an interruption when the Prince's father Timur, and Liù, are dragged in. Ping saw them with the Prince, and they presumably know the secret of his name. They are threatened by the mob if they do not immediately disclose it. The civil servants rush to fetch

---

[14] We begin to hear, at first in the strings and then the woodwind, the love theme, later the basis of *Nessun dorma*.

[15] The surging orchestra depicts their voluptuous figures. Their 'Page 3' aspects are characterised by their conversation being limited to a repetition of the single word 'Ah'. Puccini has a marvellous sense of humour.

Turandot, who reappears, taunts the Prince, and orders Timur to disclose the name.

The Prince's father remains silent. Before he can be tortured, Liù declares that she alone knows the name but she will not disclose it – she would rather die. Despite the crowd's baying for blood and guts, despite the threat of torture, which is implemented, she will not reveal it. Turandot in amazement wonders what has steeled her heart with so much strength. Love, true love, she declares, accompanied by a solo violin: *Principessa, l'amore, tanto amore.* Indeed, so much love, secret and undisclosed, that the torture is sweetness for her. Liù bequeaths the Prince to her, and thereby loses any hope she herself ever had.

When the mighty executioner is called in to exert more pressure, Liù fears she will not have the strength to resist. She foretells that, despite Turandot's icy frigidity, *Tu che di gel sei cinta*, she too will eventually come to love him. The crowd calls for her to reveal the name. She manages to rush through the crowd, grab a dagger from a soldier and plunge it into her heart. As she falls at the feet of Prince, he and his father are distraught. Turandot seizes a whip and strikes the soldier in the face.

Ping tells the father that she is dead: he might as well get up. The old man warns that Liù's spirit will take revenge. The victim of injustice will become a vampire. In what has been described as 'one of the most moving scenes in all opera', the crowd's attitude changes. With the basses descending to E, (F flat), the crowd prays for forgiveness. The dead Liù is taken away, the old man holding her hand, going, as he knows, to die of grief. (This was the point Puccini reached and at which Alfano took over.)

Everyone disperses, apart from the Prince and Turandot, who haughtily still resists him. The Prince rips her veil away. 'Keep back,' she protests. She is the daughter of Heaven, and her soul is on high. The Prince responds, *la tua anima è in alto, ma il tuo corpo è vicino* ('Your soul may be on high but your body is here!'). He grabs her and kisses her passionately. She yields. The kiss transforms her from the ice-cold princess into a loving woman.

Voices behind the scenes hail the rising dawn. In an aria that provides a considerable contrast to her Act 2 narration, Turandot admits to the Prince that, when she first saw him, she knew he was special, and feared she would love him: *Del primo pianto*. But she still tries to resist him. Surely, he has achieved his objective with the kiss. 'Go no further: go away and carry your mystery (your name) with you.' 'There's no mystery any more,' shouts the Prince, 'You're mine!' He gives her his name, Calaf, the son of Timur, and thereby places his life in her hands. They leave for the ceremonial questioning of his name.

Outside the palace, Turandot, conquered at last, tells her father she knows the Prince's name: it is Love (on B flat). The couple embrace passionately, to the applause of the crowd (to the tune of *Nessun dorma*).

BRITTEN: *PETER GRIMES*

THE OPERA AND ITS COMPOSER

'One of the most significant events in British operatic history' is how the première of *Peter Grimes* has been described. It 'stamped Britten as the most gifted music dramatist England had produced since Purcell.'[1] It was adopted eagerly by foreign houses,[2] and it secured his international reputation.

It has been included 'amongst the greatest of all operas.' Although the smaller stage at London's Sadlers Wells, where it was premièred, gave it a suitably claustrophobic atmosphere, *Peter Grimes* is intended for a large audience in a large theatre. It consists of three acts, with a total running time of about two-and-a-half hours.

In 1941, during the Second World War, Benjamin Britten was living in self-imposed exile in California. He read an article by E.M. Forster – the novelist best known for *A Passage to India* and *Howard's End* and who was a member of Britten's homosexual circle – about George Crabbe, the Suffolk poet who left his birthplace at Aldeburgh, but never escaped from it 'in spirit'. Crabbe and his poem *The Borough*, alias Aldeburgh, struck a particular chord with Britten, who, at heart, was longing to be back home in England. He and his partner Peter Pears, who was to be the first Grimes, soon recognised the potential for creating an opera based on Crabbe's horrifying tale.

Financial support was supplied by a Foundation which Serge Koussevitsky, the Boston Symphony Orchestra conductor, had set up in memory of his second wife. Although many of the ideas and memorable phrases came from Pears, Britten used, as librettist, Montagu Slater, a communist journalist and poet. Britten was prone to change libretti to

---

[1] Sir Thomas Beecham, the conductor, had quipped: 'British music is in a state of perpetual promise. It might almost be said to be one long promissory note.'

[2] East German authorities encouraged its performance 'as a harrowing but authentic picture of the degeneracy of life in Britain as portrayed by and for Englishmen.'

suit what he wanted or had already composed. Although other great composers have also done this, the relationship with Slater was rocky.

Britten

Britten had originally wanted a libretto from the novelist Christopher Isherwood, best known for *Mr Norris Changes Trains*, but the invitation was turned down bluntly: the subject did not excite Isherwood enough 'that he wanted to make time for it'. This was probably a stroke of luck: in a tortuous way, Slater, although 'resistant to change and slow in delivering agreed revisions', generated what Britten wanted, and he gave constructive advice. The strong-willed composer took all the decisions. A libretto handed over by the more prominent Isherwood might have been a fait accompli, and very difficult to change.

An astonishing amount of effort and redrafting went into relentlessly developing the text. There were long sessions between Slater, producer Eric Crozier, Britten and Pears; they went over it line by line. Even after the score was finished in February 1945, Britten wrote, 'Peter & I are pretty well rewriting his part … Montagu has agreed to the new Mad Scene.' The result was an opera very different from the poem; indeed, 'an independent masterpiece, with a life of its own.'

The 'spectacularly triumphant' première of *Peter Grimes* was on 7 June 1945, exactly a month after VE (Victory in Europe) Day.[3] It marked the reopening of the Sadler's Wells Theatre.

---

[3] It was conducted by Reginald Goodall, and produced by Eric Crozier (1914–1994), the theatrical director who wrote the libretto for Britten's *Albert Herring*. The designer was Kenneth

Britten's own image was tainted with his having been a conscientious objector during the war. Some have suggested that his pacifism was the motivating force for the opera. Peter Pears said that in the early stages of planning the opera, the sea stood for war and the horrors of war. Others have asserted, especially in more recent times, that *Peter Grimes* represents an endeavour to win sympathy for homosexuality, at a time when homosexuals were excluded and lonely because their sexuality was illegal and openly attacked.[4] However, there is no attempt to portray Grimes himself as homosexual.

Aldeburgh in Suffolk, on the East Coast of England, is to the north of the modern port of Felixstowe, and some 30 miles south of Britten's birthplace, Lowestoft. It is located on a narrow strip of sand and gravel that lies between a river and the North Sea, by which it is relentlessly pounded, eroded and silted up. At a time when its struggle with the geographical consequences of a changing climate permitted, it was a prosperous port with its own parliamentary representation. E.M. Forster surprisingly called it 'a bleak little place … not beautiful', whereas in fact it has great charm, redolent of Britten's comic opera *Albert Herring*. Aldeburgh produced Britain's first female qualified doctor of medicine, Elizabeth Garrett Anderson (1836–1917).

The lonely, timeless sea,[5] and Britten's haunting musical description, provide the cruel backdrop for the town and the relentless struggle of those whose livelihood depends on it. Britten and Pears 'imagined

Green, art master at Wellington College, whose father had been a patient of Britten's dentist father. Britten used Green's sketches as a reference when composing.

[4] The couplet 'Did you ever see such [adjective] queers, as Benjamin Britten and Peter Pears' featured in a revue performed at the Royal Court Theatre, London, in the mid-1950s.

[5] Four of the interludes, Dawn, Sunday Morning, Moonlight and Storm, were published as a separate orchestral suite, 'Four Sea Interludes, from Peter Grimes'. With the Passacaglia, also from the opera, it comprises Opus 33.

the sea as being in the orchestra, so it was not necessary to see it on the stage.'

The bustling little fishing town, depicted around 1830, provides a complete contrast, which those who know the sea will understand. Britten realistically and wittily paints the town: its pub brawls and barn dances, its hypocrisy and sanctimoniousness, its pomposity. We see the irreproachable mayor (and the apothecary) chasing the 'nieces' of the pub landlady; the drunken Methodist leering at them; the ineffectual parson, the rich widow addicted to opium, and so on. Dr Crabbe himself is even included as a walk-on part. And we have the dark side: the hysteria, busybodies, and lynch-mobs being whipped up into a frenzy.

Peter Grimes, one of the town's fishermen, is a loner and 'different'. But he longs for social acceptance, which he will attain through material success, and by marrying the retired schoolmistress. Whereas Crabbe's Grimes was simply a thug, or 'lout' as Forster called him, Britten's is more complex. He is a visionary, a 'misunderstood Byronic hero'. The cruel, lonely sea and the sky provide 'a metaphor for Grimes's subconscious', or at least that second side of his personality.

Britten, himself an individual in conflict with the society to which he had returned from America, related to Grimes. For, as well as being at odds with the town, Grimes is at odds with himself. He is tormented by the censure of The Borough and his own moral conscience. The Borough – society – though claiming it 'lives and lets live', nevertheless determines to destroy him because he does not conform.

With Britten's reputation for pacifism and homosexuality, there was unease backstage and considerable apprehension at the time of the première: many of the company were ex-servicemen. Besides, there was considerable hostility to such 'a piece of cacophony'. Joan Cross (the first Ellen) remembered the moment on the first night when the curtain came down: there was silence, then the shouting broke out. Some of those on stage wondered if it was a demonstration! It wasn't: it was applause.

Today, an audience is still left almost drained at the end. What is so shocking, so compelling about *Peter Grimes*? Is it the music which infuses the words so beautifully and clearly? Is it the accident to Boy John, or the suicide to avoid a lynching? Or is it that the sinner is society itself, not Grimes, and that it is the community – including perhaps the audience – which is to blame? Or is it just the moral perplexity engendered by feeling sorry for a bully, 'an outlaw and an enemy of society'?

The audience is left wondering, and troubled. When Grimes is told by Balstrode to go and sink himself in his boat, 'you feel that you are in the same boat as him.'

Sir Geraint Evans, the baritone, wrote, 'To me *Peter Grimes* is a truly fantastic opera and makes a thrilling evening in the theatre. I mentioned this once to Ben, and all he said was: "Can't stand it now!"' Britten, like Grimes, was enigmatic as well. Ironically, it is possibly because Grimes is such a complex character, because we suspect that there is 'something of a Grimes in each one of us', and because we do not really feel confident that we know what this seemingly simple story is actually about, that the opera is so successful dramatically.

Benjamin Britten (1913–1976) was born on St Cecilia's Day, 22 November. His father was a dentist in Lowestoft, on the East Anglian coast, where the family lived in a house facing the sea. Britten felt that he had his roots there and had a nostalgic longing for it when he spent time elsewhere. He was educated at Gresham's School, Holt, studied under the composer Frank Bridge and was briefly at the Royal College of Music. He began by earning his living largely from editing film unit music. After some difficult relationships, around 1936–1937 Britten met Peter Pears, who was about three-and-a-half years older than him. They fell in love and settled down to a stable relationship. Britten and Pears set out for the USA in April 1939. They lived with, among others, W.H. Auden and E.M. Forster. But Britten longed for his roots, and when they returned in 1943, the pair registered as conscientious objectors and gave concerts. At the start of 1944, Britten began composing *Peter Grimes*.

Britten formed the English Opera Group. This led to the foundation, in June 1948, of the Festival at Aldeburgh, where he lived with Pears. Compositions poured forth, such as *The Rape of Lucretia*, *Albert Herring*, *Billy Budd*, *The Turn of the Screw*, *A Midsummer Night's Dream*. *Gloriana* was written to mark the Queen's Coronation in 1953. One of his most significant works was the *War Requiem* written for the consecration of the reconstructed Coventry Cathedral.

Speaking about the 1930s, the daughter of *Peter Grimes* librettist Montagu Slater said that Britten was unpredictable, irritable. She was 'never sure when he would turn in a fractious fury or gently join us in a game.'

In the early 1970s, Britten's health deteriorated. He was advised to have a heart valve replacement, but he was determined first to finish composing *Death in Venice*. The operation was not a success, and he suffered a stroke in the operating theatre. He continued composing but continued to go downhill. He died in Peter Pears' arms.

WHO'S WHO AND WHAT'S WHAT

The story below is based on the libretto. Certain directors may amend opera stories to suit their production.

An inquest is being held in The Borough, a small fishing town on the East Coast of England, around 1830. **Swallow**, its pompous, unimpeachable mayor and coroner, presides. It concerns the death at sea of an apprentice of one of the town's fishermen, **Peter Grimes**, who in the view of the town is 'callous, brutal and coarse', and fails to conform. The verdict is 'accidental death'. **Ellen Orford**, a widow of about 40, the schoolmistress of the town, comforts Grimes, who needs a replacement apprentice to help him at his work.

The orchestra depicts dawn rising over the sea. Down by the

beach, townspeople and **fisher-folk**[6] are about their work. One, **Bob Boles**, a Methodist, is outraged when '**Auntie**', the landlady of The Boar, invites people into her pub, where her **two** '**nieces**' are the main attraction. Captain **Balstrode**, a retired merchant skipper, and generally a sympathetic character,[7] sees a storm out to sea.

Dr Crabbe (the poet himself, but a silent part) is seen going to the pub, and **the Rector** (Mr Horace Adams) goes to church, accompanied by **Mrs Sedley**, the affluent widow of an East India Company manager, with the nickname Mrs Nabob. She is inquisitive and interfering, and she survives on opiates.

When Peter calls for help with his boat, he is given the cold shoulder.[8] But **Ned Keene**, the apothecary and quack has found him a new apprentice. **Hobson**, the carter, declines to fetch the boy from the workhouse – until Ellen volunteers to go too.

When alone with Balstrode, Grimes declares his intention to stand up to The Borough and earn enough money from fishing to set up in comfort with Ellen.

The orchestra depicts the storm from which people shelter in The Boar. There, Mrs Sedley, an improbable pub patron, awaits the arrival of Hobson with the apprentice; she has arranged to collect her pills from him. But he is held up: the cliff has collapsed by Grimes's hut. The pub is rowdy and there is a scuffle between Balstrode and Boles, the Methodist. Grimes comes in from the storm, which he describes with Byronic flamboyance. He has a scuffle with Boles. By singing a song, order is restored. Eventually, Hobson arrives with Ellen and **Boy John** (another silent part).[9] Grimes drags John off home.

---

[6] The chorus has a big role in the opera, and several of its members have solo parts.

[7] Sir Geraint Evans enjoyed playing Balstrode: 'such an honest, straightforward, no nonsense character.' He added, 'I had no difficulty in portraying him – all I did was to think of my grandfather.'

[8] It would be difficult, even impossible, to haul single-handed a fishing boat up Aldeburgh's beach of heavy shingle. In the old days, winches were used; today, tractors.

[9] By making the part silent, Britten avoided having to find a suitable Boy John. At one stage, he thought of making John physically dumb, but he dropped this plan, probably because John's death would have put Grimes beyond any sympathy whatsoever. Slater wanted John to have a part, but it seems that Slater's wife Enid got fed up with the rows about the role, and, much to Britten's relief, intervened with 'For God's sake, make the Boy a dumb role.'

Some weeks later, on a Sunday morning outside church, Ellen sits outside and embroiders a jersey for John. She is shocked to see a tear in his coat and a bruise on his neck. Peter has seen a shoal, and, despite Ellen's protests, drags John off to help him fish. The rough conversation has been overheard, and townspeople round on Ellen. She explains that she and Peter had planned to have a new start, and to look after the boy properly. But the others are not impressed. A procession of men goes to inspect Grimes's hut.

In the hut, Grimes roughly orders the wretched boy to get ready. He gets very angry when he hears the procession in the distance. He makes John go down the cliff-side[10] to the boat. We hear John scream as he falls. By the time the procession arrives, Grimes also has gone down to the sea.

A few nights later, dark but moonlit, a dance is taking place in the Moot Hall. Outside, Mrs Sedley points out that neither Grimes nor the boy has been seen for two days. She overhears Ellen and Balstrode, who have discovered that Grimes has indeed sailed in. Ominously, they have found John's jersey, which Ellen embroidered. They know the score, but Balstrode is determined to go and help Grimes.

Mrs Sedley, scenting 'murder', calls on Swallow et al. to go and arrest Grimes. A posse, drummed up by Hobson, sets off again to the hut.

In the hut, in a 'Mad Scene', Grimes is raving. Ellen and Balstrode watch him, and then Balstrode tells him to head out in the boat and sink it out of sight of land. By the time that dawn rises, with everybody once more going about their business, the posse has returned without finding Grimes – but there is a report that a boat has been seen sinking out at sea, too far out to help.

[10] The geography at Aldeburgh – the flat land, the shallow marshes full of wildfowl – seems to preclude, at least today, the existence of a cliff in the vicinity.

440

Montagu Slater (1902–1956), the librettist, a very shy man from Cumberland, was a journalist between the wars, including working for *The Observer*. He was a colleague of Britten's at the GPO Film Unit, where Britten was working on sound effects and music for documentary films. Britten composed incidental music for Slater's left-wing plays such as 'Stay Down Miner' (Slater was a Communist).

The Slater home provided a haven for Britten in his twenties; but when writing the Grimes libretto, he was 'difficult and argumentative', and he separately published his own version of what he thought the libretto should be, thereby 'making a point' and causing a row. They drifted apart: Slater felt that Britten had become a 'court musician' and also was deeply hurt that Britten did not use him for a subsequent opera.

THE INTERVAL: TALKING POINTS

Fishermen's apprenticeships

This system, a veritable 'slave-shop', whereby the Parish got pauper children off its hands, was much abused. Parish Overseers, 'workhouse clearing men', would 'toiling slaves of piteous orphans make': a child would be bound in an apprenticeship in another Parish, and after 40 days the child would become the other Parish's responsibility. The Master was usually paid a fee of £5 for taking on the apprentice: as Crabbe put it, 'such Peter sought, and when a lad was found, the sum was dealt him, and the slave was bound.' This, one might imagine, could have been an alternative career path for Dickens's Oliver Twist.

Apparently, 'fishermen's and watermen's apprentices were notoriously ill-treated.' They were 'pinn'd, beaten, cold, pinch'd, threatened, and abused.'

Crabbe's Grimes

Crabbe's poem *The Borough* takes the form of a series of 24 'letters' written to a distant friend, in which the goings-on in the town are described: its church, professions and trades, the inn, the hospital, the prison and so forth. The work is modelled to a very considerable extent upon Aldeburgh. 'Peter Grimes' is Letter XXII and, with only 375 lines, is not long.

Crabbe's Grimes was a fisherman and part-time thief who attacked his old father with a knife, and on another occasion actually felled him, leading to his death. After his father's death, he took an apprentice. The town was aware of Peter's sadism, 'But none enquired how Peter used the rope, Or what the bruise that made the stripling stoop' ... 'and some, on hearing cries, said calmly, 'Grimes is at his exercise'. Even though the townswomen were worried, they turned a blind eye.

After Crabbe's Grimes's third apprentice died (in circumstances similar to those described in the inquest), he was prohibited from having further ones. He had to fish without help, and thus ineffectively. He was increasingly haunted, and eventually taken to the madhouse. On his deathbed, he described being haunted by the ghost of his father with two[11] of the apprentices grinning gleefully on either hand. Whenever he went out fishing, and whenever he reached three particular places, the spectres would appear. They threatened 'unremitted torments every day', and tried to lure him to his death. Finally, according to Grimes, his father 'scoop'd the flood, and there came flame about him mix'd with blood; he bade me stoop and look upon the place, then flung the hot-red liquor in my face'.

As the opera evolved, Britten, Pears and Slater made major changes to Crabbe's story, including the means of Grimes's death. Grimes's father at one time was going to have a role, but he was deleted. In particular, Grimes himself was re-characterised. Britten's Grimes is sensitive, remorseful, at odds with a cruel society of which he is the victim,

---

[11] Possibly, one of Crabbe's boys was actually driven to suicide.

and by which he is classed as a criminal and destroyed. By contrast, Crabbe's Grimes was without sensitivity or remorse (and morally a murderer). It is inconceivable that he would have had the imagination or character to sing 'Now the Great Bear and the Pleiades'.

Dr George Crabbe (1754–1832), a contemporary of Wordsworth, was born in Aldeburgh. He was the son of a saltmaster (collector of salt tax), who was alcoholic and violent towards his son. Crabbe gave up the medical profession and went to London to take up a literary career, where he managed to survive on the financial help he received from his future wife, Sarah. He sent his poems to Edmund Burke, the author and politician, who introduced him to the circle of Dr Johnson, Sir Joshua Reynolds and the Duke of Rutland. He became a clergyman and returned briefly to be curate at Aldeburgh. However, he disliked the 'venal little borough in Suffolk' and quickly moved away to be the Duke's domestic chaplain. *The Borough* was published in 1810, at the height of his fame.

After his wife's death, he became Rector of Trowbridge in Wiltshire, close to Bath. At this time, he formed 'a series of semi-romantic attachments to various young ladies'. Jane Austen's nephew records that the writer 'thoroughly enjoyed Crabbe … and would sometimes say, in jest, that if she ever married at all she could fancy being Mrs Crabbe.'

Forster thought that, although Crabbe had merit, 'he was not one of our great poets.' A nineteenth-century commentator thought he was 'one of the most original of our poets … even with naturally pleasing subjects, he was apt to blend disagreeable images' – for he told of grim, realistic incidents of rural, humble, life, with force, accuracy, great sincerity and an eye for detail.

More than a sadist

Britten insisted that Peter Pears should be his Grimes. But Pears did not convince the critics at the première that he was sufficiently thuggish for the role depicted by Crabbe: Crabbe's Grimes was a heartless sadist with whom nobody should sympathise.

Britten did not want Grimes to be portrayed thus (the part was originally intended for a baritone), nor was the role to be too lyric, which would just be dull. Peter Pears' voice was ideal.

A more robust Grimes was later performed by Jon Vickers, the leading tenor, whose interpretation was loathed by both Britten and Pears. One of the bizarre features of opera is that opera personnel often pay scant attention to the composer's intentions, performances of Wagner's operas being notorious for this. In the end, it is often the producer's opera we are seeing, rather than that of the composer.

It has been pointed out that 'the further away from its creators a stage-work gets, the greater it becomes: it is freed from the protective carapace those creators understandably fashion around it.' Some have the arrogance to assume that they can do something better than that which the composer intended. And like it or not, it has been called 'perfectly justifiable' to ignore the composer's intentions when evolving a 'valid' interpretation of a work.

Grimes's divided character

At the time of the première, critics were perplexed by what they called Grimes's 'divided nature'. They could not take on board the realistic complexity of the character. 'We never really meet the man,' said one. 'His death breaks no heart. His suicide is a mere item of police court news.'

Grimes's collision with the community, a crowd bent on vengeance and retribution, has led many to suggest that the opera is about Britten's homosexuality. Possibly 'it is Britten's awareness of his own difference that the work attempts to depict.'

Peter Pears, possibly wisely at the time, denied that there was a homosexual aspect. There is no attempt to depict Grimes himself as homosexual: he just wanted to settle down and marry Ellen and enjoy 'fruit in the garden, children by the shore, a whitened doorstep and a woman's care.' He is undeniably an outcast, 'an individual against the crowd'. Britten related this specifically to him and Pears being conscientious objectors.[12] With his music, he will (as Grimes sings at the end of the Prologue) 'thrust into their mouths, the Truth itself, the simple truth.'[13]

Musical style

Britten is not setting words to a tune in the way that some composers a hundred years earlier might have done. Like his contemporaries, and other great composers, he is infusing the words and action with his music to create a work of art; he uses a modern idiom, pleasant, although not tuneful. That said, Ellen's 'embroidery aria' in Act 3 is beautifully lyrical, in a modern way.

Volumes have been written analysing Britten's music, its key structures and so forth. Various conclusions or speculations have been put forward: for example, 'it would appear that chains of thirds are associated generally with women and femininity'; one critic has speculated that, for Britten, 'the minor third signifies homosexuality.'

An audience's concern is more likely to be with the story, the sound and the operatic experience. Much of the musical detail is likely to be beyond all but the most musically perceptive. Even if the detail is heard, the opera moves too fast for much of it to be appreciated, but there are some details which the audience can listen for.

Britten's melody often sharpens or flattens the notes in the scale which adherents of classical music otherwise might expect to hear.[14] This 'prevents the staleness' that the ear might detect if the 'classical' melody was used.

'Grace notes', clipped notes usually a semitone apart, conjure up the loneliness of the sea, 'a metaphor for Grimes's subconscious.' Their depiction is reinforced by the haunting sound of the brass. The effect

[12] Britten's and Pears' graves, side by side in the churchyard at Aldeburgh, noticeably lack the prominence which one would normally associate with people of such distinction.
[13] Britten seems to have been kind and charming, but he also had a sadistic streak, and a terrible temper. He has been described by a friend as 'psychologically crippled and bent ... Ben was one of the most tortured people I have ever known: he was on the rack, the rack of his own making.'
[14] This provides a 'modal' sound, as if the music does not use the traditional scales of classical music but (crudely) as if in the scale, the sharps and flats are ignored, and, on a piano, all the notes are white notes regardless of which scale it is.

is somewhat similar to that created by Debussy in his *La Mer* (*The Sea*). The counterpart to the grace note, where an octave is inserted, the ninth, is associated with Peter's isolation.

Key structures play an important part, although they are very unlikely to be appreciated in performance by the general listener. The antagonism between the town and Grimes is emphasised by Grimes's music being centred around A–E–B; this conflicts with the music of The Borough, which is centred around B flat (with F and E flat playing a subsidiary role). Grimes's name at the opening is sung on A whereas Swallow's description of the apprentice's death is centred on B flat.

High E has 'a crucial dramatic function' in the opera. It is reiterated in Interlude I, which depicts coastal dawn, and in 'Now the Great Bear'. Grimes finally succumbs to E flat, and The Borough.

Balstrode's abandonment of music

The abandonment of music when Balstrode tell Grimes to go and sink his boat has been criticised as a cop-out. This is odd: Balstrode's order is hardly the subject for some lyrical aria, and we may find it hard to imagine how music could have enhanced the drama at this point. The sudden use of the spoken line can be immensely effective. There is good precedent: in Beethoven's *Fidelio*, a great soprano, when intervening to prevent the murder of her husband in the dungeon, shrieked the line 'First kill his wife' rather than singing it.[15]

---

[15] The performances of this soprano, Wilhelmine Schröder-Devrient, are said to have been what inspired Wagner to compose opera. Richard Strauss used spoken voice to great effect in *Arabella*, at the moment when the heroine takes offence at her fiancé's insinuations about her behaviour with another man.

ACT BY ACT

Prologue

A coroner's inquest has convened in the Moot Hall[16] in The Borough, a small fishing town on the East Coast of England, around 1830. The case concerns the death of William Spode, the apprentice of one of the town's fishermen, Peter Grimes. The boy's body was brought ashore from Grimes's boat after it had apparently been caught in a storm heading for London with an exceptionally large catch. They were blown off course and the boy died when they ran out of drinking water. In the view of the town (voiced by its coroner Swallow), Peter Grimes is 'callous, brutal and coarse'. Swallow is the leading lawyer and the mayor, a man of unimpeachable qualities. Hobson, the carrier or carter, is acting as the constable, trying to keep order in the excitable crowd of townspeople and fisher-folk.

On sailing in, Grimes had called Ned Keene, the apothecary and quack, for help. There was a rumpus, and Grimes shouted abuse at an affluent busybody, Mrs Sedley. The schoolmistress Ellen Orford, a widow of about 40, helped carry the boy home.

The verdict of the inquest is 'accidental death'. Swallow warns Grimes that this event will not be forgotten. He tells him not to get another boy apprentice, but to get himself a fisherman to assist. Grimes protests that he cannot do without an apprentice. He is told that, if that is the case, he should get a woman to help him. But he does not want to do this, not yet, until he has 'stopped people's mouths'. When the inquest is stood down, Peter protests that there should be a proper trial, otherwise his reputation will be tarnished. The crowd leaves.

Ellen is left comforting Peter, who is pessimistic about gossip, peeping Toms and The Borough's hatred of him. He warns her that she too will be tainted, as an 'outlaw', for supporting him. In unison, they express their affinity with each other.

---

[16] Aldeburgh's tiny town hall, known as its Moot Hall, was built during the sixteenth-century Tudor period, when the town was a very prosperous shipbuilding and trading town.

Interlude I: With haunting brass and grace notes on the strings, this depicts coastal dawn.

Act 1

On a cold, grey morning in the street down by the beach, the people are about their work, hauling in boats, mending nets and so on. Captain Balstrode, a retired merchant skipper, looks out to sea.[17] He sees the storm coming. Much to his amusement, Bob Boles, a fisherman and Methodist, is outraged when 'Auntie', the landlady of The Boar pub, encourages people to come in. The main attraction of the pub is provided by her two 'nieces', who are a 'little worn', and who behave musically like twins, 'as though each has only half a personality.' Dr Crabbe (a silent role) is seen heading for the pub. The Rector (Mr Horace Adams) and Mrs Sedley are seen heading for the church.

When Peter Grimes calls out 'Give us a hand', he is given the brush-off: there are no volunteers, apart from Balstrode and Ned Keene, the apothecary. Boles looks on and says that Grimes must be shunned. Ned Keene tells Grimes that he has found and paid for an apprentice for him, but Hobson, the carter, tries to excuse himself from fetching him, until Ned insists. Boles deplores child labour.

Ellen intervenes and says that she will go and fetch the apprentice: the boy needs looking after. The crowd warns that she will share the blame. Ellen responds with 'Let her among you without fault cast the first stone.'[18]

Mrs Sedley wants her pills, which the carter is due to collect. Ned says she can collect them from the pub, a notion which horrifies her – but she agrees. Balstrode predicts a colossal tide which will flood and erode the coast.

[17] The sea may be regarded as the primary 'character' in the opera. It only appears in the orchestra: it is mysterious and timeless, independent of the petty hustle and bustle of humans. A visitor to Aldeburgh is awestruck by the impression of infinite space, as sea and sky meet each other (land, which is flat all around, forms a relatively small part of the field of vision, and the continental coast is miles beyond the horizon). Britten conveys this image in his music.

[18] The music, with its succession of downward phrases, is so moving that the first Ellen, Joan Cross, said that often she would end up in tears off stage.

Balstrode suggests to Grimes that he should leave: he should sign up for the merchant fleet or a privateer. He has little future in the town: mothers threaten their naughty children that they will be 'sent to Grimes'. But Grimes's roots are in The Borough and he does not warm to the suggestion that he should go. Balstrode knows that the dead boy was probably starved in the workhouse. Grimes describes the boy's death and how his 'silent reproach turned to illness.' He accuses The Borough gossips of being only interested in money. But he'll show them: he'll catch an enormous hoard of fish and make his fortune; and he'll marry Ellen. Balstrode suggests that he could have her now, but he does not want her because she pities him. Balstrode predicts a repeat disaster, but Peter will not listen. Balstrode goes into the pub and Peter is left alone, but optimistic for the future.

Interlude II: The storm

It is after closing time at The Boar pub and Mrs Sedley is still there awaiting the arrival of her pills. Balstrode and a fisherman come in from the storm. Mrs Sedley, being wholly out of place, is not welcomed by Auntie. Auntie's nieces are frightened by the storm, much to Balstrode's amusement. Auntie is not amused: 'A joke's a joke and fun is fun'.

Boles comes in, leaving the door open. The wind blows a window in. The nieces dislike the howling of the wind. Mrs Sedley thinks it is time to leave. Boles, the Methodist, gets drunk and tries to chat up the nieces. Auntie wants him thrown out, and there is a scuffle: Balstrode forcibly sits Boles down and orders him to keep his hands to himself: 'We live and let live, and look, we keep our hands to ourselves', the overriding ethic of The Borough. In the middle of it all, a fisherman reports that there has been a landslide up the coast, and Ned Keene reports that the cliff has collapsed near Grimes's hut. This has delayed the carter. But Mrs Sedley still wants her pills, and is horrified by the pub, the tipsy nieces and the brawls.

When Grimes makes his way in, looking wild, conversation stops and Mrs Sedley faints. Grimes comments on the storm: 'Now the

Great Bear and the Pleiades, who can decipher the stars?'[19] Everyone thinks he is drunk or mad; they want him chucked out. Boles starts moralising to Grimes and declares, 'His exercise is not with men but with killing boys.' He is about to attack him with a bottle of gin when Balstrode intervenes. Tempers become strained; Auntie fears she will lose her licence to sell alcohol.

Balstrode cools the atmosphere by suggesting that they should sing a song, 'Old Joe has gone fishing'.[20]

Ellen Orford, the carrier and the boy arrive, bedraggled and chilled to the bone. The bridge had been down. The nieces look after the boy. Peter just wants to get back home (only the cliff has collapsed – his hut remains intact), although Auntie says they should first have time to recover. Peter drags the apprentice off 'home', out into the storm. 'Do you call that home?' asks the crowd, in what has been described as 'a tremendous curtain line'.

Act 2

Interlude III: Sunday morning

Out in the street by the beach again, some weeks later, people are going to church. Ellen appears with the Boy John. She decides to stay outside, do her sewing and to talk to the boy. The religious aspirations of the church service provide a counterpoint to reality. Ellen tries to encourage John. She suggests that life was not too bad in the workhouse. And although he may have heard about the fate of his predecessor, she has made it absolutely clear to Peter that he must change.

---

[19] 'Now the Great Bear' is designed to portray a better side of Grimes's nature. The image of the firmament represents the feeling of infinite space. Arguably, this is 'the dramatic, musical and theatrical apex of the opera': in it, 'Grimes temporarily transcends the storm which is raging outside and the malicious gossip of The Borough within.'

[20] Britten suggested that the singing of 'Old Joe' is typical of a pub: tempers fray and, to ease the tension, somebody suggests that a song is sung. Someone starts up, and others follow on, one by one. The round, or canon ('Three Blind Mice' being the standard example), provides a suitable form in which to depict this: one voice comes in after another in imitation, and, at the end of the melody, begins again. Grimes shows his exclusion by holding back, and, as the score notes, 'Peter's entry upsets the course of the round.'

She is horrified to see a tear in John's coat and that his neck is bruised. Mrs Sedley overhears this.

Peter comes to take the boy out fishing against the background, ironically, of the congregation singing the 'Benedicite', the canticle from Morning Prayer ('O all ye works of the Lord, bless ye the Lord'). He has seen an enormous shoal. Ellen tries to persuade him to desist: it is Sunday, a day of rest after a week's arduous fishing. She wonders about Peter's bargain with her, that he would change. She wonders why he is so obsessed with his work. He explains that he wants to have enough money for them to have a home free from pain and gossip.

She enquires where John got the bruise. 'Out of the hurly burly,' he replies. She suggests that Peter's ways are too rough for the small boy. She wonders whether they were right to plan as they did. Surely they were mistaken to think that they could stop the gossip by obtaining wealth: the problems will never be solved with all the fish of the sea. They were too ambitious: 'We have failed,' she declares. Peter, enraged by this, strikes her. Echoing the Amen in the congregation, he declares, 'So be it, and God have mercy upon me,' and hauls the boy off. Ellen goes away, weeping.

Meanwhile, other people, including Mrs Sedley, have been watching and listening. Auntie, Ned and Boles come out. The people emerge from church. Grimes, everyone thinks, is a sadist: 'Grimes is at his exercise'.[21] But Balstrode says they should leave him alone. He warns that when gossip gets going, somebody will suffer. Boles, however, goes up the Moot Hall steps and criticises the apprentice system. Balstrode thinks it gives employment to the illegitimate.[22] Boles criticises the parson for not giving a lead.

When Ellen reappears, to collect her things, they round on her, to Balstrode's fury. She explains that they planned to have a new start, to look after the boy properly. But the others are not impressed. The

---

[21] This can seem cryptic. Crabbe's poem explains: 'Some, on hearing Cries, Said calmly, "Grimes is at his exercise".' The community wilfully abdicates its responsibility: 'We live and let live'. The Borough has its standards, and relies on the parson to lead them.

[22] The observation on the apprentice system that 'Something of the sort befits brats conceived outside the sheets' (marked *leggiero* to indicate a lightness of delivery) seems uncharacteristic for the phlegmatic Balstrode.

Rector suggests that the men should visit Grimes in his hut and put the gossip to the test. Off they go, led by Hobson. Auntie, the nieces and Ellen are left behind. Why should Auntie and the nieces get involved? As women, they count for little with the men, who, despite all they do for them, treat them like dirt and leave them 'in the gutter'.

Interlude IV: Passacaglia[23]

Later on the same morning, Grimes is in his hut, which is an upturned boat with the path to the town at one end and the collapsed cliff down to the sea at the other. 'In a towering rage', he roughly orders the wretched John to get ready. For a moment, he sees the jersey that Ellen knitted, and the music is appropriately lyrical. He tells the boy not to be frightened. Alternating between harshness and softness, he looks out over the cliff to the sea, which appears boiling with fish. The gossips listen to money: he will make a fortune and marry Ellen. He imagines a warmer home, where there is no more fear and no more storm; but, with the sound of the posse steadily approaching in the background, he also imagines that he can see the previous dead apprentice asking for drinking water when there was none to be had.

He hears the procession in the distance. His calm turns to rage again. He accuses the boy of gossiping with Ellen and the town. The boy's behaviour, cowering in the corner, sends him wild. He violently forces him to get up and he sends him down the cliff to the sea, ordering him to watch his step as the climb is dangerous. Peter's attention is distracted by a knocking at the path door. And we hear John scream and fall.[24] Peter has followed by the time the Rector and the others arrive and look down the 40ft drop, the scene of the landslide.

[23] Although a Passacaglia was a Spanish dance in the baroque period, it became associated with instrumental music in the form of variations composed over a recurring theme in the bass. The bass melody here is derived from Grimes's melodic phrase 'God have mercy upon me' and the chorus's 'Grimes is at his exercise'.

[24] The score states, 'There is a knocking at the path door. Peter turns towards it, then retreats: While Peter is between the two doors, the Boy loses his hold, screams and falls. Peter runs to the cliff door and climbs quickly out.' Based on this, Peter clearly did not push John, as some

The hut, though, is neat and empty. Swallow 'draws the moral' that they should interfere less. They leave by the path, but Balstrode goes out down the way Peter and the boy went.

Act 3

Interlude V: Moonlight[25]

A few nights later, it is dark but moonlit, outside the Moot Hall where a barn dance is taking place. And the Boar is doing good business. Swallow is chasing the nieces who find safety in numbers. The girls fool around, and Swallow grabs the first niece. Mrs Sedley, who rates herself as an amateur detective, confides in Ned Keene (who has been chasing the other niece). According to her, an earlier version of Miss Marple, neither Grimes nor the boy has been seen for two days. In her opinion, clearly Grimes has murdered him. Ned tells her to mind her own business: where's the body? he asks. She thinks he has been drowned: without doubt, there has been 'murder most foul'. Ned thinks she is mad or has had too much of the laudanum to which she is addicted.

The old townspeople head for home and, led by the Rector, bid each other good night, leaving the young behind. Mrs Sedley contin-ues to ponder the circumstances. She is out of sight but within earshot when Ellen and Balstrode come up from the beach. Grimes's boat is in but he has disappeared and Ellen has found the boy's jersey embroi-dered with an anchor. She had made it to give comfort and joy, a little luxury,[26] but now it provides the clue: they realise that the situation is hopeless. But Balstrode is determined to go and help Grimes; they cannot just turn their backs.

have suggested. Productions diverge at this key moment, depending on the intentions of the producer, not Britten.
[25] Britten marks the orchestra parts with a gentle crescendo and diminuendo on each beat of the syncopated rhythms, to depict the rolling of the sea.
[26] In this 'embroidery aria', 'the music is ingeniously contrived by Britten to suggest the very act of embroidery with weaving and tugging of thread.'

Mrs Sedley however calls in at the inn door and demands to see the lawyer, Swallow. Auntie tries to get rid of her. Swallow calls Hobson (the constable of The Borough and the carter) and orders him to search everywhere and find Grimes. The villagers congregate outside the hall when the dance has ended. There, they whip themselves up into a vengeful mob. They dislike loners: 'him who despises us we shall destroy'. A posse is formed. They all determine to get Grimes.

Interlude VI

It is some hours later. The mob and the foghorn (sounded on the tuba) can be heard in the background. Grimes, off his head in the 'Mad Scene', rambles fragments from earlier in the opera. He imagines he is bringing the boat in; he thinks of Ellen. Ellen and Balstrode watch him and then approach him. Balstrode tells him he will help him push the boat out. When he is out of sight of the Moot Hall, he must sink it. Ellen utters a horrified 'No'. 'Good-bye Peter,' says Balstrode emphatically.

* * *

Dawn rises. The Borough goes about its daily business. Britten provides a framing effect to the work, by returning to the haunting sounds of the first interlude and Act 1, and to the sea. The posse has returned without finding Grimes. Swallow says that the coastguard has reported that there is a boat sinking, too far out to help. They cannot see it. It can be ignored. The routine goes on. The curtain slowly falls.

SOURCES

Information in the Preface is taken from Berlioz, H., *Mémoires de Hector Berlioz* (Paris: Michel Lévy Frères, 1870) p. 179; Carner, M., *Puccini* (London: Duckworth, 1974) p. 140; *Times Literary Supplement* 27 June 2003 (Andrew Porter's review of *Idomeneo* at Glyndebourne).

Handel: *Giulio Cesare*

Sources of quotes: Dean, W. and Knapp, J., *Handel's Operas 1704–1726* (Oxford: Clarendon Press, 1995) pp. 7, 25, 406, 484, 488, 489, 490, 508; Winton Dean in Burrows, D. (ed.), *The Cambridge Companion to Handel* (Cambridge: Cambridge University Press, 1997) pp. 252, 258; Burrows, D. (ed.), op. cit. p. 78 (quoting Matheson); *The Spectator*, 21 March 1711 and 6 December 1711 (a letter signed jointly by Haym, Clayton and Dieupart); Grout, D., *A History of Western Music* (London: J.M. Dent & Sons, 1962) p. 405; Braddon, R., *Joan Sutherland* (London: Collins, 1962) p. 133; Lang, P.H., *Music in Western Civilisation* (London: J.M. Dent & Sons Ltd, 1963) p. 518, quoting Richard Steele; Bukofzer, M., *Music in the Baroque Era* (London: J.M. Dent & Sons Ltd, 1975) p. 7, quoting Caccini; *Encyclopaedia Britannica* ninth edition, vol. XIX, p. 451; vol. XIX, p. 452; Lebrecht, N., *The Book of Musical Anecdotes* (London: André Deutsch, 1985) p. 31; Pelham, H., *Outlines of Roman History* (London: Rivingtons, 1905) pp. 312, 316; *New Grove Dictionary of Music and Musicians* (ed. S. Sadie), (London: Macmillan, 1980) vol. 16, p. 74, Robinson (W. Dean).

Other sources: *New Oxford Companion to Music* (ed. Denis Arnold) (Oxford: Oxford University Press, 1983); Dean, W., *Giulio Cesare, in Perfect Balance*, (Glyndebourne programme, 2005); *New Grove Dictionary of Music and Musicians* (ed. S. Sadie), (London: Macmillan, 1980) vol. 16, Sartorio (E. Tarr); vol. 8, Haym (W. Dean); vol. 17, Senesino (W. Dean); vol. 3, Cuzzoni (W. Dean); vol. 3, Bordoni (W. Dean); vol. 5, Durastanti (W. Dean); vol. 16, Boschi (W. Dean); Wilkinson, T., *The Rise and Fall of Ancient Egypt* (London: Bloomsbury, 2010); Brewer, E.C., *Dictionary of Phrase and Fable* (London: Cassell, Petter, Galpin & Co. 14th edition); *Encyclopaedia Britannica* ninth edition, vol. II, p. 141; vol. IV, pp. 633, 639; vol. V, p. 826; Steen, M., *The Lives and Times of the Great Composers* (Cambridge: Icon Books, 2003); Steen, M., *Enchantress of Nations: Pauline Viardot, Soprano, Muse and Lover* (Cambridge: Icon Books, 2007).

Mozart: *The Marriage of Figaro*

Sources of quotes: Beales, D., *Joseph II, Against the World* (Cambridge: Cambridge University Press, 2009) p. 470, 474; Heartz, D., *Mozart's Operas*, (London: University of California Press, 1990) pp. 111, 123, 129, 152; Bukofzer, M., *Music in the Baroque Era* (London: J.M. Dent & Sons Ltd, 1975) p. 7, quoting Caccini; Carter, T., *Monteverdi's Musical Theatre* (New Haven and London: Yale University Press, 2002) p. 58; Kelly, M.,

Solo Recital, The Reminiscences of Michael Kelly (London: The Folio Society, 1972), p.131; FitzLyon, A., *Lorenzo da Ponte* (London: Calder, 1982) pp. 136, 228, 242, 264; Lang, P.H., *Music in Western Civilisation* (London: J.M. Dent & Sons Ltd, 1963) pp. 660, 661, 912, 913; Beaumarchais (transl. J. Wood), *The Barber of Seville and The Marriage of Figaro* (London: Penguin, 2004) p. 176; Braddon, R., *Joan Sutherland* (London: Collins, 1962) p. 56; Jenkins, G. and d'Antal, S., *Kiri* (London: HarperCollins, 1998) p. 183; *Encyclopaedia Britannica* ninth edition, vol. XIII, p. 750.

Other sources: Steptoe, A., *The Mozart–Da Ponte Operas* (Oxford: Clarendon Press, 1990); Glover, J., *Mozart's Women* (London: Macmillan, 2005); Cardus, N., *Sir Thomas Beecham, A Memoir* (London: Collins, 1961); Douglas, N., *Legendary Voices* (London: André Deutsch, 1992); Edwards, O.D., *City of a Thousand Worlds* (Edinburgh: Mainstream Publishing, 1991); Gowan, C. D'O., *France from the Regent to the Romantics* (London: Harrap, 1961); Hewlett-Davies, B., *A Night at the Opera* (London: Weidenfeld & Nicolson, 1980); *Encyclopaedia Britannica* ninth edition, vol. III, p 467; Anderson, E. (trans. and ed.), *The Letters of Mozart and His Family* (London: Macmillan, 1938); Evans, G., *A Knight at the Opera* (London: Futura, 1985); Kobbé, G., *The Complete Opera Book* (London: G.P. Putnam's Sons, 1930); Keys, I., *Mozart: His Music in His Life* (London: Elek, 1980); Cairns, D., *Viva, Viva, Grande Mozart* (Glyndebourne programme, 2001) ; Till, N., *Le Nozze di Figaro and Don Giovanni, Variations on a Theme,* (Glyndebourne programme, 1994); Vickers, H., *Even Greater Operatic Disasters* (London: Jill Norman & Hobhouse Ltd, 1982); *Le Nozze di Figaro* (London: Ernst Eulenburg) p 139; *Così fan tutte* (London: Ernst Eulenburg) p. 366; Steen, M., *The Lives and Times of the Great Composers* (Cambridge: Icon Books, 2003).

Mozart: *Don Giovanni*

Sources of quotes: Mozart, W.A., *Don Giovanni* miniature score (London: Eulenburg); Lang, P.H., *Music in Western Civilisation* (London: J.M. Dent & Sons Ltd, 1963) pp. 644, 658, 663; Rushton, J., *Mozart's Don Giovanni* (Cambridge: Cambridge University Press, 1981) pp. 2, 45, 54, 60; Berlioz, H. (transl D. Cairns), *Memoirs* (London: Cardinal, 1990) p. 54; Heartz, D., *Mozart's Operas,* (London: University of California Press, 1990) pp. 181, 210; Jefferson, A., *Elisabeth Schwarzkopf* (London: Gollancz, 1996) p. 202 quoting E.J. Dent; Walter, B, *Theme and Variations,* (London: Hamish Hamilton, 1947) p. 178; FitzLyon, A,. *Lorenzo da Ponte* (London: Calder, 1982) pp. 134, 136, 141,142, 143, 144, 207, 228, 242, 245; Kelly, M., *Solo Recital: The Reminiscences of Michael Kelly* (London: The Folio Society, 1972) p. 131; Gounod, C., (transl. W Clark & J Hutchinson) *Don Giovanni* (New York: Da Capo Press, 1970) pp. v, 53; Lebrecht, N., *The Book of Musical Anecdotes* (London: André Deutsch, 1985) p. 52; Domingo, P., *My First Forty Years* (London: Weidenfeld & Nicolson, 1983) p. 165, 166; Vickers, H., *Even Greater Operatic Disasters* (London: Jill Norman & Hobhouse Ltd, 1982) p. 32; Shaw, G.B., *Music in London 1890–94* (London: Constable, 1949) vol. i, pp. 187, 296; vol. ii, p. 283; Kobbé, G., *The Complete Opera Book* (London: G.P. Putnam's Sons, 1930) p. 43; Nilsson, B., *La Nilsson* (Boston: Northeastern University Press, 2007) p. 72.

Other sources: Steptoe, A., *The Mozart–Da Ponte Operas* (Oxford: Clarendon Press, 1990); Spaethling, R., (ed. and transl.) *Mozart's Letters, Mozart's Life* (London: Faber & Faber, 2000); Carnegy, P., *Wagner and the art of the theatre* (New Haven and London: Yale University Press, 2006); Chorley, H.F., *Thirty years' Musical Recollections* (London: Hurst & Blackett, 1862) vol. 1, vol. 2; Hewlett-Davies, B., *A Night at the Opera* (London: Weidenfeld & Nicolson, 1980); *New Grove Dictionary of Music and Musicians* (ed. S. Sadie), (London: Macmillan, 1980) vol. 5, p. 236, Da Ponte (Rudolph Angermüller); vol 7, p. 205. Gazzaniga (R. Angermüller); vol 7. p. 460 Gluck (G. Croll); vol. 12. p. 97 Melani (R.L. Weaver); Kemp, I., *Talent Transcended* (Glyndebourne programme 2000); Steen, M., *Enchantress of Nations: Pauline Viardot, Soprano, Muse and Lover* (Cambridge: Icon Books, 2007).

Mozart: *Così fan tutte*

Sources of quotes: Mozart, W.A., *Così fan tutte* full score, (London: Edition Eulenburg); Rice, J.A., *Antonio Salieri and Viennese Opera* (Chicago: University of Chicago Press, 1998) pp. 474–478; Cardus, N., *Sir Thomas Beecham, A Memoir* (London: Collins, 1961) p.92; Stendhal, (transl. R.N. Coe) *Life of Rossini* (London: John Calder, 1956) p. 468; Canning, H., *Volcanic emotions* (Glyndebourne programme, 2007) p. 56, 58, 59; Heartz, D., *Mozart's Operas* (London: University of California Press, 1990) pp. 217, 218; Jenkins, G. and d'Antal, S., *Kiri* (London: HarperCollins, 1998), p. 252; Lang, P.H., *Music in Western Civilisation* (London: J.M. Dent & Sons Ltd, 1963) p. 645, 660, 661, 673; Hall, P., *The School for Lovers or Getting Near the Truth* (Glyndebourne programme, 1987) p. 127; Chorley, H.F., *Thirty years' Musical Recollections* (London: Hurst & Blackett, 1862) vol. 1, p 215; Deutsch, O.E., *Mozart: A Documentary Biography* (Stanford: Stanford University Press, 1966) p. 508; Glover, J., *Mozart's Women* (London: Macmillan, 2005) pp. 283, 284, 287; Evans, G., *A Knight at the Opera* (London: Futura, 1985) pp. 196; Jefferson, A., *Elisabeth Schwarzkopf* (London: Victor Gollancz, 1996) p. 169.

Other sources: FitzLyon, A., *Lorenzo da Ponte* (London: Calder, 1982); Beales, D., *Joseph II* (Cambridge: Cambridge University Press, 1997); Woodfield, I., *Mozart's Così fan tutte* (Woodbridge: Boydell Press, 2008); Steptoe, A., *The Mozart–Da Ponte Operas* (Oxford: Clarendon Press, 1990); Kelly, M., *Solo Recital: The Reminiscences of Michael Kelly* (London: The Folio Society, 1972); Melitz, L., *The Opera Goer's Complete Guide* (London: J.M. Dent & Sons Ltd, 1926); Bukofzer, M., *Music in the Baroque Era* (London: J.M. Dent & Sons Ltd, 1975); *New Grove Dictionary of Music and Musicians* (ed. S. Sadie), (London: Macmillan, 1980) vol. 5, Da Ponte, p. 236 (R. Angermüller); vol. 6, Ferrarese, p. 490 (C. Raeburn); Anderson, E., *The Letters of Mozart and His Family* (London: Macmillan, 1938) vol. III, pp. 1391, 1392, 1464; Christiansen, R., *Opera* (London: Faber & Faber, 2002); *Encyclopaedia Britannica* ninth edition, vol. XV, p. 277; Halliwell, R., *The Mozart Family* (Oxford: Clarendon Press, 1998); Steen, M., *The Lives and Times of the Great Composers* (Cambridge: Icon Books, 2003).

Mozart: *The Magic Flute*

Sources of quotes: Abert, H., *The Magic Flute* (London: Eulenburg miniature score) p. iv; Shakespeare, W., *The Tempest* Act 1 Scene 2; Anderson, E. (trans. and ed.), *The Letters of Mozart and his Family* (London: Macmillan, 1938) vol. III, p. 1442; Kobbé, G., *The Complete Opera Book* (London: G.P. Putnam's Sons, 1930) pp. 46, 51; Heartz, D., *Mozart's Operas* (London: University of California Press, 1990) pp. 292; Henry, J., *Mozart the Freemason* (Rochester Vermont: Inner Traditions, 2006) pp. 15, 104; Shaw, G.B., *Music in London 1890–94* (London: Constable, 1949) vol. ii p. 261, vol. iii, p. 202; Evans, G., *A Knight at the Opera* (London: Futura, 1985) p. 54; Mackerras, C., *Die Zauberflöte, its Music and its Performance* (Glyndebourne 2005 programme) p. 65; Milnes, R., *Clashing Symbols: A Defence of the Flute libretto* (Glyndebourne 2004 programme) p. 55; Thomson, K., *The Masonic Thread in Mozart* (London: Lawrence and Wishart, 1977) p. 158; Somerset-Ward, R., *Angels & Monsters* (London: Yale University Press, 2004) p. 108; Beales, D., *Joseph II: In the Shadow of Maria Theresa 1741–1780* (Cambridge: Cambridge University Press, 1987) pp. 533, 537, 543; Chorley, H.F., *Thirty Years' Musical Recollections* (London: Hurst & Blackett, 1862) vol. 2, p. 147; Walter, B., *Theme and Variations* (London: Hamish Hamilton, 1947) p. 107; Glover, J., *Mozart's Women* (London: Macmillan, 2005) p. 305; M. Tanner, *Simplicity and Depth in Die Zauberflöte* (Glyndebourne 2005 programme) pp. 68, 69; *Musical Times* 1/6/1897 pp. 369–71.

Other sources: *New Grove Dictionary of Music and Musicians* (ed. S. Sadie) (London: Macmillan, 1980) vol. 10, p. 340, Lablache (P. Robinson); vol. 11, p. 509, Mahler (P. Banks); vol. 16, p. 296, Rubini (J. Budden), p. 644, Schikaneder (P. Branscombe); *New Oxford Companion to Music* (ed. Denis Arnold) (Oxford: Oxford University Press, 1983) pp. 1301, 1689; Beyle, H. (pseudonym Stendhal) (trans. R.N. Coe), *Life of Rossini* (London: John Calder, 1956); Müller, U. and Wapnewski, P., (trans. and ed. J. Deathridge) *Wagner Handbook* (London: Harvard University Press, 1992) p. 528 (J.M. Fischer); Jenkins, G. and d'Antal, S., *Kiri* (London: HarperCollins, 1998); Vickers, H., *Great Operatic Disasters* (London: Macmillan, 1981); Vickers, H., *Even Greater Operatic Disasters* (London: Jill Norman & Hobhouse Ltd, 1982); Spaethling, R., *Mozart's Letters, Mozart's Life* (London: Faber and Faber, 2001); Chrysalia (pseudonym): *Calaf, A Rejected Drama* (London: T. Hookham, 1826); Hewlett-Davies, B., *A Night at the Opera* (London: Weidenfeld and Nicolson, 1980); Stassinopoulos, A., *Maria* (London: Weidenfeld & Nicolson, 1980); Major, N., *Joan Sutherland* (London: Little, Brown, 1993); Steen, M., *The Lives and Times of the Great Composers* (Cambridge: Icon Books, 2003); Wilkinson T., *The Rise and Fall of Ancient Egypt* (London: Bloomsbury, 2010).

Rossini: *The Barber of Seville*

Sources of quotes: Rossini, G., *The Barber of Seville* full score (New York: Dover Publications, 1989); Lebrecht, N., *The Book of Musical Anecdotes* (London: André Deutsch, 1985) pp. 51, 104, 105; Chorley, H.F., *Thirty Years' Musical Recollections* (London: Hurst & Blackett, 1862) vol. 1, pp. 34, 36, 38, 42; Hewlett-Davies, B., *A Night at the Opera* (London: Weidenfeld & Nicolson, 1980) p. 131; Stendhal, (transl. R.N. Coe) *Life of*

Rossini (London: John Calder, 1956) pp. 55, 167, 173, 181, 183, 186, 393; Gowan, C. D'O., *France from the Regent to the Romantics* (London: Harrap, 1961) p. 102; Chissell, J., *Schumann* (London: J.M. Dent, 1977) p. 195; *Encyclopaedia Britannica* ninth edition, vol. III, p. 467; Beaumarchais (transl. J. Wood), *The Barber of Seville and The Marriage of Figaro* (London: Penguin Books, 2004); Kobbé, G., *The Complete Opera Book* (London: G.P. Putnam's Sons, 1930) pp. 300, 303; Stassinopoulos, A., *Maria* (London: Weidenfeld & Nicolson, 1980) p. 129; *New Grove Dictionary of Music and Musicians* (ed. S. Sadie) (London: Macmillan, 1980) vol. 4, p. 524 (E. Forbes); vol. 14, pp. 97–98, Paisiello (Michael F. Robinson); vol. 18, p. 126, Sterbini (F. Cella); vol. 16, p. 19, Righetti (B. Cagli); vol. 16, Rossini (Philip Gossett) pp. 228, 232, 233, 237–239, 242, 244; Evans, G., *A Knight at the Opera* (London: Futura, 1985) p. 234 ; Steen, M., *The Lives and Times of the Great Composers* (Cambridge: Icon Books, 2003) p. 245.

Other sources: Lang, P.H., *Music in Western Civilisation* (London: J.M. Dent & Sons Ltd, 1963); Weinstock, H., *Rossini: A Biography* (Oxford: Oxford University Press, 1968); Héritte-Viardot, L. (transl. E.S. Buchheim), *Memories and Adventures* (London: Mills & Boon Ltd, 1913); Müller, U. and Wapnewski, P. (transl. J. Deathridge), *The Wagner Handbook* (Cambridge, MA: Harvard University Press, 1992); Rutherford, S., *The Prima Donna and Opera 1815–1930* (Cambridge, Cambridge University Press, 2006); Lacombe, H., *The Keys to French Opera in the Nineteenth Century* (London: University of California Press, 2001) p. 367; *New Oxford Companion to Music* (ed. Denis Arnold) (Oxford: Oxford University Press, 1983) pp. 424, 1399; Steptoe, A., *The Mozart–Da Ponte Operas* (Oxford: Clarendon Press 1990); Kelly, M., *Solo Recital: The Reminiscences of Michael Kelly* (London: The Folio Society, 1972); FitzLyon, A,. *Lorenzo da Ponte* (London: Calder, 1982) p. 106; Steen, M., *Enchantress of Nations: Pauline Viardot, Soprano, Muse and Lover* (Cambridge: Icon Books, 2007) p. 34.

Rossini: *La Cenerentola*

Sources of quotes: *New Grove Dictionary of Music and Musicians* (ed. S. Sadie), (London: Macmillan, 1980) vol. 16, Rossini (Philip Gossett) p. 232; vol. 9, Isouard (M. Briquet/D. Charlton) p. 354; Shaw, G.B., *Music in London 1890–94* (London: Constable, 1949) vol. ii, pp. 42, 44; Stendhal (transl. R.N. Coe), *Life of Rossini* (London: John Calder, 1956) pp. 237, 238 244, 253; Weinstock, H., *Rossini* (Oxford, Oxford University Press, 1968) p. 70; Osborne, R., *Rossini* (London: J.M. Dent & Sons Ltd, 1986) p. 126; Lebrecht, N., *The Book of Musical Anecdotes* (London: André Deutsch, 1985) p. 105; Milnes, R., *A Journey through La Cenerentola*, (Glyndebourne programme, 2007), p. 66; Till, N., *Rossini: Some Popular Misconceptions and an Attempt to Right Some Wrongs* (Glyndebourne programme, 1985) p. 132.

Other sources: Senici, E. (ed.): *The Cambridge Companion to Rossini*, (Cambridge: Cambridge University Press, 2004); *New Grove* op. cit. vol. 6. p. 497, Ferretti (F. Cella); *Encyclopaedia Britannica* ninth edition, vol. XVIII, p. 556; Lang, P.H., *Music in Western Civilisation* (London: J.M. Dent & Sons Ltd, 1963); Müller, U. and Wapnewski, P. (trans.

J. Deathridge), *The Wagner Handbook* (Cambridge, MA: Harvard University Press, 1992); Carner, M., *Puccini* (London: Duckworth, 1974. 2nd edition); Steptoe, A., *The Mozart–Da Ponte Operas* (Oxford: Clarendon Press 1990); *New Oxford Companion to Music* (ed. Denis Arnold) (Oxford: Oxford University Press, 1983); Rutherford, S., *The Prima Donna and Opera, 1815–1930* (Cambridge: Cambridge University Press, 2006); Steen, M., *The Lives and Times of the Great Composers* (Cambridge: Icon Books, 2003); Steen, M., *Enchantress of Nations: Pauline Viardot, Soprano, Muse and Lover* (Cambridge: Icon Books, 2007).

Donizetti: *L'Elisir d'Amore*

Sources of quotes: Pavarotti, L. and Wright, W., *My World* (London: Chatto & Windus, 1995) pp. 6, 30; Breslin, H. and Midgette, A., *The King and I: Luciano Pavarotti's Rise to Fame* (Edinburgh: Mainstream Publishing, 2004) p. 164; Weinstock, H., *Donizetti and the World of Opera* (London: Methuen, 1964) pp. 58, 333; Berlioz, H. (transl. D. Cairns), *The Memoirs of Hector Berlioz* (London: Sphere Books, 1990) pp. 158, 159; Berlioz, H., *Mémoires de Hector Berlioz* (Paris: Michel Lévy Frères, 1870) p. 179; *New Grove Dictionary of Music and Musicians* (ed. S. Sadie), (London: Macmillan, 1980) vol. 5, pp. 557, 558, 562 Donizetti (J. Budden); Hewlett-Davies, B., *A Night at the Opera* (London: Weidenfeld & Nicolson, 1980) p. 116; Davidson, G., *Stories from Gilbert and Sullivan* (London: Werner Laurie, 1957) p. 170.

Other sources: Lebrecht, N., *The Book of Musical Anecdotes* (London: André Deutsch, 1985); *New Oxford Companion to Music* (ed. Denis Arnold) (Oxford: Oxford University Press, 1983) p. 113; New Grove *Dictionary of Music and Musicians* (ed. S. Sadie), (London: Macmillan, 1980) vol. 16, p. 127 Romani (W. Weaver); Bleiler, E.H. (transl. and intro.), *Lucia di Lammermoor* (New York: Dover Publications Inc., 1972); Steen, M., *The Lives and Times of the Great Composers* (Cambridge: Icon Books, 2003); Steen, M., *Enchantress of Nations: Pauline Viardot, Soprano, Muse and Lover* (Cambridge: Icon Books, 2007).

Donizetti: *Lucia di Lammermoor*

Sources of quotes: Donizetti, G., *Lucia di Lammermoor* full-score (New York: Dover Publications, 1992); *New Grove Dictionary of Music and Musicians* (ed. S. Sadie), (London: Macmillan, 1980) vol. 5, p. 558, Donizetti (J. Budden); Bleiler, E.H. (trans. and intro), *Lucia di Lammermoor* (New York: Dover Publications, Inc., 1972) pp. 27, 31, 82; *The Oxford Companion to Music* (ed. Percy Scholes) ninth edition, (Oxford: Oxford University Press, 1955) p. 1100; Weinstock, H., *Donizetti and the World of Opera* (London: Methuen, 1964), p. 131; Chorley, H.F., *Thirty Years' Musical Recollections* (Cambridge: Cambridge University Press, 2009) vol. 1 pp. 145, 146, 147, 149, 151, 154, 159; Cruttwell, P., 'Walter Scott' in *Pelican Guide to English Literature: From Blake to Byron* (Harmondsworth: Penguin, 1957) pp. 107, 110; Braddon, R., *Joan Sutherland* (London: Collins, 1962) pp. 104, 119; Scott, Sir W., *The Bride of Lammermoor* (Edinburgh: Adam & Charles Black, 1886) ch. 8, 9, 16, 18, 19; Kobbé, G., *The Complete Opera Book* (London: G.P. Putnam's Sons, 1930) p. 344, 348; Shaw, G.B., *Music in London 1890–94* (London: Constable,

1949) vol. ii, p. 151; Zviguilsky, A. (ed), *Ivan Tourguénev: Nouvelle Correspondance inédites* (Paris: Librairie des Cinq Continents, 1971) p. 21; Stassinopoulos, A., *Maria* (London: Weidenfeld & Nicolson, 1980) p. 181; Major, N., *Joan Sutherland* (London: Little, Brown, 1993) p. 227; Breslin, H., and Midgette, A., *The King and I: Luciano Pavarotti's Rise to Fame* (Edinburgh: Mainstream Publishing, 2004).

Other sources: *New Grove Dictionary of Music and Musicians* (ed. S. Sadie), (London: Macmillan, 1980) vol. 18, p. 516, Tacchinardi-Persiani, (Francesco Bussi); vol. 3, p. 651, Cammarano (W. Weaver); vol. 17, p. 84, Scott (R. Fiske); vol. 5, p. 285, Davy (R. Fiske); Ashbrook, W., *Donizetti* (London: Cassell & Company, 1965); Rutherford S., *The Prima Donna and Opera 1815–1930* (Cambridge: Cambridge University Press, 2006); Tolstoy, L. (trans. K. Zinovieff and J. Hughes), *Anna Karenina* (London: Oneworld Classics, 2008); Flaubert, G. (trans. G. Hopkins), *Madame Bovary* (Oxford: Oxford University Press, 1981); Berlioz, H. (trans. D. Cairns), *Memoirs* (London: Sphere Books, 1990); Steen, M., *The Lives and Times of the Great Composers* (Cambridge: Icon Books, 2003); *Encyclopaedia Britannica* ninth edition, vol. XXI. pp. 550, 548; Evans, I., *A Short History of English Literature* (Harmondsworth: Penguin, 1963); *Cambridge Opera Journal* vol. 16, 2004; Domingo, P., *My First Forty Years* (London: Weidenfeld & Nicolson, 1983); Steen, M., *Enchantress of Nations: Pauline Viardot, Soprano, Muse and Lover* (Cambridge: Icon Books, 2007).

Wagner: *Tannhäuser*

Sources of quotes: Wagner, R., *Tannhäuser in full score* (New York: Dover Publications); Newman, E., *The Life of Richard Wagner* (London: Cambridge University Press, 1976) vol. 1, pp. 398, 399, 481; vol. 2, p. 125; vol. 3, p. 72; Magee, B., *Wagner and Philosophy* (London: Hamish Hamilton, 2000) pp. 98, 178, 243; Bauer, O. and Wapnewski, P. in Müller, U. and Wapnewski, P. (transl. J. Deathridge), *The Wagner Handbook* (Cambridge, MA: Harvard University Press, 1992) pp. 22, 27, 28, 30, 504; Carnegy, P., *Wagner and the Art of the Theatre* (New Haven and London: Yale University Press, 2006) p. 34; Deathridge, J., *Wagner beyond Good and Evil* (London: University of California Press, 2008) pp. x, 229; Cooke, D., *Lohengrin, introduction to score* (London: Eulenburg, no date) p. x; Lacombe, H. (transl. E. Schneider), *The Keys to French Opera in the Nineteenth Century* (Berkeley, CA: University of California Press, 2001) pp. 142, 358.

Other sources: Reese, G., *Music in the Middle Ages* (London: J.M. Dent & Sons Ltd, 1941); Lebrecht, N., *The Book of Musical Anecdotes* (London: André Deutsch, 1985); *New Oxford Companion to Music* (ed. Denis Arnold) (Oxford: Oxford University Press, 1983) p. 1180; Mertens, V., Breig, W., Eger, M. in Müller, U. and Wapnewski, P. (transl. J. Deathridge), *The Wagner Handbook* (Cambridge, MA: Harvard University Press, 1992); Millington, B., *Wagner* (Master Musicians) (London: J.M. Dent, 1984); *New Grove Dictionary of Music and Musicians* (ed. S. Sadie), (London: Macmillan, 1980) vol. 20 (Wagner) p. 106 (A. Porter); Chadwick, O., *The Reformation* (London: Pelican, 1964); Insight Guide; Wartburg tourist leaflet; Nilsson, B., *La Nilsson* (Boston: Northeastern University Press, 2007); *Encyclopadia*

Britannica fifteenth edition; Zola, E. (transl. D. Parmée), *Nana* (Oxford: Oxford University Press, 1998; first published 1880); *The Book of Saints*, compiled by the Benedictine Monks of St Augustine's Abbey, Ramsgate, 6th edition (London: A&C Black, 1989); Rutherford, S., *The Prima Donna and Opera, 1815–1930* (Cambridge: Cambridge University Press, 2006); Jost, P., *Tannhäuser is Killing Me* (Bayreuth programme, 2005) p. 90; Steen, M., *The Lives and Times of the Great Composers* (Cambridge: Icon Books, 2003).

Wagner: *Tristan und Isolde*

Sources of quotes: Wagner, R., *Tristan und Isolde* full score (London: Eulenberg); Gottfried von Strassburg (transl. A. Hatto), *Tristan* (Harmondsworth: Penguin, 1967) pp. 173, 185; Mann, T. (transl. A. Blunden), *Pro and Contra Wagner*, (London: Faber and Faber, 1985) p. 124; Schopenhauer, A. (transl. E. Payne), *The World as Will and Representation* (New York: Dover Publications, 1958) vol II, p. 533 (Supplement to Book IV, *The Metaphysics of Sexual Love*); Müller, U. and Wapnewski, P. (transl. J. Deathridge), *The Wagner Handbook* (Cambridge, MA: Harvard University Press, 1992) pp. 66, 70, 72, 73 (P. Wapnewski); p. 257 (V. Mertens); p. 291 (H. Reinhardt); p. 509 (O. Bauer); Carner, M., *Puccini* (London: Duckworth, 1974 2nd edition) pp. 171, 272; Walter, B., *Theme and Variations*, (London: Hamish Hamilton, 1947) p. 42; Lang, P.H., *Music in Western Civilisation* (London: J.M. Dent & Sons Ltd, 1963) pp. 886, 887, 888, 892, 982; Carnegy, P., *Wagner and the Art of the Theatre* (New Haven and London: Yale University Press, 2006) pp. 50, 55, 58, 288; Newman, E., *The Life of Richard Wagner* (London: Cassell, 1976) vol 2, pp. 153, 152, 174, 531, 532, 542; Blunt, W., *The Dream King* (London: Hamish Hamilton, 1970) pp. 50, 51; Kobbé, G., *The Complete Opera Book* (London: G.P. Putnam's Sons, 1930) pp. 141, 228, 230; Grout, D., *A History of Western Music* (London: J.M. Dent & Sons, 1962) p. 567; *New Oxford Companion to Music* (ed. Denis Arnold) (Oxford: Oxford University Press, 1983) pp. 1064, 1056; Lebrecht, N., *The Book of Musical Anecdotes* (London: André Deutsch, 1985) p. 188; Einstein, A., *Music in the Romantic Era* (London: J.M. Dent & Sons Ltd, 1947) pp. 34, 240, 241; Nilsson, B., *La Nilsson* (Boston: Northeastern University Press, 2007) pp. 7, 10, 157, 165; Lampedusa, G. di, *The Leopard* (London: William Collins, Fontana books, 1963) ch. 4, pp. 117, 133; Breslin, H., and Midgette, A., *The King and I: Luciano Pavarotti's Rise to Fame* (Edinburgh: Mainstream Publishing, 2004) p. 53; Heyworth, P., *Otto Klemperer* (Cambridge: Cambridge University Press, 1983) pp. 27, 250; Atkins, H., and Newman, A., *Beecham Stories* (London: Futura, 1983), p. 41; Cardus, N., *Sir Thomas Beecham: A Memoir* (London: Collins, 1961) p. 118.

Other sources: Deathridge, J., *Wagner beyond Good and Evil* (London: University of California Press, 2008); Steen, J., *Verse and Virtuosity* (Toronto: University of Toronto Press, 2008); Vickers, H., *Even Greater Operatic Disasters* (London: Jill Norman & Hobhouse Ltd, 1982); Magee, B., *Wagner and Philosophy* (London: Hamish Hamilton, 2000); Steen, M., *Enchantress of Nations: Pauline Viardot, Soprano, Muse and Lover* (Cambridge: Icon Books, 2007); Müller, U. and Wapnewski, P. (transl. J. Deathridge), *The Wagner Handbook* (Cambridge, MA: Harvard University Press, 1992) W. Breig, P. Branscombe; C. Dahlhaus; E. Koppen; U. Müller; *New Grove Dictionary of Music and Musicians* (ed. S. Sadie),

(London: Macmillan, 1980) vol. 3, p. 452 Bülow (J. Warrack); vol. 8, p. 636 Hofmansthal (R. Henderson); vol. 9, p. 843 Keilberth (G. Brunner); vol. 12, p. 103 Melchior (D. Shawe-Taylor); Stassinopoulos, A., *Maria* (London: Weidenfeld & Nicolson, 1980).

Verdi: *Rigoletto*

Sources of quotes: Phillips-Matz, M.J., *Verdi* (Oxford: Oxford University Press, 1993) pp. 265, 284; Budden, J., *The Operas of Verdi* (New York: Oxford University Press, 1984) vol. 2, pp. 480, 491, 498, 504, 510; Walter, B., *Theme and Variations* (London: Hamish Hamilton, 1947) p. 139; Evans, G., *A Knight at the Opera* (London: Futura, 1985) p. 109; Douglas, N., *Legendary Voices* (London: André Deutsch, 1992) pp. 47, 107; Chorley, H.F., *Thirty Years' Musical Recollections*, (London: Hurst & Blackett, 1862) vol. 1, pp. 27, 288; Héritte-Viardot, L. (transl. E.S. Bucheim), *Memories and Adventures* (London: Mills & Boon, 1913) p. 95; Lang, P.H., *Music in Western Civilisation* (London: J.M. Dent & Sons Ltd, 1963) pp. 331, 829; Einstein, A., *Music in the Romantic Era* (London: J.M. Dent & Sons Ltd, 1947) p. 273; *New Grove Dictionary of Music and Musicians* (ed. S. Sadie), (London: Macmillan, 1980) vol. 19, p. 641 Verdi (A. Porter); Burton, W.E. (transl.), *The Court Fool, or, A King's Amusement*, 1834, Act 1 scene 4, p. 288; Act 2 pp. 292, 294; Gobbi, T., *On His World of Italian Opera* (London: Hamish Hamilton, 1984) p. 94; Steen, M., *Enchantress of Nations: Pauline Viardot, Soprano, Muse and Lover* (Cambridge: Icon Books, 2007) p. 256.

Other sources: Lebrecht, N., *The Book of Musical Anecdotes* (London: André Deutsch, 1985); Kobbé, G., *The Complete Opera Book* (London: G.P. Putnam's Sons, 1930); *New Grove* op. cit. vol. 18, p. 268 Strepponi (J. Budden); *New Grove* op. cit. vol. 19, p. 534 Varesi (E. Forbes); Hewlett-Davies, B., *A Night at the Opera* (London: Weidenfeld & Nicolson, 1980); Bernas, R., in John, N., (ed.) *The Force of Destiny: Opera Guide* (London: John Calder, 1983); Vickers, H., *Great Operatic Disasters* (London: Macmillan, 1981); Steen, M., *The Lives and Times of the Great Composers* (Cambridge: Icon Books, 2003).

Verdi: *Il Trovatore*

Sources of quotes: Verdi, G., *Il Trovatore* (full score) (Milan: Ricordi, 1918); Chorley, H.F., *Thirty Years' Musical Recollections* (London: Hurst & Blackett, 1862) vol. 2, pp. 219, 221, 222; Phillips-Matz, M.J., *Verdi* (Oxford: Oxford University Press, 1993) p. 331; Héritte-Viardot, Louise (transl. E.S. Bucheim), *Memories and Adventures* (London: Mills & Boon, 1913) p. 63; Rutherford, S., *The Prima Donna and Opera 1815–1930* (Cambridge: Cambridge University Press, 2006) p. 227; Kobbé, G., *The Complete Opera Book* (London: G.P. Putnam's Sons, 1930) pp. 403, 407, 413; Shaw, G.B., *Music in London 1890–94* (London: Constable, 1949) vol. 1, p. 6; Budden, J., *The Operas of Verdi*, (New York: Oxford University Press, 1984) vol. 2, pp. 67, 75, 86, 89, 100, 104, 112; FitzLyon, A., *The Price of Genius* (London: John Calder, 1964) p. 301; Walter, B., *Theme and Variations*, (London: Hamish Hamilton, 1947) p. 139; Steen, M., *The Lives and Times of the Great Composers* (Cambridge: Icon Books, 2003) ch. 16; Gutiérrez, A.G. (transl. R.G. Trimble), *El Trovador*

(The Troubadour) (Lewiston NY: The Edward Mellen Press, 2004) p. ix, quoting R. Milnes; Domingo, P., *My First Forty Years* (London: Weidenfeld & Nicolson, 1983) p. 87.

Other sources: *New Grove Dictionary of Music and Musicians* (ed. S. Sadie), (London: Macmillan, 1980) vol. 3, p. 651, Cammarano (W. Weaver); *Encyclopaedia Britannica* ninth edition, vol. XXII, p 361; vol. XXIV, p. 619; Davidson, G., *Stories from Gilbert and Sullivan* (London: Werner Laurie, 1957); Major, N., *Joan Sutherland* (London: Little Brown, 1993); Douglas, N., *Legendary Voices* (London: André Deutsch, 1992).

Verdi: *La Traviata*

Sources of quotes: Verdi, G., *La Traviata* full score (New York: Dover Publications, 1990); Rutherford, S., *The Prima Donna and Opera, 1815–1930*, (Cambridge: Cambridge University Press, 2006) p. 40; Dumas, A., fils, *Camille* (Paris: D. Giraud et J. Dagneau, 1851) frontispiece: 'S'adresser, pour la musique exacte à M.R. Taranne, 15, rue Montmartre'; Dumas, A., fils, *La Dame aux Camélias*, (Bruxelles and Leipzig: Kiessling, Schnée et Cie, 1854) vol. 1, pp. 179, 182, 196: 'je la possédais'; Dumas, A., fils, *The Lady with the Camelias* (London: George Vickers, 1856); introduction by Jules Janin, p. viii, p. 91; Dumas, A. (transl. B. Bray), *La Dame aux Camélias* (London: The Folio Society, 1975) p. 22; Dumas, A., fils, *Camille or The Fate of a Coquette* (New York: Samuel French, 1856) Act 1, p. 12; *The Lady with the Camelias* (Edinburgh: The New University Society, no date) pp. 84, 155; Shakespeare: *Othello*, Act IV Scene 1 line 112; *New Grove Dictionary of Music and Musicians* (ed. S. Sadie), (London: Macmillan, 1980) vol. 14, p. 718 Piave (W.Weaver); Phillips-Matz, M.J., *Verdi* (Oxford: Oxford University Press, 1993) pp. 324, 328, 329; Douglas, N., *Legendary Voices* (London: André Deutsch, 1992) p. 21; *Encyclopaedia Britannica* ninth edition, vol. XVIII, p. 855; vol. VII, p. 522; McPhee, P., *A Social History of France 1780–1880*, (London: Palgrave Macmillan, 2004) p. 193; Horne, A., *The Fall of Paris*, (London: Macmillan, 1965) p. 19; Gobbi, T., *On His World of Italian Opera* (London: Hamish Hamilton, 1984) p. 108; Budden, J., *The Operas of Verdi*, (New York: Oxford University Press, 1984) vol. 2, pp. 115, 144; Shaw, B., *Music in London 1890–94* (London: Constable, 1949) vol. 1, p. 177; Somerset-Ward, R., *Angels and Monsters* (New Haven and London: Yale University Press 2004) p. 184; Chorley, H.F., *Thirty Years' Musical Recollections* (London: Hurst & Blackett, 1862) vol. 1, pp. 27, 289; vol. 2, pp. 236, 238–40, 276, 290, 302; Stassinopoulos, A., *Maria* (London: Weidenfeld and Nicolson, 1980) p. 221; Domingo, P., *My First Forty Years* (London: Weidenfeld & Nicolson, 1983) p. 1; Walter, B., *Theme and Variations,* (London: Hamish Hamilton, 1947) p. 139; Steen, M., *The Lives and Times of the Great Composers* (Cambridge: Icon Books, 2003) ch. 16.

Other sources: Christiansen, R., *Prima Donna – A History*, (London: Pimlico, 1995); *New Grove Dictionary of Music and Musicians* (ed. S. Sadie), (London: Macmillan, 1980) Salvini-Donatelli (C. Jahant); Kobbé, G., *The Complete Opera Book* (London: G.P. Putnam's Sons, 1930); Hewlett-Davies, B., *A Night at the Opera* (London: Weidenfeld & Nicolson, 1980); *Black's Medical Dictionary* (London: A&C Black, 1999); Carner, M., *Puccini*

(London: Duckworth, 1974 2nd edition); Barbier, P. (transl. R. Luoma), *Opera in Paris 1800–1850* (Portland, OR: Amadeus Press, 1995); Richardson, J., *The Courtesans – The Demi-monde in 19th Century France*, (London: Weidenfeld & Nicolson, 1967); Jenkins, G. & d'Antal, S., *Kiri* (London: HarperCollins, 1998); Jefferson, A., *Elisabeth Schwarzkopf* (London: Victor Gollancz 1996); Braddon, R., *Joan Sutherland* (London: Collins, 1962); Zola, E. (transl. M. Mauldon), *L'Assommoir* (Oxford: Oxford University Press, 1998); Maupassant, G. de, *The Sign*, (London: The Folio Society, 1959); Breslin, H., & Midgette, A., *The King and I, Luciano Pavarotti's Rise to Fame* (Edinburgh: Mainstream Publishing, 2004); Steen, M., *Enchantress of Nations, Pauline Viardot, Soprano, Muse and Lover* (Cambridge: Icon Books, 2007).

Verdi: *Aïda*

Sources of quotes: Verdi, G., *Aïda* full score (New York: Dover Publications, 1989); Shaw, G.B., *Music in London 1890–94* (London: Constable, 1949). vol. ii, p. 282; Douglas, N., *Legendary Voices* (London: André Deutsch, 1992) p. 5; Kobbé, G., *The Complete Opera Book* (London: G.P. Putnam's Sons, 1930) p. 454; Steen, M., *The Lives and Times of the Great Composers* (Cambridge: Icon Books, 2003) ch. 16; Phillips-Matz, M.J., *Verdi* (Oxford: Oxford University Press, 1993) pp. 580, 590, 597, 598; Budden, J., *The Operas of Verdi*, (New York: Oxford University Press, 1984) vol. 3, pp. 189, 211, 220, 223, 225, 233, 235, 244, 255, 258.

Other sources: *New Grove Dictionary of Music and Musicians* (ed. S. Sadie), (London: Macmillan, 1980) vol. 2, p. 760 Bizet (W. Dean); vol. 7, p. 342 Ghislanzoni (W. Weaver); vol. 19, p. 655 Verdi (A. Porter); Rutherford, S., *The Prima Donna and Opera* (Cambridge: Cambridge University Press, 2006); *Encyclopaedia Britannica* ninth edition, vol. IV, p. 789; vol. VII, pp. 715, 766; vol. XV, p. 542; vol. XXII, p. 620; Shaw, I., *The Oxford History of Ancient Egypt* (Oxford: Oxford University Press, 2000); Kobbé, G., *The Complete Opera Book* (London: G.P. Putnam's Sons, 1930); Walter, B., *Theme and Variations* (London: Hamish Hamilton, 1947); Somerset-Ward, R., *Angels & Monsters* (New Haven and London: Yale University Press, 2004); Breslin, H. and Midgette, A., *The King and I: Luciano Pavarotti's Rise to Fame* (Edinburgh: Mainstream, 2004); Stassinopoulos, A., *Maria* (London: Weidenfeld & Nicolson, 1980); *New Oxford Companion to Music* (ed. Denis Arnold) (Oxford: Oxford University Press, 1983) p. 1170; Horne, A., *The Fall of Paris* (London: Macmillan, 1965); Zola, E. (transl. M. Mauldon), *L'Assommoir* (Oxford: Oxford University Press, 1995); Vickers, H., *Great Operatic Disasters* (London: Macmillan, 1981); Nilsson, B., *La Nilsson* (Boston: Northeastern University Press, 2007).

Gounod: *Faust*

Sources of quotes: Gounod, C., (transl. Chorley, ed. Sullivan) *Faust* (London: Boosey & Co. no date); Harding, J., *Gounod* (London: George Allen & Unwin, 1973) pp. 13, 109; Huebner, S., *The Operas of Charles Gounod* (Oxford: Clarendon Press, 1992) p. 114; *New Grove Dictionary of Opera* (ed. S. Sadie), (London: Macmillan, 1992) vol. 2, p. 135

(W. Ashbrook); *New Oxford Companion to Music* (ed. Denis Arnold) (Oxford: Oxford University Press, 1983) p. 664; Moore, G., *Am I Too Loud?* (London: Hamish Hamilton, 1962) p. 30; Kobbé, G., *The Complete Opera Book* (London: G.P. Putnam's Sons, 1930) p. 570; Poesio, G., *Temptations on Pointe Shoes* (London: Royal Opera House Covent Garden programme, 2004) pp. 30, 32; Zviguilsky, A. (ed.), *Ivan Tourguénev: Nouvelle Correspondance inédites* (Paris: Librairie des Cinq Continents, 1971) p. 121; Lang, P.H., *Music in Western Civilisation* (London: J.M. Dent & Sons Ltd, 1963) pp. 624, 863; Barbier, P. (transl. R. Luoma), *Opera in Paris 1800–1850* (Portland, OR: Amadeus Press, 1995) p. 111; Einstein, A., *Music in the Romantic Era* (London: J.M. Dent & Sons Ltd, 1947) pp. 258, 259; Müller, U. and Wapnewski, P. (transl. J. Deathridge), *The Wagner Handbook* (Cambridge, MA: Harvard University Press, 1992) p. 611; Shaw, G.B., *Music in London 1890–94* (London: Constable, 1949) vol. ii, p. 251; Brewer, E.C., *Dictionary of Phrase and Fable* (London: Cassell, Petter Galpin & Co. 14th edition) p. 683; *Encyclopaedia Britannica* ninth edition, vol. IX, p.55; vol. X, p. 734; Santley, C., *Student and Singer* (London: Edward Arnold, 1892) p. 207; Cardus, N., *Sir Thomas Beecham, A Memoir* (London: Collins, 1961) p. 100; Steen, M., *The Lives and Times of the Great Composers* (Cambridge: Icon Books, 2003).

Other sources: *New Grove Dictionary of Music and Musicians* (ed. S. Sadie), (London: Macmillan, 1980) vol. 7, p. 583 Gounod (Martin Cooper); vol. 3, pp. 840, 842 Carvalho (H. Rosenthal); vol. 20, p. 690, Zimmermann (Frédéric Robert); *Encyclopaedia Britannica* ninth edition; vol. X, pp. 723, 725, 734, 735, 736; Bury, J., *France 1814–1940* (London: Methuen, 1969); Royal Opera House Covent Garden 2004 programme; Grout, D., *A History of Western Music* (London: J.M. Dent & Sons, 1962); Walsh, T.J., *Second Empire Opera* (London: Calder, 1981); Curtiss, M., 'Unpublished Letters by Georges Bizet', *Musical Quarterly* vol. 36, 1950, p. 395; *Book of Saints*, (London: A&C Black, 1989); Irvine, D., *Massenet: A Chronicle of His Life and Times*, Amadeus Press 1997; Steen, M., *Enchantress of Nations: Pauline Viardot, Soprano, Muse and Lover* (Cambridge: Icon Books, 2007); Solomon, M., *Beethoven* (New York: Schirmer, 1998); Waddington, P., 'Turgenev's Relations with H.F. Chorley', *New Zealand Slavonic Journal*, 1978, No. 2, p. 27.

Johann Strauss: *Die Fledermaus*

Sources of quotes: Strauss, J., *Die Fledermaus* Vocal Score (New York: Dover Publications 2001); *New Grove Dictionary of Music and Musicians* (ed. S. Sadie), (London: Macmillan, 1980) vol. 18, p. 211, Strauss (M. Carner/M. Schönherr); Crittenden, C., *Johann Strauss and Vienna* (Cambridge: Cambridge University Press, 2000) p. 167; Fantel, H., *Johann Strauss* (Newton Abbott: David & Charles, 1971) p. 181; Clark, A., *The Unbearable Lightness of Being* (Glyndebourne programme, 2006) pp. 70, 71, 73; Gartenberg, E., *Johann Strauss* (New York: Da Capo, 1974) p. 218; Douglas, N., *Legendary Voices* (London: André Deutsch, 1992) p. 144; Okey, R., *The Habsburg Monarchy c. 1765–1918* (London: Macmillan, 2001) pp. 229, 231; Lang, P.H., *Music in Western Civilisation* (London: J.M. Dent & Sons Ltd, 1963) p. 1004; Goncharov, I. (transl. D Magarshack), *Oblomov* (London: Penguin, 1954) part III, ch. 5, p. 321; Turgenev, I. (transl. C. Garnett), *Virgin*

Soil (New York: New York Review Books, 2000) part II, ch. 37, p. 340; Turgenev, I. (transl. R. Freeborn), *First Love and other stories* (Oxford: Oxford University Press, 1999) pp. 13, 33, 72; Seton-Watson, H., *The Russian Empire 1801–1917* (Oxford: The Clarendon Press, 1988) p. 24; Saunders, D., *Russia in the Age of Reaction and Reform* (London: Longman, 1992) p.18; Steen, M., *The Lives and Times of the Great Composers* (Cambridge: Icon Books, 2003) pp. 492, 508.

Other sources: Walker, A., *Franz Liszt Vol. 1: The Virtuoso Years, 1811–47* (London: Faber and Faber, 1983); Vickers, H., *Even Greater Operatic Disasters* (London: Jill Norman & Hobhouse Ltd, 1982); Tauber, R., *From Vaudeville Bluebird to Operetta Bat* (Glyndebourne programme, 2003) pp. 89, 90; Grout, D.J., *A History of Western Music,* (London: J.M. Dent & Sons Ltd, 1962); Pushkin, A. (transl. C. Johnston), *Eugene Onegin* (Penguin, London 2003); *New Oxford Companion to Music* (ed. Denis Arnold) (Oxford: Oxford University Press, 1983) pp.1464, 1966; Steen, M., *Enchantress of Nations: Pauline Viardot, Soprano, Muse and Lover* (Cambridge: Icon Books, 2007).

Bizet: *Carmen*

Sources of quotes: Bizet, G., *Carmen* full score (New York: Dover Publications, 1989); Hewlett-Davies, B., *A Night at the Opera* (London: Weidenfeld & Nicolson, 1980) pp. 79, 118; Jenkins, G. and d'Antal, S., *Kiri* (London: HarperCollins, 1998) pp. 157, 162, 163; *New Grove Dictionary of Music and Musicians* (ed. S. Sadie), (London: Macmillan, 1980) Bizet (Winton Dean) vol. 2, p. 760; *Encyclopaedia Britannica* ninth edition, vol. XVI, pp. 37, 39; Somerset-Ward, R., *Angels and Monsters* (New Haven and London: Yale University Press, 2004) p. 184; Holden, A., *Tchaikovsky* (London: Bantam Press, 1995) p. 103; Vickers, H., *Even Greater Operatic Disasters* (London: Jill Norman & Hobhouse Ltd, 1982) p. 59; Lucas, J., *Thomas Beecham* (Woodbridge, Suffolk: The Boydell Press, 2008) pp. 277, 290; Atkins, H. and Newman, A., *Beecham Stories* (London: Futura, 1983) p. 37; Cobbe, H. (ed.), *Letters of Ralph Vaughan Williams* (Oxford: Oxford University Press, 2008) p. 420; Lang, P.H., *Music in Western Civilisation* (London: J.M. Dent & Sons Ltd, 1963) pp. 907, 908, 923, 924; Budden, J., *The Operas of Verdi,* (New York: Oxford University Press, 1984) vol. 3, p. 445; *New Grove* op. cit. Galli-Marié (Harold Rosenthal) vol. 7, p. 127; Domingo, P., *My First Forty Years* (London: Weidenfeld & Nicolson, 1983) p. 93.

Other sources: Lacombe, H., *The Keys to French Opera in the Nineteenth Century,* (London: University of California Press, 2001); *New Oxford Companion to Music* (ed. Denis Arnold) (Oxford: Oxford University Press, 1983); Rees, B., *Camille Saint-Saëns* (London: Chatto & Windus, 1999), p. 185; Braddon, R., *Joan Sutherland* (London: Collins, 1962); *The Concise Oxford Dictionary*; Vickers, H., *Great Operatic Disasters* (London: Macmillan, 1981); *New Grove* op. cit. Guiraud (Hugh MacDonald) vol. 7; Beales, D., *Joseph II: Against the World 1780–1790* (Cambridge: Cambridge University Press, 2009); *New Oxford Companion to Music* (ed. Denis Arnold) (Oxford: Oxford University Press, 1983) p. 799; Steen, M., *The Lives and Times of the Great Composers* (Cambridge: Icon Books, 2003).

Tchaikovsky: *Eugene Onegin*

Sources of quotes: Tchaikovsky, P., *Eugene Onegin* full score (New York: Dover Publications, 1997); Shaw, G.B., *Music in London 1890–94* (London: Constable, 1949) vol. ii, p. 172; Turgenev, I., *On the Eve* ch. 2; Goncharov, *Oblomov* part II ch. 3, ch. 4, part III, ch. 5; *The Times Literary Supplement*, 27 June 2008, p. 32; *New Grove Dictionary of Music and Musicians* (ed. S. Sadie), (London: Macmillan, 1980) Tchaikovsky (David Brown) vol. 18, p. 617; Lermontov, M. (trans. P. Foote), *A Hero of Our Time* (London: Penguin, 2001) p. xvii, part II, ch. 2 (*Princess Mary*); Freeborn, R., *Turgenev, the Novelist's Novelist* (Oxford: Oxford University Press, 1960) p. 20; Turgenev, I. (trans. and intro. R. Freeborn), *First Love and other stories* (Oxford: Oxford University Press, 1999) p. 32; Turgenev, I. (trans. R. Freeborn), *Rudin* (London: Penguin, 1975) p. 9; FitzLyon, A., *The Price of Genius* (London: John Calder, 1964) p. 243; Tolstoy, L., *War and Peace* book VIII ch. 3; Tolstoy, L. (trans. K. Zinovieff and J. Hughes), *Anna Karenina* (Richmond: Oneworld Classics, 2008) part III, ch. 26.

Other sources: Holden, A., *Tchaikovsky* (London: Transworld, 1995); Pushkin, A. (trans. C. Johnston), *Eugene Onegin* (London: Penguin, 2003) preface by J. Bayley; Pushkin, A. (trans. V. Nabokov), *Eugene Onegin* (London: Routledge & Kegan Paul, 1964) vol. 1; Pushkin, A., *The Complete Works* (Downham Market: Milner & Co., 1999) vol. 4; *Encyclopaedia Britannica* ninth edition, vol. XIX p. 649; Saunders, D., *Russia in the Age of Reaction and Reform*, (London: Longman, 1992); Figes, O., *Natasha's Dance* (London: Allen Lane, 2002); Waller, B. (ed), *Themes in Modern European History 1830–1890*, (London: Unwin Hyman, 1990); Turgenev, I., *Punin and Baburin*; Turgenev, I., *Khor and Kalinych*; Turgenev, I. (trans. Constance Garnett), *Virgin Soil* (New York: New York Review Books, 2000) part II, ch. 37; *The Oxford Book of Saints* (London: A&C Black, 1989); *New Oxford Companion to Music* (ed. Denis Arnold), (Oxford: Oxford University Press, 1983) pp. 501, 694, 1144, 1465; Steen, M., *The Lives and Times of the Great Composers* (Cambridge: Icon Books, 2003); Greenish, A., *The Student's Dictionary of Musical Terms* (London: Joseph Williams, 1953); Steen, M., *Enchantress of Nations: Pauline Viardot, Soprano, Muse and Lover* (Cambridge: Icon Books, 2007).

'Cav & Pag'

Sources of quotes: Mascagni, P., *Cavalleria Rusticana* full score (New York: Dover Publications, 1993); Leoncavallo, R., *Pagliacci* full score (New York: Dover Publications, 1992); Carner, M., *Puccini* (London: Duckworth, 1974 2nd edition) pp. 258, 260, 261; Walter, B., *Theme and Variations*, (London: Hamish Hamilton, 1947) p. 54; Kobbé, G., *The Complete Opera Book* (London: G.P. Putnam's Sons, 1930) pp. 613, 617, 632; Barrie Jones, J. (transl. and ed.), *Gabriel Fauré: A Life in Letters* (London: Batsford, 1988) p. 111; Shaw, B., *Music in London 1890–94* (London: Constable, 1949) vol. 1, pp. 264, 267, 270; vol. 3, p. 219; *New Grove Dictionary of Music and Musicians* (ed. S. Sadie), (London: Macmillan, 1980) vol. 10, p. 673, Leoncavallo (W. Ashbrook); vol. 11, p. 743, Mascagni (W. Ashbrook); Lebrecht, N., *The Book of Musical Anecdotes* (London: André Deutsch, 1985), pp. 242, 266.

Other sources: Domingo, P., *My First Forty Years* (London: Weidenfeld & Nicolson, 1983); Lang, P.H., *Music in Western Civilisation* (London: J.M. Dent & Sons Ltd, 1963); *New Oxford Companion to Music* (ed. Denis Arnold) (Oxford: Oxford University Press, 1983) pp. 1306, 1909; Phillips-Matz, M.J., *Verdi* (Oxford: Oxford University Press, 1993); Vickers, H., *Great Operatic Disasters* (London: Macmillan, 1981); *Encyclopaedia Britannica* ninth edition, vol. VII, p. 418; Steen, M., *The Lives and Times of the Great Composers* (Cambridge: Icon Books, 2003).

Puccini: *La Bohème*

Sources of quotes: Puccini, G., *La Bohème*, full score (Milan: Ricordi, 1999); Carner, M., *Puccini* (London: Duckworth, 1992. 3rd edition) pp. 86, 88, 93, 341, 342, 345; *Encyclopaedia Britannica* ninth edition, vol. XVII, p. 54; vol XVIII, pp. 405 (pathology), 855, 858 (Phthisis); *New Grove Dictionary of Music and Musicians* (ed. S. Sadie), (London: Macmillan, 1980) vol. 15, Puccini (M. Carner) pp. 437, 435; Barrie Jones, J. (trans. and ed.) *Gabriel Fauré: A Life in Letters* (London: Batsford, 1988) p. 103; Lang, P.H., *Music in Western Civilisation* (London: J.M. Dent & Sons Ltd, 1963) pp. 999, 1000; Pavarotti, L. and Wright, W., *My World* (London: Chatto & Windus 1995) pp. 36, 37, 284; Hewlett-Davies, B., *A Night at the Opera* (London: Weidenfeld & Nicolson, 1980) p. 45; Atkins, H., and Newman, A., *Beecham Stories* (London: Futura 1983) p. 37; Breslin, H., and Midgette, A., *The King and I: Luciano Pavarotti's Rise to Fame* (Edinburgh: Mainstream Publishing, 2004) p. 175; McPhee, P., *A Social History of France 1789–1914* (Basingstoke: Palgrave Macmillan, 2004) pp. 130, 138, 141, 189.

Other sources: Jenkins, G. and d'Antal, S., *Kiri* (London: HarperCollins, 1998); Mansel, P., *Paris Between Empires, 1814–1852* (London: John Murray, 2001); *New Grove op. cit.* vol. 7, Giacosa (W. Weaver); vol. 9 Illica (W. Weaver); Shaw, B., *Music in London 1890–94* (London: Constable, 1949); Vickers, H., *Even Greater Operatic Disasters* (London: Jill Norman & Hobhouse Ltd, 1982); Steen, M., *The Lives and Times of the Great Composers* (Cambridge: Icon Books, 2003) ch. 27; Lucas, J., *Thomas Beecham* (Woodbridge: The Boydell Press, 2008).

Puccini: *Tosca*

Sources of quotes: Carner, M., *Puccini* (London: Duckworth, 1974 2nd edition) pp. 102, 110, 349, 364, 366, 369; Barrie Jones, J. (transl. and ed.), *Gabriel Fauré: A Life in Letters* (London: Batsford, 1988) p. 111; Lang, P.H., *Music in Western Civilisation* (London: J.M. Dent & Sons Ltd, 1963) p. 999; Stassinopoulos, A., *Maria* (London: Weidenfeld & Nicolson, 1980) pp. 138, 155, 220, 222; *New Grove Dictionary of Music and Musicians* (ed. S. Sadie), (London: Macmillan, 1980) Puccini (M. Carner) vol. 15, pp. 432, 435; Vandiver Nicassio, S., *Tosca's Rome: The Play and the Opera in Historical Perspective* (Chicago: University of Chicago Press, 2002) p. 2; Pavarotti, L. and Wright, W., *My World* (London: Chatto & Windus, 1995) pp. 35, 36, 72; Kobbé, G., *The Complete Opera Book* (London: G.P. Putnam's Sons, 1930) p. 662; Douglas, N., *Legendary Voices* (London: André Deutsch,

1992), p. 222; (Nilsson, B., *La Nilsson* (Boston: Northeastern University Press, 2007) p. 69; Steen, M., *The Lives and Times of the Great Composers* (Cambridge: Icon Books, 2003) ch. 27.

Other sources: *Encyclopaedia Britannica* ninth edition, vol. XVII, p 204; vol. XX, p 806; *New Grove Dictionary of Music and Musicians* (ed. S. Sadie), (London: Macmillan, 1980) vol. 7, p. 346, Giacosa (W. Weaver); vol. 9, p. 25 Illica (W. Weaver); vol. 12, p. 765 Mugnone (C. Casini); Shaw, G.B., *Music in London 1890–94* (London: Constable, 1949) vol. iii, p. 220; Lebrecht, N., *The Book of Musical Anecdotes* (London: André Deutsch, 1985); Domingo, P., *My First Forty Years* (London: Weidenfeld & Nicolson, 1983); Vickers, H., *Great Operatic Disasters* (London: Macmillan, 1981); Vickers, H., *Even Greater Operatic Disasters* (London: Jill Norman & Hobhouse Ltd, 1982); Hewlett-Davies, B., *A Night at the Opera* (London: Weidenfeld & Nicolson, 1980); Jenkins, G. and d'Antal, S., *Kiri* (London: HarperCollins, 1998); *Times Literary Supplement*, 6 June 2008, p. 7.

Puccini: *Madama Butterfly*

Sources of quotes: Puccini, G., *Madama Butterfly* full score (San Giuliano Milanese: UMP Ricordi, 1999); Carner, M., *Puccini* (London: Duckworth, 3rd edition 1992), pp. 131, 136, 140, 142, 389, 392, 398; Barrie Jones, J., (trans. and ed.), *Gabriel Fauré: a Life in Letters* (London: Batsford, 1988) pp. 103, 111; Lang, P.H., *Music in Western Civilisation* (London: J.M. Dent & Sons Ltd, 1963) p. 999; Rutherford, S., *The Prima Donna and Opera 1815–1930* (Cambridge: Cambridge University Press 2006) p. 217; Kobbé, G., *The Complete Opera Book* (London: G.P. Putnam's Sons, 1930) p. 673; Stassinopoulos, A., *Maria* (London: Weidenfeld & Nicolson, 1980) p. 124; Hewlett-Davies, B., *A Night at the Opera* (London: Weidenfeld & Nicolson, 1980) p. 33; Allen, T., *Foreign Parts* (London: Sinclair-Stevenson 1993) pp. 126, 127.

Other sources: Domingo, P., *My First Forty Years* (London: Weidenfeld & Nicolson, 1983); *New Grove* vol. 15, Puccini (M. Carner); vol. 7, p. 346, Giacosa (W. Weaver); vol. 9, p. 25, Illica (W. Weaver); Shaw, G.B., *Music in London 1890–94* (London: Constable, 1949) vol. iii; *Encyclopaedia Britannica* 9th edition, vol. XIII p. 581; Fowler, H., *A Dictionary of Modern English Usage*, (Oxford: Clarendon Press 1963) p. 295; Steen, M., *The Lives and Times of the Great Composers* (Cambridge: Icon Books 2003).

Puccini: *Turandot*

Sources of quotes: Puccini, G., *Turandot*, full score, (Milan: Ricordi, 2000); Carner, M., *Puccini* (London: Duckworth, 1992 3rd edition) pp. 172, 439, 465, 473, 479, 486, 488; Shakespeare, W., *The Merchant of Venice*, Act II sc. I; Pavarotti, L. and Wright, W., *Pavarotti, My World* (London: Chatto & Windus, 1995) p. 67; Breslin, H. and Midgette, A., *The King and I: Luciano Pavarotti's Rise to Fame* (Edinburgh: Mainstream Publishing, 2004) p. 208; Lebrecht, N., *The Book of Musical Anecdotes* (London: André Deutsch, 1985) p. 245; DiGaetani, J., *Carlo Gozzi: A Life in the 18th Century Venetian Theater* (Jefferson,

North Carolina: McFarland & Company, Inc., 2000) pp. 4, 125, 127; Douglas, N., *Legendary Voices* (London: André Deutsch, 1992) p. 257; Nilsson, B., *La Nilsson* (Boston: Northeastern University Press, 2007) pp 89, 185, 188, 200; Domingo, P., *My First Forty Years* (London: Weidenfeld & Nicolson, 1983) p. 19; Chrysalia (pseudonym): *Calaf, A Rejected Drama* (London: T. Hookham, 1826) Act 1, pp. 13, 15, 17; Gozzi, C. (ed. A. Bermel and T. Emery), *Five tales for the Theatre* (Chicago: University of Chicago Press 1989) p. 1.

Other sources: *New Grove Dictionary of Music and Musicians* (ed. S. Sadie), (London: Macmillan, 1980) vol. 1, p. 250 Alfano (J. Waterhouse); vol. 15, Puccini (M. Carner) pp. 437, 435; *Encyclopaedia Britannica* ninth edition, vol. xi, p. 24, vol. x, p. 759; Shaw, G.B., *Music in London 1890–94* (London: Constable, 1949) vol. iii, p. 220; Stassinopoulos, A., *Maria* (London: Weidenfeld & Nicolson 1980 p. 181; Major, N., *Joan Sutherland* (London: Little Brown, 1993) p. 227; P. Casali, 'The Pronunciation of Turandot, Puccini's Last Enigma', *Opera Quarterly* (1997) vol. 13 no. 4 pp. 77–91; Vickers, H., *Great Operatic Disasters* (London: Macmillan, 1981) p. 59; Steen, M., *The Lives and Times of the Great Composers* (Cambridge: Icon Books, 2003) ch. 27.

Britten: *Peter Grimes*

Sources of quotes: Crabbe, G., *London Life in the Eighteenth Century* (London: Kegan Paul, Trench, Trubner, 1925) lines 60, 64–66, 69, 70, 77–79, 119, 359, 367 and pp. 13, 173, 231; Lucas, T., *Thomas Beecham* (Woodbridge: The Boydell Press, 2008) pp. 58, 312; Milnes, R., *Some Questions About Peter Grimes, But No Answers* (Glyndebourne programme, 2000) pp. 96, 98, 99; *Encyclopaedia Britannica* ninth edition, vol. VI, p. 539; Evans, I., *A Short History of English Literature* (Harmondsworth: Penguin, 1963) p. 46; Britten, B. (ed. D. Mitchell and P. Reed), *Letters from a Life* (London: Faber & Faber, 1991) vol. II (February 24, 1945 to R. Duncan) p. 160; Evans, G., *A Knight at the Opera* (London: Futura, 1985) pp. 61, 212; Oliver, M., *Benjamin Britten* (London: Phaidon, 1996) p. 211; *New Grove Dictionary of Music and Musicians* (ed. S. Sadie), (London: Macmillan, 1980) vol. III, pp. 293, 301 Britten (P. Evans); Austen Leigh, J.E., *Memoir of Jane Austen*, ch. V, quoted in Crabbe op. cit. p. 14; Atkins, H., and Newman, A., *Beecham Stories* (London: Futura, 1983) p. 62; *Peter Grimes* Vocal Score (London: Boosey & Hawkes, 2003) Act I, 5, 81; Act 2, 27, 55, 62, 69; Abbate, T., *Elektra's Voice* (Cambridge: Cambridge University Press, 1989) p. 111; Seymour, C., *The Operas of Benjamin Britten*, (Woodbridge: The Boydell Press, 2004) pp. 43 (Hans Keller), 47, 63, 74; Brett, P. (compiled), *Benjamin Britten Peter Grimes* (Cambridge: Cambridge University Press, 1983) pp. 60, 74, 100, 104, 180, 186, 190; D. Mitchell in Brett op. cit. pp. 29, 30, 35, 38–40; E.M. Forster in Brett op. cit. pp. 7, 10, 16, 20; E. Wilson in Brett op. cit. p. 162; Cooke, M., (ed.) *The Cambridge Companion to Benjamin Britten* (Cambridge: Cambridge University Press, 1999) p. 3; Allen, A., in Cooke op. cit. pp. 93, 280.

Other sources: Hughes, D., *Aldeburgh's Moot Hall* (The Aldeburgh Museum); *Erosion: Aldeburgh's Fight against the Sea* (Aldeburgh Museum Trust, 1993); Whittall, A., *The*

Chamber Operas, in Cooke (op. cit); Del Mar, N., *Richard Strauss*, (London: Barrie & Jenkins, 1972) vol. II; Carnegy, P., *Wagner and the Art of the Theatre* (New Haven and London: Yale University Press, 2006); Lebrecht, N., *The Book of Musical Anecdotes* (London: André Deutsch, 1985); *New Oxford Companion to Music* (ed. Denis Arnold) (Oxford: Oxford University Press, 1983) pp. 1394, 1591; Steen, M., *The Lives and Times of the Great Composers* (Cambridge: Icon Books, 2003).

PICTURE CREDITS

Images were supplied by the following people and organisations (numbers indicate page references):

3, 24, 129, 138, 208, 233, 283, 303, 320, 340, 357, 358, 434
  Royal College of Music, London
15, 16 Gerald Coke Handel Collection, The Foundling Museum
48 The Bridgeman Art Library
67 Internationale Stiftung Mozarteum (ISM)
116, 246 Pamela, Lady Vestey, *Melba a Family Memoir* and
  www.nelliemelbamuseum.com.au
310 The Brahms Institute
394, 421 The Press Association

Other images are from the author's collection.

INDEX

Short Guides
to Great Operas

Various guides to individual operas are available as ebooks:

See greatoperas.net for more information

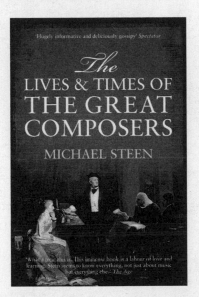

Enchantress of Nations

Pauline Viardot:
Soprano, Muse and Lover

MICHAEL STEEN

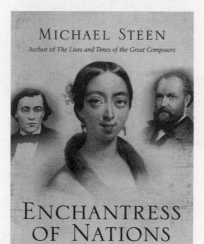

This is a picturesque but painstakingly researched biography
of the life – and the times – of the nineteenth century's
Maria Callas. She was among 'the most brilliant dramatic stars
of our time', according to Franz Liszt, and billed as 'the most
talked of opera singer in Europe'. *Enchantress of Nations* is a
lavish biography of this amazing woman whose life spanned most
of the nineteenth century; and it also weaves a rich tapestry of
music and literature in France, England and Russia.

ISBN: 9781840468434